EP Fourth Reader
Days 1-90

EP Reader Series

Volume 4

Second Edition

CONTENTS

ACKNOWLEDGEMENTS

Thank you to Abigail Baia for her beautiful cover art.

Welcome to Easy Peasy All-in-One Homeschool's Fourth Reader Lessons 1-90

We hope you enjoy curling up with this book of books.

This is the first half of Easy Peasy's offline version of its assignments for the first half of Reading 4. The novels and poetry included are found in the public domain and have been gathered here along with each day's assignment directions. There are differences between this course and the online version because some reading assignments are not found in the public domain and had to be replaced.

In addition to the readings, online lessons and activities from Easy Peasy's website have been replaced with offline versions found in this book.

This is only the first half of the course, Lessons 1-90. The rest of the course is in EP Fourth Reader Lessons 91-180.

Lesson 1

1. Write **quench** (story 3), **dismay** (story 4) and **retort** (story 5), each on its own line. Pay attention to those words while you read.
2. Read stories 1-5 in *McGuffey's Third Eclectic Reader*.
3. Guess what you think those words mean.
4. Look up each word in the answers section to see if you are right. Write the correct definition of the words. (Answers)

STORY I THE SHEPHERD BOY.

1. Little Roy led his sheep down to pasture,

   And his cows, by the side of the brook;

   But his cows never drank any water,

   And his sheep never needed a crook.

2. For the pasture was gay as a garden,

   And it glowed with a flowery red;

   But the meadows had never a grass blade,

   And the brooklet—it slept in its bed:

3. And it lay without sparkle or murmur,

   Nor reflected the blue of the skies;

   But the music was made by the shepherd,

   And the sparkle was all in his eyes.

4. Oh, he sang like a bird in the summer!

   And, if sometimes you fancied a bleat,

   That, too, was the voice of the shepherd,

   And not of the lambs at his feet.

5. And the glossy brown cows were so gentle

   That they moved at the touch of his hand

   O'er the wonderful, rosy-red meadow,

   And they stood at the word of command.

6. So he led all his sheep to the pasture,

   And his cows, by the side of the brook;

   Though it rained, yet the rain never pattered

   O'er the beautiful way that they took.

7. And it wasn't in Fairyland either,

   But a house in the midst of the town,

   Where Roy, as he looked from the window,

   Saw the silvery drops trickle down.

8. For his pasture was only a table,

   With its cover so flowery fair,

   And his brooklet was just a green ribbon,

   That his sister had lost from her hair.

9. And his cows were but glossy horse-chestnuts,

   That had grown on his grandfather's tree;

   And his sheep only snowy-white pebbles,

   He had brought from the shore of the sea.

10. And at length when the shepherd was weary,

    And had taken his milk and his bread,

    And his mother had kissed him and tucked him,

    And had bid him "good night" in his bed;

11. Then there entered his big brother Walter,

    While the shepherd was soundly asleep,

    And he cut up the cows into baskets,

    And to jackstones turned all of the sheep.

STORY II JOHNNY'S FIRST SNOWSTORM.

1. Johnny Reed was a little boy who never had seen a snowstorm till he was six years old. Before this, he had lived in a warm country, where the sun shines down on beautiful orange groves, and fields always sweet with flowers.

2. But now he had come to visit his grandmother, who lived where the snow falls in winter. Johnny was standing at the window when the snow came down.

3. "O mamma!" he cried, joyfully, "do come quick, and see these little white birds flying down from heaven."

4. "They are not birds, Johnny," said mamma, smiling.

5. "Then maybe the little angels are losing their feathers! Oh! do tell me what it is; is it sugar? Let me taste it," said Johnny. But when he tasted it, he gave a little jump—it was so cold.

6. "That is only snow, Johnny," said his mother.

7. "What is snow, mother?"

8. "The snowflakes, Johnny, are little drops of water that fall from the clouds. But the air through which they pass is so cold it freezes them, and they come down turned into snow."

9. As she said this, she brought out an old black hat from the closet. "See, Johnny! I have caught a snowflake on this hat. Look quick through this glass, and you will see how beautiful it is."

10. Johnny looked through the glass. There lay the pure, feathery snowflake like a lovely little star.

11. "Twinkle, twinkle, little star!" he cried in delight. "Oh! please show me more snow-flakes, mother."

12. So his mother caught several more, and they were all beautiful.

13. The next day Johnny had a fine play in the snow, and when he came in, he said, "I love snow; and I think snowballs are a great deal prettier than oranges."

STORY III LET IT RAIN

Rose. See how it rains! Oh dear, dear, dear! how dull it is! Must I stay in doors all day?

Father. Why, Rose, are you sorry that you had any bread and butter for breakfast, this morning?

Rose. Why, father, what a question! I should be sorry, indeed, if I could not get any.

Father. Are you sorry, my daughter, when you see the flowers and the trees growing in the garden?

Rose. Sorry? No, indeed. Just now, I wished very much to go out and see them,--they look so pretty.

Father. Well, are you sorry when you see the horses, cows, or sheep drinking at the brook to quench their thirst?

Rose. Why, father, you must think I am a cruel girl, to wish that the poor horses that work so hard, the beautiful cows that give so much nice milk, and the pretty lambs should always be thirsty.

Father. Do you not think they would die, if they had no water to drink?

Rose. Yes, sir, I am sure they would. How shocking to think of such a thing!

Father. I thought little Rose was sorry it rained. Do you think the trees and flowers would grow, if they never had any water on them?

Rose. No, indeed, father, they would be dried up by the sun. Then we should not have any pretty flowers to look at, and to make wreaths of for mother.

Father. I thought you were sorry it rained. Rose, what is our bread made of?

Rose. It is made of flour, and the flour is made from wheat, which is ground in the mill.

Father. Yes, Rose, and it was rain that helped to make the wheat grow, and it was water that turned the mill to grind the wheat. I thought little Rose was sorry it rained.

Rose. I did not think of all these things, father. I am truly very glad to see the rain falling.

STORY IV CASTLE-BUILDING

1. "O pussy!" cried Herbert, in a voice of anger and dismay, as the blockhouse he was building fell in sudden ruin. The playful cat had rubbed against his mimic castle, and tower and wall went rattling down upon the floor.

2. Herbert took up one of the blocks and threw it fiercely at pussy. Happily, it passed over her and did no harm. His hand was reaching for another block, when his little sister Hetty sprang toward the cat, and caught her up.

3. "No, no, no!" said she, "you sha'n't hurt pussy! She didn't mean to do it!"

4. Herbert's passion was over quickly, and, sitting down upon the floor, he covered his face with his hands, and began to cry.

5. "What a baby!" said Joe, his elder brother, who was reading on the sofa. "Crying over spilled milk does no good. Build it up again."

6. "No, I won't," said Herbert, and he went on crying.

7. "What's all the trouble here?" exclaimed papa, as he opened the door and came in.

8. "Pussy just rubbed against Herbert's castle, and it fell down," answered Hetty. "But she didn't mean to do it; she didn't know it would fall, did she, papa?"

9. "Why, no! And is that all the trouble?"

10. "Herbert!" his papa called, and held out his hands. "Come." The little boy got up from the floor, and came slowly, his eyes full of tears, and stood by his father.

11. "There is a better way than this, my boy," said papa. "If you had taken that way, your heart would have been light already. I should have heard you singing over your blocks instead of crying. Shall I show you that way?"

12. Herbert nodded his head, and papa sat down on the floor by the pile of blocks, with his little son by his side, and began to lay the foundation for a new castle.

STORY V CASTLE-BUILDING (CONCLUDED)

1. Soon, Herbert was as much interested in castle-building as he had been a little while before. He began to sing over his work. All his trouble was gone.

2. "This is a great deal better than crying, isn't it?" said papa.

3. "Crying for what?" asked Herbert, forgetting his grief of a few minutes before.

4. "Because pussy knocked your castle over."

5. "Oh!" A shadow flitted across his face, but was gone in a moment, and he went on building as eagerly as ever.

6. "I told him not to cry over spilled milk," said Joe, looking down from his place on the sofa.

7. "I wonder if you didn't cry when your kite string broke," retorted Herbert.

8. "Losing a kite is quite another thing," answered Joe, a little dashed. "The kite was gone forever; but your blocks were as good as before, and you had only to build again."

9. "I don't see," said papa, "that crying was of any more use in your case than in Herbert's. Sticks and paper are easily found, and you had only to go to work and make another kite." Joe looked down at his book, and went on reading. By this time the castle was finished.

10. "It is ever so much nicer than the one pussy knocked down," said Hetty. And so thought Herbert, as he looked at it proudly from all sides.

11. "If pussy knocks that down, I'll-"

12. "Build it up again," said papa, finishing the sentence for his little boy.

13. "But, papa, pussy must not knock my castles down. I can't have it," spoke out Herbert, knitting his forehead.

14. "You must watch her, then. Little boys, as well as grown up people, have to be often on their guard. If you go into the street, you have to look out for the carriages, so as not to be run over, and you have to keep out of people's way.

15. "In the house, if you go about heedlessly, you will be very apt to run against some one. I have seen a careless child dash suddenly into a room just as a servant was leaving it with a tray of dishes in her hands. A crash followed."

16. "It was I, wasn't it?" said Hetty.

17. "Yes, I believe it was, and I hope it will never happen again."

18. Papa now left the room, saying, "I don't want any more of this crying over spilled milk, as Joe says. If your castles get knocked down, build them up again."

Lesson 2

1. Write **toil** and **strife**. Pay attention to those words while you read.
2. Read this stanza of the poem in story 6 in the *McGuffey's Third Eclectic Reader*.

> Lend a hand to one another
> In the daily toil of life
> When we meet a weaker brother,
> Let us help him in the strife
> There is none so rich but may

> In his turn, be forced to borrow;
> And the poor man's lot to-day
> May become our own to-morrow.

3. Guess what you think those words in bold mean.

4. Look up each word in the answers section to see if you are right. Write the correct definition of the words. (Answers)

5. Now tell or rewrite the paragraph in your own words. What is it saying? Example: For the first line you could write, "Help each other."

Lesson 3

1. Write **malicious** and **adrift**. Pay attention to those words while you read.
2. Read the second stanza of the poem in story 6 in the *McGuffey's Third Eclectic Reader*.

> Lend a hand to one another;
> When malicious tongues have thrown
> Dark suspicion on your brother,
> Be not prompt to cast a stone.
> There is none so good but may
> Run adrift in shame and sorrow,
> And the good man of to-day
> May become the bad to-morrow.

3. What do you think the new words mean? Write their correct definitions. (Answers)
4. Tell or rewrite what the paragraph means in your own words.

Lesson 4

1. Write **envy**. The phrase "Honor's crown" is in today's reading. It means gaining some honor, getting recognition for something.
2. Read the third stanza of the poem in story 6 in the *McGuffey's Third Eclectic Reader*.

> Lend a hand to one another:
> In the race for Honor's crown;
> Should it fall upon your brother,
> Let not envy tear it down.

Lend a hand to all, we pray,
In their sunshine or their sorrow;
And the prize they've won today
May become our own to-morrow.

3. Guess what you think today's vocabulary word means.

4. Look it up to see if you are right. Write the correct definition. (Answers)

5. Tell or rewrite the paragraph in your own words.

Lesson 5

1. Write **ignorant**, **haste** (story 7) and **inquire** (story 10). Pay attention to these words as you read.
2. Read stories 7 through 10 in the *McGuffey's Third Eclectic Reader*.
3. Guess what you think those words mean.
4. Look up their definitions in the answers section to see if you are correct. Write the correct definitions. (Answers)
5. In story 9 there is the word "inhuman." When "in" is used in front of a word, it means not. So, inhuman means not human. Indescribable also has "in" for a prefix (the part added onto the front of a word). Can you think of another word with the prefix "in"?

STORY VII THE TRUANT

1. James Brown was ten years old when his parents sent him to school. It was not far from his home, and therefore they sent him by himself.

2. But, instead of going to school, he was in the habit of playing truant. He would go into the fields, or spend his time with idle boys.

3. But this was not all. When he went home, he would falsely tell his mother that he had been to school, and had said his lessons very well.

4. One fine morning, his mother told James to make haste home from school, for she wished, after he had come back, to take him to his aunt's.

5. But, instead of minding her, he went off to the water, where there were some boats. There he met plenty of idle boys.

6. Some of these boys found that James had money, which his aunt had given him; and he was led by them to hire a boat, and to go with them upon the water.

7. Little did James think of the danger into which he was running. Soon the wind began to blow, and none of them knew how to manage the boat.

8. For some time, they struggled against the wind and the tide. At last, they became so tired that they could row no longer.

9. A large wave upset the boat, and they were all thrown into the water. Think of James Brown, the truant, at this time!

10. He was far from home, known by no one. His parents were ignorant of his danger. He was struggling in the water, on the point of being drowned.

11. Some men, however, saw the boys, and went out to them in a boat. They reached them just in time to save them from a watery grave.

12. They were taken into a house, where their clothes were dried. After a while, they were sent home to their parents.

13. James was very sorry for his conduct, and he was never known to be guilty of the same thing again.

14. He became regular at school, learned to attend to his books, and, above all, to obey his parents perfectly.

STORY VIII THE WHITE KITTEN

1. My little white kitten's asleep on my knee;
   As white as the snow or the lilies is she;
     She wakes up with a pur
     When I stroke her soft fur:
   Was there ever another white kitten like her?

2. My little white kitten now wants to go out
   And frolic, with no one to watch her about;
     "Little kitten," I say,
     "Just an hour you may stay,
   And be careful in choosing your places to play."

3. But night has come down, when I hear a loud "mew;"
   I open the door, and my kitten comes through;
     My white kitten! ah me!
     Can it really be she--
   This ill-looking, beggar-like cat that I see?

4. What ugly, gray streaks on her side and her back!
   Her nose, once as pink as a rosebud, is black!
     Oh, I very well know,
     Though she does not say so,
   She has been where white kittens ought never to go.

5. If little good children intend to do right,
    If little white kittens would keep themselves white,
        It is needful that they
        Should this counsel obey,
    And be careful in choosing their places to play.

STORY IX THE BEAVER

1. The beaver is found chiefly in North America. It is about three and a half feet long, including the flat, paddle- shaped tail, which is a foot in length.

2. The long, shining hair on the back is chestnut-colored, while the fine, soft fur that lies next the skin, is grayish brown.

3. Beavers build themselves most curious huts to live in, and quite frequently a great number of these huts are placed close together, like the buildings in a town.

4. They always build their huts on the banks of rivers or lakes, for they swim much more easily than they walk, and prefer moving about in the water.

5. When they build on the bank of a running stream, they make a dam across the stream for the purpose of keeping the water at the height they wish.

6. These dams are made chiefly of mud, and stones, and the branches of trees. They are sometimes six or seven hundred feet in length, and are so constructed that they look more like the work of man than of little dumb beasts.

7. Their huts are made of the same material as the dams, and are round in shape. The walls are very thick, and the roofs are finished off with a thick layer of mud, sticks, and leaves.

8. They commence building their houses late in the summer, but do not get them finished before the early frosts. The freezing makes them tighter and stronger.

9. They obtain the wood for their dams and huts by gnawing through the branches of trees, and even through the trunks of small ones, with their sharp front teeth. They peel off the bark, and lay it up in store for winter food.

10. The fur of the beaver is highly prized. The men who hunt these animals are called trappers.

11. A gentleman once saw five young beavers playing. They would leap on the trunk of a tree that lay near a beaver dam, and would push one another off into the water.

12. He crept forward very cautiously, and was about to fire on the little creatures; but their amusing tricks reminded him so much of some little children he knew at home, that he thought it would be inhuman to kill them. So he left them without even disturbing their play.

STORY X THE YOUNG TEACHER.

1. Charles Rose lived in the country with his father, who taught him to read and to write.

2. Mr. Rose told his son that, when his morning lessons were over, he might amuse himself for one hour as he pleased.

3. There was a river near by. On its bank stood the hut of a poor fisherman, who lived by selling fish.

4. His careful wife kept her wheel going early and late. They both worked very hard to keep themselves above want.

5. But they were greatly troubled lest their only son should never learn to read and to write. They could not teach him themselves, and they were too poor to send him to school.

6. Charles called at the hut of this fisherman one day, to inquire about his dog, which was missing.

7. He found the little boy, whose name was Joe, sitting by the table, on which he was making marks with a piece of chalk. Charles asked him whether he was drawing pictures.

8. "No, I am trying to write," said little Joe, "but I know only two words. Those I saw upon a sign, and I am trying to write them."

9. "If I could only learn to read and write," said he, "I should be the happiest boy in the world."

10. "Then I will make you happy," said Charles. "I am only a little boy, but I can teach you that.

11. "My father gives me an hour every day for myself. Now, if you will try to learn, you shall soon know how to read and to write."

12. Both Joe and his mother were ready to fall on their knees to thank Charles. They told him it was what they wished above all things.

13. So, on the next day when the hour came, Charles put his book in his pocket, and went to teach Joe. Joe learned very fast, and Charles soon began to teach him how to write.

14. Some time after, a gentleman called on Mr. Rose, and asked him if he knew where Charles was. Mr. Rose said that he was taking a walk, he supposed.

15. "I am afraid," said the gentleman, "that he does not always amuse himself thus. I often see him go to the house of the fisherman. I fear he goes out in their boat."

16. Mr. Rose was much troubled. He had told Charles that he must never venture on the river, and he thought he could trust him.

17. The moment the gentleman left, Mr. Rose went in search of his son. He went to the river, and walked up and down, in hope of seeing the boat.

18. Not seeing it, he grew uneasy. He thought Charles must have gone a long way off. Unwilling to leave without learning some thing of him, he went to the hut.

19. He put his head in at the window, which was open. There a pleasant sight met his eyes.

20. Charles was at the table, ruling a copybook Joe was reading to him, while his mother was spinning in the corner.

21. Charles was a little confused. He feared his father might not be pleased; but he had no need to be uneasy, for his father was delighted.

22. The next day, his father took him to town, and gave him books for himself and Joe, with writing paper, pens, and ink.

23. Charles was the happiest boy in the world when he came home. He ran to Joe, his hands filled with parcels, and his heart beating with joy.

Lesson 6

1. Read this poem from story 11 in the *McGuffey's Third Eclectic Reader*.

    STORY XI THE BLACKSMITH

    1. Clink, clink, clinkerty clink!
            We begin to hammer at morning's blink,
                And hammer away
            Till the busy day,
                Like us, aweary, to rest shall sink.

    2. Clink, clink, clinkerty clink!
            From labor and care we never will shrink;
                But our fires we'll blow
                Till our forges glow
            With light intense, while our eyelids wink.

    3. Clink, clink, clinkerty clink;
        The chain we'll forge with many a link.
                We'll work each form
                While the iron is warm,
            With strokes as fast as we can think.

    4. Clink, clink, clinkerty clink!
            Our faces may be as black as ink,
                But our hearts are true
                As man ever knew,
            And kindly of all we shall ever think.

2. Write **forge**. In this context forge is a verb, an action, and means to form by heating and pounding into shape. This is how metal is molded into different shapes. Write this definition.

3. This type of poem is called a limerick. It is in the form: AABBA. In this type of poem the B lines not only rhyme but they are shorter in length than the other lines.
4. How many lines are in this form of poem? (Answers)
5. Which lines rhyme in a limerick? (Answers)
6. Read some other limericks. They are fun poems and are often humorous.

> There was an old man with a beard.
> Who said, "It is just as I feared!"
> Two owls and a wren
> Four larks and a hen
> Have all built their nests in my beard!
> – Edward Lear

> There was an Old Man of Nantucket
> Who kept all his cash in a bucket.
> His daughter, called Nan,
> Ran away with a man,
> And as for the bucket, Nantucket.
> – Anonymous

"Nantucket" — get it? Nan took it. She ran off with all the old man's money.

Vocabulary

1. Choose the correct definition for each word. Write the question number and letter of each answer on a separate piece of paper. (Answers)

1. intending to harm
a) ignorant   b) adrift   c) malicious   d) toil

2. work hard
a) quench   b) haste   c) toil   d) ignorant

3. hurry
a) haste   b) strife   c) inquire   d) adrift

4. conflict
a) strife   b) haste   c) malicious   d) quench

5. lacking knowledge
a) adrift   b) toil   c) ignorant   d) malicious

6. ask
a) retort   b) toil   c) quench   d) inquire

7. satisfy
a) quench   b) strife   c) inquire   d) retort

8. lost and confused
a) malicious   b) retort   c) adrift   d) inquire

9. distress
a) strife   b) dismay   c) haste   d) ignorant

10. to say something in answer, typically in a sharp or witty fashion
a) inquire   b) adrift   c) haste   d) retort

Lesson 7

1. Write **assure** (story 12), **earnest** (story 13), **grove** (story 16)
2. Read stories 12 through 16 in your reader.
3. What do you think the words mean?
4. Check the definitions in the answers section and write the correct definitions. (Answers)

STORY XII A WALK IN THE GARDEN

1. Frank was one day walking with his mother, when they came to a pretty garden. Frank looked in, and saw that it had clean gravel walks, and beds of beautiful flowers all in bloom.

2. He called to his mother, and said, "Mother, come and look at this pretty garden. I wish I might open the gate, and walk in."

3. The gardener, being near, heard what Frank said, and kindly invited him and his mother to come into the garden.

4. Frank's mother thanked the man. Turning to her son, she said, "Frank, if I take you to walk in this garden, you must take care not to meddle with anything in it."

5. Frank walked along the neat gravel paths, and looked at everything, but touched nothing that he saw.

6. He did not tread on any of the borders, and was careful that his clothes should not brush the

tops of the flowers, lest he might break them.

7. The gardener was much pleased with Frank, because he was so careful not to do mischief. He showed him the seeds, and told him the name of many of the flowers and plants.

8. While Frank was admiring the beauty of a flower, a boy came to the gate, and finding it locked, he shook it hard. But it would not open. Then he said, "Let me in; let me in; will you not let me in this garden?"

9. "No, indeed," said the gardener, "I will not let you in, I assure you; for when I let you in yesterday, you meddled with my flowers, and pulled some of my rare fruit. I do not choose to let a boy into my garden who meddles with the plants."

10. The boy looked ashamed, and when he found that the gardener would not let him in, he went slowly away.

11. Frank saw and felt how much happier a boy may be by not meddling with what does not belong to him.

12. He and his mother then continued their walk in the garden, and enjoyed the day very much. Before they left, the gardener gave each of them some pretty flowers.

STORY XIII THE WOLF

1. A boy was once taking care of some sheep, not far from a forest. Near by was a village, and he was told to call for help if there was any danger.

2. One day, in order to have some fun, he cried out, with all his might, "The wolf is coming! the wolf is coming!"

3. The men came running with clubs and axes to destroy the wolf. As they saw nothing they went home again, and left John laughing in his sleeve.

4. As he had had so much fun this time, John cried out again, the next day, "The wolf! the wolf!"

5. The men came again, but not so many as the first time. Again they saw no trace of the wolf; so they shook their heads, and went back.

6. On the third day, the wolf came in earnest. John cried in dismay, "Help! help! the wolf! the wolf!" But not a single man came to help him.

7. The wolf broke into the flock, and killed a great many sheep. Among them was a beautiful lamb, which belonged to John.

8. Then he felt very sorry that he had deceived his friends and neighbors, and grieved over the loss of his pet lamb.

> The truth itself is not believed,
> From one who often has deceived.

STORY XIV THE LITTLE BIRD'S SONG

1. A little bird, with feathers brown,
   Sat singing on a tree;
   The song was very soft and low,
   But sweet as it could be.

2. The people who were passing by,
   Looked up to see the bird
   That made the sweetest melody,
   That ever they had heard.

3. But all the bright eyes looked in vain;
   Birdie was very small,
   And with his modest, dark-brown coat,
   He made no show at all.

4. "Why, father," little Gracie said,
   "Where can the birdie be?
   If I could sing a song like that,
   I'd sit where folks could see."

5. "I hope my little girl will learn,
   A lesson from the bird,
   And try to do what good she can,
   Not to be seen or heard.

6. "This birdie is content to sit,
   Unnoticed on the way,
   And sweetly sing his Maker's praise,
   From dawn to close of day.

7. "So live, my child, all through your life,
   That, be it short or long,
   Though others may forget your looks,
   They'll not forget your song."

STORY XV HARRY AND ANNIE

1. Harry and Annie lived a mile from town, but they went there to school every day. It was a pleasant walk down the lane, and through the meadow by the pond.

2. I hardly know whether they liked it better in summer or in winter. They used to pretend that they were travelers exploring a new country, and would scatter leaves on the road that they might find their way back again.

3. When the ice was thick and firm, they went across the pond. But their mother did not like to

15

have them do this unless some one was with them.

4. "Don't go across the pond today, children," she said, as she kissed them and bade them goodbye one morning; "it is beginning to thaw."

5. "All right, mother," said Harry, not very good naturedly, for he was very fond of running and sliding on the ice. When they came to the pond, the ice looked hard and safe.

6. "There," said he to his sister, "I knew it hadn't thawed any. Mother is always afraid we shall be drowned. Come along, we will have a good time sliding. The school bell will not ring for an hour at least."

7. "But you promised mother," said Annie.

8. "No, I didn't. I only said 'All right,' and it is all right."

9. "I didn't say anything; so I can do as I like," said Annie.

10. So they stepped on the ice, and started to go across the pond. They had not gone far before the ice gave way, and they fell into the water.

11. A man who was at work near the shore, heard the screams of the children, and plunged into the water to save them. Harry managed to get to the shore without any help, but poor Annie was nearly drowned before the man could reach her.

12. Harry went home almost frozen, and told his mother how disobedient he had been. He remembered the lesson learned that day as long as he lived.

STORY XVI BIRD FRIENDS

1. I once knew a man who was rich in his love for birds, and in their love for him. He lived in the midst of a grove full of all kinds of trees. He had no wife or children in his home.

2. He was an old man with gray beard, blue and kind eyes, and a voice that the birds loved; and this was the way he made them his friends.

3. While he was at work with a rake on his nice walks in the grove, the birds came close to him to pick up the worms in the fresh earth he dug up. At first, they kept a rod or two from him, but they soon found he was a kind man, and would not hurt them, but liked to have them near him. (Note: A "rod" here means about 5 meters.)

4. They knew this by his kind eyes and voice, which tell what is in the heart. So, day by day their faith in his love grew in them.

5. They came close to the rake. They would hop on top of it to be first at the worm. They would turn up their eyes into his when he spoke to them, as if they said, "He is a kind man; he loves us; we need not fear him."

6. All the birds of the grove were soon his fast friends. They were on the watch for him, and would fly down from the green tree tops to greet him with their chirp.

7. When he had no work on the walks to do with his rake or his hoe, he took crusts of bread with him, and dropped the crumbs on the ground. Down they would dart on his head and feet to catch them as they fell from his hand.

8. He showed me how they loved him. He put a crust of bread in his mouth, with one end of it out of his lips. Down they came like bees at a flower, and flew off with it crumb by crumb.

9. When they thought he slept too long in the morning, they would fly in and sit on the bedpost, and call him up with their chirp.

10. They went with him to church, and while he said his prayers and sang his hymns in it, they sat in the trees, and sang their praises to the same good God who cares for them as he does for us.

11. Thus the love and trust of birds were a joy to him all his life long; and such love and trust no boy or girl can fail to win with the same kind heart, voice, and eye that he had.

Lesson 8

1. Read story 17.
2. What is the lesson of this poem? (Answers)
3. What form is this poem in? (For instance the limerick was in the form: AABBA) (Answers)

STORY XVII WHAT THE MINUTES SAY

1. We are but minutes--little things!
   Each one furnished with sixty wings,
   With which we fly on our unseen track,
   And not a minute ever comes back.

2. We are but minutes; use us well,
   For how we are used we must one day tell.
   Who uses minutes, has hours to use;
   Who loses minutes, whole years must lose.

Lesson 9

1. Write **distress** and **hesitation**.
2. Read story 18.
3. How much does the woman ask for? (Answers)
4. How much does the man give her at first? (Answers)
5. Why does the man give her $500? (Answers)
6. What is the moral of the story? (Answers)

7. What do you think the day's vocabulary words mean?
8. Write their correct definitions. (Answers)

STORY XVIII THE WIDOW AND THE MERCHANT

1. A merchant, who was very fond of music, was asked by a poor widow to give her some assistance. Her husband, who was a musician, had died, and left her very poor indeed.

2. The merchant saw that the widow and her daughter, who was with her, were in great distress. He looked with pity into their pale faces, and was convinced by their conduct that their sad story was true.

3. "How much do you want, my good woman?" said the merchant.

4. "Five dollars will save us," said the poor widow, with some hesitation.

5. The merchant sat down at his desk, took a piece of paper, wrote a few lines on it, and gave it to the widow with the words, "Take it to the bank you see on the other side of the street."

6. The grateful widow and her daughter, without stopping to read the note, hastened to the bank. The banker at once counted out fifty dollars instead of five, and passed them to the widow.

7. She was amazed when she saw so much money. "Sir, there is a mistake here," she said. "You have given me fifty dollars, and I asked for only five."

8. The banker looked at the note once more, and said, "The check calls for fifty dollars."

9. "It is a mistake--indeed it is," said the widow.

10. The banker then asked her to wait a few minutes, while he went to see the merchant who gave her the note.

11. "Yes." said the merchant, when he had heard the banker's story, "I did make a mistake. I wrote fifty instead of five hundred. Give the poor widow five hundred dollars, for such honesty is poorly rewarded with even that sum."

Lesson 10

1. Write **adorn** (story 21) and **dispute** (story 22).
2. Read stories 19 – 23.
3. Look at the word "downy" in paragraph 1 of story 20. What does downy mean? It tells us by partnering it with what word? Soft. Often when we don't know a word, if we read the rest of the sentence or the next sentence, it will explain it to us.
4. What is the moral, or lesson, of the poem in story 20? (Answers)
5. What is the form of the poem in story 23? (Answers)
6. Guess what you think the vocabulary words mean.
7. Look them up and write the correct definition. (Answers)

STORY XIX THE BIRDS SET FREE

1. A man was walking one day through a large city. On a street corner he saw a boy with a number of small birds for sale, in a cage.

2. He looked with sadness upon the little prisoners flying about the cage, peeping through the wires, beating them with their wings, and trying to get out.

3. He stood for some time looking at the birds. At last he said to the boy, "How much do you ask for your birds?"

4. "Fifty cents apiece, sir," said the boy. "I do not mean how much apiece," said the man, "but how much for all of them? I want to buy them all."

5. The boy began to count, and found they came to five dollars. "There is your money," said the man. The boy took it, well pleased with his morning's trade.

6. No sooner was the bargain settled than the man opened the cage door, and let all the birds fly away.

7. The boy, in great surprise, cried, "What did you do that for, sir? You have lost all your birds."

8. "I will tell you why I did it," said the man. "I was shut up three years in a French prison, as a prisoner of war, and I am resolved never to see anything in prison which I can make free."

STORY XX A MOMENT TOO LATE

1. A moment too late, my beautiful bird,
   A moment too late are you now;
   The wind has your soft, downy nest disturbed—
   The nest that you hung on the bough.

2. A moment too late; that string in your bill,
   Would have fastened it firmly and strong;
   But see, there it goes, rolling over the hill!
   Oh, you staid a moment too long.

3. A moment, one moment too late, busy bee;
   The honey has dropped from the flower:
   No use to creep under the petals and see;
   It stood ready to drop for an hour.

4. A moment too late; had you sped on your wing,
   The honey would not have been gone;
   Now you see what a very, a very sad thing
   is to stay a moment too long.

5. Little girl, never be a moment too late,
   It will soon end in trouble or crime;

Better be an hour early, and stand and wait,
Than a moment behind the time.

6. If the bird and the bee, little boy, were too late,
Remember, as you play along,
On your way to school, with pencil and slate,
Never stay a moment too long.

STORY XXI HUMMING BIRDS

1. The most beautiful humming birds are found in the West Indies and South America. The crest of the tiny head of one of these shines like a sparkling crown of colored light.

2. The shades of color that adorn its breast, are equally brilliant. As the bird flits from one object to another, it looks more like a bright flash of sunlight than it does like a living being.

3. But, you ask, why are they called humming birds? It is because they make a soft, humming noise by the rapid motion of their wings--a motion so rapid, that as they fly you can only see that they have wings.

4. One day when walking in the woods, I found the nest of one of the smallest humming birds. It was about half the size of a very small hen's egg, and was attached to a twig no thicker than a steel knitting needle.

5. It seemed to have been made of cotton fibers, and was covered with the softest bits of leaf and bark. It had two eggs in it, quite white, and each about as large as a small sugarplum.

6. When you approach the spot where one of these birds has built its nest, it is necessary to be careful. The mother bird will dart at you and try to peck your eyes. Its sharp beak may hurt your eyes most severely, and even destroy the sight.

7. The poor little thing knows no other way of defending its young, and instinct teaches it that you might carry off its nest if you could find it.

STORY XXII THE WIND AND THE SUN

1. A dispute once arose between the Wind and the Sun, as to which was the stronger.

2. To decide the matter, they agreed to try their power on a traveler. That party which should first strip him of his cloak, was to win the day.

3. The Wind began. He blew a cutting blast, which tore up the mountain oaks by their roots, and made the whole forest look like a wreck.

4. But the traveler, though at first he could scarcely keep his cloak on his back, ran under a hill for shelter, and buckled his mantle about him more closely.

5. The Wind having thus tried his utmost power in vain, the Sun began.

6. Bursting through a thick cloud, he darted his sultry beams so forcibly upon the traveler's head, that the poor fellow was almost melted.

7. "This," said he, "is past all bearing. It is so hot, that one might as well be in an oven."

8. So he quickly threw off his cloak, and went into the shade of a tree to cool himself.

9. This fable teaches us, that gentle means will often succeed where forcible ones will fail.

STORY XXIII SUNSET

Now the sun is sinking,
In the golden west;
Birds and bees and children,
All have gone to rest;
And the merry streamlet
As it runs along,
With a voice of sweetness
Sings its evening song.

Cowslip, daisy, violet
In their little beds
All among the grasses,
Hide their heavy heads;
There they'll all, sweet darlings,
Lie in happy dreams,
Till the rosy morning
Wakes them with its beams.

Lesson 11

1. Write **coarse** (story 24), **peevish** (story 25), and **perplexed** (story 26). Pay attention to these words as you read.
2. Read stories 24-27.
3. Guess what you think those words mean.
4. Look them up and write the correct definitions. (Answers)
5. What are some of the things from story 25 that you should remember?

Vocabulary

1. Replace the underlined words with your vocabulary words: assure, envy, forge, adorn, earnest, grove, dispute. Write the sentence number and the correct vocabulary word on a separate piece of paper. (Answers)

1. He was <u>sincere</u> in his efforts to please me.

2. There was an <u>argument </u>over whether or not to bring him along.

3. I chose to hang the lights in the room <u>to make</u> it<u> more beautiful.</u>

4. We played tag in the <u>small group of trees</u>.

5. The pewter cross necklace I wear was <u>created by heating the metal.</u>

6. There was <u>jealousy</u> between the two brothers after they each got what the other wanted.

7. I want to <u>encourage</u> you<u> that it will come about</u> if you will just wait patiently for it.

STORY XXIV BEAUTIFUL HANDS

1. "O Miss Roberts! what coarse-looking hands Mary Jessup has!" said Daisy Marvin, as she walked home from school with her teacher.

2. "In my opinion, Daisy, Mary's hands are the prettiest in the class."

3. "Why, Miss Roberts, they are as red and hard as they can be. How they would look if she were to try to play on a piano!" exclaimed Daisy.

4. Miss Roberts took Daisy's hands in hers, and said, "Your hands are very soft and white, Daisy-- just the hands to look beautiful on a piano; yet they lack one beauty that Mary's hands have. Shall I tell you what the difference is?"

5. "Yes, please, Miss Roberts."

6. "Well, Daisy, Mary's hands are always busy. They wash dishes; they make fires; they hang out clothes, and help to wash them, too; they sweep, and dust, and sew; they are always trying to help her poor, hard-working mother.

7. "Besides, they wash and dress the children; they mend their toys and dress their dolls; yet, they find time to bathe the head of the little girl who is so sick in the next house to theirs.

8. "They are full of good deeds to every living thing. I have seen them patting the tired horse and the lame dog in the street. They are always ready to help those who need help."

9. "I shall never think Mary's hands are ugly any more, Miss Roberts."

10. "I am glad to hear you say that, Daisy; and I must tell you that they are beautiful because they do their work gladly and cheerfully."

11. "O Miss Roberts! I feel so ashamed of myself, and so sorry," said Daisy, looking into her teacher's face with tearful eyes.

 12. "Then, my dear, show your sorrow by deeds of kindness. The good alone are really beautiful."

STORY XXV THINGS TO REMEMBER

1. When you rise in the morning, remember who kept you from danger during the night. Remember who watched over you while you slept, and whose sun shines around you, and gives you the sweet light of day.

2. Let God have the thanks of your heart, for his kindness and his care; and pray for his protection during the wakeful hours of day.

3. Remember that God made all creatures to be happy, and will do nothing that may prevent their being so, without good reason for it.

4. When you are at the table, do not eat in a greedy manner, like a pig. Eat quietly, and do not reach forth your hand for the food, but ask some one to help you.

5. Do not become peevish and pout, because you do not get a part of everything. Be satisfied with what is given you.

6. Avoid a pouting face, angry looks, and angry words. Do not slam the doors. Go quietly up and down stairs; and never make a loud noise about the house.

7. Be kind and gentle in your manners; not like the howling winter storm, but like the bright summer morning.

8. Do always as your parents bid you. Obey them with a ready mind, and with a pleasant face.

9. Never do anything that you would be afraid or ashamed that your parents should know. Remember, if no one else sees you, God does, from whom you can not hide even your most secret thought.

10. At night, before you go to sleep, think whether you have done anything that was wrong during the day, and pray to God to forgive you. If anyone has done you wrong, forgive him in your heart.

11. If you have not learned something useful, or been in some way useful, during the past day, think that it is a day lost, and be very sorry for it.

12. Trust in the Lord, and He will guide you in the way of good men. The path of the just is as the shining light that shineth more and more unto the perfect day.

13. We must do all the good we can to all men, for this is well pleasing in the sight of God. He delights to see his children walk in love, and do good one to another.

STORY XXVI THREE LITTLE MICE

1. I will tell you the story of three little mice,
   If you will keep still and listen to me,
   Who live in a cage that is cozy and nice,
   And are just as cunning as cunning can be.
   They look very wise, with their pretty red eyes,
   That seem just exactly like little round beads;

They are white as the snow, and stand up in a row
Whenever we do not attend to their needs;--

2. Stand up in a row in a comical way,--
Now folding their forepaws as if saying, please;"
Now rattling the lattice, as much as to say,
"We shall not stay here without more bread and cheese,"
They are not at all shy, as you'll find, if you try
To make them run up in their chamber to bed;
If they don't want to go, why, they won't go-- ah! no,
Though you tap with your finger each queer little head.

3. One day as I stood by the side of the cage,
Through the bars there protruded a funny, round tail;
Just for mischief I caught it, and soon; in a rage,
Its owner set up a most pitiful wail.
He looked in dismay,--there was something to pay,--
But what was the matter he could not make out;
What was holding him so, when he wanted
To go to see what his brothers upstairs were about?

4. But soon from the chamber the others rushed down,
Impatient to learn what the trouble might be;
I have not a doubt that each brow wore a frown,
Only frowns on their brows are not easy to see.
For a moment they gazed, perplexed and amazed;
Then began both together to--gnaw off the tail!
So, quick I released him,--do you think that it pleased him?
And up the small staircase they fled like a gale.

STORY XXVII THE NEW YEAR

1. One pleasant New-year morning, Edward rose, and washed and dressed himself in haste. He wanted to be first to wish a happy New Year.

2. He looked in every room, and shouted the words of welcome. He ran into the street, to repeat them to those he might meet.

3. When he came back, his father gave him two bright, new silver dollars.

4. His face lighted up as he took them. He had wished for a long time to buy some pretty books that he had seen at the bookstore.

5. He left the house with a light heart, intending to buy the books.

6. As he ran down the street, he saw a poor German family, the father, mother, and three children shivering with cold.

7. "I wish you a happy New Year," said Edward, as he was gayly passing on. The man shook his head.

8. "You do not belong to this country," said Edward. The man again shook his head, for he could not understand or speak our language.

9. But he pointed to his mouth, and to the children, as if to say, "These little ones have had nothing to eat for a long time."

10. Edward quickly understood that these poor people were in distress. He took out his dollars, and gave one to the man, and the other to his wife.

11. How their eyes sparkled with gratitude! They said something in their language, which doubtless meant, "We thank you a thousand times, and will remember you in our prayers."

12. When Edward came home, his father asked what books he had bought. He hung his head a moment, but quickly looked up.

13. "I have bought no books," said he, "I gave my money to some poor people, who seemed to be very hungry and wretched.

14. "I think I can wait for my books till next New Year. Oh, if you had seen how glad they were to receive the money!"

15. "My dear boy;" said his father, "here is a whole bundle of books. I give them to you, more as a reward for your goodness of heart than as a New-year gift.

16. "I saw you give the money to the poor German family. It was no small sum for a little boy to give cheerfully.

17. "Be thus ever ready to help the poor, and wretched, and distressed; and every year of your life will be to you a happy New Year."

Lesson 12

1. Write **reproach** (story 30) and **stroke** (story 31).
2. Read stories 28-31.
3. Write definitions of both words. (Answers)

STORY XXVIII THE CLOCK AND THE SUNDIAL A FABLE

1. One gloomy day, the clock on a church steeple, looking down on a sundial, said, "How stupid it is in you to stand there all the while like a stock!

2. "You never tell the hour till a bright sun looks forth from the sky, and gives you leave. I go

merrily round, day and night, in summer and winter the same, without asking his leave.

3. "I tell the people the time to rise, to go to dinner, and to come to church.

4. "Hark! I am going to strike now; one, two, three, four. There it is for you. How silly you look! You can say nothing."

5. The sun, at that moment, broke forth from behind a cloud, and showed, by the sundial, that the clock was half an hour behind the right time.

6. The boasting clock now held his tongue, and the dial only smiled at his folly.

7. MORAL.--Humble modesty is more often right than a proud and boasting spirit.

STORY XXIX REMEMBER

1. Remember, child, remember,
   That God is in the sky;
   That He looks down on all we do,
   With an ever-wakeful eye.

2. Remember, oh remember,
   That, all the day and night,
   He sees our thoughts and actions
   With an ever-watchful sight.

3. Remember, child, remember,
   That God is good and true;
   That He wishes us to always be
   Like Him in all we do.

4. Remember that He ever hates
   A falsehood or a lie;
   Remember He will punish, too,
   The wicked, by and by.

5. Remember, oh remember,
   That He is like a friend,
   And wishes us to holy be,
   And happy, in the end.

6. Remember, child, remember,
   To pray to Him in heaven;
   And if you have been doing wrong,
   Oh, ask to be forgiven.

7. Be sorry, in your little prayer,
   And whisper in his ear;
   Ask his forgiveness and his love.
   And He will surely hear.

8. Remember, child, remember,
   That you love, with all your might,
   The God who watches o'er us,
   And gives us each delight;
   Who guards us ever through the day,
   And saves us in the night.

STORY XXX COURAGE AND COWARDICE

1. Robert and Henry were going home from school, when, on turning a corner, Robert cried out, "A fight! let us go and see!"

2. "No," said Henry; "let us go quietly home and not meddle with this quarrel. We have nothing to do with it, and may get into mischief."

3. "You are a coward, and afraid to go," said Robert, and off he ran. Henry went straight home, and in the afternoon went to school, as usual.

4. But Robert had told all the boys that Henry was a coward, and they laughed at him a great deal.

5. Henry had learned, however, that true courage is shown most in bearing reproach when not deserved, and that he ought to be afraid of nothing but doing wrong.

6. A few days after, Robert was bathing with some schoolmates, and got out of his depth. He struggled, and screamed for help, but all in vain.

7. The boys who had called Henry a coward, got out of the water as fast as they could, but they did not even try to help him.

8. Robert was fast sinking, when Henry threw off his clothes, and sprang into the water. He reached Robert just as he was sinking the last time.

9. By great effort, and with much danger to himself, he brought Robert to the shore, and thus saved his life.

10. Robert and his schoolmates were ashamed at having called Henry a coward. They owned that he had more courage than any of them.

11. Never be afraid to do good, but always fear to do evil.

STORY XXXI WEIGHING AN ELEPHANT

1. "An eastern king," said Teddy's mother, "had been saved from some great danger. To show his gratitude for deliverance, he vowed he would give to the poor the weight of his favorite elephant in silver."

2. "Oh! what a great quantity that would be," cried Lily, opening her eyes very wide. "But how could you weigh an elephant?" asked Teddy, who was a quiet, thoughtful boy.

3. "There was the difficulty," said his mother. "The wise and learned men of the court stroked their long beards, and talked the matter over, but no one found out how to weigh the elephant.

4. "At last, a poor old sailor found safe and simple means by which to weigh the enormous beast. The thousands and thousands of pieces of silver were counted out to the people; and crowds of the poor were relieved by the clever thought of the sailor."

5. "O mamma," said Lily, "do tell us what it was!"

6. "Stop, stop!" said Teddy. "I want to think for myself-- think hard--and find out how an elephant's weight could be known, with little trouble and expense."

7. "I am well pleased," said his mother, "that my little boy should set his mind to work on the subject. If he can find out the sailor's secret before night, he shall have that orange for his pains."

8. The boy thought hard and long. Lily laughed at her brother's grave looks, as he sat leaning his head on his hands. Often she teased him with the question, "Can you weigh an elephant, Teddy?"

9. At last, while eating his supper, Teddy suddenly cried out, "I have it now!"

10. "Do you think so?" asked his mother.

11. "How would you do it," asked Lily.

12. "First, I would have a big boat brought very close to the shore, and would have planks laid across, so that the elephant could walk right into it."

13. "Oh, such a great, heavy beast would make it sink low in the water," said Lily.

14. "Of course it would," said her brother. Then I would mark on the outside of the boat the exact height to which the water had risen all around it while the elephant was inside. Then he should march on shore, leaving the boat quite empty."

15. "But I don't see the use of all this," said Lily.

16. "Don't you?" cried Teddy, in surprise. "Why, I should then bring the heaps of silver, and throw them into the boat till their weight would sink it to the mark made by the elephant. That would show that the weight of each was the same."

17. "How funny!" cried Lily; "you would make a weighing machine of the boat?"

18. "That is my plan," said Teddy.

19. "That was the sailor's plan," said his mother. "You have earned the orange, my boy."

Lesson 13

1. Write **clad, array** (32), **scarlet** (34), **revere** (35) and **torment** (36).
2. Pay attention to them as you read.
3. Read stories 32 – 36.
   - Deign means to stoop to a level lower than your station.
   - Hallow means to honor or respect greatly.
   - Transgressions are sins.
   - Plumage means feathers.
4. What do you think your new words mean?
5. Write the correct definitions. (Answers)
6. Complete the vocabulary activity.

Vocabulary

1. Match the words to their definitions. Write the letters and numbers of the matches on a separate sheet of paper. (Answers)

1. ask	A. assure
2. hurry	B. forge
3. pause	C. envy
4. sincere	D. strife
5. argument	E. distress
6. conflict	F. haste
7. to feel distress	G. malicious
8. jealousy	H. ignorant
9. hard work	I. earnest
10. lacking knowledge	J. dismay
11. intended to cause harm	K. adorn
12. to answer back sharply	L. hesitation
13. extreme worry or sorrow	M. inquire
14. without direction, lost	N. toil
15. put out, satisfy by drinking	O. adrift
16. small wood or group of trees	P. retort
17. make something more beautiful	Q. quench
18. create something new by heating metal	R. dispute
19. encourage someone to be sure of something	S. grove

STORY XXXII THE SOLDIER.

1. A soldier! a soldier! I'm longing to be:
   The name and the life of a soldier for me!

I would not be living at ease and at play;
True honor and glory I'd win in my day.

2. A soldier! a soldier! in armor arrayed;
My weapons in hand, of no contest afraid;
I'd ever be ready to strike the first blow,
And to fight my way through the ranks of the foe.

3. But then, let me tell you, no blood would I shed,
No victory seek o'er the dying and dead;
A far braver soldier than this would I be;
A warrior of Truth, in the ranks of the free.

4. A soldier! a soldier! Oh, then, let me be!
My friends, I invite you, enlist now with me.
Truth's bands shall be mustered, love's foes shall give way!
Let's up, and be clad in our battle array!

STORY XXXIII THE ECHO

1. As Robert was one day rambling about, he happened to cry out, "Ho, ho!" He instantly heard coming back from a hill nearby, the same words, "Ho, ho!"

2. In great surprise, he said with a loud voice, "Who are you?" Upon this, the same words came back, "Who are you?"

3. Robert now cried out harshly, "You must be a very foolish fellow." "Foolish fellow!" came back from the hill.

4. Robert became angry, and with loud and fierce words went toward the spot whence the sounds came. The words all came back to him in the same angry tone.

5. He then went into the thicket, and looked for the boy who, as he thought, was mocking him; but he could find nobody anywhere.

6. When he went home, he told his mother that some boy had hid himself in the wood, for the purpose of mocking him.

7. "Robert," said his mother, "you are angry with yourself alone. You heard nothing but your own words."

8. "Why, mother, how can that be?" said Robert. "Did you never hear an echo?" asked his mother. "An echo, dear mother? No, ma'am. What is it?"

9. "I will tell you," said his mother. "You know, when you play with your ball, and throw it against the side of a house, it bounds back to you." "Yes, mother," said he, "and I catch it again."

10. "Well," said his mother, "if I were in the open air, by the side of a hill or a large barn, and should

speak very loud, my voice would be sent back, so that I could hear again the very words which I spoke.

11. "That, my son, is an echo. When you thought some one was mocking you, it was only the hill before you, echoing, or sending back, your own voice.

12. "The bad boy, as you thought it was, spoke no more angrily than yourself. If you had spoken kindly, you would have heard a kind reply.

13. "Had you spoken in a low, sweet, gentle tone, the voice that came back would have been as low, sweet, and gentle as your own.

14. "The Bible says, 'A soft answer turneth away wrath.' Remember this when you are at play with your school mates.

15. "If any of them should be offended, and speak in a loud, angry tone, remember the echo, and let your words be soft and kind.

16. "When you come home from school, and find your little brother cross and peevish, speak mildly to him. You will soon see a smile on his lips, and find that his tones will become mild and sweet.

17. "Whether you are in the fields or in the woods, at school or at play, at home or abroad, remember,

> The good and the kind,
> By kindness their love ever proving,
> Will dwell with the pure and the loving."

STORY XXXIV GEORGE'S FEAST

1. George's mother was very poor. Instead of having bright, blazing fires in winter, she had nothing to burn but dry sticks, which George picked up from under the trees and hedges.

2. One fine day in July, she sent George to the woods, which were about two miles from the village in which she lived. He was to stay there all day, to get as much wood as he could collect.

3. It was a bright, sunny day, and George worked very hard; so that by the time the sun was high, he was hot, and wished for a cool place where he might rest and eat his dinner.

4. While he hunted about the bank he saw among the moss some fine, wild strawberries, which were a bright scarlet with ripeness.

5. "How good these will be with my bread and butter!" thought George; and lining his little cap with leaves, he set to work eagerly to gather all he could find, and then seated himself by the brook.

6. It was a pleasant place, and George felt happy and contented. He thought how much his mother would like to see him there, and to be there herself, instead of in her dark, close room in the village.

7. George thought of all this, and just as he was lifting the first strawberry to his mouth, he said to himself, "How much mother would like these;" and he stopped, and put the strawberry back again.

8. "Shall I save them for her?" said he, thinking how much they would refresh her, yet still looking at them with a longing eye.

9. "I will eat half, and take the other half to her," said he at last; and he divided them into two heaps. But each heap looked so small, that he put them together again.

10. "I will only taste one," thought he; but, as he again lifted it to his mouth, he saw that he had taken the finest, and he put it back. "I will keep them all for her," said he, and he covered them up nicely, till he should go home.

11. When the sun was beginning to sink, George set out for home. How happy he felt, then, that he had all his strawberries for his sick mother. The nearer he came to his home, the less he wished to taste them.

12. Just as he had thrown down his wood, he heard his mother's faint voice calling him from the next room. "Is that you, George? I am glad you have come, for I am thirsty, and am longing for some tea."

13. George ran in to her, and joyfully offered his wild strawberries. "And you saved them for your sick mother, did you?" said she, laying her hand fondly on his head, while the tears stood in her eyes. "God will bless you for all this, my child."

14. Could the eating of the strawberries have given George half the happiness he felt at this moment?

STORY XXXV THE LORD'S PRAYER

1. Our Father in heaven,
   We hallow thy name;
   May thy kingdom holy
   On earth be the same;
   Oh, give to us daily,
   Our portion of bread;
   It is from thy bounty
   That all must be fed.

2. Forgive our transgressions.
   And teach us to know
   The humble compassion
   that pardons each foe;
   Keep us from temptation,
   From weakness and sin,
   And thine be the glory
   Forever! Amen!

AN EVENING PRAYER.

1. Before I close my eyes to sleep,
   Lord, hear my evening prayer,
   And deign a helpless child to keep,
   With thy protecting care.

2. Though young in years, I have been taught
   Thy name to love and fear;
   Of thee to think with solemn thought,
   Thy goodness to revere.

3. That goodness gives each simple flower
   Its scent and beauty, too;
   And feeds it in night's darkest hour
   With heaven's refreshing dew.

4. The little birds that sing all day
   In many a leafy wood,
   By thee are clothed in plumage gay,
   By thee supplied with food.

5. And when at night they cease to sing,
   By thee protected still,
   Their young ones sleep beneath their wing,
   Secure from every ill.

6. Thus may'st thou guard with gracious arm
   The bed whereon I lie,
   And keep a child from every harm
   By thine own watchful eye.

STORY XXXVI FINDING THE OWNER

1. "It's mine," said Fred, showing a white-handled pocketknife, with every blade perfect and shining. "Just what I've always wanted." And he turned the prize over and over with evident satisfaction.

2. "I guess I know who owns it," said Tom, looking at it with a critical eye.

3. "I guess you don't," was the quick response. "It isn't Mr. Raymond's," said Fred, shooting wide of the mark.

4. "I know that; Mr. Raymond's is twice as large," observed Tom, going on with his drawing lesson.

5. Do you suppose Fred took any comfort in that knife? Not a bit of comfort did he take. He was conscious all the time of having something in his possession that did not belong to him; and Tom's suspicion interfered sadly with his enjoyment.

6. Finally, it became such a torment to him, that he had serious thoughts of burning it, or burying it, or giving it away; but a better plan suggested itself.

7. "Tom," said he, one day at recess, "didn't you say you thought you knew who owned that knife I found?"

8. "Yes, I did; it looked like Doctor Perry's." And Tom ran off to his play, without giving the knife another thought.

9. Dr. Perry's! Why, Fred would have time to go to the doctor's office before recess closed: so he started in haste, and found the old gentleman getting ready to visit a patient. "Is this yours?" cried Fred, in breathless haste, holding up the cause of a week's anxiety.

10. "It was," said the doctor; "but I lost it the other day."

11. "I found it," said Fred, "and have felt like a thief ever since. Here, take it; I've got to run."

12. "Hold on!" said the doctor. "I've got a new one, and you are quite welcome to this."

13. "Am I? May I? Oh! thank you!" And with what a different feeling he kept it from that which he had experienced for a week!

Lesson 14

1.   Write **crevice and prowl** (story 37).
2.   A chandelier is a fancy light that hangs from the ceiling with lots of branches that hold many light bulbs or candles.
3.   A pendulum usually is found in old fashioned clocks. It swings back and forth, regulating the time.
4.   Lowing is the sound cows make; lance is the long spear thing a knight uses; sheaves are bundles of cut grain.
5.   Read stories 37 – 40 (in Roman Numerals L means 50)
6.   Guess what you think those words mean.
7.   Look up the definitions and write the correct definitions. (Answers)

STORY XXXVII BATS

1. Bats are very strange little animals, having hair like mice, and wings like birds. During the day, they live in crevices of rocks, in caves, and in other dark places.

2. At night, they go forth in search of food; and, no doubt, you have seen them flying about, catching such insects as happen to be out rather late at night.

3. The wings of a bat have no quills. They are only thin pieces of skin stretched upon a framework of bones. Besides this, it may be said that while he is a quadruped, he can rise into the air and fly from place to place like a bird.

4. There is a funny fable about the bat, founded upon this double character of beast and bird, which I will tell you.

5. An owl was once prowling about, when he came across a bat. So he caught him in his claws, and was about to devour him. Upon this, the bat began to squeal terribly; and he said to the owl, "Pray, what do you take me for, that you use me thus?"

6. "Why, you are a bird, to be sure," said the owl, "and I am fond of birds. I love dearly to break their little bones."

7. "Well," said the bat, "I thought there was some mistake. I am no bird. Don't you see, Mr. Owl, that I have no feathers, and that I am covered with hair like a mouse?"

8. "Sure enough," said the owl, in great surprise; "I see it now. Really, I took you for a bird, but it appears you are only a kind of mouse. I ate a mouse last night, and it gave me the nightmare. I can't bear mice! Bah! it makes me sick to think of it." So the owl let the bat go.

9. The very next night, the bat encountered another danger. He was snapped up by puss, who took him for a mouse, and immediately prepared to eat him.

10. "I beg you to stop one moment," said the bat. "Pray, Miss Puss, what do you suppose I am?" "A mouse, to be sure!" said the cat. "Not at all," said the bat, spreading his long wings.

11. "Sure enough," said the cat: "you seem to be a bird, though your feathers are not very fine. I eat birds sometimes, but I am tired of them just now, having lately devoured four young robins; so you may go. But, bird or mouse, it will be your best policy to keep out of my way hereafter."

12. The meaning of this fable is, that a person playing a double part may sometimes escape danger; but he is always, like the bat, a creature that is disgusting to everybody, and shunned by all.

STORY XXXVIII A SUMMER DAY

1. This is the way the morning dawns:
Rosy tints on flowers and trees,
Winds that wake the birds and bees,
Dewdrops on the fields and lawns—
This is the way the morning dawns.

2. This is the way the sun comes up:
Gold on brook and glossy leaves,
Mist that melts above the sheaves,
Vine, and rose, and buttercup—
This is the way the sun comes up.

3. This is the way the river flows:
Here a whirl, and there a dance;

Slowly now, then, like a lance,
Swiftly to the sea it goes—
This is the way the river flows.

4. This is the way the rain comes down:
Tinkle, tinkle, drop by drop,
Over roof and chimney top;
Boughs that bend, and skies that frown—
This is the way the rain comes down.

5. This is the way the birdie sings:
"Baby birdies in the nest,
You I surely love the best;
Over you I fold my wings"—
This is the way the birdie sings.

6. This is the way the daylight dies:
Cows are lowing in the lane,
Fireflies wink on hill and plain;
Yellow, red, and purple skies—
This is the way the daylight dies.

STORY XXXIX I WILL THINK OF IT

1. "I will think of it." It is easy to say this; but do you know what great things have come from thinking?

2. We can not see our thoughts, or hear, or taste, or feel them; and yet what mighty power they have!

3. Sir Isaac Newton was seated in his garden on a summer's evening, when he saw an apple fall from a tree. He began to think, and, in trying to find out why the apple fell, discovered how the earth, sun, moon, and stars are kept in their places.

4. A boy named James Watt sat quietly by the fireside, watching the lid of the tea kettle as it moved up and down. He began to think; he wanted to find out why the steam in the kettle moved the heavy lid.

5. From that time he went on thinking and thinking; and when he became a man, he improved the steam engine so much that it could, with the greatest ease, do the work of many horses.

6. When you see a steamboat, a steam mill, or a locomotive, remember that it would never have been built if it had not been for the hard thinking of some one.

7. A man named Galileo was once standing in the cathedral of Pisa, when he saw a chandelier swaying to and fro.

8. This set him thinking, and it led to the invention of the pendulum.

9. James Ferguson was a poor Scotch shepherd boy. Once, seeing the inside of a watch, he was filled with wonder. "Why should I not make a watch?" thought he.

10. But how was he to get the materials out of which to make the wheels and the mainspring? He soon found how to get them: he made the mainspring out of a piece of whalebone. He then made a wooden clock which kept good time.

11. He began, also, to copy pictures with a pen, and portraits with oil colors. In a few years, while still a small boy, he earned money enough to support his father.

12. When he became a man, he went to London to live. Some of the wisest men in England, and the king himself, used to attend his lectures. His motto was, "I will think of it;" and he made his thoughts useful to himself and the world.

13. Boys, when you have a difficult lesson to learn, don't feel discouraged, and ask some one to help you before helping yourselves. Think, and by thinking you will learn how to think to some purpose.

STORY XL CHARLIE AND ROB

1. "Don't you hate splitting wood?" asked Charlie, as he sat down on a log to hinder Rob for a while.

2. "No, I rather like it. When I get hold of a tough old fellow, I say, 'See here, now, you think you're the stronger, and are going to beat me; so I'll split you up into kindling wood."

3. "Pshaw!" said Charlie, laughing; "and it's only a stick of wood."

4. "Yes; but you see I pretend it's a lesson, or a tough job of any kind, and it's nice to conquer it."

5. "I don't want to conquer such things; I don't care what becomes of them. I wish I were a man, and a rich one."

6. "Well, Charlie, if you live long enough you'll be a man, without wishing for it; and as for the rich part, I mean to be that myself."

7. "You do. How do you expect to get your money? By sawing wood?"

8. "May be--some of it; that's as good a way as any, so long as it lasts. I don't care how I get rich, you know, so that it's in an honest and useful way."

9. "I'd like to sleep over the next ten years, and wake up to find myself a young man with a splendid education and plenty of money."

10. "Humph! I am not sleepy--a night at a time is enough for me. I mean to work the next ten years. You see there are things that you've got to work out--you can't sleep them out."

11. "I hate work," said Charlie, "that is, such work as sawing and splitting wood, and doing chores. I'd like to do some big work, like being a clerk in a bank or something of that sort."

12. "Wood has to be sawed and split before it can be burned," said Rob. "I don't know but I'll be a clerk in a bank some time; I'm working towards it. I'm keeping father's accounts for him."

13. How Charlie laughed! "I should think that was a long way from being a bank clerk. I suppose your father sells two tables and six chairs, some days, doesn't he?"

14. "Sometimes more than that, and some times not so much," said Rob, in perfect good humor.

15. "I didn't say I was a bank clerk now. I said I was working towards it. Am I not nearer it by keeping a little bit of a book than I should be if I didn't keep any book at all?"

16. "Not a whit--such things happen," said Charlie, as he started to go.

17. Now, which of these boys, do you think, grew up to be a rich and useful man, and which of them joined a party of tramps before he was thirty years old?

Lesson 15

1. Read stories 41 – 45.
2. Tell someone about the stories.

STORY XLI. RAY AND HIS KITE.

1. Ray was thought to be an odd boy. You will think him so, too, when you have read this story.

2. Ray liked well enough to play with the boys at school; yet he liked better to be alone under the shade of some tree, reading a fairy tale or dreaming daydreams. But there was one sport that he liked as well as his companions; that was kite flying.

3. One day when he was flying his kite, he said to himself, "I wonder if anybody ever tried to fly a kite at night. It seems to me it would be nice. But then, if it were very dark, the kite could not be seen. What if I should fasten a light to it, though? That would make it show. I'll try it this very night."

4. As soon as it was dark, without saying a word to anybody, he took his kite and lantern, and went to a large, open lot, about a quarter of a mile from his home. "Well," thought he, "this is queer. How lonely and still it seems without any other boys around! But I am going to fly my kite, anyway."

5. So he tied the lantern, which was made of tin punched full of small holes, to the tail of his kite. Then he pitched the kite, and, after several attempts, succeeded in making it rise. Up it went, higher and higher, as Ray let out the string. When the string was all unwound, he tied it to a fence; and then he stood and gazed at his kite as it floated high up in the air.

6. While Ray was enjoying his sport, some people who were out on the street in the village, saw a strange light in the sky. They gathered in groups to watch it. Now it was still for a few seconds, then it seemed to be jumping up and down; then it made long sweeps back and forth through the

air.

7. "What can it be?" said one person. "How strange!" said another. "It can not be a comet; for comets have tails," said a third. "Perhaps it's a big firefly," said another.

8. At last some of the men determined to find out what this strange light was-- whether it was a hobgoblin dancing in the air, or something dropped from the sky. So off they started to get as near it as they could.

9. While this was taking place, Ray, who had got tired of standing, was seated in a fence corner, behind a tree. He could see the men as they approached; but they did not see him.

10. When they were directly under the light, and saw what it was, they looked at each other, laughing, and said, "This is some boy's trick; and it has fooled us nicely. Let us keep the secret, and have our share of the joke."

11. Then they laughed again, and went back to the village; and some of the simple people there have not yet found out what that strange light was.

12. When the men had gone, Ray thought it was time for him to go; so he wound up his string, picked up his kite and lantern, and went home. His mother had been wondering what had become of him.

13. When she heard what he had been doing, she hardly knew whether to laugh or scold; but I think she laughed, and told him that it was time for him to go to bed.

STORY XLII BEWARE OF THE FIRST DRINK

1. "Uncle Philip, as the day is fine, will you take a walk with us this morning?"

2. "Yes, boys. Let me get my hat and cane, and we will take a ramble. I will tell you a story as we go. Do you know poor old Tom Smith?"

3. "Know him! Why, Uncle Philip, everybody knows him. He is such a shocking drunkard, and swears so horribly."

4. "Well, I have known him ever since we were boys together. There was not a more decent, well-behaved boy among us. After he left school, his father died, and he was put into a store in the city. There, he fell into bad company.

5. "Instead of spending his evenings in reading, he would go to the theater and to balls. He soon learned to play cards, and of course to play for money. He lost more than he could pay.

6. "He wrote to his poor mother, and told her his losses. She sent him money to pay his debts, and told him to come home.

7. "He did come home. After all, he might still have been useful and happy, for his friends were willing to forgive the past. For a time, things went on well. He married a lovely woman, gave up his bad habits, and was doing well.

8. "But one thing, boys, ruined him forever. In the city, he had learned to take strong drink, and he said to me once, that when a man begins to drink, he never knows where it will end. 'Therefore,' said Tom, 'beware of the first drink!'

9. "It was not long before he began to follow his old habit. He knew the danger, but it seemed as if he could not resist his desire to drink. His poor mother soon died of grief and shame. His lovely wife followed her to the grave.

10. "He lost the respect of all, went on from bad to worse, and has long been a perfect sot. Last night, I had a letter from the city, stating that Tom Smith had been found guilty of stealing, and sent to the state prison for ten years.

11. "There I suppose he will die, for he is now old. It is dreadful to think to what an end he has come. I could not but think, as I read the letter, of what he said to me years ago, 'Beware of the first drink!'

12. "Ah, my dear boys, when old Uncle Philip is gone, remember that he told you the story of Tom Smith, and said to you, 'Beware of the first drink!' The man who does this will never be a drunkard."

STORY XLIII SPEAK GENTLY

1. Speak gently; it is better far
   To rule by love than fear:
   Speak gently; let no harsh words mar
   The good we might do here.

2. Speak gently to the little child;
   Its love be sure to gain;
   Teach it in accents soft and mild;
   It may not long remain.

3. Speak gently to the aged one;
   Grieve not the careworn heart:
   The sands of life are nearly run;
   Let such in peace depart.

4. Speak gently, kindly, to the poor;
   Let no harsh tone be heard;
   They have enough they must endure,
   Without an unkind word.

5. Speak gently to the erring;
   Know they must have toiled in vain;
   Perhaps unkindness made them so;
   Oh, win them back again.

6. Speak gently: 'tis a little thing

Dropped in the heart's deep well;
The good, the joy, which it may bring,
Eternity shall tell.

STORY XLIV THE SEVEN STICKS

1. A man had seven sons, who were always quarreling. They left their studies and work, to quarrel among themselves. Some bad men were looking forward to the death of their father, to cheat them out of their property by making them quarrel about it.

2. The good old man, one day, called his sons around him. He laid before them seven sticks, which were bound together. He said, "I will pay a hundred dollars to the one who can break this bundle."

3. Each one strained every nerve to break the bundle. After a long but vain trial, they all said that it could not be done.

4. "And yet, my boys," said the father, "nothing is easier to do." He then untied the bundle, and broke the sticks, one by one, with perfect ease.

5. "Ah!" said his sons, "it is easy enough to do it so; anybody could do it in that way."

6. Their father replied, "As it is with these sticks, so is it with you, my sons. So long as you hold fast together and aid each other, you will prosper, and none can injure you.

7. "But if the bond of union be broken, it will happen to you just as it has to these sticks, which lie here broken on the ground." Home, city, country, all are prosperous found, when by the powerful link of union bound.

STORY XLV THE MOUNTAIN SISTER

1. The home of little Jeannette is far away, high up among the mountains. Let us call her our mountain sister.

2. There are many things you would like to hear about her, but I can only tell you now how she goes with her father and brother, in the autumn, to help gather nuts for the long winter.

3. A little way down the mountain side is a chestnut wood. Did you ever see a chestnut tree? In the spring its branches are covered with bunches of creamy flowers, like long tassels. All the hot summer these are turning into sweet nuts, wrapped safely in large, prickly, green balls.

4. But when the frost of autumn comes, these prickly balls turn brown, and crack open. Then you may see inside one, two, three, and even four, sweet, brown nuts.

5. When her father says, one night at supper time, "I think there will be a frost tonight," Jeannette knows very well what to do. She dances away early in the evening to her little bed, made in a box built up against the wall.

6. Soon she falls asleep to dream about the chestnut wood, and the little brook that springs from rock to rock down under the tall, dark trees. She wakes with the first daylight, and is out of bed in

a minute, when she hears her father's cheerful call, "Come, children; it is time to be off."

7. Their dinner is ready in a large basket. The donkey stands before the door with great bags for the nuts hanging at each side. They go merrily over the crisp, white frost to the chestnut trees. How the frost has opened the burs! It has done half their work for them already.

8. How they laugh and sing, and shout to each other as they fill their baskets! The sun looks down through the yellow leaves; the rocks give them mossy seats; the birds and squirrels wonder what these strange people are doing in their woods.

9. Jeannette really helps, though she is only a little girl; and her father says at night, that his Jane is a dear, good child. This makes her very happy. She thinks about it at night, when she says her prayers. Then she goes to sleep to dream of the merry autumn days.

10. Such is our little mountain sister, and here is a picture of her far-away home. The mountain life is ever a fresh and happy one.

Lesson 16

1. Read stories 46 – 50.
2. Tell someone about what you read.
3. Complete the vocabulary activity.

Vocabulary

1. Match the words and their definitions. Write the letters and numbers of the matches on a separate piece of paper. (Answers)

1.	revere	A.	to move around stealthily
2.	clad	B.	deeply respect
3.	prowl	C.	narrow opening
4.	crevice	D.	to cause suffering
5.	torment	E.	covered
6.	peevish	F.	to run your hand along something, esp. hair or fur
7.	coarse	G.	an ordered arrangement of something
8.	stroke	H.	rough
9.	array	I.	easily irritated
10.	scarlet	J.	bright red

STORY XLVI HARRY AND THE GUIDEPOST

1. The night was dark, the sun was hid
Beneath the mountain gray,

And not a single star appeared
To shoot a silver ray.

2. Across the heath the owlet flew,
   And screamed along the blast;
   And onward, with a quickened step,
   Benighted Harry passed.

3. Now, in thickest darkness plunged,
   He groped his way to find;
   And now, he thought he saw beyond,
   A form of horrid kind.

4. In deadly white it upward rose,
   Of cloak and mantle bare,
   And held its naked arms across,
   To catch him by the hair.

5. Poor Harry felt his blood run cold,
   At what before him stood;
   But then, thought he, no harm, I'm sure,
   Can happen to the good.

6. So, calling all his courage up,
   He to the monster went;
   And eager through the dismal gloom
   His piercing eyes he bent.

7. And when he came well nigh
   The ghost that gave him such affright,
   He clapped his hands upon his side,
   And loudly laughed outright.

8. For't was a friendly guidepost stood,
   His wandering steps to guide;
   And thus he found that to the good,
   No evil could betide.

9. Ah well, thought he, one thing I've learned,
   Nor shall I soon forget;
   Whatever frightens me again,
   I'll march straight up to it.

10. And when I hear an idle tale,
    Of monster or of ghost,
    I'll tell of this, my lonely walk,
    And one tall, white guidepost.

STORY XLVII THE MONEY AMY DIDN'T EARN

1. Amy was a dear little girl, but she was too apt to waste time in getting ready to do her tasks, instead of doing them at once as she ought.

2. In the village in which she lived, Mr. Thornton kept a store where he sold fruit of all kinds, including berries in their season. One day he said to Amy, whose parents were quite poor, "Would you like to earn some money?"

3. "Oh, yes," replied she, "for I want some new shoes, and papa has no money to buy them with."

4. "Well, Amy," said Mr. Thornton, "I noticed some fine, ripe blackberries in Mr. Green's pasture to-day, and he said that anybody was welcome to them. I will pay you thirteen cents a quart for all you will pick for me."

5. Amy was delighted at the thought of earning some money; so she ran home to get a basket, intending to go immediately to pick the berries.

6. Then she thought she would like to know how much money she would get if she picked five quarts. With the help of her slate and pencil, she found out that she would get sixty-five cents.

7. "But supposing I should pick a dozen quarts," thought she, "how much should I earn then?" "Dear me," she said, after figuring a while, "I should earn a dollar and fifty-six cents."

8. Amy then found out what Mr. Thornton would pay her for fifty, a hundred, and two hundred quarts. It took her some time to do this, and then it was so near dinner time that she had to stay at home until afternoon.

9. As soon as dinner was over, she took her basket and hurried to the pasture. Some boys had been there before dinner, and all the ripe berries were picked. She could not find enough to fill a quart measure.

10. As Amy went home, she thought of what her teacher had often told her--"Do your task at once; then think about it," for "one doer is worth a hundred dreamers."

STORY XLVIII WHO MADE THE STARS?

1. "Mother, who made the stars, which light
The beautiful blue sky?
Who made the moon, so clear and bright,
That rises up so high?"

2. "T'was God, my child, the Glorious One,
He formed them by his power;
He made alike the brilliant sun,
And every leaf and flower.

3. "He made your little feet to walk;
Your sparkling eyes to see;

Your busy, prattling tongue to talk,
And limbs so light and free.

4. "He paints each fragrant flower that blows,
With loveliness and bloom;
He gives the violet and the rose
Their beauty and perfume.

5. "Our various wants his hands supply;
He guides us every hour;
We're kept beneath his watchful eye,
And guarded by his power.

6. "Then let your little heart, my love,
Its grateful homage pay
To that kind Friend, who, from above,
Thus guides you every day.

7. "In all the changing scenes of time,
On Him our hopes depend;
In every age, in every clime,
Our Father and our Friend."

STORY XLIX DEEDS OF KINDNESS

1. One day, as two little boys were walking along the road, they overtook a woman carrying a large basket of apples.

2. The boys thought the woman looked very pale and tired; so they said, "Are you going to town? If you are, we will carry your basket."

3. "Thank you," replied the woman, "you are very kind: you see I am weak and ill." Then she told them that she was a widow, and had a lame son to support.

4. She lived in a cottage three miles away, and was now going to market to sell the apples which grew on the only tree in her little garden. She wanted the money to pay her rent.

5. "We are going the same way you are," said the boys. "Let us have the basket;" and they took hold of it, one on each side, and trudged along with merry hearts.

6. The poor widow looked glad, and said that she hoped their mother would not be angry with them. "Oh, no," they replied; "our mother has taught us to be kind to everybody, and to be useful in any way that we can."

7. She then offered to give them a few of the ripest apples for their trouble. "No, thank you," said they; "we do not want any pay for what we have done."

8. When the widow got home, she told her lame son what had happened on the road, and they were both made happier that day by the kindness of the two boys.

9. The other day, I saw a little girl stop and pick up a piece of orange peel, which she threw into the gutter. "I wish the boys would not throw orange peel on the sidewalk," said she. "Some one may tread upon it, and fall."

10. "That is right, my dear," I said. "It is a little thing for you to do what you have done, but it shows that you have a thoughtful mind and a feeling heart."

11. Perhaps some may say that these are little things. So they are; but we must not wait for occasions to do great things. We must begin with little labors of love.

STORY L THE ALARM CLOCK

1. A lady, who found it not easy to wake in the morning as early as she wished, bought an alarm clock. These clocks are so made as to strike with a loud whirring noise at any hour the owner pleases to set them.

2. The lady placed her clock at the head of the bed, and at the right time she found herself roused by the long, rattling sound.

3. She arose at once, and felt better all day for her early rising. This lasted for some weeks. The alarm clock faithfully did its duty, and was plainly heard so long as it was obeyed.

4. But, after a time, the lady grew tired of early rising. When she was waked by the noise, she merely turned over in bed, and slept again.

5. In a few days, the clock ceased to rouse her from her sleep. It spoke just as loudly as ever; but she did not hear it, because she had been in the habit of not obeying it.

6. Finding that she might as well be without it, she resolved that when she heard the sound she would jump up.

7. Just so it is with conscience. If we will obey its voice, even in the most trifling things, we can always hear it, clear and strong.

8. But if we allow ourselves to do what we have some fears may not be quite right, we shall grow more and more sleepy, until the voice of conscience has no longer power to wake us.

Lesson 17

1. Read stories 51 – 56.
2. Tell someone about what you read.

STORY LI SPRING

1. The alder by the river
   Shakes out her powdery curls;

The willow buds in silver
For little boys and girls.

2. The little birds fly over,
   And oh, how sweet they sing!
   To tell the happy children
   That once again 'tis Spring.

3. The gay green grass comes creeping
   So soft beneath their feet;
   The frogs begin to ripple
   A music clear and sweet.

4. And buttercups are coming,
   And scarlet columbine,
   And in the sunny meadows
   The dandelions shine.

5. And just as many daisies
   As their soft hands can hold,
   The little ones may gather,
   All fair in white and gold.

6. Here blows the warm red clover,
   There peeps the violet blue;
   Oh, happy little children!
   God made them all for you.

STORY LII TRUE COURAGE

One cold winter's day, three boys were passing by a schoolhouse. The oldest was a bad boy, always in trouble himself, and trying to get others into trouble. The youngest, whose name was George, was a very good boy.

George wished to do right, but was very much wanting in courage. The other boys were named Henry and James. As they walked along, they talked as follows:

Henry: What fun it would be to throw a snowball against the schoolroom door, and make the teacher and scholars all jump!

James: You would jump, if you should. If the teacher did not catch you and whip you, he would tell your father, and you would get a whipping then; and that would make you jump higher than the scholars, I think.

Henry: Why, we would get so far off, before the teacher could come to the door, that he could not tell who we are. Here is a snowball just as hard as ice, and George would as soon throw it against the door as not.

James: Give it to him, and see. He would not dare to throw it.

Henry: Do you think George is a coward? You do not know him as well as I do. Here, George, take this snowball, and show James that you are not such a coward as he thinks you are.

George: I am not afraid to throw it; but I do not want to. I do not see that it will do any good, or that there will be any fun in it.

James: There! I told you he would not dare to throw it.

Henry: Why, George, are you turning coward? I thought you did not fear anything. Come, save your credit, and throw it. I know you are not afraid.

George: Well, I am not afraid to throw. Give me the snowball. I would as soon throw it as not.

Whack! went the snowball against the door; and the boys took to their heels. Henry was laughing as heartily as he could, to think what a fool he had made of George.

George had a whipping for his folly, as he ought to have had. He was such a coward, that he was afraid of being called a coward. He did not dare refuse to do as Henry told him, for fear that he would be laughed at.

If he had been really a brave boy, he would have said, "Henry, do you suppose that I am so foolish as to throw that snowball, just because you want to have me? You may throw your own snowballs, if you please!" Henry would, perhaps, have laughed at him, and called him a coward.

But George would have said, "Do you think that I care for your laughing? I do not think it right to throw the snowball. I will not do that which I think to be wrong, if the whole town should join with you in laughing."

This would have been real courage. Henry would have seen, at once, that it would do no good to laugh at a boy who had so bold a heart. You must have this fearless spirit, or you will get into trouble, and will be, and ought to be, disliked by all.

STORY LIII THE OLD CLOCK

1. In the old, old hall the old clock stands,
   And round and round move the steady hands;
   With its tick, tick, tick, both night and day,
   While seconds and minutes pass away.

2. At the old, old clock oft wonders Nell,
   For she can't make out what it has to tell;
   She has ne'er yet read, in prose or rhyme,
   That it marks the silent course of time.

3. When I was a child, as Nell is now,
   And long ere Time had wrinkled my brow,

The old, old clock both by night and day
Said,--"Tick, tick, tick!" Time passes away.

STORY LIV THE WAVES

1. "Where are we to go?" said the little waves to the great, deep sea. "Go, my darlings, to the yellow sands: you will find work to do there."

2. "I want to play," said one little wave; "I want to see who can jump the highest." "No; come on, come on," said an earnest wave; "mother must be right. I want to work."

3. "Oh, I dare not go," said another; "look at those great, black rocks close to the sands; I dare not go there, for they will tear me to pieces."

4. "Take my hand, sister," said the earnest wave; "let us go on together. How glorious it is to do some work."

5. "Shall we ever go back to mother?" "Yes, when our work is done."

6. So one and all hurried on. Even the little wave that wanted to play, pressed on, and thought that work might be fun after all. The timid ones did not like to be left behind, and they became earnest as they got nearer the sands.

7. After all, it was fun, pressing on one after another-- jumping, laughing, running on to the broad, shining sands.

8. First, they came in their course to a great sand castle. Splash, splash! they all went over it, and down it came. "Oh, what fun!" they cried.

9. "Mother told me to bring these seaweeds; I will find a pretty place for them," said one--and she ran a long way over the sands, and left them among the pebbles. The pebbles cried, "We are glad you are come. We wanted washing."

10. "Mother sent these shells; I don't know where to put them," said a little fretful wave. "Lay them one by one on the sand, and do not break them," said the eldest wave.

11. And the little one went about its work, and learned to be quiet and gentle, for fear of breaking the shells.

12. "Where is my work?" said a great, full-grown wave. "This is mere play. The little ones can do this and laugh over it. Mother said there was work for me." And he came down upon some large rocks.

13. Over the rocks and into a pool he went, and he heard the fishes say, "The sea is coming. Thank you, great sea; you always send a big wave when a storm is nigh. Thank you, kind wave; we are all ready for you now."

14. Then the waves all went back over the wet sands, slowly and carelessly, for they were tired.

15. "All my shells are safe," said one.

16. And, "My seaweeds are left behind," said another.

17. "I washed all of the pebbles," said a third.

18. "And I--I only broke on a rock, and splashed into a pool," said the one that was so eager to work. "I have done no good, mother--no work at all."

19. "Hush!" said the sea. And they heard a child that was walking on the shore, say, "O mother, the sea has been here! Look, how nice and clean the sand is, and how clear the water is in that pool."

20. Then the sea, said, "Hark!" and far away they heard the deep moaning of the coming storm.

21. "Come, my darlings," said she; "you have done your work, now let the storm do its work."

STORY LV DON'T KILL THE BIRDS

1. Don't kill the birds! the little birds,
   That sing about your door
   Soon as the joyous Spring has come,
   And chilling storms are o'er.

2. The little birds! how sweet they sing!
   Oh, let them joyous live;
   And do not seek to take the life
   Which you can never give.

3. Don't kill the birds! the pretty birds,
   That play among the trees;
   For earth would be a cheerless place,
   If it were not for these.

4. The little birds! how fond they play!
   Do not disturb their sport;
   But let them warble forth their songs,
   Till winter cuts them short.

5. Don't kill the birds! the happy birds,
   That bless the field and grove;
   So innocent to look upon,
   They claim our warmest love.

6. The happy birds, the tuneful birds,
   How pleasant 't is to see!
   No spot can be a cheerless place
   Where'er their presence be.

STORY LVI WHEN TO SAY NO

1. Though "No" is a very little word, it is not always easy to say it; and the not doing so, often causes trouble.

2. When we are asked to stay away from school, and spend in idleness or mischief the time which ought to be spent in study, we should at once say "No."

3. When we are urged to loiter on our way to school, and thus be late, and interrupt our teacher and the school, we should say "No." When some schoolmate wishes us to whisper or play in the schoolroom, we should say "No."

4. When we are tempted to use angry or wicked words, we should remember that the eye of God is always upon us, and should say "No."

5. When we have done anything wrong, and are tempted to conceal it by falsehood, we should say "No, we can not tell a lie; it is wicked and cowardly."

6. If we are asked to do anything which we know to be wrong, we should not fear to say "No."

7. If we thus learn to say "No," we shall avoid much trouble, and be always safe.

Lesson 18

1. Read stories 57 – 60.
2. Write in your notebook the moral, or lesson, from each of your readings today. Label each one with the story number.

Vocabulary

1. Review your vocabulary words by going to Lesson 16.

STORY LVII WHICH LOVED BEST?

1. "I love you, mother," said little John;
   Then, forgetting work, his cap went on,
   And he was off to the garden swing,
   Leaving his mother the wood to bring.

2. "I love you, mother," said rosy Nell;
   "I love you better than tongue can tell;"
   Then she teased and pouted full half the day,
   Till her mother rejoiced when she went to play.

3. "I love you, mother," said little Fan;
   "Today I'll help you all I can;
   How glad I am that school doesn't keep!"
   So she rocked the baby till it fell asleep.

4. Then, stepping softly, she took the broom,
   And swept the floor, and dusted the room;
   Busy and happy all day was she,
   Helpful and cheerful as child could be.

5. "I love you, mother," again they said –
   Three little children going to bed;
   How do you think that mother guessed
   Which of them really loved her best?

STORY LVIII JOHN CARPENTER

1. John Carpenter did not like to buy toys that somebody else had made. He liked the fun of making them himself. The thought that they were his own work delighted him.

2. Tom Austin, one of his playmates, thought a toy was worth nothing unless it cost a great deal of money. He never tried to make anything, but bought all his toys.

3. "Come and look at my horse," said he, one day. "It cost a dollar, and it is such a beauty! Come and see it."

4. John was soon admiring his friend's horse; and he was examining it carefully, to see how it was made. The same evening he began to make one for himself.

5. He went into the wood shed, and picked out two pieces of wood--one for the head of his horse, the other for the body. It took him two or three days to shape them to his satisfaction.

6. His father gave him a bit of red leather for a bridle, and a few brass nails, and his mother found a bit of old fur with which he made a mane and tail for his horse.

7. But what about the wheels? This puzzled him. At last he thought he would go to a turner's shop, and see if he could not get some round pieces of wood which might suit his purpose.

8. He found a large number of such pieces among the shavings on the floor, and asked permission to take a few of them. The turner asked him what he wanted them for, and he told him about his horse.

9. "Oh," said the man, laughing, "if you wish it, I will make some wheels for your horse. But mind, when it is finished, you must let me see it."

10. John promised to do so, and he soon ran home with the wheels in his pocket. The next evening, he went to the turner's shop with his horse all complete, and was told that he was an ingenious little fellow.

11. Proud of this compliment, he ran to his friend Tom, crying, "Now then, Tom, here is my horse, look!"

12. "Well, that is a funny horse," said Tom; "where did you buy it?" "I didn't buy it," replied John; I made it."

13. "You made it yourself! Oh, well, it's a good horse for you to make. But it is not so good as mine. Mine cost a dollar, and yours didn't cost anything."

14. "It was real fun to make it, though," said John, and away he ran with his horse rolling after him.

15. Do you want to know what became of John? Well, I will tell you. He studied hard in school, and was called the best scholar in his class. When he left school, he went to work in a machine shop. He is now a master workman, and will soon have a shop of his own.

STORY LIX PERSEVERE

1. The fisher who draws in his net too soon,
   Won't have any fish to sell;
   The child who shuts up his book too soon,
   Won't learn any lessons well.

2. If you would have your learning stay,
   Be patient, don't learn too fast:
   The man who travels a mile each day,
   May get round the world at last.

STORY LX THE CONTENTED BOY

Mr. Lenox was one morning riding by himself. He got off from his horse to look at something on the roadside. The horse broke away from him, and ran off. Mr. Lenox ran after him, but soon found that he could not catch him.

A little boy at work in a field near the road, heard the horse. As soon as he saw him running from his master, the boy ran very quickly to the middle of the road, and, catching the horse by the bridle, stopped him till Mr. Lenox came up.

Mr. Lenox: Thank you, my good boy, you have caught my horse very nicely. What shall I give you for your trouble?

Boy: I want nothing, sir.

Mr. L: You want nothing? So much the better for you. Few men can say as much. But what were you doing in the field?

Boy: I was rooting up weeds, and tending the sheep that were feeding on turnips.

Mr. L: Do you like to work?

Boy: Yes, sir, very well, this fine weather.

Mr. L: But would you not rather play?

Boy: This is not hard work. It is almost as good as play.

Mr. L: Who set you to work?

Boy: My father, sir.

Mr. L: What is your name?

Boy: Peter Hurdle, sir.

Mr. L: How old are you?

Boy: Eight years old, next June.

Mr. L: How long have you been here?

Boy: Ever since six o'clock this morning.

Mr. L: Are you not hungry?

Boy: Yes, sir, but I shall go to dinner soon.

Mr. L: If you had a dime now, what would you do with it?

Boy: I don't know, sir. I never had so much.

Mr. L: Have you no playthings?

Boy: Playthings? What are they?

Mr. L: Such things as ninepins, marbles, tops, and wooden horses.

Boy: No, sir. Tom and I play at football in winter, and I have a jumping rope. I had a hoop, but it is broken.

Mr. L: Do you want nothing else?

Boy: I have hardly time to play with what I have. I have to drive the cows, and to run on errands, and to ride the horses to the fields, and that is as good as play.

Mr. L: You could get apples and cakes, if you had money, you know.

Boy: I can have apples at home. As for cake, I do not want that. My mother makes me a pie now and then, which is as good.

Mr. L: Would you not like a knife to cut sticks?

Boy: I have one. Here it is. Brother Tom gave it to me.

Mr. L: Your shoes are full of holes. Don't you want a new pair?

Boy: I have a better pair for Sundays.

Mr. L: But these let in water.

Boy: I do not mind that, sir.

Mr. L: Your hat is all torn, too.

Boy: I have a better one at home.

Mr. L: What do you do when it rains?

Boy: If it rains very hard when I am in the field, I get under a tree for shelter.

Mr. L: What do you do, if you are hungry before it is time to go home?

Boy: I sometimes eat a raw turnip.

Mr. L: But if there is none?

Boy: Then I do as well as I can without. I work on, and never think of it.

Mr. L: Why, my little fellow, I am glad to see that you are so contented. Were you ever at school?

Boy: No, sir. But father means to send me next winter.

Mr. L: You will want books then.

Boy: Yes, sir; each boy has a Spelling Book, a Reader, and a Testament.

Mr. L: Then I will give them to you. Tell your father so, and that it is because you are an obliging, contented little boy.

Boy: I will, sir. Thank you.

Mr. L: Good by, Peter.

Boy: Good morning, sir.

Lesson 19

1. Read stories 61 – 64.
2. Tell someone about what you read.
3. Based on the character of the "insolent boy," what do you think insolent means? (Answers)

STORY LXI LITTLE GUSTAVA

1. Little Gustava sits in the sun, safe in the porch, and the little drops run from the icicles under the eaves so fast, for the bright spring sun shines warm at last, And glad is little Gustava.

2. She wears a quaint little scarlet cap, and a little green bowl she holds in her lap, filled with bread and milk to the brim, and a wreath of marigolds round the rim: "Ha! ha!" laughs little Gustava.

3. Up comes her little gray, coaxing cat, with her little pink nose, and she mews, "What's that?" Gustava feeds her,--she begs for more, and a little brown hen walks in at the door: "Good day!" cries little Gustava.

4. She scatters crumbs for the little brown hen, There comes a rush and a flutter, and then Down fly her little white doves so sweet, with their snowy wings and their crimson feet: "Welcome!" cries little Gustava.

5. So dainty and eager they pick up the crumbs. But who is this through the doorway comes? Little Scotch terrier, little dog Rags, looks in her face, and his funny tail wags: "Ha! ha!" laughs little Gustava.

6. "You want some breakfast, too?" and down She sets her bowl on the brick floor brown, and little dog Rags drinks up her milk, while she strokes his shaggy locks, like silk: "Dear Rags!" says little Gustava.

7. Waiting without stood sparrow and crow, cooling their feet in the melting snow. "Won't you come in, good folk?" she cried, but they were too bashful, and staid outside, though "Pray come in!" cried Gustava.

8. So the last she threw them, and knelt on the mat, with doves, and biddy, and dog, and cat. And her mother came to the open house door: "Dear little daughter, I bring you some more, my merry little Gustava."

9. Kitty and terrier, biddy and doves, all things harmless Gustava loves, the shy, kind creatures 'tis joy to feed, and, oh! her breakfast is sweet indeed to happy little Gustava!

STORY LXII THE INSOLENT BOY

1. James Selton was one of the most insolent boys in the village where he lived. He would rarely pass people in the street without being guilty of some sort of abuse.

2. If a person were well dressed he would cry out, "Dandy!" If a person's clothes were dirty or torn, he would throw stones at him, and annoy him in every way.

3. One afternoon, just as the school was dismissed, a stranger passed through the village. His dress was plain and somewhat old, but neat and clean. He carried a cane in his hand, on the end of which was a bundle, and he wore a broad-brimmed hat.

4. No sooner did James see the stranger, than he winked to his playmates, and said, "Now for some fun!" He then silently went toward the stranger from behind, and, knocking off his hat, ran away.

5. The man turned and saw him, but James was out of hearing before he could speak. The stranger put on his hat, and went on his way. Again did James approach; but this time, the man caught him by the arm, and held him fast.

6. However, he contented himself with looking James a moment in the face, and then pushed him from him. No sooner did the naughty boy find himself free again, than he began to pelt the stranger

with dirt and stones.

7. But he was much frightened when the "rowdy," as he foolishly called the man, was struck on the head by a brick, and badly hurt. All the boys now ran away, and James skulked across the fields to his home.

8. As he drew near the house, his sister Caroline came out to meet him, holding up a beautiful gold chain and some new books for him to see.

9. She told James, as fast as she could talk, that their uncle, who had been away several years, had come home, and was now in the house; that he had brought beautiful presents for the whole family; that he had left his carriage at the tavern, a mile or two off, and walked on foot, so as to surprise his brother, their father.

10. She said, that while he was coming through the village, some wicked boys threw stones at him, and hit him just over the eye, and that mother had bound up the wound. "But what makes you look so pale?" asked Caroline, changing her tone.

11. The guilty boy told her that nothing was the matter with him; and running into the house, he went upstairs into his chamber. Soon after, he heard his father calling him to come down. Trembling from head to foot, he obeyed. When he reached the parlor door, he stood, fearing to enter.

12. His mother said, "James, why do you not come in? You are not usually so bashful. See this beautiful watch, which your uncle has brought for you."

13. What a sense of shame did James now feel! Little Caroline seized his arm, and pulled him into the room. But he hung down his head, and covered his face with his hands.

14. His uncle went up to him, and kindly taking away his hands, said, "James, will you not bid me welcome?" But quickly starting back, he cried, "Brother, this is not your son. It is the boy who so shamefully insulted me in the street!"

15. With surprise and grief did the good father and mother learn this. His uncle was ready to forgive him, and forget the injury. But his father would never permit James to have the gold watch, nor the beautiful books, which his uncle had brought for him.

16. The rest of the children were loaded with presents. James was obliged to content himself with seeing them happy. He never forgot this lesson so long as he lived. It cured him entirely of his low and insolent manners.

STORY LXIII WE ARE SEVEN

1. I met a little cottage girl:
   She was eight years old, she said;
   Her hair was thick with many a curl,
   That clustered round her head.

2. She had a rustic, woodland air,
   And she was wildly clad:

Her eyes were fair, and very fair;--
Her beauty made me glad.

3. "Sisters and brothers, little maid,
   How many may you be?"
   "How many? Seven in all," she said,
   And, wondering, looked at me.

4. "And where are they? I pray you tell."
   She answered, "Seven are we;
   And two of us at Conway dwell,
   And two are gone to sea.

5. "Two of us in the churchyard lie,
   My sister and my brother;
   And, in the churchyard cottage,
   I dwell near them with my mother,"

6. "You say that two at Conway dwell,
   And two are gone to sea,
   Yet ye are seven! I pray you tell,
   Sweet maid, how this may be."

7. Then did the little maid reply,
   "Seven boys and girls are we;
   Two of us in the churchyard lie,
   Beneath the churchyard tree."

8. "You run about, my little maid,
   Your limbs, they are alive;
   If two are in the churchyard laid,
   Then ye are only five."

9. "Their graves are green, they may be seen,"
   The little maid replied,
   "Twelve steps or more from mother's door,
   And they are side by side.

10. "My stockings there I often knit,
    My kerchief there I hem;
    And there upon the ground I sit,
    And sing a song to them.

11. "And often after sunset, sir,
    When it is light and fair,
    I take my little porringer,
    And eat my supper there.

12. "The first that died was sister Jane;

In bed she moaning lay,
Till God released her from her pain;
And then she went away.

13. "So in the churchyard she was laid;
And, when the grass was dry,
Together round her grave
We played, my brother John and I.

14. "And when the ground was white with snow,
And I could run and slide,
My brother John was forced to go,
And he lies by her side."

15. "How many are you, then?" said I,
"If they two are in heaven?"
Quick was the little maid's reply,
"O master! we are seven."

16. "But they are dead; those two are dead!
Their spirits are in heaven!"
'Twas throwing words away: for still
The little maid would have her will, and said,
"Nay, we are seven."

STORY LXIV MARY'S DIME

1. There! I have drawn the chairs into the right corners, and dusted the room nicely. How cold papa and mamma will be when they return from their long ride! It is not time to toast the bread yet, and I am tired of reading.

2. What shall I do? Somehow, I can't help thinking about the pale face of that little beggar girl all the time. I can see the glad light filling her eyes, just as plain as I did when I laid the dime in her little dirty hand.

3. How much I had thought of that dime, too! Grandpa gave it to me a whole month ago, and I had kept it ever since in my red box upstairs; but those sugar apples looked so beautiful, and were so cheap--only a dime apiece--that I made up my mind to have one.

4. I can see her--the beggar girl, I mean--as she stood there in front of the store, in her old hood and faded dress, looking at the candies laid all in a row. I wonder what made me say, "Little girl what do you want?"

5. How she stared at me, just as if nobody had spoken kindly to her before. I guess she thought I was sorry for her, for she said, so earnestly and sorrowfully, "I was thinking how good one of those gingerbread rolls would taste. I haven't had anything to eat today."

6. Now, I thought to myself, "Mary Williams, you have had a good breakfast and a good dinner

this day, and this poor girl has not had a mouthful. You can give her your dime; she needs it a great deal more than you do."

7. I could not resist that little girl's sorrowful, hungry look--so I dropped the dime right into her hand, and, without waiting for her to speak, walked straight away. I'm so glad I gave her the dime, if I did have to go without the apple lying there in the window, and looking just like a real one.

Lesson 20

1. Read stories 65 – 69.
2. Tell someone what you read.

STORY LXV MARY DOW

1. "Come in, little stranger," I said,
   A she tapped at my half open door;
   While the blanket, pinned over her head,
   Just reached to the basket she bore.

2. A look full of innocence fell
   From her modest and pretty blue eye,
   As she said, "I have matches to sell,
   And hope you are willing to buy.

3. "A penny a bunch is the price,
   I think you'll not find it too much;
   They are tied up so even and nice,
   And ready to light with a touch."

4. I asked, "'What's your name, little girl?"
   "'Tis Mary," said she, "Mary Dow;"
   And carelessly tossed off a curl,
   That played on her delicate brow.

5. "My father was lost on the deep;
   The ship never got to the shore;
   And mother is sad, and will weep,
   To hear the wind blow and sea roar.

6. "She sits there at home, without food,
   Beside our poor, sick Willy's bed;
   She paid all her money for wood,
   And so I sell matches for bread.

7. "I'd go to the yard and get chips,
   But then it would make me too sad

    To see the men building the ships,
    And think they had made one so bad.

8. "But God, I am sure, who can take
    Such fatherly care of a bird,
    Will never forget nor forsake
    The children who trust in his word.

9. "And now, if I only can sell
    The matches I brought out today,
    I think I shall do very well,
    And we shall rejoice at the pay."

10. "Fly home, little bird," then I thought,
    "Fly home, full of joy, to your nest;"
    For I took all the matches she brought,
    And Mary may tell you the rest.

STORY LXVI THE LITTLE LOAF

1. Once when there was a famine, a rich baker sent for twenty of the poorest children in the town, and said to them, "In this basket there is a loaf for each of you. Take it, and come back to me every day at this hour till God sends us better times."

2. The hungry children gathered eagerly about the basket, and quarreled for the bread, because each wished to have the largest loaf. At last they went away without even thanking the good gentleman.

3. But Gretchen, a poorly-dressed little girl, did not quarrel or struggle with the rest, but remained standing modestly in the distance. When the ill-behaved girls had left, she took the smallest loaf, which alone was left in the basket, kissed the gentleman's hand, and went home.

4. The next day the children were as ill behaved as before, and poor, timid Gretchen received a loaf scarcely half the size of the one she got the first day. When she came home, and her mother cut the loaf open, many new, shining pieces of silver fell out of it.

5. Her mother was very much alarmed, and said, "Take the money back to the good gentleman at once, for it must have got into the dough by accident. Be quick, Gretchen! be quick!"

6. But when the little girl gave the rich man her mother's message, he said, "No, no, my child, it was no mistake. I had the silver pieces put into the smallest loaf to reward you. Always be as contented, peaceable, and grateful as you now are. Go home now, and tell your mother that the money is your own."

STORY LXVII SUSIE AND ROVER

1. "Mamma," said Susie Dean, one summer's morning, "may I go to the woods, and pick berries?"

2. "Yes," replied Mrs. Dean, "but you must take Rover with you."

3. Susie brought her little basket, and her mother put up a nice lunch for her. She tied down the cover, and fastened a tin cup to it.

4. The little girl called Rover--a great Newfoundland dog--and gave him a tin pail to carry. "If I bring it home full, mamma," she said, "won't you make some berry cakes for tea?"

5. Away she tripped, singing as she went down the lane and across the pasture. When she got to the woods, she put her dinner basket down beside a tree, and began to pick berries.

6. Rover ran about, chasing a squirrel or a rabbit now and then, but never straying far from Susie.

7. The tin pail was not a very small one. By the time it was two thirds full, Susie began to feel hungry, and thought she would eat her lunch.

8. Rover came and took his place at her side as soon as she began to eat. Did she not give him some of the lunch? No, she was in a selfish mood, and did no such thing.

9. "There, Rover, run away! there's a good dog," she said; but Rover staid near her, watching her steadily with his clear brown eyes.

10. The meat he wanted so much, was soon eaten up; and all he got of the nice dinner, was a small crust of gingerbread that Susie threw away.

11. After dinner, Susie played a while by the brook. She threw sticks into the water, and Rover swam in and brought them back. Then she began to pick berries again.

12. She did not enjoy the afternoon as she did the morning. The sunshine was as bright, the berries were as sweet and plentiful, and she was neither tired nor hungry.

13. But good, faithful Rover was hungry, and she had not given him even one piece of meat. She tried to forget how selfish she had been; but she could not do so, and quite early she started for home.

14. When she was nearly out of the woods, a rustling in the underbrush attracted her attention. "I wonder if that is a bird or a squirrel," said she to herself. "If I can catch it, how glad I shall be!"

15. She tried to make her way quietly through the underbrush; but what was her terror when she saw it large snake coiled up before her, prepared for a spring!

16. She was so much frightened that she could not move; but brave Rover saw the snake, and, springing forward, seized it by the neck and killed it.

17. When the faithful dog came and rubbed his head against her hand, Susie put her arms 'round his neck, and burst into tears. "O Rover," she cried, "you dear, good dog! How sorry I am that I was so selfish!"

18. Rover understood the tone of her voice, if he did not understand her words, and capered about in great glee, barking all the time. You may be sure that he had a plentiful supper that evening.

19. Susie never forgot the lesson of that day. She soon learned to be on her guard against a selfish spirit, and became a happier and more lovable little girl.

STORY LXVIII THE VIOLET

. Down in a green and shady bed,
   A modest violet grew;
   Its stalk was bent, it hung its head,
   As if to hide from view.

2. And yet it was a lovely flower,
   Its colors bright and fair;
   It might have graced a rosy bower
   Instead of hiding there.

3. Yet there it was content to bloom,
   In modest tints arrayed,
   And there it spread its sweet perfume,
   Within the silent shade.

4. Then let me to the valley go,
   This pretty flower to see;
   That I may also learn to grow
   In sweet humility.

STORY LXIX NO CROWN FOR ME

1. "Will you come with us, Susan?" cried several little girls to a schoolmate. "We are going to the woods; do come, too."

2. "I should like to go with you very much," replied Susan, with a sigh; "but I can not finish the task grandmother set me to do."

3. "How tiresome it must be to stay at home to work on a holiday!" said one of the girls, with a toss of her head. "Susan's grandmother is too strict."

4. Susan heard this remark, and, as she bent her head over her task, she wiped away a tear, and thought of the pleasant afternoon the girls would spend gathering wild flowers in the woods.

5. Soon she said to herself, "What harm can there be in moving the mark grand mother put in the stocking? The woods must be very beautiful today, and how I should like to be in them!"

6. "Grandmother," said she, a few minutes afterwards, "I am ready, now." "What, so soon, Susan?" Her grandmother took the work, and looked at it very closely.

7. "True, Susan," said she, laying great stress on each word; "true, I count twenty turns from the mark; and, as you have never deceived me, you may go and amuse yourself as you like the rest of the day."

8. Susan's cheeks were scarlet, and she did not say, "Thank you." As she left the cottage, she walked slowly away, not singing as usual.

9. "Why, here is Susan!" the girls cried, when she joined their company; "but what is the matter? Why have you left your dear, old grandmother?" they tauntingly added.

10. "There is nothing the matter." As Susan repeated these words, she felt that she was trying to deceive herself. She had acted a lie. At the same time she remembered her grandmother's words, "You have never deceived me."

11. "Yes, I have deceived her," said she to herself. "If she knew all, she would never trust me again."

12. When the little party had reached an open space in the woods, her companions ran about enjoying themselves; but Susan sat on the grass, wishing she were at home confessing her fault.

13. After a while Rose cried out, "Let us make a crown of violets, and put it on the head of the best girl here."

14. "It will be easy enough to make the crown, but not so easy to decide who is to wear it," said Julia.

15. "Why, Susan is to wear it, of course," said Rose: "is she not said to be the best girl in school and the most obedient at home?"

16. "Yes, yes; the crown shall be for Susan," cried the other girls, and they began to make the crown. It was soon finished.

17. "Now, Susan," said Rose, "put it on in a very dignified way, for you are to be our queen."

18. As these words were spoken, the crown was placed on her head. In a moment she snatched it off, and threw it on the ground, saying, "No crown for me; I do not deserve it."

19. The girls looked at her with surprise. "I have deceived my grandmother," said she, while tears flowed down her cheeks. "I altered the mark she put in the stocking, that I might join you in the woods."

20. "Do you call that wicked?" asked one of the girls. "I am quite sure it is; and I have been miserable all the time I have been here."

21. Susan now ran home, and as soon as she got there she said, with a beating heart, "O grandmother! I deserve to be punished, for I altered the mark you put in the stocking. Do forgive me; I am very sorry and unhappy."

22. "Susan," said her grandmother, "I knew it all the time; but I let you go out, hoping that your own conscience would tell you of your sin. I am so glad that you have confessed your fault and your sorrow."

23. "When shall I be your own little girl again?" "Now," was the quick reply, and Susan's grandmother kissed her forehead.

Lesson 21

1. Read this summary of *Swiss Family Robinson*.

"The Swiss Family Robinson follows a close family who has found themselves stranded on an island after a shipwreck. The story is told from the point of view of the father. The religious family is made up of their intelligent and resourceful father, a kind and caring mother, and their four sons named Fritz, Ernest, Jack, and Franz. Fritz is the eldest son, 15-years-old when the family lands on the island, and he is often tough on his brothers despite his good intentions. Ernest is the second oldest, and he is intelligent and well-formed though indolent. Jack is the third oldest son. He is bold, but often thoughtless. Last is Franz, the youngest son, nearly 8-years-old when the family first is stranded. The story begins with the family's good fortune when they survive a shipwreck in a terrible storm. They find themselves stuck on a ship, after being abandoned by their shipmates, but not too far from shore. Luckily, the family discovers many supplies on the ship including clothing, tools, fish hooks, guns and gun powder, and various useful animals. They find even more treasures on the endlessly fruitful island and continue to prosper and make new and exciting discoveries for years."

(excerpt from http://www.childrensnursery.org.uk/ swiss-family-robinson/swiss-family-robinson.html)

2. Look at the picture from the book. What do you think they are doing? (on the next page)
3. Based on the book summary, what do you think just happened?
4. What are all the things that you observe in the picture?

Lesson 22

1. Read *Swiss Family Robinson* chapter 1.
2. The story starts with them on a boat in the middle of a big storm. The word he uses for storm is "tempest." That's a really bad storm.
3. As you read, if you get stuck, especially on a word you don't know, read the next few sentences to see if you can figure out what's going on. If a word you don't know is keeping you from following the story, then stop. Ask for help. There's no use reading the whole chapter and not knowing what happened at the end. Stop and think. The reading should make sense. It's a story. Things are happening. Make a picture in your mind of what is going on. You don't have to understand every word, but you should know what's going on. Don't get lost in the book. If you don't know what's happening, go back to what you last knew and start again from there.
4. What is "she" referring to in this sentence? "As all hope from this direction was over, I examined the ship to see if she would hold together for a little while, and was reassured."
5. Who is narrating this story? (Who is I?)
6. Tell someone about the chapter.

Chapter 1

The tempest had raged for six days, and on the seventh seemed to increase. The ship had been so far driven from its course, that no one on board knew where we were. Every one was exhausted with fatigue and watching. The shattered vessel began to leak in many places, the oaths of the sailors were changed to prayers, and each thought only how to save his own life. "Children," said I, to my terrified boys, who were clinging round me, "God can save us if he will. To him nothing is impossible; but if he thinks it good to call us to him, let us not murmur; we shall not be separated." My excellent wife dried her tears, and from that moment became more tranquil. We knelt down to pray for the help of our Heavenly Father; and the fervor and emotion of my innocent boys proved to me that even children can pray, and find in prayer consolation and peace. (When you get to the end of a paragraph, think about what's happening. Are you picturing the storm? They are on a ship. How are the children feeling? Terrified! What do they do about it? They pray. Picture the story as you read.)

We rose from our knees strengthened to bear the afflictions that hung over us. Suddenly we heard amid the roaring of the waves the cry of "Land! land!" At that moment the ship struck on a rock; the concussion threw us down. We heard a loud cracking, as if the vessel was parting asunder; we felt that we were aground, and heard the captain cry, in a tone of despair, "We are lost! Launch the boats!" These words were a dagger to my heart, and the lamentations of my children were louder than ever. I then recollected myself, and said, "Courage, my darlings, we are still, above water, and the land is near. God helps those who trust in him. Remain here, and I will endeavour to save us." (In America we spell it, endeavor. When you see words with that "our" ending, it's the British spelling. To en-dev-er is to try hard to achieve something. You'll see this word a lot.)

"Let us take some food," said my wife; "with the body, the mind is strengthened; this must be a night of trial."

Night came, and the tempest continued its fury; tearing away the planks from the devoted vessel with a fearful crashing. It appeared absolutely impossible that the boats could have out-lived the storm. (What's happening? The boat is falling apart.)

At length Fritz, overcome with fatigue, lay down and slept with his brothers. My wife and I, too anxious to rest, spent that dreadful night in prayer, and in arranging various plans. How gladly we welcomed the light of day, shining through an opening. The wind was subsiding, the sky serene, and I watched the sun rise with renewed hope. I called my wife and children on deck. The younger ones were surprised to find we were alone. They inquired what had become of the sailors, and how we should manage the ship alone.

"Children," said I, "one more powerful than man has protected us till now, and will still extend a saving arm to us, if we do not give way to complaint and despair. Let all hands set to work. Remember that excellent maxim, God helps those who help themselves. Let us all consider what is best to do now."

"Let us leap into the sea," cried Fritz, "and swim to the shore."

"Very well for you," replied Ernest, "who can swim; but we should be all drowned. Would it not be better to construct a raft and go all together?"

"That might do," added I, "if we were strong enough for such a work, and if a raft was not always so dangerous a conveyance. But away, boys, look about you, and seek for anything that may be useful to us."

We all dispersed to different parts of the vessel. For my own part I went to the provision-room, to look after the casks of water and other necessaries of life; my wife visited the livestock and fed them, for they were almost famished; Fritz sought for arms and ammunition; Ernest for the carpenter's tools. Jack had opened the captain's cabin, and was immediately thrown down by two large dogs, who leaped on him so roughly that he cried out as if they were going to devour him. However, hunger had rendered them so docile that they licked his hands, and he soon recovered his feet, seized the largest by the ears, and mounting his back, gravely rode up to me as I was coming from the hold. I could not help laughing; I applauded his courage; but recommended him always to be prudent with animals of that kind, who are often dangerous when hungry.

My little troop began to assemble. Fritz had found two fowling-pieces, some bags of powder and shot, and some balls, in horn flasks. Ernest was loaded with an axe and hammer, a pair of pincers, a large pair of scissors, and an auger showed itself half out of his pocket.

Francis had a large box under his arm, from which he eagerly produced what he called little pointed hooks. His brothers laughed at his prize. "Silence," said I, "the youngest has made the most valuable addition to our stores. These are fish-hooks, and may be more useful for the preservation of our lives than anything the ship contains. However, Fritz and Ernest have not done amiss."

"For my part," said my wife, "I only contribute good news; I have found a cow, an ass, two goats, six sheep, and a sow with young. I have fed them, and hope we may preserve them."

"Very well," said I to my little workmen, "I am satisfied with all but Master Jack, who, instead of anything useful, has contributed two great eaters, who will do us more harm than good."

"They can help us to hunt when we get to land," said Jack.

"Yes," replied I, "but can you devise any means of our getting there?"

"It does not seem at all difficult," said the spirited little fellow; "put us each into a great tub, and let us float to shore."

"A very good idea, Jack; good counsel may sometimes be given even by a child. Be quick, boys, give me the saw and auger, with some nails, we will see what we can do." I remembered seeing some empty casks in the hold. We went down and found them floating. This gave us less difficulty in getting them upon the lower deck, which was but just above the water. They were of strong wood, bound with iron hoops, and exactly suited my purpose; my sons and I therefore began to saw them through the middle. After long labour, we had eight tubs all the same height. We refreshed ourselves with wine and biscuit, which we had found in some of the casks. I then contemplated with delight my little squadron of boats ranged in a line; and was surprised that my wife still continued depressed. She looked mournfully on them. "I can never venture in one of these tubs," said she. (You can see the wooden tubs/casks in the picture I put in the beginning.)

"Wait a little, till my work is finished," replied I, "and you will see it is more to be depended on than this broken vessel."

I sought out a long flexible plank, and arranged eight tubs on it, close to each other, leaving a piece at each end to form a curve upwards, like the keel of a vessel. We then nailed them firmly to the plank, and to each other. We nailed a plank at each side, of the same length as the first, and succeeded in producing a sort of boat, divided into eight compartments, in which it did not appear difficult to make a short voyage, over a calm sea.

But, unluckily, our wonderful vessel proved so heavy, that our united efforts could not move it an inch. I sent Fritz to bring me the jack-screw, and, in the mean time, sawed a thick round pole into pieces; then raising the fore-part of our work by means of the powerful machine, Fritz placed one of these rollers under it.

Ernest was very anxious to know how this small machine could accomplish more than our united strength. I explained to him, as well as I could, the power of the lever of Archimedes, with which he had declared he could move the world, if he had but a point to rest it on; and I promised my son to take the machine to pieces when we were on shore, and explain the mode of operation. I then told them that God, to compensate for the weakness of man, had bestowed on him reason, invention, and skill in workmanship. The result of these had produced a science which, under the name of *Mechanics*, taught us to increase and extend our limited powers incredibly by the aid of instruments.

Jack remarked that the jack-screw worked very slowly.

"Better slowly, than not at all," said I. "It is a principle in mechanics, that what is gained in time is lost in power. The jack is not meant to work rapidly, but to raise heavy weights; and the heavier the weight, the slower the operation. But, can you tell me how we can make up for this slowness?"

"Oh, by turning the handle quicker, to be sure!"

"Quite wrong; that would not aid us at all. Patience and Reason are the two fairies, by whose potent help I hope to get our boat afloat."

The day had passed in toil, and we were compelled to spend another night on the wreck, though we knew it might not remain till morning. We took a regular meal, for during the day we had scarcely had time to snatch a morsel of bread and a glass of wine. More composed than on the preceding night, we retired to rest. I took the precaution to fasten the swimming apparatus across the shoulders of my three younger children and my wife, for fear another storm might destroy the vessel, and cast us into the sea. I also advised my wife to put on a sailor's dress, as more convenient for her expected toils and trials. She reluctantly consented, and, after a short absence, appeared in the dress of a youth who had served as a volunteer in the vessel. She felt very timid and awkward in her new dress; but I showed her the advantage of the change, and, at last, she was reconciled, and joined in the laughter of the children at her strange disguise. She then got into her hammock, and we enjoyed a pleasant sleep, to prepare us for new labours. (Here's another word spelled with "ou." This is the word "labor." You'll see this word a lot because the father believes in working hard. How did you do with the reading? Did you picture it? What's the family doing now? This is a tough book, but you can do it. Take your time. Keep thinking. Ask for help when you don't know what it's talking about, go back if you get lost, and never give up!)

Lesson 23

1. Read *Swiss Family Robinson* chapter 2.
2. List the four boys and write a word to describe each one.
3. What's the first thing they do when they get on the beach? (Answers)
4. If a word you don't know is keeping you from understanding what's going on, look it up or ask someone what it means.
5. I'll tell you what one weird word means right now. A hogshead is a cask used to store liquids.
6. If you aren't following the story, go back to where you last knew what was going on and start from there. Ask for help when you need it. Don't get to the end of the chapter and not know what you read!
7. Tell someone about the chapter.

Chapter 2

At break of day we were awake and ready, and after morning prayer, I addressed my children thus: "We are now, my dear boys, with the help of God, about to attempt our deliverance. Before we go, provide our poor animals with food for some days: we cannot take them with us, but if our voyage succeed, we may return for them. Are you ready?

Collect what you wish to carry away, but only things absolutely necessary for our actual wants." I planned that our first cargo should consist of a barrel of powder, three fowling-pieces, three muskets, two pair of pocket pistols, and one pair larger, ball, shot, and lead as much as we could carry, with a bullet-mould (mold); and I wished each of my sons, as well as their mother, should have a complete game-bag, of which there were several in the officers' cabins. We then set apart a box of portable soup, another of biscuit, an iron pot, a fishing-rod, a chest of nails, and one of carpenter's tools, also some sailcloth to make a tent. In fact my boys collected so many things, we were compelled to leave some behind, though I exchanged all the useless ballast for necessaries. (So, maybe you don't know what ballast is. That's a boat term. But you do know what the words useless and necessary mean. He's getting rid of what's not useful and only taking what's necessary.)

When all was ready, we implored the blessing of God on our undertaking, and prepared to embark in our tubs. At this moment the cocks crowed a sort of reproachful farewell to us; we had forgotten them; I immediately proposed to take our poultry with us, geese, ducks, fowls and pigeons, for, as I observed to my wife, if we could not feed them, they would, at any rate, feed us. We placed our ten hens and two cocks in a covered tub; the rest we set at liberty, hoping the geese and ducks might reach the shore by water, and the pigeons by flight.

We waited a little for my wife, who came loaded with a large bag, which she threw into the tub that contained her youngest son. I concluded it was intended to steady him, or for a seat, and made no observation on it. Here follows the order of our embarkation. In the first division, sat the tender mother, the faithful and pious wife. In the second, our amiable little Francis, six years old, and of a sweet disposition.

In the third, Fritz, our eldest, fourteen or fifteen years old, a curly-headed, clever, intelligent and lively youth.

In the fourth, the powder-cask, with the fowls and the sailcloth.

Our provisions filled the fifth.

In the sixth, our heedless Jack, ten years old, enterprising, bold, and useful.

In the seventh, Ernest, twelve years of age, well-informed and rational, but somewhat selfish and indolent. In the eighth, myself, an anxious father, charged with the important duty of guiding the vessel to save my dear family. Each of us had some useful tools beside us; each held an oar, and had a swimming apparatus at hand, in case we were unfortunately upset. The tide was rising when we left, which I considered might assist my weak endeavours. We turned our out-riggers length-ways, and thus passed from the cleft of the ship into the open sea. We rowed with all our might, to reach the blue land we saw at a distance, but for some time in vain, as the boat kept turning round, and made no progress.

At last I contrived to steer it, so that we went straight forward.

As soon as our dogs saw us depart, they leaped into the sea, and followed us; I could not let them get into the boat, for fear they should upset it. I was very sorry, for I hardly expected they would be able to swim to land; but by occasionally resting their forepaws on our out-riggers, they managed to keep up with us. Turk was an English dog, and Flora of a Danish breed.

We proceeded slowly, but safely. The nearer we approached the land, the more dreary and unpromising it appeared. The rocky coast seemed to announce to us nothing but famine and misery. The waves, gently rippling against the shore, were scattered over with barrels, bales, and chests from the wreck. Hoping to secure some good provisions, I called on Fritz for assistance; he held a cord, hammer, and nails, and we managed to seize two hogsheads in passing, and fastening them with cords to our vessel, drew them after us to the shore.

As we approached, the coast seemed to improve. The chain of rock was not entire, and Fritz's hawk eye made out some trees, which he declared were the cocoa-nut tree; Ernest was delighted at the prospect of eating these nuts, so much larger and better than any grown in Europe. I was regretting not having brought the large telescope from the captain's cabin, when Jack produced from his pocket a smaller one, which he offered me with no little pride.

All that were able leaped on shore in a moment. Even little Francis, who had been laid down in his tub, like a salted herring, tried to crawl out, but was compelled to wait for his mother's assistance. The dogs, who had preceded us in landing, welcomed us in a truly friendly manner, leaping playfully around us; the geese kept up a loud cackling, to which the yellow-billed ducks quacked a powerful bass. This, with the clacking of the liberated fowls, and the chattering of the boys, formed a perfect Babel; mingled with these, were the harsh cries of the penguins and flamingoes, which hovered over our heads, or sat on the points of the rocks. They were in immense numbers, and their notes almost deafened us, especially as they did not accord with the harmony of our civilized fowls. However I rejoiced to see these feathered creatures, already fancying them on my table, if we were obliged to remain in this desert region.

Our first care, when we stepped in safety on land, was to kneel down and thank God, to whom we owed our lives; and to resign ourselves wholly to his Fatherly kindness.

We then began to unload our vessel. How rich we thought ourselves with the little we had saved! We sought a convenient place for our tent, under the shade of the rocks. We then inserted a pole into a fissure in the rock; this, resting firmly on another pole fixed in the ground, formed the frame of the tent. The sailcloth was then stretched over it, and fastened down at proper distances, by pegs, to which, for greater security, we added some boxes of provision; we fixed some hooks to the canvas at the opening in front, that we might close the entrance during the night. I sent my sons to seek some moss and withered grass, and spread it in the sun to dry, to form our beds; and while all, even little Francis, were busy with this, I constructed a sort of cooking-place, at some distance from the tent, near the river which was to supply us with fresh water. It was merely a hearth of flat stones from the bed of the stream, fenced round with some thick branches. I kindled a cheerful fire with some dry twigs, put on the pot, filled with water and some squares of portable soup, and left my wife, with Francis for assistant, to prepare dinner. He took the portable soup for glue, and could not conceive how mamma could make soup, as we had no meat, and there were no butchers' shops here.

On returning, I congratulated Jack on being the first who had been successful in foraging. Ernest remarked, that he had seen some oysters attached to a rock, but could not get at them without wetting his feet, which he did not like.

"Indeed, my delicate gentleman!" said I, laughing, "I must trouble you to return and procure us some. We must all unite in working for the public good, regardless of wet feet. The sun will soon dry us."

"I might as well bring some salt at the same time," said he; "I saw plenty in the fissures of the rock, left by the sea, I should think, papa?"

He went, and returned with some salt, so mixed with sand and earth, that I should have thrown it away as useless; but my wife dissolved it in fresh water, and, filtering it through a piece of canvas, managed to flavour our soup with it.

Jack asked why we could not have used sea-water; and I explained to him that the bitter and nauseous taste of sea-water would have spoiled our dinner. My wife stirred the soup with a little stick, and, tasting it, pronounced it very good, but added, "We must wait for Fritz. And how shall we eat our soup without plates or spoons? We cannot possibly raise this large boiling pot to our heads, and drink out of it."

It was too true. We gazed stupified at our pot, and, at last, all burst into laughter at our destitution, and our folly in forgetting such useful necessaries.

"If we only had cocoa-nuts," said Ernest, "we might split them, and make basins and spoons."

"If!" replied I "but we have none! We might as well wish for a dozen handsome silver spoons at once, if wishes were of any use."

"But," observed he, "we can use oyster-shells."

"A useful thought, Ernest; go directly and get the oysters; and, remember, gentlemen, no complaints, though the spoons are without handles, and you should dip your fingers into the bowl."

Off ran Jack, and was mid-leg in the water before Ernest got to him. He tore down the oysters, and threw them to his idle brother, who filled his handkerchief, taking care to put a large one into his pocket for his own use; and they returned with their spoil.

Fritz spoke, "Beyond the river there is rich grass for pasturage, and a shady wood. Why should we remain in this barren wilderness?"

"Softly!" replied I, "there is a time for all things. To-morrow, and the day after to-morrow will have their work. But first tell me, did you see anything of our shipmates?"

"Not a trace of man, living or dead, on land or sea; but I saw an animal more like a hog than this, but with feet like a hare; it leaped among the grass, sometimes sitting upright, and rubbing its mouth with its forepaws; sometimes seeking for roots, and gnawing them like a squirrel. If I had not been afraid it would escape me, I would have tried to take it alive, it seemed so very tame."

As we were talking, Jack had been trying, with many grimaces, to force an oyster open with his knife. I laughed at his vain endeavours, and putting some on the fire, showed him them open of themselves. I had no taste for oysters myself; but as they are everywhere accounted a delicacy, I advised my sons to try them. They all at first declined the unattractive repast, except Jack, who, with great courage, closed his eyes, and desperately swallowed one as if it had been medicine. The rest followed his example, and then all agreed with me that oysters were not good. The shells were soon plunged into the pot to bring out some of the good soup; but scalding their fingers, it was who could cry out the loudest. Ernest took his large shell from his pocket, cautiously filled it with a good portion of soup, and set it down to cool, exulting in his own prudence.

"You have been very thoughtful, my dear Ernest," said I; "but why are your thoughts always for yourself; so seldom for others? As a punishment for your egotism, that portion must be given to our faithful dogs. We can all dip our shells into the pot, the dogs cannot. Therefore, they shall have your soup, and you must wait, and eat as we do." My reproach struck his heart, and he placed his shell obediently on the ground, which the dogs emptied immediately. We were almost as hungry as they were, and were watching anxiously till the soup began to cool; when we perceived that the dogs were tearing and gnawing Fritz's agouti (that's a sort of rodent). The boys all cried out; Fritz was in a fury, took his gun, struck the dogs, called them names, threw stones at them, and would have killed them if I had not held him. He had actually bent his gun with striking them. As soon as he would listen to me, I reproached him seriously for his violence, and represented to him how much he had distressed us, and terrified his mother; that he had spoiled his gun, which might have been so useful to us, and had almost killed the poor animals, who might be more so. "Anger," said I, "leads to every crime. Remember Cain, who killed his brother in a fit of passion." "Oh, father!" said he, in a voice of terror; and, acknowledging his error, he asked pardon, and shed bitter tears.

Our pigeons now flew among the rocks, the cocks and hens perched on the frame of the tent, and the geese and ducks chose to roost in a marsh, covered with bushes, near the sea. We prepared for our rest; we loaded all our arms, then offered up our prayers together, thanking God for his signal mercy to us, and commending ourselves to his care. When the last ray of light departed, we closed our tent, and lay down on our beds, close together. The children had remarked how suddenly the darkness came on, from which I concluded we were not far from the equator; for I explained to them, the more perpendicularly the rays of the sun fall, the less their refraction; and consequently night comes on suddenly when the sun is below the horizon.

Once more I looked out to see if all was quiet, then carefully closing the entrance, I lay down. Warm as the day had been, the night was so cold that we were obliged to crowd together for warmth. The children soon slept, and when I saw their mother in her first peaceful sleep, my own eyes closed, and our first night on the island passed comfortably.

Lesson 24

1. Read *Swiss Family Robinson* chapter 3.
2. What are some of the foods they find?
3. How did they gets nuts from the tree? (Answers)
4. Tell someone about the chapter.

Chapter 3

At break of day I was waked by the crowing of the cock. I summoned my wife to council, to consider on the business of the day. We agreed that our first duty was to seek for our shipmates, and to examine the country beyond the river before we came to any decisive resolution.

My wife saw we could not all go on this expedition, and courageously agreed to remain with her three youngest sons, while Fritz, as the eldest and boldest, should accompany me. I begged her to prepare breakfast immediately, which she warned me would be scanty, as no soup was provided.

We began our preparation; we each took a game-bag and a hatchet. I gave Fritz a pair of pistols in addition to his gun, equipped myself in the same way, and took care to carry biscuit and a flask of fresh water. The lobster proved so hard at breakfast, that the boys did not object to our carrying off the remainder; and, though the flesh is coarse, it is very nutritious.

I proposed before we departed, to have prayers, and my thoughtless Jack began to imitate the sound of church-bells "Ding, dong! to prayers! to prayers! ding, dong!" I was really angry, and reproved him severely for jesting about sacred things. Then, kneeling down, I prayed God's blessing on our undertaking, and his pardon for us all, especially for him who had now so grievously sinned. Poor Jack came and kneeled by me, weeping and begging for forgiveness from me and from God. I embraced him, and enjoined him and his brothers to obey their mother. I then loaded the guns I left with them, and charged my wife to keep near the boat, their best refuge. We took leave of our friends with many tears, as we did not know what dangers might assail us in an unknown region. But the murmur of the river, which we were now approaching, drowned the sound of their sobs, and we bent our thoughts on our journey.

The bank of the river was so steep, that we could only reach the bed at one little opening, near the sea, where we had procured our water; but here the opposite side was guarded by a ridge of lofty perpendicular rocks. We were obliged to ascend the river to a place where it fell over some rocks, some fragments of which having fallen, made a sort of stepping-stones, which enabled us to cross with some hazard. We made our way, with difficulty, through the high grass, withered by the sun, directing our course towards the sea, in hopes of discovering some traces of the boats, or the crew. We had scarcely gone a hundred yards, when we heard a loud noise and rustling in the grass, which was as tall as we were. We imagined we were pursued by some wild beast, and I was gratified to observe the courage of Fritz, who, instead of running away, calmly turned round and presented his piece. What was our joy when we discovered that the formidable enemy was only our faithful Turk, whom we had forgotten in our distress, and our friends had doubtless dispatched him after us! I applauded my son's presence of mind; a rash act might have deprived us of this valuable friend.

We proceeded, and entering a little wood that extended to the sea, we rested in the shade, near a clear stream, and took some refreshment. We were surrounded by unknown birds, more remarkable for brilliant plumage than for the charm of their voice. Fritz thought he saw some monkeys among the leaves, and Turk began to be restless, smelling about, and barking very loud. Fritz was gazing up into the trees, when he fell over a large round substance, which he brought to me, observing that it might be a bird's nest. I thought it more likely to be a cocoa-nut. The fibrous covering had reminded him of the description he had read of the nests of certain birds; but, on breaking the shell, we found it was indeed a cocoa-nut, but quite decayed and uneatable.

Fritz was astonished; where was the sweet milk that Ernest had talked of?

I told him the milk was only in the half-ripe nuts; that it thickened and hardened as the nut ripened, becoming a kernel. This nut had perished from remaining above ground. If it had been in the earth, it would have vegetated, and burst the shell. I advised my son to try if he could not find a perfect nut.

After some search, we found one, and sat down to eat it, keeping our own provision for dinner. The nut was somewhat rancid; but we enjoyed it, and then continued our journey. We were some time before we got through the wood, being frequently obliged to clear a road for ourselves, through the entangled brushwood, with our hatchets. At last we entered the open plain again, and had a clear view before us. The forest still extended about a stone's throw to our right, and Fritz, who was always on the look-out for discoveries, observed a remarkable tree, here and there, which he approached to examine; and he soon called me to see this wonderful tree, with wens growing on the trunk.

On coming up, I was overjoyed to find this tree, of which there were a great number, was the gourd-tree, which bears fruit on the trunk. Fritz asked if these were sponges. I told him to bring me one, and I would explain the mystery.

"There is one," said he, "very like a pumpkin, only harder outside."

"Of this shell," said I, "we can make plates, dishes, basins, and flasks. We call it the gourd-tree."

Fritz leaped for joy. "Now my dear mother will be able to serve her soup properly." I asked him if he knew why the tree bore the fruit on its trunk, or on the thick branches only. He immediately replied, that the smaller branches would not bear the weight of the fruit. He asked me if this fruit was eatable. "Harmless, I believe," said I; "but by no means delicate. Its great value to these nations consists in the shell, which they use to contain their food, and drink, and even cook in it." Fritz could not comprehend how they could cook in the shell without burning it. I told him the shell was not placed on the fire; but, being filled with cold water, and the fish or meat placed in it, red-hot stones are, by degrees, introduced into the water, till it attains sufficient heat to cook the food, without injuring the vessel.

We then set about making our dishes and plates. I showed Fritz a better plan of dividing the gourd than with a knife. I tied a string tightly round the nut, struck it with the handle of my knife till an incision was made, then tightened it till the nut was separated into two equally-sized bowls. Fritz had spoiled his gourd by cutting it irregularly with his knife. I advised him to try and make spoons of it, as it would not do for basins now. I told him I had learnt my plan from books of travels. It is the practice of the natives, who have no knives, to use a sort of string, made from the bark of trees, for this purpose. "But how can they make bottles," said he. "That requires some preparation," replied I. "They tie a bandage round the young gourd near the stalk, so that the part at liberty expands in a round form, and the compressed part remains narrow. They then open the top, and extract the contents by putting in pebbles and shaking it. By this means they have a complete bottle."

We worked on. Fritz completed a dish and some plates, to his great satisfaction, but we considered, that being so frail, we could not carry them with us. We therefore filled them with sand, that the sun might not warp them, and left them to dry, till we returned.

As we went on, Fritz amused himself with cutting spoons from the rind of the gourd, and I tried to do the same with the fragments of the cocoa-nut; but I must confess my performances were inferior to those I had seen in the museum in London, the work of the South Sea islanders. We laughed at our spoons, which would have required mouths from ear to ear to eat with them. Fritz declared that the curve of the rind was the cause of that defect: if the spoons had been smaller, they would have been flat; and you might as well eat soup with an oyster-shell as with a shovel.

We proceeded towards a pleasant wood of palm-trees; but before reaching it, had to pass through an immense number of reeds, which greatly obstructed our road. We were, moreover, fearful of treading on the deadly serpents who choose such retreats. We made Turk walk before us to give notice, and I cut a long, thick cane as a weapon of defence. I was surprised to see a glutinous juice oozing from the end of the cut cane; I tasted it, and was convinced that we had met with a plantation of sugar-canes. I sucked more of it, and found myself singularly refreshed. I said nothing to Fritz, that he might have the pleasure of making the discovery himself. He was walking a few paces before me, and I called to him to cut himself a cane like mine, which he did, and soon found out the riches it contained. He cried out in ecstasy, "Oh, papa! papa! syrup of sugar-cane! delicious! How delighted will dear mamma, and my brothers be, when I carry some to them!" He went on, sucking pieces of cane so greedily, that I checked him, recommending moderation. He was then content to take some pieces to regale himself as he walked home, loading himself with a huge burden for his mother and brothers.

We now entered the wood of palms to eat our dinner, when suddenly a number of monkeys, alarmed by our approach, and the barking of the dog, fled like lightning to the tops of the trees; and then grinned frightfully at us, with loud cries of defiance. As I saw the trees were cocoa-palms, I hoped to obtain, by means of the monkeys, a supply of the nuts in the half-ripe state, when filled with milk. I held Fritz's arm, who was preparing to shoot at them, to his great vexation, as he was irritated against the poor monkeys for their derisive gestures; but I told him, that though no patron of monkeys myself, I could not allow it. We had no right to kill any animal except in defence, or as a means of supporting life. Besides, the monkeys would be of more use to us living than dead, as I would show him. I began to throw stones at the monkeys, not being able, of course, to reach the place of their retreat, and they, in their anger, and in the spirit of imitation, gathered the nuts and hurled them on us in such quantities, that we had some difficulty in escaping from them. We had soon a large stock of cocoa-nuts. Fritz enjoyed the success of the stratagem, and, when the shower subsided, he collected as many as he wished.

We then got up, I tied some nuts together by their stems, and threw them over my shoulder. Fritz took his bundle of canes, and we set out homewards.

Lesson 25

1. Read chapter 4 of *Swiss Family Robinson*.
2. "If the Lord will, He can save us even from this fearful peril; if not, let us calmly yield our lives into His hand, and think of the joy and blessedness of finding ourselves forever and ever united in that happy home above." What does this quote by Father tell us about what their family believes?
3. Tell someone about the chapter.

Chapter 4

Perfectly refreshed, we went on cheerfully to the place where we had left our gourd utensils. We found them quite dry, and hard as bone; we had no difficulty in carrying them in our game-bags. ("Game" is hunted animals, so those bags must be where they carried any small game they shot.) We had scarcely got through the little wood where we had breakfasted, when Turk darted furiously on a troop of monkeys, who were sporting about, and had not perceived him. He immediately seized a female, holding a young one in her arms, which impeded her flight, and had killed and devoured the poor mother before we could reach him. The young one had hidden itself among the long grass, when Fritz arrived; he had run with all his might, losing his hat, bottle, and canes, but could not prevent the murder of the poor mother.

The little monkey no sooner saw him than it leaped upon his shoulders, fastening its paws in his curls, and neither cries, threats, nor shaking could rid him of it. I ran up to him laughing, for I saw the little creature could not hurt him, and tried in vain to disengage it. I told him he must carry it thus. It was evident the sagacious little creature, having lost its mother, had adopted him for a father. (Are you picturing it? Who's Turk? What did he do? Who's attached to Fritz?)

I succeeded, at last, in quietly releasing him, and took the little orphan, which was no bigger than a cat, in my arms, pitying its helplessness. The mother appeared as tall as Fritz.

I was reluctant to add another mouth to the number we had to feed; but Fritz earnestly begged to keep it, offering to divide his share of cocoa-nut milk with it till we had our cows. I consented, on condition that he took care of it, and taught it to be obedient to him.

Turk, in the mean time, was feasting on the remains of the unfortunate mother. Fritz would have driven him off, but I saw we had not food sufficient to satisfy this voracious animal, and we might ourselves be in danger from his appetite.

We left him, therefore, with his prey, the little orphan sitting on the shoulder of his protector, while I carried the canes. Turk soon overtook us, and was received very coldly; we reproached him with his cruelty, but he was quite unconcerned, and continued to walk after Fritz. The little monkey seemed uneasy at the sight of him, and crept into Fritz's bosom, much to his inconvenience. But a thought struck him; he tied the monkey with a cord to Turk's back, leading the dog by another cord, as he was very rebellious at first; but our threats and caresses at last induced him to submit to his burden. We proceeded slowly, and I could not help anticipating the mirth of my little ones, when they saw us approach like a pair of show-men.

I advised Fritz not to correct the dogs for attacking and killing unknown animals. Heaven bestows the dog on man, as well as the horse, for a friend and protector. Fritz thought we were very fortunate, then, in having two such faithful dogs; he only regretted that our horses had died on the passage, and only left us the ass.

"Let us not disdain the ass," said I; "I wish we had him here; he is of a very fine breed, and would be as useful as a horse to us."

In such conversations, we arrived at the banks of our river before we were aware. Flora barked to announce our approach, and Turk answered so loudly, that the terrified little monkey leaped from his back to the shoulder of its protector, and would not come down. Turk ran off to meet his companion, and our dear family soon appeared on the opposite shore, shouting with joy at our happy return. We crossed at the same place as we had done in the morning, and embraced each other. Then began such a noise of exclamations. "A monkey! a real, live monkey! Ah! how delightful! How glad we are! How did you catch him?"

"He is very ugly," said little Francis, who was almost afraid of him.

"He is prettier than you are," said Jack; "see how he laughs! how I should like to see him eat!"

"If we only had some cocoa-nuts," said Ernest. "Have you found any, and are they good?"

"Have you had any unpleasant adventures?" asked my wife.

It was in vain to attempt replying to so many questions and exclamations.

At length, when we got a little peace, I told them that, though I had brought them all sorts of good things, I had, unfortunately, not met with any of our companions.

"God's will be done!" said my wife; "let us thank Him for saving us, and again bringing us together now. This day has seemed an age. But put down your loads, and let us hear your adventures; we have not been idle, but we are less fatigued than you. Boys, assist your father and brother."

Jack took my gun, Ernest the cocoa-nuts, Francis the gourd-rinds, and my wife the game-bag. Fritz distributed his sugar-canes, and placed the monkey on Turk's back, to the amusement of the children. He begged Ernest to carry his gun, but he complained of being overloaded with the great bowls. His indulgent mother took them from him, and we proceeded to the tent.

Fritz thought Ernest would not have relinquished the bowls, if he had known what they contained, and called out to tell him they were cocoa-nuts.

"Give them to me," cried Ernest. "I will carry them, mamma, and the gun too."

His mother declined giving them.

"I can throw away these sticks," said he, "and carry the gun in my hand."

"I would advise you not," observed Fritz, "for the sticks are sugar-canes."

"Sugar-canes!" cried they all, surrounding Fritz, who had to give them the history, and teach them the art of sucking the canes.

My wife, who had a proper respect for sugar in her housekeeping, was much pleased with this discovery, and the history of all our acquisitions, which I displayed to her. Nothing gave her so much pleasure as our plates and dishes, which were actual necessaries. We went to our kitchen, and were gratified to see preparations going on for a good supper. My wife had planted a forked stick on each side the hearth; on these rested a long thin wand, on which all sorts of fish were roasting, Francis being intrusted to turn the spit. On the other side was impaled a goose on another spit, and a row of oyster-shells formed the dripping-pan: besides this, the iron pot was on the fire, from which arose the savoury odour of a good soup. Behind the hearth stood one of the hogsheads, opened, and containing the finest Dutch cheeses, enclosed in cases of lead. All this was very tempting to hungry travellers, and very unlike a supper on a desert island. I could not think my family had been idle, when I saw such a result of their labours; I was only sorry they had killed the goose, as I wished to be economical with our poultry.

"Have no uneasiness," said my wife, "this is not from our poultry-yard, it is a wild goose, killed by Ernest."

"It is a sort of penguin, I believe," said Ernest, "distinguished by the name of *booby*, and so stupid, that I knocked it down with a stick. It is web-footed, has a long narrow beak, a little curved downwards. I have preserved the head and neck for you to examine; it exactly resembles the penguin of my book of natural history."

I pointed out to him the advantages of study, and was making more inquiries about the form and habits of the bird, when my wife requested me to defer my catechism of natural history.

"Ernest has killed the bird," added she; "I received it; we shall eat it. What more would you have? Let the poor child have the pleasure of examining and tasting the cocoa-nuts."

"Very well," replied I, "Fritz must teach them how to open them; and we must not forget the little monkey, who has lost his mother's milk."

"I have tried him," cried Jack, "and he will eat nothing."

I told them he had not yet learnt to eat, and we must feed him with cocoa-nut milk till we could get something better. Jack generously offered all his share, but Ernest and Francis were anxious to taste the milk themselves.

"But the monkey must live," said Jack, petulantly.

"And so must we all," said mamma. "Supper is ready, and we will reserve the cocoa-nuts for dessert."

We sat down on the ground, and the supper was served on our gourd-rind service, which answered the purpose admirably. My impatient boys had broken the nuts, which they found excellent, and they made themselves spoons of the shell. Jack had taken care the monkey had his share; they dipped the corner of their handkerchiefs in the milk, and let him suck them. They were going to break up some more nuts, after emptying them through the natural holes, but I stopped them, and called for a saw. I carefully divided the nuts with this instrument, and soon provided us each with a neat basin for our soup, to the great comfort of my dear wife, who was gratified by seeing us able to eat like civilized beings. Fritz begged now to enliven the repast by introducing his champaign. I consented; requesting him, however, to taste it himself before he served it. What was his mortification to find it vinegar! But we consoled ourselves by using it as sauce to our goose; a great improvement also to the fish. We had now to hear the history of our supper. Jack and Francis had caught the fish at the edge of the sea. My active wife had performed the most laborious duty, in rolling the hogshead to the place and breaking open the head.

The sun was going down as we finished supper, and, recollecting how rapidly night succeeded, we hastened to our tent, where we found our beds much more comfortable, from the kind attention of the good mother, who had collected a large addition of dried grass. After prayers, we all lay down; the monkey between Jack and Fritz, carefully covered with moss to keep him warm. The fowls went to their roost, as on the previous night, and, after our fatigue, we were all soon in a profound sleep.

We had not slept long, when a great commotion among the dogs and fowls announced the presence of an enemy. My wife, Fritz, and I, each seizing a gun, rushed out.

By the light of the moon, we saw a terrible battle going on: our brave dogs were surrounded by a dozen jackals, three or four were extended dead, but our faithful animals were nearly overpowered by numbers when we arrived. I was glad to find nothing worse than jackals; Fritz and I fired on them; two fell dead, and the others fled slowly, evidently wounded. Turk and Flora pursued and completed the business, and then, like true dogs, devoured their fallen foes, regardless of the bonds of relationship.

All being quiet again, we retired to our beds; Fritz obtaining leave to drag the jackal he had killed towards the tent, to save it from the dogs, and to show to his brothers next morning. This he accomplished with difficulty, for it was as big as a large dog.

We all slept peacefully the remainder of the night, till the crowing of the cock awoke my wife and myself to a consultation on the business of the day.

Lesson 26

1. Read chapter 5 of *Swiss Family Robinson*.
2. Read chapter 6 as well.
3. While you are reading, if you are stuck, stop and go back to where you understood. Try again. Make a mental picture of what's happening. Sound out unfamiliar words. Ask for help when you need it. Use these suggestions to make sure you are following the book.
4. Tell someone about the chapters when you are done reading.

Chapter 5

"Well, my dear," I began, "I feel rather alarmed at all the labours I see before me. A voyage to the vessel is indispensable, if we wish to save our cattle, and many other things that may be useful to us; on the other hand, I should like to have a more secure shelter for ourselves and our property than this tent."

"With patience, order, and perseverance, all may be done," said my good counselor; "and whatever uneasiness your voyage may give me, I yield to the importance and utility of it. Let it be done to-day; and have no care for the morrow: sufficient unto the day is the evil thereof, as our blessed Lord has said."

It was then agreed that the three youngest children should remain with my wife; and Fritz, the strongest and most active, should accompany me.

While Fritz made ready the boat, I erected a signal-post, with a piece of sailcloth for a flag, to float as long as all was going on well; but if we were wanted, they were to lower the flag, and fire a gun three times, when we would immediately return; for I had informed my dear wife it might be necessary for us to remain on board all night; and she consented to the plan, on my promising to pass the night in our tubs, instead of the vessel. We took nothing but our guns and ammunition; relying on the ship's provisions. Fritz would, however, take the monkey, that he might give it some milk from the cow.

We took a tender leave of each other, and embarked. When we had rowed into the middle of the bay, I perceived a strong current formed by the water of the river which issued at a little distance, which I was glad to take advantage of, to spare our labour. It carried us three parts of our voyage, and we rowed the remainder; and entering the opening in the vessel, we secured our boat firmly, and went on board.

The first care of Fritz was to feed the animals, who were on deck, and who all saluted us after their fashion, rejoiced to see their friends again, as well as to have their wants supplied. We put the young monkey to a goat, which he sucked with extraordinary grimaces, to our infinite amusement. We then took some refreshment ourselves, and Fritz, to my great surprise, proposed that we should begin by adding a sail to our boat. He said the current which helped us to the vessel, could not carry us back, but the wind which blew so strongly against us, and made our rowing so fatiguing, would be of great service, if we had a sail.

I thanked my counsellor for his good advice, and we immediately set to the task. I selected a strong pole for a mast, and a triangular sail, which was fixed to a yard. We made a hole in a plank, to receive the mast, secured the plank on our fourth tub, forming a deck, and then, by aid of a block used to hoist and lower the sails, raised our mast. Finally, two ropes fastened by one end to the yard, and by the other to each extremity of the boat, enabled us to direct the sail at pleasure. Fritz next ornamented the top of the mast with a little red streamer. He then gave our boat the name of the *Deliverance*, and requested it might henceforward be called the little vessel. To complete its equipment, I contrived a rudder, so that I could direct the boat from either end.

After signalling to our friends that we should not return that night, we spent the rest of the day in emptying the tubs of the stones we had used for ballast, and replacing them with useful things. Powder and shot, nails and tools of all kinds, pieces of cloth; above all, we did not forget knives, forks, spoons, and kitchen utensils, including a roasting-jack. In the captain's cabin we found some services of silver, pewter plates and dishes, and a small chest filled with bottles of choice wines. All these we took, as well as a chest of eatables, intended for the officers' table, portable soup, Westphalian hams, Bologna sausages, &c.; also some bags of maize, wheat, and other seeds, and some potatoes. We collected all the implements of husbandry we could spare room for, and, at the request of Fritz, some hammocks and blankets; two or three handsome guns, and an armful of sabres, swords, and hunting-knives. Lastly, I embarked a barrel of sulphur, all the cord and string I could lay my hands on, and a large roll of sailcloth. The sulphur was intended to produce matches with. Our tubs were loaded to the edge; there was barely room left for us to sit, and it would have been dangerous to attempt our return if the sea had not been so calm.

Night arrived, we exchanged signals, to announce security on sea and land, and, after prayers for the dear islanders, we sought our tubs, not the most luxurious of dormitories, but safer than the ship. Fritz slept soundly; but I could not close my eyes, thinking of the jackals. I was, however, thankful for the protection they had in the dogs.

Chapter 6

As soon as day broke, I mounted on deck, to look through the telescope. I saw my wife looking towards us; and the flag, which denoted their safety, floating in the breeze. Satisfied on this important point, we enjoyed our breakfast of biscuit, ham, and wine, and then turned our thoughts to the means of saving our cattle. Even if we could contrive a raft, we could never get all the animals to remain still on it. We might venture the huge sow in the water, but the rest of the animals we found would not be able to swim to shore. At last Fritz suggested the swimming apparatus. We passed two hours in constructing them. For the cow and ass it was necessary to have an empty cask on each side, well bound in strong sailcloth, fastened by leather thongs over the back and under each animal. For the rest, we merely tied a piece of cork under their bodies; the sow only being unruly, and giving us much trouble. We then fastened a cord to the horns or neck of each animal, with a slip of wood at the end, for a convenient handle. Luckily, the waves had broken away part of the ship, and left the opening wide enough for the passage of our troop. We first launched the ass into the water, by a sudden push; he swam away, after the first plunge, very gracefully. The cow, sheep, and goats, followed quietly after. The sow was furious, and soon broke loose from us all, but fortunately reached the shore long before the rest.

We now embarked, fastening all the slips of wood to the stern of the boat, thus drawing our train after us; and the wind filling our sail, carried us smoothly towards the shore. Fritz exulted in his plan, as we certainly could never have rowed our boat, loaded as we were. I once more took out my telescope, and was remarking that our party on shore seemed making ready for some excursion, when a loud cry from Fritz filled me with terror. "We are lost! we are lost! see, what a monstrous fish!" Though pale with alarm, the bold boy had seized his gun, and, encouraged by my directions, he fired two balls into the head of the monster, as it was preparing to dart on the sheep. It immediately made its escape, leaving a long red track to prove that it was severely wounded.

Being freed from our enemy, I now resumed the rudder, and we lowered the sail and rowed to shore. The animals, as soon as the water became low enough, walked out at their own discretion, after we had relieved them from their swimming girdles. We then secured our boat as before, and landed ourselves, anxiously looking round for our friends.

We had not long to wait, they came joyfully to greet us; and, after our first burst of pleasure, we sat down to tell our adventures in a regular form. My wife was overjoyed to see herself surrounded by these valuable animals; and especially pleased that her son Fritz had suggested so many useful plans. We next proceeded to disembark all our treasures. I noticed that Jack wore a belt of yellow skin, in which were placed a pair of pistols, and inquired where he had got his brigand costume.

"I manufactured it myself," said he; "and this is not all. Look at the dogs!"

The dogs wore each a collar of the same skin as his belt, bristling with long nails, the points outwards a formidable defense.

"It is my own invention," said he; "only mamma helped me in the sewing."

"But where did you get the leather, the needle and thread?" inquired I.

"Fritz's jackal supplied the skin," said my wife, "and my wonderful bag the rest. There is still more to come from it, only say what you want."

Fritz evidently felt a little vexation at his brother's unceremonious appropriation of the skin of the jackal, which displayed itself in the tone in which he exclaimed, holding his nose, "Keep at a distance, Mr. Skinner, you carry an intolerable smell about with you."

I gave him a gentle hint of his duty in the position of eldest son, and he soon recovered his good humour. However, as the body as well as the skin of the jackal was becoming offensive, they united in dragging it down to the sea, while Jack placed his belt in the sun to dry.

As I saw no preparation for supper, I told Fritz to bring the ham; and, to the astonishment and joy of all, he returned with a fine Westphalian ham, which we had cut into in the morning.

"I will tell you," said my wife, "why we have no supper prepared; but first, I will make you an omelet;" and she produced from a basket a dozen turtle's eggs.

"You see," said Ernest, "they have all the characteristics of those Robinson Crusoe had in his island. They are white balls, the skin of which resembles moistened parchment."

My wife promised to relate the history of the discovery after supper, and set about preparing her ham and omelet, while Fritz and I proceeded in unloading our cargo, assisted by the useful ass.

Supper was now ready. A tablecloth was laid over the butter-cask, and spread with the plates and spoons from the ship. The ham was in the middle, and the omelet and cheese at each end; and we made a good meal, surrounded by our subjects, the dogs, the fowls, the pigeons, the sheep, and the goats, waiting for our notice. The geese and ducks were more independent, remaining in their marsh, where they lived in plenty on the small crabs which abounded there.

After supper, I sent Fritz for a bottle of the captain's Canary wine, and then requested my wife to give us her recital.

Lesson 27

1. Read chapter 7 of *Swiss Family Robinson*.
2. Read chapter 8.
3. What are they going to have to build to get their things to their new home? (Answers)
4. Tell someone about the chapters.

Chapter 7

"I will spare you the history of the first day," said my good Elizabeth, "spent in anxiety about you, and attending to the signals; but this morning, being satisfied that all was going right, I sought, before the boys got up, a shady place to rest in, but in vain; I believe this barren shore has not a single tree on it. Then I began to consider on the necessity of searching for a more comfortable spot for our residence; and determined, after a slight repast, to set out with my children across the river, on a journey of discovery. The day before, Jack had busied himself in skinning the jackal with his knife, sharpened on the rock; Ernest declining to assist him in his dirty work, for which I reproved him, sorry that any fastidiousness should deter him from a labour of benefit to society.

"When we attained the hill, I was charmed with the smiling prospect, and, for the first time since our shipwreck, ventured to hope for better things. I had remarked a beautiful wood, to which I determined to make our way, for a little shade, and a most painful progress it was, through grass that was higher than the children's heads. As we were struggling through it, we heard a strange rustling sound among the grass, and at the same moment a bird of prodigious size rose, and flew away, before the poor boys could get their guns ready. They were much mortified, and I recommended them always to have their guns in readiness, for the birds would not be likely to wait till they loaded them.

"We found that what we thought a wood was merely a group of a dozen trees, of a height far beyond any I had ever seen; and apparently belonging rather to the air than the earth; the trunks springing from roots which formed a series of supporting arches. Jack climbed one of the arches, and measured the trunk of the tree with a piece of packthread. He found it to be thirty-four feet. I made thirty-two steps round the roots. Between the roots and the lowest branches, it seemed about forty or fifty feet. The branches are thick and strong, and the leaves are of a moderate size, and resemble our walnut-tree. A thick, short, smooth turf clothed the ground beneath and around the detached roots of the trees, and everything combined to render this one of the most delicious spots the mind could conceive.

"We were astonished at the sight of a sail. Ernest was certain it was papa and Fritz, and though Francis was in dread that it should be the those who visited Robinson Crusoe's island, coming to eat us up, we were soon enabled to calm his fears. We crossed the river by leaping from stone to stone, and, hastening to the landing-place, arrived to greet you on your happy return."

"And I understand, my dear," said I, "that you have discovered a tree sixty feet high, where you wish we should perch like fowls. But how are we to get up?"

"Oh! you must remember," answered she, "the large lime-tree near our native town, in which was a ball-room. We used to ascend to it by a wooden staircase. Could you not contrive something of the sort in one of these gigantic trees, where we might sleep in peace, fearing neither jackals nor any other terrible nocturnal enemy?"

I promised to consider this plan, hoping at least that we might make a commodious and shady dwelling among the roots. To-morrow we were to examine it. We then performed our evening devotions, and retired to rest.

Chapter 8

"Now, my dear Elizabeth," said I, waking early next morning, "let us talk a little on this grand project of changing our residence; to which there are many objections. First, it seems wise to remain on the spot where Providence has cast us, where we can have at once means of support drawn from the ship, and security from all attacks, protected by the rock, the river, and the sea on all sides."

My wife distrusted the river, which could not protect us from the jackals, and complained of the intolerable heat of this sandy desert, of her distaste for such food as oysters and wild geese; and, lastly, of her agony of mind, when we ventured to the wreck; willingly renouncing all its treasures, and begging we might rest content with the blessings we already had.

"There is some truth in your objections," said I, "and perhaps we may erect a dwelling under the roots of your favourite tree; but among these rocks we must have a storehouse for our goods, and a retreat in case of invasion. I hope, by blowing off some pieces of the rock with powder, to be able to fortify the part next the river, leaving a secret passage known only to ourselves. This would make it impregnable. But before we proceed, we must have a bridge to convey our baggage across the river.

"A bridge," said she, in a tone of vexation; "then when shall we get from here? Why cannot we ford it as usual? The cow and ass could carry our stores."

I explained to her how necessary it was for our ammunition and provision to be conveyed over without risk of wetting, and begged her to manufacture some bags and baskets, and leave the bridge to me and my boys. If we succeeded, it would always be useful; as for fear of danger from lightning or accident, I intended to make a powder-magazine among the rocks.

The important question was now decided. I called up my sons, and communicated our plans to them. They were greatly delighted, though somewhat alarmed, at the formidable project of the bridge; besides, the delay was vexatious; they were all anxious for a removal into the *Land of Promise*, as they chose to call it.

We read prayers, and then thought of breakfast. The monkey sucked one of the goats, as if it had been its mother. My wife milked the cow, and gave us boiled milk with biscuit for our breakfast; part of which she put in a flask, for us to take on our expedition. We then prepared our boat for a voyage to the vessel, to procure planks and timber for our bridge. I took both Ernest and Fritz, as I foresaw our cargo would be weighty, and require all our hands to bring it to shore.

At last, we reached our landing-place, and, securing our boat, and calling out loudly, we soon saw our friends running from the river; each carried a handkerchief filled with some new acquisition, and Francis had over his shoulder a small fishing-net. Jack reached us first, and threw down before us from his handkerchief some fine crawfish. They had each as many, forming a provision for many days.

Francis claimed the merit of the discovery. Jack related, that Francis and he took a walk to find a good place for the bridge.

"Thank you, Mr. Architect," said I; "then you must superintend the workmen. Have you fixed on your place?"

"Yes, yes!" cried he; "only listen. When we got to the river, Francis, who was looking about, called out, 'Jack! Jack! Fritz's jackal is covered with crabs! Come! come!' I ran to tell mamma, who brought a net that came from the ship, and we caught these in a few minutes, and could have got many more, if you had not come."

I commanded them to put the smaller ones back into the river, reserving only as many as we could eat. I was truly thankful to discover another means of support.

We now landed our timber. I had looked at Jack's site for the bridge, and thought my little architect very happy in his selection; but it was at a great distance from the timber. I recollected the simplicity of the harness the Laplanders used for their reindeer. I tied cords to the horns of the cow as the strength of this animal is in the head and then fastened the other ends round the piece of timber we wanted moving. I placed a halter round the neck of the ass, and attached the cords to this. We were thus enabled, by degrees, to remove all our wood to the chosen spot, where the sides of the river were steep, and appeared of equal height.

It was necessary to know the breadth of the river, to select the proper planks; and Ernest proposed to procure a ball of packthread from his mother, to tie a stone to one end of the string, and throw it across the river, and to measure it after drawing it back. This expedient succeeded admirably. We found the breadth to be eighteen feet; but, as I proposed to give the bridge strength by having three feet, at least, resting on each shore, we chose some planks of twenty-four feet in length. How we were to get these across the river was another question, which we prepared to discuss during dinner, to which my wife now summoned us.

Our dinner consisted of a dish of crawfish, and some very good rice-milk. But, before we began, we admired her work. She had made a pair of bags for the ass, sewed with packthread; but having no large needles, she had been obliged to pierce holes with a nail, a tedious and painful process. Well satisfied with her success, we turned to our repast, talking of our bridge, which the boys, by anticipation, named the *Nonpareil* (meaning incomparable, unsurpassed). We then went to work.

There happened to be an old trunk of a tree standing on the shore. To this I tied my main beam by a strong cord, loose enough to turn round the trunk. Another cord was attached to the opposite end of the beam, long enough to cross the river twice. I took the end of my rope over the stream, where we had previously fixed the block, used in our boat, to a tree, by the hook which usually suspended it. I passed my rope, and returned with the end to our own side. I then harnessed my cow and ass to the end of my rope, and drove them forcibly from the shore. The beam turned slowly round the trunk, then advanced, and was finally lodged over the river, amidst the shouts of the boys; its own weight keeping it firm. Fritz and Jack leaped on it immediately to run across, to my great fear.

We succeeded in placing four strong beams in the same way; and, by the aid of my sons, I arranged them at a convenient distance from each other, that we might have a broad and good bridge. We then laid down planks close together across the beams; but not fixed, as in time of danger it might be necessary rapidly to remove the bridge. My wife and I were as much excited as the children, and ran across with delight. Our bridge was at least ten feet broad.

Thoroughly fatigued with our day of labour, we returned home, supped, and offered thanks to God, and went to rest.

Lesson 28

1. Read chapter 9 of *Swiss Family Robinson*.
2. Read chapter 10 and tell someone about the chapters.

Vocabulary

1. What does "**convey**" mean in this sentence?
   o Finally, we conveyed inside the tent all we could not carry away, closing the entrance, and barricading it with chests and casks, thus confiding all our possessions to the care of God. (from *Swiss Family Robinson*)
2. Look up the word and write two definitions for this word.
3. Where are they building their new home? (Answers)

Chapter 9

The next morning, after prayers, I assembled my family. We took a solemn leave of our first place of refuge. I cautioned my sons to be prudent, and on their guard; and especially to remain together during our journey. We then prepared for departure. We assembled the cattle: the bags were fixed across the backs of the cow and the ass, and loaded with all our heavy baggage; our cooking utensils; and provisions, consisting of biscuits, butter, cheese, and portable soup; our hammocks and blankets; the captain's service of plate, were all carefully packed in the bags, equally poised on each side the animals.

All was ready, when my wife came in haste with her inexhaustible bag, requesting a place for it. Neither would she consent to leave the poultry, as food for the jackals; above all, Francis must have a place; he could not possibly walk all the way. I was amused with the exactions of the sex; but consented to all, and made a good place for Francis between the bags, on the back of the ass.

The elder boys returned in despair, they could not succeed in catching the fowls; but the experienced mother laughed at them, and said she would soon capture them.

"If you do," said my pert little Jack, "I will be contented to be roasted in the place of the first chicken taken."

"Then, my poor Jack," said his mother, "you will soon be on the spit. Remember, that intellect has always more power than mere bodily exertion. Look here!" She scattered a few handfuls of grain before the tent, calling the fowls; they soon all assembled, including the pigeons; then throwing more down inside the tent, they followed her. It was now only necessary to close the entrance; and they were all soon taken, tied by the wings and feet, and, being placed in baskets covered with nets, were added to the rest of our luggage on the backs of the animals.

Finally, we conveyed inside the tent all we could not carry away, closing the entrance, and barricading it with chests and casks, thus confiding all our possessions to the care of God. We set out on our pilgrimage, each carrying a game-bag and a gun. My wife and her eldest son led the way, followed by the heavily-laden cow and ass; the third division consisted of the goats, driven by Jack, the little monkey seated on the back of its nurse, and grimacing, to our great amusement; next came Ernest, with the sheep; and I followed, superintending the whole. Our gallant dogs acted as *aides-de-camp,* and were continually passing from the front to the rear rank.

Our march was slow, but orderly, and quite patriarchal. "We are now traveling across the deserts, as our first fathers did," said I, "and as the Arabs, Tartars, and other *nomad nations do* to this day, followed by their flocks and herds. But these people generally have strong camels to bear their burdens, instead of a poor ass and cow. I hope this may be the last of our pilgrimages." My wife also hoped that, once under the shade of her marvelous trees, we should have no temptation to travel further.

We now crossed our new bridge, and here the party was happily augmented by a new arrival. The sow had proved very mutinous at setting out, and we had been compelled to leave her; she now voluntarily joined us, seeing we were actually departing; but continued to grunt loudly her disapprobation of our proceedings. After we had crossed the river, we had another embarrassment. The rich grass tempted our animals to stray off to feed, and, but for our dogs, we should never have been able to muster them again. But, for fear of further accident, I commanded my advanced guard to take the road by the coast, which offered no temptation to our troops.

We had scarcely left the high grass when our dogs rushed back into it, barking furiously, and howling as if in combat; Fritz immediately prepared for action, Ernest drew near his mother, Jack rushed forward with his gun over his shoulder, and I cautiously advanced, commanding them to be discreet and cool. But Jack, with his usual impetuosity, leaped among the high grass to the dogs; and immediately returned, clapping his hands, and crying out, "Be quick, papa! a huge porcupine, with quills as long as my arm!"

When I got up, I really found a porcupine, whom the dogs were warmly attacking. It made a frightful noise, erecting its quills so boldly, that the wounded animals howled with pain after every attempt to seize it. As we were looking at them Jack drew a pistol from his belt, and discharged it directly into the head of the porcupine, which fell dead. Jack was very proud of his feat, and Fritz, not a little jealous, suggested that such a little boy should not be trusted with pistols, as he might have shot one of the dogs, or even one of us. I forbade any envy or jealousy among the brothers, and declared that all did well who acted for the public good. Mamma was now summoned to see the curious animal her son's valour had destroyed. Her first thought was to dress the wounds made by the quills which had stuck in the noses of the dogs during their attack.

At last, we arrived at the end of our journey, and, certainly, the size of the trees surpassed anything I could have imagined. Jack was certain they were gigantic walnut-trees; for my own part, I believed them to be a species of fig-tree probably the Antilles fig. But all thanks were given to the kind mother who had sought out such a pleasant home for us; at all events, we could find a convenient shelter among the roots. And, if we should ever succeed in perching on the branches, I told her we should be safe from all wild beasts. I would defy even the bears of our native mountains to climb these immense trunks, totally destitute of branches.

We released our animals from their loads, tying their fore legs together, that they might not stray; except the sow, who, as usual, did her own way. The fowls and pigeons we released, and left to their own discretion. We then sat down on the grass, to consider where we should establish ourselves. I wished to mount the tree that very night. Suddenly we heard, to our no slight alarm, the report of a gun. But the next moment the voice of Fritz re-assured us. He had stolen out unnoticed, and shot a beautiful tiger-cat, which he displayed in great triumph.

"Well done, noble hunter!" said I; "you deserve the thanks of the fowls and pigeons; they would most probably have all fallen a sacrifice to-night, if you had not slain their deadly foe. Pray wage war with all his kind, or we shall not have a chicken left for the pot."

Still occupied with the idea of our castle in the air, I thought of making a ladder of ropes; but this would be useless, if we did not succeed in getting a cord over the lower branches, to draw it up. Neither my sons nor myself could throw a stone, to which I had fastened a cord, over these branches, which were thirty feet above us. It was necessary to think of some other expedient. In the mean time, dinner was ready. The porcupine made excellent soup, and the flesh was well-tasted, though rather hard. My wife could not make up her mind to taste it, but contented herself with a slice of ham and some cheese.

Chapter 10

After dinner, as I found we could not ascend at present, I suspended our hammocks under the arched roots of our tree, and, covering the whole with sailcloth, we had a shelter from the dew and the insects.

While my wife was employed making harness for the cow and ass, I went with my sons to the shore, to look for wood fit for our use next day. We saw a great quantity of wreck, but none fit for our purpose, till Ernest met with a heap of bamboo canes, half buried in sand and mud. These were exactly what I wanted. I drew them out of the sand, stripped them of their leaves, cut them in pieces of about four or five feet long, and my sons each made up a bundle to carry home. I then set out to seek some slender stalks to make arrows, which I should need in my project.

I now ordered Fritz to measure our strong cord, and the little ones to collect all the small string, and wind it. I then took a strong bamboo and made a bow of it, and some arrows of the slender canes, filling them with wet sand to give them weight, and feathering them from the dead flamingo. As soon as my work was completed, the boys crowded round me, all begging to try the bow and arrows. I begged them to be patient, and asked my wife to supply me with a ball of thick strong thread. The enchanted bag did not fail us; the very ball I wanted appeared at her summons. This, my little ones declared, must be magic; but I explained to them, that prudence, foresight, and presence of mind in danger, such as their good mother had displayed, produced more miracles than magic.

I then tied the end of the ball of thread to one of my arrows, fixed it in my bow, and sent it directly over one of the thickest of the lower branches of the tree, and, falling to the ground, it drew the thread after it. Charmed with this result, I hastened to complete my ladder. Fritz had measured our ropes, and found two of forty feet each, exactly what I wanted. These I stretched on the ground at about one foot distance from each other; Fritz cut pieces of cane two feet long, which Ernest passed to me. I placed these in knots which I had made in the cords, at about a foot distance from each other, and Jack fastened each end with a long nail, to prevent it slipping. In a very short time our ladder was completed; and, tying it to the end of the cord which went over the branch, we drew it up without difficulty. All the boys were anxious to ascend; but I chose Jack, as the lightest and most active. Accordingly, he ascended, while his brothers and myself held the ladder firm by the end of the cord. Fritz followed him, conveying a bag with nails and hammer. They were soon perched on the branches, huzzaing to us.

Fritz secured the ladder so firmly to the branch, that I had no hesitation in ascending myself. I carried with me a large pulley fixed to the end of a rope, which I attached to a branch above us, to enable us to raise the planks necessary to form the groundwork of our habitation. I smoothed the branches a little by aid of my axe, sending the boys down to be out of my way. After completing my day's work, I descended by the light of the moon, and was alarmed to find that Fritz and Jack were not below; and still more so, when I heard their clear, sweet voices, at the summit of the tree, singing the evening hymn, as if to sanctify our future abode. They had climbed the tree, instead of descending, and, filled with wonder and reverence at the sublime view below them, had burst out into the hymn of thanksgiving to God.

I could not scold my dear boys, when they descended, but directed them to assemble the animals, and to collect wood, to keep up fires during the night, in order to drive away any wild beasts that might be near.

My wife then displayed her work, complete harness for our two beasts of burden, and, in return, I promised her we would establish ourselves next day in the tree. Supper was now ready, one piece of the porcupine was roasted by the fire, smelling deliciously; another piece formed a rich soup; a cloth was spread on the turf; the ham, cheese, butter, and biscuits, were placed upon it.

My wife first assembled the fowls, by throwing some grain to them, to accustom them to the place. We soon saw the pigeons fly to roost on the higher branches of the trees, while the fowls perched on the ladder; the beasts we tied to the roots, close to us. Now, that our cares were over, we sat down to a merry and excellent repast by moonlight. Then, after the prayers of the evening, I kindled our watch-fires, and we all lay down to rest in our hammocks. The boys were rather discontented, and complained of their cramped position, longing for the freedom of their beds of moss; but I instructed them to lie, as the sailors do, diagonally, and swinging the hammock, and told them that brave Swiss boys might sleep as the sailors of all nations were compelled to sleep. After some stifled sighs and groans, all sank to rest except myself, kept awake by anxiety for the safety of the rest.

Lesson 29

1. Read chapters 11 and 12 of *Swiss Family Robinson*.
2. He tells his children a parable, a story that has a meaning. The "Great King" in the story is Jesus. He's teaching his children about the Bible.
3. Tell someone about the chapters.

Chapter 11

My anxiety kept me awake till near morning, when, after a short sleep, I rose, and we were soon all at work. My wife, after milking the cow and goats, harnessed the cow and ass, and set out to search for drift-wood for our use. In the mean time, I mounted the ladder with Fritz, and we set to work stoutly, with axe and saw, to rid ourselves of all useless branches. Some, about six feet above our foundation, I left, to suspend our hammocks from, and others, a little higher, to support the roof, which, at present, was to be merely sailcloth. My wife succeeded in collecting us some boards and planks, which, with her assistance, and the aid of the pulley, we hoisted up. We then arranged them on the level branches close to each other, in such a manner as to form a smooth and solid floor. I made a sort of parapet round, to prevent accidents.

By degrees, our dwelling began to assume a distinct form; the sailcloth was raised over the high branches, forming a roof; and, being brought down on each side, was nailed to the parapet. The immense trunk protected the back of our apartment, and the front was open to admit the breeze from the sea, which was visible from this elevation. We hoisted our hammocks and blankets by the pulley, and suspended them; my son and I then descended, and, as our day was not yet exhausted, we set about constructing a rude table and some benches, from the remainder of our wood, which we placed beneath the roots of the tree, henceforward to be our dining-room. The little boys collected the chips and pieces of wood for fire-wood; while their mamma prepared supper, which we needed much after the extraordinary fatigues of this day.

The next day, however, being Sunday, we looked forward to as a day of rest, of recreation, and thanksgiving to the great God who had preserved us.

Chapter 12

Next morning, all awoke in good spirits; I told them that on this, the Lord's day, we would do no work. That it was appointed, not only for a day of rest, but a day when we must, as much as possible, turn our hearts from the vanities of the world, to God himself; thank him, worship him, and serve him. Jack thought we could not do this without a church and a priest; but Ernest believed that God would hear our prayers under his own sky, and papa could give them a sermon; Francis wished to know if God would like to hear them sing the beautiful hymns mamma had taught them, without an organ accompaniment.

"Yes, my dear children," said I, "God is everywhere; and to bless him, to praise him in all his works, to submit to his holy will, and to obey him, is to serve him. But everything in its time. Let us first attend to the wants of our animals, and breakfast, and we will then begin the services of the day by a hymn."

We descended, and breakfasted on warm milk, fed our animals, and then, my children and their mother seated on the turf, I placed myself on a little eminence before them, and, after the service of the day, which I knew by heart, and singing some portions of the 119th Psalm, I told them a little allegory.

"There was once on a time a great king, whose kingdom was called the Land of *Light* and *Reality*, because there reigned there constant light and incessant activity. On the most remote frontier of this kingdom, towards the north, there was another large kingdom, equally subject to his rule, and of which none but himself knew the immense extent. From time immemorial, an exact plan of this kingdom had been preserved in the archives. It was called the Land of Obscurity, or *Night,* because everything in it was dark and inactive.

"In the most fertile and agreeable part of the empire of Reality, the king had a magnificent residence, called *The Heavenly City,* where he held his brilliant court. Millions of servants executed his wishes still more were ready to receive his orders. The first were clothed in glittering robes, whiter than snow for white was the colour of the Great King, as the emblem of purity. Others were clothed in armour, shining like the colours of the rainbow, and carried flaming swords in their hands. Each, at his master's nod, flew like lightning to accomplish his will. All his servants faithful, vigilant, bold, and ardent were united in friendship, and could imagine no happiness greater than the favour of their master. There were some, less elevated, who were still good, rich, and happy in the favours of their sovereign, to whom all his subjects were alike, and were treated by him as his children.

"Not far from the frontiers, the Great King possessed a desert island, which he desired to people and cultivate, in order to make it, for a time, the abode of those of his subjects whom he intended to admit, by degrees, into his *Heavenly City* a favour he wished to bestow on the greatest number possible.

"This island was called *Earthly Abode*; and he who had passed some time there, worthily, was to be received into all the happiness of the heavenly city. To attain this, the Great King equipped a fleet to transport the colonists, whom he chose from the kingdom of *Night*, to this island, where he gave them light and activity advantages they had not known before. Think how joyful their arrival would be! The island was fertile when cultivated; and all was prepared to make the time pass agreeably, till they were admitted to their highest honours.

"At the moment of embarkation, the Great King sent his own son, who spoke thus to them in His name:

"'My dear children, I have called you from inaction and insensibility to render you happy by feeling, by action, by life. Never forget I am your king, and obey my commands, by cultivating the country I confide to you. Every one will receive his portion of land, and wise and learned men are appointed to explain my will to you. I wish you all to acquire the knowledge of my laws, and that every father should keep a copy, to read daily to his children, that they may never be forgotten. And on the first day of the week you must all assemble, as brothers, in one place, to hear these laws read and explained. Thus it will be easy for every one to learn the best method of improving his land, what to plant, and how to cleanse it from the *tares* that might choke the good seed. All may ask what they desire, and every reasonable demand will be granted, if it be conformable to the great end.

"'If you feel grateful for these benefits, and testify it by increased activity, and by occupying yourself on this day in expressing your gratitude to me, I will take care this day of rest shall be a benefit, and not a loss. I wish that all your useful animals, and even the wild beasts of the plains, should on this day repose in peace.

"'He who obeys my commands in *Earthly Abode,* shall receive a rich reward in the *Heavenly City;* but the idle, the negligent, and the evil-disposed, shall be condemned to perpetual slavery, or to labour in mines, in the bowels of the earth.

"'From time to time, I shall send ships, to bring away individuals, to be rewarded or punished, as they have fulfilled my commands. None can deceive me; a magic mirror will show me the actions and thoughts of all,'

"The colonists were satisfied, and eager to begin their labour. The portions of land and instruments of labour were distributed to them, with seeds, and useful plants, and fruit-trees. They were then left to turn these good gifts to profit.

"But what followed? Every one did as he wished. Some planted their ground with groves and gardens, pretty and useless. Others planted wild fruit, instead of the good fruit the Great King had commanded. A third had sowed good seed; but, not knowing the *tares* from the wheat, he had torn up all before they reached maturity. But the most part left their land uncultivated; they had lost their seeds, or spoiled their implements. Many would not understand the orders of the great king; and others tried, by subtlety, to evade them.

"A few laboured with courage, as they had been taught, rejoicing in the hope of the promise given them. Their greatest danger was in the disbelief of their teachers. Though every one had a copy of the law, few read it; all were ready, by some excuse, to avoid this duty. Some asserted they knew it, yet never thought on it: some called these the laws of past times; not of the present. Other said the Great King did not regard the actions of his subjects, that he had neither mines nor dungeons, and that all would certainly be taken to the *Heavenly City*. They began to neglect the duties of the day dedicated to the Great King. Few assembled; and of these, the most part were inattentive, and did not profit by the instruction given them.

"But the Great King was faithful to his word. From time to time, frigates arrived, bearing the name of some disease. These were followed by a large vessel called *The Grave*, bearing the terrible flag of the Admiral *Death*; this flag was of two colours, green and black; and appeared to the colonists, according to their state, the smiling colour of *Hope*, or the gloomy hue of *Despair*.

"This fleet always arrived unexpectedly, and was usually unwelcome. The officers were sent out, by the admiral, to seize those he pointed out: many who were unwilling were compelled to go; and others whose land was prepared, and even the harvest ripening, were summoned; but these went joyfully, sure that they went to happiness. The fleet being ready, sailed for the *Heavenly City*. Then the Great King, in his justice, awarded the punishments and recompenses. Excuses were now too late; the negligent and disobedient were sent to labour in the dark mines; while the faithful and obedient, arrayed in bright robes, were received into their glorious abodes of happiness.

"I have finished my parable, my dear children; reflect on it, and profit by it. Fritz, what do you think of it?"

"I am considering the goodness of the Great King, and the ingratitude of his people," answered he.

"And how very foolish they were," said Ernest, "with a little prudence, they might have kept their land in good condition, and secured a pleasant life afterwards."

"Away with them to the mines!" cried Jack, "they richly deserved such a doom."

"How much I should like," said Francis, "to see those soldiers in their shining armour!"

"I hope you will see them some day, my dear boy, if you continue to be good and obedient." I then explained my parable fully, and applied the moral to each of my sons directly.

"You, Fritz, should take warning from the people who planted wild fruit, and wished to make them pass for good fruit. Such are those who are proud of natural virtues, easy to exercise, such as bodily strength, or physical courage; and place these above the qualities which are only attained by labour and patience.

"You, Ernest, must remember the subjects who laid out their land in flowery gardens; like those who seek the pleasures of life, rather than the duties. And you, my thoughtless Jack, and little Francis, think of the fate of those who left their land untilled, or heedlessly sowed *tares* (weeds) for wheat. These are God's people who neither study nor reflect; who cast to the winds all instruction, and leave room in their minds for evil. Then let us all be, like the good labourers of the parable, constantly cultivating our ground, that, when Death comes for us, we may willingly follow him to the feet of the Great King, to hear these blessed words: 'Good and faithful servants! enter into the joy of your Lord!'"

This made a great impression on my children. We concluded by singing a hymn. Then my good wife produced from her unfailing bag, a copy of the Holy Scripture, from which I selected such passages as applied to our situation; and explained them to my best ability. My boys remained for some time thoughtful and serious, and though they followed their innocent recreations during the day, they did not lose sight of the useful lesson of the morning, but, by a more gentle and amiable manner, showed that my words had taken effect.

Lesson 30

1. Read chapters 13 and 14 of *Swiss Family Robinson*.
2. Tell someone about the chapters.

Chapter 13

The next morning, all were engaged in archery: I completed the bow for Francis, and at his particular request made him a quiver too. The delicate bark of a tree, united by glue, obtained from our portable soup, formed an admirable quiver; this I suspended by a string round the neck of my boy, furnished with arrows; then taking his bow in his hand, he was as proud as a knight armed at all points.

After dinner, I proposed that we should give names to all the parts of our island known to us, in order that, by a pleasing delusion, we might fancy ourselves in an inhabited country. My proposal was well received, and then began the discussion of names. Jack wished for something high-sounding and difficult, such as *Monomotapa* or *Zanguebar*; very difficult words, to puzzle any one that visited our island. But I objected to this, as *we* were the most likely to have to use the names ourselves, and we should suffer from it. I rather suggested that we should give, in our own language, such simple names as should point out some circumstance connected with the spot. I proposed we should begin with the bay where we landed, and called on Fritz for his name.

"*The Bay of Oysters*" said he, "we found so many there."

"Oh, no!" said Jack, "let it be *Lobster Bay*; for there I was caught by the leg."

"Then we ought to call it the *Bay of Tears*," said Ernest, "to commemorate those you shed on the occasion."

"My advice," said my wife, "is, that in gratitude to God we should name it *Safety Bay*."

We were all pleased with this name, and proceeded to give the name of *Tent House* to our first abode; *Shark Island*, to the little island in the bay, where we had found that animal; and, at Jack's desire, the marshy spot where we had cut our arrows was named *Flamingo Marsh*. There the height from which we had vainly sought traces of our shipmates, received the name of *Cape Disappointment*. The river was to be *Jackal River*, and the bridge, *Family Bridge*. The most difficult point was, to name our present abode. At last we agreed on the name of *Falcon's Nest*. This was received with *acclamations*, and I poured out for my young nestlings each a glass of sweet wine, to drink Prosperity to *Falcon's Nest*. We thus laid the foundation of the geography of our new country, promising to forward it to Europe by the first post.

After dinner, my sons returned to their occupation as tanners, Fritz to complete his belt, and Jack to make a sort of cuirass, of the formidable skin of the porcupine, to protect the dogs. He finished by making a sort of helmet from the head of the animal, as strange as the cuirasses.

The heat of the day being over, we prepared to set out to walk to Tent House, to renew our stock of provisions, and endeavour to bring the geese and ducks to our new residence; but, instead of going by the coast, we proposed to go up the river till we reached the chain of rocks, and continue under their shade till we got to the cascade, where we could cross, and return by Family Bridge.

This was approved, and we set out. Fritz, decorated with his beautiful belt of skin, Jack in his porcupine helmet. Each had a gun and game-bag; except Francis, who, with his pretty fair face, his golden hair, and his bow and quiver, was a perfect Cupid. My wife was loaded with a large butter-pot for a fresh supply. Turk walked before us with his coat of mail, and Flora followed, keeping at a respectful distance from him, for fear of the darts. *Knips*, as my boys called the monkey, finding this new saddle very inconvenient, jumped off, with many contortions, but soon fixed on Flora, who, not being able to shake him off, was compelled to become his palfrey.

The road by the river was smooth and pleasant. When we reached the end of the wood, the country seemed more open; and now the boys, who had been rambling about, came running up, out of breath; Ernest was holding a plant with leaves and flowers, and green apples hanging on it.

"Potatoes!" said he; "I am certain they are potatoes!"

"God be praised," said I; "this precious plant will secure provision for our colony."

"Well," said Jack, "if his superior knowledge discovered them, I will be the first to dig them up;" and he set to work so ardently, that we had soon a bag of fine ripe potatoes, which we carried on to Tent House.

Chapter 14

We had been much delighted with the new and lovely scenery of our road: the prickly cactus, and aloe, with its white flowers; the Indian fig; the white and yellow jasmine; the fragrant vanilla, throwing round its graceful festoons. Above all, the regal pineapple grew in profusion, and we feasted on it, for the first time, with avidity.

Among the prickly stalks of the cactus and aloes, I perceived a plant with large pointed leaves, which I knew to be the *karata*. I pointed out to the boys its beautiful red flowers; the leaves are an excellent application to wounds, and thread is made from the filaments, and the pith of the stem is used by the tribes for tinder.

When I showed the boys, by experiment, the use of the pith, they thought the *tinder-tree* would be almost as useful as the potatoes.

"At all events," I said, "it will be more useful than the pine-apples; your mother will be thankful for thread, when her enchanted bag is exhausted."

"How happy it is for us," said she, "that you have devoted yourself to reading and study. In our ignorance we might have passed this treasure, without suspecting its value."

Fritz inquired of what use in the world all the rest of these prickly plants could be, which wounded every one that came near.

"All these have their use, Fritz," said I; "some contain juices and gums, which are daily made use of in medicine; others are useful in the arts, or in manufactures. The Indian fig, for instance, is a most interesting tree. It grows in the most arid soil. The fruit is said to be sweet and wholesome."

In a moment, my little active Jack was climbing the rocks to gather some of these figs; but he had not remarked that they were covered with thousands of slender thorns, finer than the finest needles, which terribly wounded his fingers. He returned, weeping bitterly and dancing with pain. Having rallied him a little for his greediness, I extracted the thorns, and then showed him how to open the fruit, by first cutting off the pointed end, as it lay on the ground; into this I fixed a piece of stick, and then pared it with my knife. The novelty of the expedient recommended it, and they were soon all engaged eating the fruit, which they declared was very good.

In the mean time, I saw Ernest examining one of the figs very attentively. "Oh! papa!" said he, "what a singular sight; the fig is covered with a small red insect. I cannot shake them off." I recognized at once the precious insect, of which I explained to my sons the nature and use. "It is with this insect," said I, "that the beautiful and rich scarlet dye is made. It is found in America, and the Europeans give its weight in gold for it."

Thus discoursing on the wonders of nature, and the necessity of increasing our knowledge by observation and study, we arrived at Tent House, and found it in the same state as we left it.

We all began to collect necessaries. Fritz loaded himself with powder and shot, I opened the butter-cask, and my wife and little Francis filled the pot. Ernest and Jack went to try and secure the geese and ducks; but they had become so wild that it would have been impossible, if Ernest had not thought of an expedient. He tied pieces of cheese, for bait, to threads, which he floated on the water. The voracious creatures immediately swallowed the cheese and were drawn out by the thread. They were then securely tied, and fastened to the game-bags, to be carried home on our backs. As the bait could not be recovered, the boys contented themselves with cutting off the string close to the beak, leaving them to digest the rest.

Our bags were already loaded with potatoes, but we filled up the spaces between them with salt; and, having relieved Turk of his armour, we placed the heaviest on his back. I took the butter-pot; and, after replacing everything, and closing our tent, we resumed our march, with our ludicrous incumbrances. The geese and ducks were very noisy in their adieu to their old marsh; the dogs barked; and we all laughed so excessively, that we forgot our burdens till we sat down again under our tree. My wife soon had her pot of potatoes on the fire. She then milked the cow and goat, while I set the fowls at liberty on the banks of the river. We then sat down to a smoking dish of potatoes, a jug of milk, and butter and cheese. After supper we had prayers, thanking God especially for his new benefits; and we then sought our repose among the leaves.

Lesson 31

1. Read chapters 15 and 16 of *Swiss Family Robinson*.
2. Write a one sentence summary of these chapters. In one sentence tell what happened in each chapter, the main idea/event of the chapter.

Chapter 15

I had observed on the shore, the preceding day, a quantity of wood, which I thought would suit to make a sledge, to convey our casks and heavy stores from Tent House to Falcon's Nest. At dawn of day I woke Ernest, whose inclination to indolence I wished to overcome, and leaving the rest asleep, we descended, and harnessing the ass to a strong branch of a tree that was lying near, we proceeded to the shore. I had no difficulty in selecting proper pieces of wood; we sawed them the right length, tied them together, and laid them across the bough, which the patient animal drew very contentedly. We added to the load a small chest we discovered half buried in the sand, and we returned homewards, Ernest leading the ass, and I assisted by raising the load with a lever when we met with any obstruction. My wife had been rather alarmed; but seeing the result of our expedition, and hearing of the prospect of a sledge, she was satisfied. I opened the chest, which contained only some sailors' dresses and some linen, both wetted with sea-water; but likely to be very useful as our own clothes decayed. I found Fritz and Jack had been shooting *ortolans* (a kind of bird); they had killed about fifty, but had consumed so much powder and shot, that I checked a prodigality so imprudent in our situation. I taught them to make snares for the birds of the threads we drew from the karata leaves we had brought home. My wife and her two younger sons busied themselves with these, while I, with my two elder boys, began to construct the sledge. As we were working, we heard a great noise among the fowls, and Ernest, looking about, discovered the monkey seizing and hiding the eggs from the nests; he had collected a good store in a hole among the roots, which Ernest carried to his mother; and Knips was punished by being tied up, every morning, till the eggs were collected.

Our work was interrupted by dinner, composed of *ortolans*, milk, and cheese. After dinner, Jack had climbed to the higher branches of the trees to place his snares, and found the pigeons were making nests. I then told him to look often to the snares, for fear our own poor birds should be taken; and, above all, never in future to fire into the tree.

"Papa," said little Francis, "can we not sow some gunpowder, and then we shall have plenty?" This proposal was received with shouts of laughter, which greatly discomposed the little innocent fellow. Professor Ernest immediately seized the opportunity to give a lecture on the composition of gunpowder.

At the end of the day my sledge was finished. Two long curved planks of wood, crossed by three pieces, at a distance from each other, formed the simple conveyance. The fore and hind parts were in the form of horns, to keep the load from falling off. Two ropes were fastened to the front, and my sledge was complete. My wife was delighted with it, and hoped I would now set out immediately to Tent House for the butter-cask. I made no objection to this; and Ernest and I prepared to go, and leave Fritz in charge of the family.

Chapter 16

When we were ready to set out, Fritz presented each of us with a little case he had made from the skin of the *margay*. They were ingeniously contrived to contain knife, fork, and spoon, and a small hatchet. We then harnessed the ass and the cow to the sledge, took a flexible bamboo cane for a whip, and, followed by Flora, we departed, leaving Turk to guard the tree.

We went by the shore, as the better road for the sledge, and crossing Family Bridge, were soon at Tent House. After unharnessing the animals, we began to load. We took the cask of butter, the cheese, and the biscuit; all the rest of our utensils, powder, shot, and Turk's armour, which we had left there. These labours had so occupied us, that we had not observed that our animals, attracted by the pasturage, had crossed the bridge, and wandered out of sight. I sent Ernest to seek them, and in the mean time went to the bay, where I discovered some convenient little hollows in the rock, that seemed cut out for baths. I called Ernest to come, and till he arrived, employed myself in cutting some rushes, which I thought might be useful. When my son came, I found he had ingeniously removed the first planks from the bridge, to prevent the animals straying over again. We then had a very pleasant bath, and Ernest being out first, I sent him to the rock, where the salt was accumulated, to fill a small bag, to be transferred to the large bags on the ass. He had not been absent long, when I heard him cry out, "Papa! papa! a huge fish! I cannot hold it; it will break my line." I ran to his assistance, and found him lying on the ground on his face, tugging at his line, to which an enormous salmon was attached, that had nearly pulled him into the water. I let it have a little more line, then drew it gently into a shallow, and secured it. It appeared about fifteen pounds weight; and we pleased ourselves with the idea of presenting this to our good cook. Ernest said, he remembered having remarked how this place swarmed with fish, and he took care to bring his rod with him; he had taken about a dozen small fishes, which he had in his handkerchief, before he was overpowered by the salmon. I cut the fishes open, and rubbed the inside with salt, to preserve them; then placing them in a small box on the sledge, and adding our bags of salt, we harnessed our animals, and set off homewards.

When we were about half-way, Flora left us, and, by her barking, raised a singular animal, which seemed to leap instead of ran. The irregular bounds of the animal disconcerted my aim, and, though very near, I missed it. Ernest was more fortunate; he fired at it, and killed it. It was an animal about the size of a sheep, with the tail of a tiger; its head and skin were like those of a mouse, ears longer than the hare; there was a curious pouch on the belly; the fore legs were short, as if imperfectly developed, and armed with strong claws, the hind legs long, like a pair of stilts. After Ernest's pride of victory was a little subdued, he fell back on his science, and began to examine his spoil.

"By its teeth," said he, "it should belong to the family of *rodentes*, or gnawers; by its legs, to the *jumpers*; and by its pouch, to the opossum tribe."

This gave me the right clue. "Then," said I, "this must be the animal Cook first discovered in New Holland, and it is called the *kangaroo*."

We now tied the legs of the animal together, and, putting a stick through, carried it to the sledge very carefully, for Ernest was anxious to preserve the beautiful skin. Our animals were heavily laden; but, giving them a little rest and some fresh grass, we once more started, and in a short time reached Falcon's Nest.

My wife had been employed during our absence in washing the clothes of the three boys, clothing them in the mean time from the sailor's chest we had found a few days before. Their appearance was excessively ridiculous, as the garments neither suited their age nor size, and caused great mirth to us all; but my wife had preferred this disguise to the alternative of their going naked.

We now began to display our riches, and relate our adventures. The butter and the rest of the provisions were very welcome, the salmon still more so, but the sight of the kangaroo produced screams of admiration. Fritz displayed a little jealousy, but soon surmounted it by an exertion of his nobler feelings; and only the keen eye of a father could have discovered it. He congratulated Ernest warmly, but could not help begging to accompany me next time.

"I promise you that," said I, "as a reward for the conquest you have achieved over your jealousy of your brother. But, remember, I could not have given you a greater proof of my confidence, than in leaving you to protect your mother and brothers. A noble mind finds its purest joy in the accomplishment of its duty, and to that willingly sacrifices its inclination. But," I added, in a low tone, lest I should distress my wife, "I propose another expedition to the vessel, and you must accompany me."

We then fed our tired animals, giving them some salt with their grass, a great treat to them. Some salmon was prepared for dinner, and the rest salted. After dinner, I hung up the kangaroo till next day, when we intended to salt and smoke the flesh. Evening arrived, and an excellent supper of fish, *ortolans*, and potatoes refreshed us; and, after thanks to God, we retired to rest.

Lesson 32

1. Read chapters 17 and 18 of *Swiss Family Robinson*.
2. What did they manage to harpoon? A harpoon is a spear used for fishing. (Answers)
3. Tell someone about the chapters.

Chapter 17

I rose early, and descended the ladder, a little uneasy about my kangaroo, and found I was but just in time to save it, for my dogs had so enjoyed their repast on the entrails, which I had given them the night before, that they wished to appropriate the rest. They had succeeded in tearing off the head, which was in their reach, and were devouring it in a sort of growling partnership. As we had no store-room for our provision, I decided to administer a little correction, as a warning to these gluttons. I gave them some smart strokes with a cane, and they fled howling to the stable under the roots. Their cries roused my wife, who came down; and, though she could not but allow the chastisement to be just and prudent, she was so moved by compassion, that she consoled the poor sufferers with some remains of last night's supper.

I now carefully stripped the kangaroo of his elegant skin, and washing myself, and changing my dress after this unpleasant operation, I joined my family at breakfast. I then announced my plan of visiting the vessel, and ordered Fritz to make preparations. My wife resigned herself mournfully to the necessity. When we were ready to depart, Ernest and Jack were not to be found; their mother suspected they had gone to get potatoes. This calmed my apprehension; but I charged her to reprimand them for going without leave. We set out towards Tent House, leaving Flora to protect the household, and taking our guns as usual.

We had scarcely left the wood, and were approaching Jackal River, when we heard piercing cries, and suddenly Ernest and Jack leaped from a thicket, delighted, as Jack said, in having succeeded in their plan of accompanying us, and, moreover, in making us believe we were beset with natives. They were, however, disappointed. I gave them a severe reproof for their disobedience, and sent them home with a message to their mother that I thought we might be detained all night, and begged she would not be uneasy.

They listened to me in great confusion, and were much mortified at their dismissal; but I begged Fritz to give Ernest his silver watch, that they might know how the time passed; and I knew that I could replace it, as there was a case of watches in the ship. This reconciled them a little to their lot, and they left us. We went forward to our boat, embarked, and, aided by the current, soon reached the vessel.

My first care was to construct some more convenient transport-vessel than our boat. Fritz proposed a raft, similar to those used by these nations, supported on skins filled with air. These we had not; but we found a number of water-hogsheads, which we emptied, and closed again, and threw a dozen of them into the sea, between the ship and our boat. Some long planks were laid on these, and secured with ropes. We added a raised edge of planks to secure our cargo, and thus had a solid raft, capable of conveying any burden. This work occupied us the whole day, scarcely interrupted by eating a little cold meat from our game-bags. Exhausted by fatigue, we were glad to take a good night's rest in the captain's cabin on an elastic mattress, of which our hammocks had made us forget the comfort. Early next morning we began to load our raft.

We began by entirely stripping our own cabin and that of the captain. We carried away even the doors and windows. The chests of the carpenter and the gunner followed. There were cases of rich jewellery, and caskets of money, which at first tempted us, but were speedily relinquished for objects of real utility. I preferred a case of young plants of European fruits, carefully packed in moss for transportation. I saw, with delight, among these precious plants, apple, pear, plum, orange, apricot, peach, almond, and chestnut trees, and some young shoots of vines. How I longed to plant these familiar trees of home in a foreign soil. We secured some bars of iron and pigs of lead, grindstones, cart-wheels ready for mounting, tongs, shovels, plough-shares, packets of copper and iron wire, sacks of maize, peas, oats, and vetches; and even a small hand-mill. The vessel had been, in fact, laden with everything likely to be useful in a new colony. We found a saw-mill in pieces, but marked, so that it could be easily put together. It was difficult to select, but we took as much as was safe on the raft, adding a large fishing-net and the ship's compass. Fritz begged to take the harpoons, which he hung by the ropes over the bow of our boat; and I indulged his fancy. We were now loaded as far as prudence would allow us; so, attaching our raft firmly to the boat, we hoisted our sail, and made slowly to the shore.

Chapter 18

The wind was favourable, but we advanced slowly, the floating mass that we had to tug retarding us. Fritz had been some time regarding a large object in the water; he called me to steer a little towards it, that he might see what it was. I went to the rudder, and made the movement; immediately I heard the whistling of the cord, and felt a shock; then a second, which was followed by a rapid motion of the boat.

"We are going to founder!" cried I. "What is the matter?"

"I have caught it," shouted Fritz; "I have harpooned it in the neck. It is a turtle."

I saw the harpoon shining at a distance, and the turtle was rapidly drawing us along by the line. I lowered the sail, and rushed forward to cut the line; but Fritz besought me not to do it. He assured me there was no danger, and that he himself would release us if necessary. I reluctantly consented, and saw our whole convoy drawn by an animal whose agony increased its strength. As we drew near the shore, I endeavoured to steer so that we might not strike and be capsized. I saw after a few minutes that our conductor again wanted to make out to sea; I therefore hoisted the sail, and the wind being in our favour, he found resistance vain, and, tugging as before, followed up the current, only taking more to the left, towards Falcon's Nest, and landing us in a shallow, rested on the shore. I leaped out of the boat, and with a hatchet soon put our powerful conductor out of his misery.

Fritz uttered a shout of joy, and fired off his gun, as a signal of our arrival. All came running to greet us, and great was their surprise, not only at the value of our cargo, but at the strange mode by which it had been brought into harbour. My first care was to send them for the sledge, to remove some of our load without delay, and as the ebbing tide was leaving our vessels almost dry on the sand, I profited by the opportunity to secure them. By the aid of the jack-screw and levers, we raised and brought to the shore two large pieces of lead from the raft. These served for anchors and, connected to the boat and raft by strong cables, fixed them safely.

As soon as the sledge arrived, we placed the turtle with some difficulty on it, as it weighed at least three hundredweight. We added some lighter articles, the mattresses, some small chests, &c., and proceeded with our first load to Falcon's Nest in great spirits. As we walked on, Fritz told them of the wondrous cases of jewellery we had abandoned for things of use; Jack wished Fritz had brought him a gold snuff-box, to hold curious seeds; and Francis wished for some of the money to buy gingerbread at the fair! Everybody laughed at the little simpleton, who could not help laughing himself, when he remembered his distance from fairs. Arrived at home, our first care was to turn the turtle on his back, to get the excellent meat out of the shell. With my hatchet I separated the *cartilages* that unite the shells: the upper shell is convex, the lower one nearly flat.

We had some of the turtle prepared for dinner, though my wife felt great repugnance in touching the green fat, notwithstanding my assurance of its being the chief delicacy to an epicure.

We salted the remainder of the flesh, and gave the offal to the dogs. The boys were all clamorous to possess the shell; but I said it belonged to Fritz, by right of conquest, and he must dispose of it as he thought best.

"Then," said he, "I will make a basin of it, and place it near the river, that my mother may always keep it full of fresh water."

"Very good," said I, "and we will fill our basin, as soon as we find some clay to make a solid foundation."

"I found some this morning," said Jack, "a whole bed of clay, and I brought these balls home to show you."

"And I have made a discovery too," said Ernest. "Look at these roots, like radishes; I have not eaten any, but the sow enjoys them very much."

"A most valuable discovery, indeed," said I; "if I am not mistaken, this is the root of the *manioc*, which with the potatoes will insure us from famine. Of this root they make in the West Indies a sort of bread, called cassava bread. In its natural state it contains a violent poison, but by a process of heating it becomes wholesome. The nutritious tapioca is a preparation from this root."

By this time we had unloaded, and proceeded to the shore to bring a second load before night came on. We brought up two chests of our own clothes and property, some chests of tools, the cart-wheels, and the hand-mill, likely now to be of use for the cassava. After unloading, we sat down to an excellent supper of turtle, with potatoes, instead of bread. After supper, my wife said, smiling, "After such a hard day, I think I can give you something to restore you." She then brought a bottle and glasses, and filled us each a glass of clear, amber-coloured wine. I found it excellent Malaga. She had been down to the shore the previous day, and there found a small cask thrown up by the waves. This, with the assistance of her sons, she had rolled up to the foot of our tree, and there covered it with leaves to keep it cool till our arrival.

We were so invigorated by this cordial, that we set briskly to work to hoist up our mattresses to our dormitory, which we accomplished by the aid of ropes and pulleys. My wife received and arranged them, and after our usual evening devotions, we gladly lay down on them, to enjoy a night of sweet repose.

Lesson 33

1. Read chapter 19 of *Swiss Family Robinson*.
2. Write a one sentence summary of the chapter.

Chapter 19

I rose before daylight, and, leaving my family sleeping, descended, to go to the shore to look after my vessels. I found all the animals moving. The dogs leaped about me; the cocks were crowing; the goats browsing on the dewy grass. The ass alone was sleeping; and, as he was the assistant I wanted, I was compelled to rouse him, a preference which did not appear to flatter him. Nevertheless, I harnessed him to the sledge, and, followed by the dogs, went forward to the coast, where I found my boat and raft safe at anchor. I took up a moderate load and came home to breakfast; but found all still as I left them. I called my family, and they sprung up ashamed of their sloth; my wife declared it must have been the good mattress that had charmed her.

I gave my boys a short admonition for their sloth. We then came down to a hasty breakfast, and returned to the coast to finish the unloading the boats, that I might, at high water, take them round to moor at the usual place in the Bay of Safety. I sent my wife up with the last load, while Fritz and I embarked, and, seeing Jack watching us, I consented that he should form one of the crew, for I had determined to make another visit to the wreck before I moored my craft. When we reached the vessel, the day was so far advanced that we had only time to collect hastily anything easy to embark. My sons ran over the ship. Jack came trundling a wheelbarrow, which he said would be excellent for fetching the potatoes in.

But Fritz brought me good news: he had found, between decks, a beautiful pinnace (a small vessel, of which the prow is square), taken to pieces, with all its fittings, and even two small guns. I saw that all the pieces were numbered, and placed in order; nothing was wanting. I felt the importance of this acquisition; but it would take days of labour to put it together; and then how could we launch it? At present, I felt I must renounce the undertaking. I returned to my loading. It consisted of all sorts of utensils: a copper boiler, some plates of iron, tobacco-graters, two grindstones, a barrel of powder, and one of flints. Jack did not forget his wheelbarrow; and we found two more, which we added to our cargo, and then sailed off speedily, to avoid the land-wind, which rises in the evening.

As we drew near, we were astonished to see a row of little creatures standing on the shore, apparently regarding us with much curiosity. They were dressed in black, with white waistcoats, and thick cravats; their arms hung down carelessly; but from time to time they raised them as if they wished to bestow on us a fraternal embrace.

"I believe," said I, laughing, "this must be the country of pigmies, and they are coming to welcome us."

"And now," said Fritz, "I begin to see our pigmies have beaks and wings."

"You are right," said I; "they are penguins, as Ernest explained to us some time since. They are good swimmers; but, unable to fly, are very helpless on land."

I steered gently to the shore, that I might not disturb them; but Jack leaped into the water up to his knees, and, dashing among the penguins, with a stick struck right and left, knocking down half a dozen of the poor stupid birds before they were aware. Some of these we brought away alive. The rest, not liking such a reception, took to the water, and were soon out of sight. I scolded Jack for his useless rashness, for the flesh of the penguin is by no means a delicacy.

We now filled our three wheelbarrows with such things as we could carry, not forgetting the sheets of iron and the graters, and trudged home. Our dogs announced our approach, and all rushed out to meet us. A curious and merry examination commenced. They laughed at my graters; but I let them laugh, for I had a project in my head. The penguins I intended for our poultry-yard; and, for the present, I ordered the boys to tie each of them by a leg to one of our geese or ducks, who opposed the bondage very clamorously; but necessity made them submissive.

My wife showed me a large store of potatoes and manioc roots, which she and her children had dug up the evening before. We then went to supper, and talked of all we had seen in the vessel, especially of the pinnace (a small boat), which we had been obliged to leave. My wife did not feel much regret on this account, as she dreaded maritime expeditions, though she agreed she might have felt less uneasiness if we had had a vessel of this description. I gave my sons a charge to rise early next morning, as we had an important business on hand; and curiosity roused them all in very good time. After our usual preparations for the day, I addressed them thus: "Gentlemen, I am going to teach you all a new business, that of a baker. Give me the plates of iron and the graters we brought yesterday." My wife was astonished; but I requested her to wait patiently and she should have bread, not perhaps light buns, but eatable flat cakes. But first she was to make me two small bags of sailcloth. She obeyed me; but, at the same time, I observed she put the potatoes on the fire, a proof she had not much faith in my bread-making. I then spread a cloth over the ground, and, giving each of the boys a grater, we began to grate the carefully-washed manioc roots, resting the end on the cloth. In a short time we had a heap of what appeared to be moist white sawdust; certainly not tempting to the appetite; but the little workmen were amused with their labour, and jested no little about the cakes made of scraped radishes.

"Laugh now, boys," said I; "we shall see, after a while. But you, Ernest, ought to know that the manioc is one of the most precious of alimentary roots, forming the principal sustenance of many nations of America, and often preferred by Europeans, who inhabit those countries, to wheaten bread."

When all the roots were grated, I filled the two bags closely with the pollard, and my wife sewed the ends up firmly. It was now necessary to apply strong pressure to extract the juice from the root, as this juice is a deadly poison. I selected an oak beam, one end of which we fixed between the roots of our tree; beneath this I placed our bags on a row of little blocks of wood; I then took a large bough, which I had cut from a tree, and prepared for the purpose, and laid it across them. We all united then in drawing down the opposite end of the plank over the bough, till we got it to a certain point, when we suspended to it the heaviest substances we possessed; hammers, bars of iron, and masses of lead. This acting upon the manioc, the sap burst through the cloth, and flowed on the ground copiously. When I thought the pressure was complete, we relieved the bags from the lever, and opening one, drew out a handful of the pollard, still rather moist, resembling coarse maize-flour.

"It only wants a little heat to complete our success," said I, in great delight. I ordered a fire to be lighted, and fixing one of our iron plates, which was round in form, and rather concave, on two stones placed on each side of the fire, I covered it with the flour which we took from the bag with a small wooden shovel. It soon formed a solid cake, which we turned, that it might be equally baked.

It smelled so good, that they all wished to commence eating immediately; and I had some difficulty in convincing them that this was only a trial, and that our baking was still imperfect. Besides, as I told them there were three kinds of manioc, of which one contained more poison than the rest, I thought it prudent to try whether we had perfectly extracted it, by giving a small quantity to our fowls. As soon, therefore, as the cake was cold, I gave some to two chickens, which I kept apart; and also some to Master Knips, the monkey, that he might, for the first time, do us a little service. He ate it with so much relish, and such grimaces of enjoyment, that my young party were quite anxious to share his feast; but I ordered them to wait till we could judge of the effect, and, leaving our employment, we went to our dinner of potatoes, to which my wife had added one of the penguins, which was truly rather tough and fishy; but as Jack would not allow this, and declared it was a dish fit for a king, we allowed him to regale on it as much as he liked. During dinner, I talked to them of the various preparations made from the manioc; I told my wife we could obtain an excellent starch from the expressed juice; but this did not interest her much, as at present she usually wore the dress of a sailor, for convenience, and had neither caps nor collars to starch.

The cake made from the root is called by the natives of the Antilles *cassava*, and in no nation such as this do we find any word signifying *bread*; an article of food unknown to them.

We spoke of poisons; and I explained to my sons the different nature and effects of them. Especially I warned them against the *manchineel*, which ought to grow in this part of the world. I described the fruit to them, as resembling a tempting yellow apple, with red spots, which is one of the most deadly poisons: it is said that even to sleep under the tree is dangerous. I forbade them to taste any unknown fruit, and they promised to obey me.

On leaving the table, we went to visit the victims of our experiment. Jack whistled for Knips, who came in three bounds from the summit of a high tree, where he had doubtless been plundering some nest; and his vivacity, and the peaceful cackling of the fowls, assured us our preparation was harmless.

"Now, gentlemen," said I, laughing, "to the bakehouse, and let us see what we can do." I wished them each to try to make the cakes. They immediately kindled the fire and heated the iron plate. In the mean time, I broke up the grated cassava, and mixed it with a little milk; and giving each of them a cocoa-nut basin filled with the paste, I showed them how to pour it with a spoon upon the plate, and spread it about; when the paste began to puff up, I judged it was baked on one side, and turned it, like a pancake, with a fork; and after a little time, we had a quantity of nice yellow biscuits, which, with a jug of milk, made us a delicious collation; and determined us, without delay, to set about cultivating the manioc.

The rest of the day was employed in bringing up the remainder of our cargo, by means of the sledge and the useful wheelbarrows.

Lesson 34

1. Read chapters 20 and 21 of *Swiss Family Robinson*.
2. Write a one sentence summary of the chapters.
3. The pinnace is a small boat that is part of the equipment of a large ship. In the beginning of this section they are getting it from the ship as a surprise to his wife.

Chapter 20

We had two days of incessant labour in fitting and loading the pinnace; finally, after putting up our masts, ropes, and sails, we selected a cargo of things our boats could not bring. When all was ready, my boys obtained permission, as a reward for their industry, to salute their mamma, as we entered the bay, by firing our two guns. Fritz was captain, and Ernest and Jack, at his command, put their matches to the guns, and fired. My wife and little boy rushed out in alarm; but our joyful shouts soon re-assured them; and they were ready to welcome us with astonishment and delight. Fritz placed a plank from the pinnace to the shore, and, assisting his mother, she came on board. They gave her a new salute, and christened the vessel, *The Elizabeth,* after her.

My wife praised our skill and perseverance, but begged we would not suppose that Francis and she had been idle during our long absence. We moored the little fleet safely to the shore, and followed her up the river to the cascade, where we saw a neat garden laid out in beds and walks.

"This is our work," said she; "the soil here, being chiefly composed of decayed leaves, is light and easy to dig. There I have my potatoes; there manioc roots: these are sown with peas, beans and lentils; in this row of beds are sown lettuces, radishes, cabbages, and other European vegetables. I have reserved one part for sugar-canes; on the high ground I have transplanted pine-apples, and sown melons. Finally, round every bed, I have sown a border of maize, that the high, bushy stems may protect the young plants from the sun."

I was delighted with the result of the labour and industry of a delicate female and a child, and could scarcely believe it was accomplished in so short a time.

"I must confess I had no great hope of success at first," said my wife, "and this made me averse to speaking of it. Afterwards, when I suspected you had a secret, I determined to have one, too, and give you a surprise."

After again applauding these useful labours, we returned to discharge our cargo; and as we went, my good Elizabeth, still full of horticultural plans, reminded me of the young fruit-trees we had brought from the vessel. I promised to look after them next day, and to establish my orchard near her kitchen-garden.

We unloaded our vessels; placed on the sledge all that might be useful at Falcon's Nest; and, arranging the rest under the tent, fixed our pinnace to the shore, by means of the anchor and a cord fastened to a heavy stone; and at length set out to Falcon's Nest, where we arrived soon, to the great comfort of my wife, who dreaded the burning plain at Tent House.

Chapter 21

After our return to Falcon's Nest, I requested my sons to continue their exercises in gymnastics. I wished to develope all the vigour and energy that nature had given them; and which, in our situation, were especially necessary. I added to archery, racing, leaping, wrestling, and climbing trees, either by the trunks, or by a rope suspended from the branches, as sailors climb. I next taught them to use the *lasso*, a powerful weapon, by aid of which the people of South America capture savage animals. I fixed two balls of lead to the ends of a cord about a fathom in length. The Patagonians, I told them, used this weapon with wonderful dexterity. Having no leaden balls, they attach a heavy stone to each end of a cord about thirty yards long. If they wish to capture an animal, they hurl one of the stones at it with singular address. By the peculiar art with which the ball is thrown, the rope makes a turn or two round the neck of the animal, which remains entangled, without the power of escaping. In order to show the power of this weapon, I took aim at the trunk of a tree which they pointed out. My throw was quite successful. The end of the rope passed two or three times round the trunk of the tree, and remained firmly fixed to it. If the tree had been the neck of a tiger, I should have been absolute master of it. This experiment decided them all to learn the use of the lasso. Fritz was soon skilful in throwing it, and I encouraged the rest to persevere in acquiring the same facility, as the weapon might be invaluable to us when our ammunition failed.

The next morning I saw, on looking out, that the sea was too much agitated for any expedition in the boats; I therefore turned to some home employments. We looked over our stores for winter provision. My wife showed me a cask of *ortolans* she had preserved in butter, and a quantity of loaves of cassava bread, carefully prepared. She pointed out, that the pigeons had built in the tree, and were sitting on their eggs. We then looked over the young fruit-trees brought from Europe, and my sons and I immediately laid out a piece of ground, and planted them.

The day passed in these employments; and as we had lived only on potatoes, cassava bread, and milk for this day, we determined to go off next morning in pursuit of game to recruit our larder. At dawn of day we all started, including little Francis and his mother, who wished to take this opportunity of seeing a little more of the country. My sons and I took our arms, I harnessed the ass to the sledge which contained our provision for the day, and was destined to bring back the products of the chase. Turk, accoutered in his coat of mail, formed the advanced guard; my sons followed with their guns; then came my wife with Francis leading the ass; and at a little distance I closed the procession, with Master Knips mounted on the patient Flora.

We crossed Flamingo Marsh, and there my wife was charmed with the richness of the vegetation and the lofty trees. Fritz left us, thinking this a favourable spot for game. We soon heard the report of his gun, and an enormous bird fell a few paces from us. I ran to assist him, as he had much difficulty in securing his prize, which was only wounded in the wing, and was defending itself vigorously with its beak and claws. I threw a handkerchief over its head, and, confused by the darkness, I had no difficulty in binding it, and conveying it in triumph to the sledge. We were all in raptures at the sight of this beautiful creature, which Ernest pronounced to be a female of the bustard tribe. My wife hoped that the bird might be domesticated among her poultry, and, attracting some more of its species, might enlarge our stock of useful fowls. We soon arrived at the Wood of Monkeys, as we called it, where we had obtained our cocoa-nuts; and Fritz related the laughable scene of the stratagem to his mother and brothers. Ernest looked up wistfully at the nuts, but there were no monkeys to throw them down.

"Do they never fall from the trees?" and hardly had he spoken, when a large cocoa-nut fell at his feet, succeeded by a second, to my great astonishment, for I saw no animal in the tree, and I was convinced the nuts in the half-ripe state, as these were, could not fall of themselves.

"It is exactly like a fairy tale," said Ernest; "I had only to speak, and my wish was accomplished."

"And here comes the magician," said I, as, after a shower of nuts, I saw a huge land-crab descending the tree quietly, and quite regardless of our presence. Jack boldly struck a blow at him, but missed, and the animal, opening its enormous claws, made up to its opponent, who fled in terror. But the laughter of his brothers made him ashamed, and recalling his courage, he pulled off his coat, and threw it over the back of the crab; this checked its movements, and going to his assistance, I killed it with a blow of my hatchet.

"But, with this," said Fritz, "we have a poor show of game. Do let us leave mamma with the young ones, and set off, to see what we can meet with."

I consented, and we left Ernest with his mother and Francis, Jack wishing to accompany us. We made towards the rocks at the right hand, and Jack preceded us a little, when he startled us by crying out, "A crocodile, papa! a crocodile!"

"You simpleton!" said I, "a crocodile in a place where there is not a drop of water!"

"Papa! I see it!" said the poor child, his eyes fixed on one spot; "it is there, on this rock, sleeping. I am sure it is a crocodile!"

As soon as I was near enough to distinguish it, I assured him his crocodile was a very harmless lizard, called the *iguana*, whose eggs and flesh were excellent food. Fritz would immediately have shot at this frightful creature, which was about five feet in length. I showed him that his scaly coat rendered such an attempt useless. I then cut a strong stick and a light wand. To the end of the former I attached a cord with a noose; this I held in my right hand, keeping the wand in my left. I approached softly, whistling. The animal awoke, apparently listening with pleasure. I drew nearer, tickling him gently with the wand. He lifted up his head, and opened his formidable jaws. I then dexterously threw the noose round his neck, drew it, and, jumping on his back, by the aid of my sons, held him down, though he succeeded in giving Jack a desperate blow with his tail. Then, plunging my wand up his nostrils, a few drops of blood came, and he died apparently without pain.

We now carried off our game. I took him on my back, holding him by the fore-claws, while my boys carried the tail behind me; and, with shouts of laughter, the procession returned to the sledge.

Poor little Francis was in great dismay when he saw the terrible monster we brought, and began to cry; but we rallied him out of his cowardice, and his mother, satisfied with our exploits, begged to return home. As the sledge was heavily laden, we decided to leave it till the next day, placing on the ass, the iguana, the crab, our gourd vessels, and a bag of the guavas, little Francis being also mounted. The bustard we loosed, and, securing it by a string tied to one of its legs, led it with us.

We arrived at home in good time. My wife prepared part of the iguana for supper, which was pronounced excellent. The crab was rejected as tough and tasteless. Our new utensils were then tried, the egg-baskets and the milk-bowls, and Fritz was charged to dig a hole in the earth, to be covered with boards, and serve as a dairy, till something better was thought of. Finally, we ascended our leafy abode, and slept in peace.

Lesson 35

1. Read chapters 22 and 23 of *Swiss Family Robinson*.
2. What is his plan for using the gum from the tree? (Answers)
3. Tell someone about the chapters.

Chapter 22

I projected an excursion with my eldest son, to explore the limits of our country, and satisfy ourselves that it was an island, and not a part of the continent. We set out, ostensibly, to bring the sledge we had left the previous evening. I took Turk and the ass with us, and left Flora with my wife and children, and, with a bag of provisions, we left Falcon's Nest as soon as breakfast was over.

We now met with a new kind of bush covered with small white berries about the size of a pea. On pressing these berries, which adhered to my fingers, I discovered that this plant was candle-berry myrtle from which a wax is obtained that may be made into candles. With great pleasure I gathered a bag of these berries, knowing how my wife would appreciate this acquisition; for she often lamented that we were compelled to go to bed with the birds, as soon as the sun set.

We forgot our fatigue, as we proceeded, in contemplation of the wonders of nature, flowers of marvellous beauty, butterflies of more dazzling colours than the flowers, and birds graceful in form, and brilliant in plumage. Fritz climbed a tree, and succeeded in securing a young green parrot, which he enveloped in his handkerchief, with the intention of bringing it up, and teaching it to speak. And now we met with another wonder: a number of birds who lived in a community, in nests, sheltered by a common roof, in the formation of which they had probably laboured jointly. This roof was composed of straw and dry sticks, plastered with clay, which rendered it equally impenetrable to sun or rain. Pressed as we were for time, I could not help stopping to admire this feathered colony. This leading us to speak of natural history, as it relates to animals who live in societies, we recalled in succession the ingenious labours of the beavers and the *marmots*; the not less marvellous constructions of the bees, the wasps, and the ants; and I mentioned particularly those immense ant-hills of America, of which the masonry is finished with such skill and solidity that they are sometimes used for ovens, to which they bear a resemblance.

We had now reached some trees quite unknown to us. They were from forty to sixty feet in height, and from the bark, which was cracked in many places, issued small balls of a thick gum. Fritz got one off with difficulty, it was so hardened by the sun. He wished to soften it with his hands, but found that heat only gave it the power of extension, and that by pulling the two extremities, and then releasing them, it immediately resumed its first form.

Fritz ran to me, crying out, "I have found some India-rubber!"

"If that be true," said I, "you have made a most valuable discovery."

He thought I was laughing at him, for we had no drawing to rub out here.

I told him this gum might be turned to many useful purposes; among the rest we might make excellent shoes of it. This interested him. How could we accomplish this?

"The *caoutchouc*," said I, "is the milky sap which is obtained from certain trees of the *Euphorbium* kind, by incisions made in the bark. It is collected in vessels, care being taken to agitate them, that the liquid may not coagulate. In this state they cover little clay bottles with successive layers of it, till it attains the required thickness. It is then dried in smoke, which gives it the dark brown colour. Before it is quite dry, it is ornamented by lines and flowers drawn with the knife. Finally, they break the clay form, and extract it from the mouth; and there remains the India-rubber bottle of commerce, soft and flexible. Now, this is my plan for shoemaking; we will fill a stocking with sand, cover it with repeated layers of the gum till it is of the proper thickness; then empty out the sand, and, if I do not deceive myself, we shall have perfect boots or shoes."

Comfortable in the hope of new boots, we advanced through an interminable forest of various trees. The monkeys on the cocoa-nut trees furnished us with pleasant refreshment, and a small store of nuts besides. Among these trees I saw some lower bushes, whose leaves were covered with a white dust. I opened the trunk of one of these, which had been torn up by the wind, and found in the interior a white farinaceous substance, which, on tasting, I knew to be the sago imported into Europe. This, as connected with our subsistence, was a most important affair, and my son and I, with our hatchets, laid open the tree, and obtained from it twenty-five pounds of the valuable sago.

This occupied us an hour; and, weary and hungry, I thought it prudent not to push our discoveries farther this day. We therefore returned to the Gourd Wood, placed all our treasures on the sledge, and took our way home. We arrived without more adventures, and were warmly greeted, and our various offerings gratefully welcomed, especially the green parrot. We talked of the *caoutchouc*, and new boots, with great delight during supper; and, afterwards, my wife looked with exceeding content at her bag of candle-berries, anticipating the time when we should not have to go to bed, as we did now, as soon as the sun set.

Chapter 23

The next morning my wife and children besought me to begin my manufacture of candles. I remembered having seen the chandler at work, and I tried to recall all my remembrances of the process. I put into a boiler as many berries as it would hold, and placed it over a moderate fire: the wax melted from the berries, and rose to the surface, and this I carefully skimmed with a large flat spoon and put in a separate vessel placed near the fire; when this was done, my wife supplied me with some wicks she had made from the threads of sailcloth; these wicks were attached, four at a time, to a small stick; I dipped them into the wax, and placed them on two branches of a tree to dry; I repeated this operation as often as necessary to make them the proper thickness, and then placed them in a cool spot to harden. But we could not forbear trying them that very night; and, thought somewhat rude in form, it was sufficient that they reminded us of our European home, and prolonged our days by many useful hours we had lost before.

This encouraged me to attempt another enterprise. My wife had long regretted that she had not been able to make butter. She had attempted to beat her cream in a vessel, but either the heat of the climate, or her want of patience, rendered her trials unsuccessful. I felt that I had not skill enough to make a churn; but I fancied that by some simple method, like that used by the Hottentots, who put their cream in a skin and shake it till they produce butter, we might obtain the same result. I cut a large gourd in two, filled it with three quarts of cream, then united the parts, and secured them closely. I fastened a stick to each corner of a square piece of sailcloth, placed the gourd in the middle, and, giving a corner to each of my sons, directed them to rock the cloth with a slow, regular motion, as you would a child's cradle. This was quite an amusement for them; and at the end of an hour, my wife had the pleasure of placing before us some excellent butter. I then tried to make a cart, our sledge being unfitted for some roads; the wheels I had brought from the wreck rendered this less difficult; and I completed a very rude vehicle, which was, nevertheless, very useful to us.

While I was thus usefully employed, my wife and children were not idle. They had transplanted the European trees, and thoughtfully placed each in the situation best suited to it. I assisted with my hands and counsels. The vines we planted round the roots of our trees, and hoped in time to form a trellis-work. Of the chesnut, walnut, and cherry-trees, we formed an avenue from Falcon's Nest to Family Bridge, which, we hoped, would ultimately be a shady road between our two mansions. We made a solid road between the two rows of trees, raised in the middle and covered with sand, which we brought from the shore in our wheelbarrows. I also made a sort of tumbril, to which we harnessed the ass, to lighten this difficult labour.

We then turned our thoughts to Tent House, our first abode, and which still might form our refuge in case of danger. Nature had not favoured it; but our labour soon supplied all deficiencies. We planted round it every tree that requires ardent heat; the citron, pistachio, the almond, the mulberry, the Siamese orange, of which the fruit is as large as the head of a child, and the Indian fig, with its long prickly leaves, all had a place here. These plantations succeeding admirably, we had, after some time, the pleasure of seeing the dry and sandy desert converted into a shady grove, rich in flowers and fruit. As this place was the magazine for our arms, ammunition, and provisions of all sorts; we made a sort of fortress of it, surrounding it with a high hedge of strong, thorny trees; so that not only to wild beasts, but even to human enemies, it was inaccessible. Our bridge was the only point of approach, and we always carefully removed the first planks after crossing it. We also placed our two cannon on a little elevation within the enclosure; and, finally, we planted some cedars, near our usual landing-place, to which we might, at a future time, fasten our vessels. These labours occupied us three months, only interrupted by a strict attention to the devotions and duties of the Sunday. I was most especially grateful to God for the robust health we all enjoyed, in the midst of our employments. All went on well in our little colony. We had an abundant and certain supply of provisions; but our wardrobe, notwithstanding the continual repairing my wife bestowed on it, was in a most wretched state, and we had no means of renewing it, except by again visiting the wreck, which I knew still contained some chests of clothes, and bales of cloth. This decided me to make another voyage; besides I was rather anxious to see the state of the vessel.

We found it much in the same condition we had left it, except being much more shattered by the winds and waves.

We selected many useful things for our cargo; the bales of linen and woollen cloth were not forgotten; some barrels of tar; and everything portable that we could remove; doors, windows, tables, benches, locks and bolts, all the ammunition, and even such of the guns as we could move. In fact we completely sacked the vessel; carrying off, after several days' labour, all our booty, with the exception of some weighty articles, amongst which were three or four immense boilers, intended for a sugar-manufactory. These we tied to some large empty casks, which we pitched completely over, and hoped they would be able to float in the water.

When we had completed our arrangements, I resolved to blow up the ship. We placed a large barrel of gunpowder in the hold, and arranging a long match from it, which would burn some hours, we lighted it, and proceeded without delay to Safety Bay to watch the event. I proposed to my wife to sup on a point of land where we could distinctly see the vessel. Just as the sun was going down, a majestic rolling, like thunder, succeeded by a column of fire, announced the destruction of the vessel, which had brought us from Europe, and bestowed its great riches on us. We could not help shedding tears, as we heard the last mournful cry of this sole remaining bond that connected us with home. We returned sorrowfully to Tent House, and felt as if we had lost an old friend.

We rose early next morning, and hastened to the shore, which we found covered with the wreck, which, with a little exertion, we found it easy to collect. Amongst the rest, were the large boilers. We afterwards used these to cover our barrels of gunpowder, which we placed in a part of the rock, where, even if an explosion took place, no damage could ensue.

My wife, in assisting us with the wreck, made the agreeable discovery, that two of our ducks, and one goose, had hatched each a brood, and were leading their noisy young families to the water. This reminded us of all our poultry and domestic comfort, at Falcon's Nest, and we determined to defer, for some time, the rest of our work at Tent House, and to return the next day to our shady summer home.

Lesson 36

1. Read chapter 24 of *Swiss Family Robinson*.
2. Tell someone about the chapter.

Vocabulary

1. Review the vocabulary in Lesson 6.

Chapter 24

As we went along the avenue of fruit-trees, I was concerned to see my young plants beginning to droop, and I immediately resolved to proceed to Cape Disappointment the next morning, to cut bamboos to make props for them. It was determined we should all go, as, on our arrival at Falcon's Nest, we discovered many other supplies wanting. The candles were failing: we must have more berries, for now my wife sewed by candlelight, while I wrote my journal. She wanted, also, some wild-fowls' eggs to set under her hens. Jack wanted some guavas, and Francis wished for some sugar-canes. So we made a family tour of it, taking the cart, with the cow and ass, to contain our provision, and a large sailcloth, to make a tent. The weather was delightful, and we set out singing, in great spirits.

We crossed the potato and manioc plantations, and the wood of guavas, on which my boys feasted to their great satisfaction. The road was rugged, but we assisted to move the cart, and rested frequently. We stopped to see the bird colony, which greatly delighted them all, and Ernest declared they belonged to the species of *Loxia gregaria*, the sociable grosbeak. He pointed out to us their wonderful instinct in forming their colony in the midst of the candle-berry bushes, on which they feed. We filled two bags with these berries, and another with guavas, my wife proposing to make jelly from them.

As it was getting late, we set about putting up our tent for the night, when suddenly our ass, who had been quietly grazing near us, began to bray furiously, erected his ears, kicking right and left, and, plunging into the bamboos, disappeared. This made us very uneasy. I could not submit to lose the useful animal; and, moreover, I was afraid his agitation announced the approach of some wild beast. The dogs and I sought for any trace of it in vain; I therefore, to guard against any danger, made a large fire before our tent, which I continued to watch till midnight, when, all being still, I crept into the tent, to my bed of moss, and slept undisturbed till morning.

In the morning we thanked God for our health and safety, and then began to lament our poor donkey, which, I hoped, might have been attracted by the light of our fire, and have returned; but we saw nothing of him, and we decided that his services were so indispensable, that I should go, with one of my sons, and the two dogs, in search of him, and cross the thickets of bamboo. I chose to take Jack with me, to his great satisfaction, for Fritz and Ernest formed a better guard for their mother in a strange place. We set out, well armed, with bags of provisions on our back, and after an hour's fruitless search among the canes, We emerged beyond them, in an extensive plain on the borders of the great bay. We saw that the ridge of rocks still extended on the right till it nearly reached the shore, when it abruptly terminated in a perpendicular precipice. A considerable river flowed into the bay here, and between the river and the rock was a narrow passage, which at high water would be overflowed. We thought it most likely that our ass had passed by this defile; and I wished to see whether these rocks merely bordered or divided the island; we therefore went forward till we met with a stream, which fell in a cascade from a mass of rocks into the river. We ascended the stream till we found a place shallow enough to cross. Here we saw the shoemarks of our ass, mingled with the footsteps of other animals, and at a distance we saw a herd of animals, but could not distinguish what they were. We ascended a little hill, and, through our telescope, saw a most beautiful and fertile country, breathing peace and repose. To our right rose the majestic chain of rocks that divided the island. On our left a succession of beautiful green hills spread to the horizon. Woods of palms and various unknown trees were scattered over the scene. The beautiful stream meandered across the valley like a silver ribbon, bordered by rushes and other aquatic plants. There was no trace of the footstep of man. The country had all the purity of its first creation; no living creatures but some beautiful birds and brilliant butterflies appeared.

But, at a distance, we saw some specks, which I concluded were the animals we had first seen, and I resolved to go nearer, in hopes our ass might have joined them. We made towards the spot, and, to shorten the road, crossed a little wood of bamboos, the stalks of which, as thick as a man's thigh, rose to the height of thirty feet. I suspected this to be the giant reed of America, so useful for the masts of boats and canoes. I promised Jack to allow him to cut some on our return; but at present the ass was my sole care. When we had crossed the wood, we suddenly came face to face on a herd of buffaloes, not numerous certainly, but formidable in appearance. At the sight, I was absolutely petrified, and my gun useless. Fortunately the dogs were in the rear, and the animals, lifting their heads, and fixing their large eyes on us, seemed more astonished than angry; we were the first men probably they had ever seen.

We drew back a little, prepared our arms, and endeavoured to retreat, when the dogs arrived, and, notwithstanding our efforts to restrain them, flew at the buffaloes. It was no time now to retreat; the combat was begun. The whole troop uttered the most frightful roars, beat the ground with their feet, and butted with their horns. Our brave dogs were not intimidated, but marched straight upon the enemy, and, falling on a young buffalo that had strayed before the rest, seized it by the ears. The creature began to bellow, and struggle to escape; its mother ran to its assistance, and, with her, the whole herd. At that moment, I tremble as I write it, I gave the signal to my brave Jack, who behaved with admirable coolness, and at the same moment we fired on the herd. The effect was wonderful: they paused a moment, and then, even before the smoke was dissipated, took to flight with incredible rapidity, forded the river, and were soon out of sight. My dogs still held their prize, and the mother, though wounded by our shot, tore up the ground in her fury, and was advancing on the dogs to destroy them; but I stepped forward, and discharging a pistol between the horns, put an end to her life.

We began to breathe. We had looked death in the face, a most horrible death; and thanked God for our preservation. I praised Jack for his courage and presence of mind; any fear or agitation on his part would have unnerved me, and rendered our fate certain. The dogs still held the young calf by the ears, it bellowed incessantly, and I feared they would either be injured or lose their prize. I went up to their assistance. I hardly knew how to act. I could easily have killed it; but I had a great desire to carry it off alive, and try to tame it, to replace our ass, whom I did not intend to follow farther. A happy idea struck Jack: he always carried his lasso in his pocket; he drew it out, retired a little, and flung it so dexterously that he completely wound it round the hind legs of the calf, and threw it down. I now approached; I replaced the lasso by a stronger cord, and used another to bind his fore legs loosely. Jack cried victory, and already thought how his mother and brothers would be delighted, when we presented it; but that was no easy matter. At last I thought of the method used in Italy to tame the wild bulls, and I resolved to try it, though it was a little cruel.

I began by tying to the foot of a tree the cords that held the legs; then making the dogs seize him again by the ears, I caught hold of his mouth, and with a sharp knife perforated the nostril, and quickly passed a cord through the opening. This cord was to serve as my rein, to guide the animal. The operation was successful; and, as soon as the blood ceased to flow, I took the cord, uniting the two ends, and the poor suffering creature, completely subdued, followed me without resistance.

I was unwilling to abandon the whole of the buffalo I had killed, as it is excellent meat; I therefore cut out the tongue, and some of the best parts from the loin, and covered them well with salt, of which we had taken a provision with us. I then carefully skinned the four legs, remembering that the American hunters use these skins for boots, being remarkably soft and flexible. We permitted the dogs to feast on the remainder; and while they were enjoying themselves, we washed ourselves, and sat down under a tree to rest and refresh ourselves. But the poor beasts had soon many guests at their banquet. Clouds of birds of prey came from every part; an incessant combat was kept up; no sooner was one troop of brigands satisfied, than another succeeded; and soon all that remained of the poor buffalo was the bones. I noticed amongst these ravenous birds the royal vulture, an elegant bird, remarkable for a brilliant collar of down. We could easily have killed some of these robbers, but I thought it useless to destroy for mere curiosity, and I preferred employing our time in cutting, with a small saw we had brought, some of the gigantic reeds that grew round us. We cut several of the very thick ones, which make excellent vessels when separated at the joints; but I perceived that Jack was cutting some of small dimensions, and I inquired if he was going to make a Pandean pipe, to celebrate his triumphal return with the buffalo.

"No," said he; "I don't recollect that Robinson Crusoe amused himself with music in his island; but I have thought of something that will be useful to mamma. I am cutting these reeds to make moulds for our candles."

"An excellent thought, my dear boy!" said I; "and if even we break our moulds in getting out the candles, which I suspect we may, we know where they grow, and can come for more."

We collected all our reeds in bundles, and then set out. The calf, intimidated by the dogs, and galled by the rein, went on tolerably well. We crossed the narrow pass in the rocks, and here our dogs killed a large jackal which was coming from her den in the rock. The furious animals then entered the den, followed by Jack, who saved, with difficulty, one of the young cubs, the others being immediately worried. It was a pretty little gold-coloured creature, about the size of a cat. Jack petitioned earnestly to have it to bring up; and I made him happy by granting his request.

In the mean time I had tied the calf to a low tree, which I discovered was the thorny dwarf palm, which grows quickly, and is extremely useful for fences. It bears an oblong fruit, about the size of a pigeon's egg, from which is extracted an oil which is an excellent substitute for butter. I determined to return for some young plants of this palm to plant at Tent House.

It was almost night when we joined our family; and endless were the questions the sight of the buffalo produced, and great was the boasting of Jack the dauntless. I was compelled to lower his pride a little by an unvarnished statement, though I gave him much credit for his coolness and resolution; and, supper-time arriving, my wife had time to tell me what had passed while we had been on our expedition.

Lesson 37

1. Read chapter 25 of *Swiss Family Robinson* and tell someone about the chapter.
2. The pith of the tree is a soft, spongy center.

Chapter 25

My wife began by saying they had not been idle in my absence. They had collected wood, and made torches for the night. Fritz and Ernest had even cut down an immense sago-palm, seventy feet high, intending to extract its precious pith; but this they had been unable to accomplish alone, and waited for my assistance. But while they were engaged in this employment, a troop of monkeys had broken into the tent and pillaged and destroyed everything; they had drunk or overturned the milk, and carried off or spoiled all our provisions; and even so much injured the palisade I had erected round the tent, that it took them an hour, after they returned, to repair the damage. Fritz had made also a beautiful capture, in a nest he had discovered in the rocks at Cape Disappointment. It was a superb bird, and, though very young, quite feathered. Ernest had pronounced it to be the eagle of Malabar, and I confirmed his assertion; and as this species of eagle is not large, and does not require much food, I advised him to train it as a falcon, to chase other birds. I took this opportunity to announce that henceforward every one must attend to his own live stock, or they should be set at liberty, mamma having sufficient to manage in her own charge.

We then made a fire of green wood, in the smoke of which we placed the buffalo-meat we had brought home, leaving it during the night, that it might be perfectly cured. We had had some for supper, and thought it excellent. The young buffalo was beginning to graze, and we gave him a little milk to-night, as well as to the jackal. Fritz had taken the precaution to cover the eyes of his eagle, and tying it fast by the leg to a branch, it rested very tranquilly. We then retired to our mossy beds, to recruit our strength for the labours of another day.

At break of day we rose, made a light breakfast, and I was about to give the signal of departure, when my wife communicated to me the difficulty they had had in cutting down the palm-tree, and the valuable provision that might be obtained from it with a little trouble. I thought she was right, and decided to remain here another day; for it was no trifling undertaking to split up a tree seventy feet long. I consented the more readily, as I thought I might, after removing the useful pith from the trunk, obtain two large spouts or channels to conduct the water from Jackal River to the kitchen garden.

Such tools as we had we carried to the place where the tree lay. We first sawed off the head; then, with the hatchet making an opening at each end, we took wedges and mallets, and the wood being tolerably soft, after four hours' labour, we succeeded in splitting it completely. When parted, we pressed the pith with our hands, to get the whole into one division of the trunk, and began to make our paste. At one end of the spout we nailed one of the graters, through which we intended to force the paste, to form the round seeds. My little bakers set vigorously to work, some pouring water on the pith, while the rest mixed it into paste. This we threw into a heap, hoping mushrooms might spring from it. We spent the rest of the day in loading the cart with our utensils and the halves of the tree. We retired to our hut at sunset, and slept in peace.

The next morning the whole caravan began to move at an early hour. The buffalo, harnessed to the cart, by the side of his nurse, the cow, took the place of our lost ass, and began his apprenticeship as a beast of draught. We took the same road on our return, that we might carry away the candle-berries and the vessels of India-rubber. The vanguard was composed of Fritz and Jack, who pioneered our way, by cutting down the underwood to make a road for the cart. Our water-pipes, being very long, somewhat impeded our progress; but we happily reached the candle-berry trees without accident, and placed our sacks on the cart. We did not find more than a quart of the *caoutchouc* gum; but it would be sufficient for our first experiment, and I carried it off.

In crossing the little wood of guavas, we suddenly heard our dogs, who were before us with Fritz and Jack, uttering the most frightful howlings. I was struck with terror lest they should have encountered a tiger, and rushed forward ready to fire. The dogs were endeavouring to enter a thicket, in the midst of which Fritz declared he had caught a glimpse of an animal larger than the buffalo, with a black, bristly skin. I was just about to discharge my gun into the thicket, when Jack, who had lain down on the ground, to look under the bushes, burst into a loud laugh. "It is another trick of that vexatious animal, our old sow! she is always making fools of us," cried he. Half merry and half angry, we made an opening into the thicket, and there discovered the lady lying, surrounded by seven little pigs, only a few days old. We were very glad to see our old friend so attended, and stroked her. She seemed to recognize us, and grunted amicably. We supplied her with some potatoes, sweet acorns, and cassava bread; intending, in return, to eat her young ones, when they were ready for the spit, though my dear wife cried out against the cruelty of the idea. At present we left them with her, but proposed afterwards to take away two, to be brought up at home, and leave the rest to support themselves on acorns in the woods, where they would become game for us. At length we arrived at Falcon's Nest, which we regarded with all the attachment of home. Our domestic animals crowded round us, and noisily welcomed us. We tied up the buffalo and jackal, as they were not yet domesticated. Fritz fastened his eagle to a branch by a chain long enough to allow it to move freely, and then imprudently uncovered its eyes; it immediately raised its head, erected its feathers, and struck on all sides with its beak and claws; our fowls took to flight, but the poor parrot fell in his way, and was torn to pieces before we could assist it. Fritz was very angry, and would have executed the murderer; but Ernest begged he would not be so rash, as parrots were more plentiful than eagles, and it was his own fault for uncovering his eyes; the falconers always keeping their young birds hooded six weeks, till they are quite tamed. He offered to train it, if Fritz would part with it; but this Fritz indignantly refused. I told them the fable of the dog in the manger, which abashed Fritz; and he then besought his brother to teach him the means of training this noble bird, and promised to present him with his monkey.

Ernest then told him that the Caribs subdue the largest birds by making them inhale tobacco smoke. Fritz laughed at this; but Ernest brought a pipe and some tobacco he had found in the ship, and began to smoke gravely under the branch where the bird was perched. It was soon calm, and on his continuing to smoke it became quite motionless. Fritz then easily replaced the bandage, and thanked his brother for his good service.

The next morning we set out early to our young plantation of fruit-trees, to fix props to support the weaker plants. We loaded the cart with the thick bamboo canes and our tools, and harnessed the cow to it, leaving the buffalo in the stable, as I wished the wound in his nostrils to be perfectly healed before I put him to any hard work. I left Francis with his mother, to prepare our dinner, begging them not to forget the maccaroni.

We began at the entrance of the avenue to Falcon's Nest, where all the trees were much bent by the wind. We raised them gently by a crowbar; I made a hole in the earth, in which one of my sons placed the bamboo props, driving them firmly down with a mallet, and we proceeded to another, while Ernest and Jack tied the trees to them with a long, tough, pliant plant, which I suspected was a species of *llana*. As we were working, Fritz inquired if these fruit-trees were wild.

"A pretty question!" cried Jack. "Do you think that trees are tamed like eagles or buffaloes? You perhaps could teach them to bow politely, so that we might gather the fruit!"

"You fancy you are a wit," said I, "but you speak like a dunce. We cannot make trees bow at our pleasure; but we can make a tree, which by nature bears sour and uneatable fruit, produce what is sweet and wholesome. This is effected by grafting into a wild tree a small branch, or even a bud, of the sort you wish. I will show you this method practically at some future time, for by these means we can procure all sorts of fruit; only we must remember, that we can only graft a tree with one of the same natural family; thus, we could not graft an apple on a cherry-tree, for one belongs to the apple tribe, and the other to the plum tribe."

"Do we know the origin of all these European fruits?" asked the inquiring Ernest.

"All our shell fruits," answered I, "such as the nut, the almond, and the chesnut, are natives of the East; the peach, of Persia; the orange and apricot, of Armenia; the cherry, which was unknown in Europe sixty years before Christ, was brought by the proconsul Lucullus from the southern shores of the Euxine; the olives come from Palestine. The first olive-trees were planted on Mount Olympus, and from thence were spread through the rest of Europe; the fig is from Lydia; the plums, your favourite fruit, with the exception of some natural sorts that are natives of our forests, are from Syria, and the town of Damascus has given its name to one sort, the *Damascene*, or Damson. The pear is a fruit of Greece; the ancients called it the fruit of Peloponnesus; the mulberry is from Asia; and the quince from the island of Crete."

Our work progressed as we talked thus, and we had soon propped all our valuable plants. It was now noon, and we returned to Falcon's Nest very hungry, and found an excellent dinner prepared, of smoked beef, and the tender bud of the cabbage-palm, the most delicious of vegetables.

After dinner, we began to discuss a plan I had long had in my head; but the execution of it presented many difficulties. It was, to substitute a firm and solid staircase for the ladder of ropes, which was a source of continual fear to my wife. It is true, that we only had to ascend it to go to bed; but bad weather might compel us to remain in our apartment; we should then have frequently to ascend and descend, and the ladder was very unsafe. But the immense height of the tree, and the impossibility of procuring beams to sustain a staircase round it, threw me into despair. However, looking at the monstrous trunk of the tree, I thought, if we cannot succeed outside, could we not contrive to mount within?

"Have you not said there was a swarm of bees in the trunk of the tree?" I inquired of my wife. "Yes," said little Francis, "they stung my face dreadfully the other day, when I was on the ladder. I was pushing a stick into the hole they came out of, to try how deep it was."

"Now, then," cried I, "I see through my difficulties. Let us find out how far the tree is hollow; we can increase the size of the tunnel, and I have already planned the sort of staircase I can construct." I had hardly spoken, when the boys leaped like squirrels, some upon the arched roots, some on the steps of the ladder, and began to strike with sticks and mallets to sound the tree. This rash proceeding had nearly been fatal to Jack, who, having placed himself just before the opening, and striking violently, the whole swarm, alarmed at an attack, which probably shook their palace of wax, issued forth, and revenged themselves amply on all the assailants. Nothing was heard but cries and stamping of feet. My wife hastened to cover the stings with moist earth, which rather relieved them; but it was some hours before they could open their eyes. They begged me to get them the honey from their foes, and I prepared a hive, which I had long thought of a large gourd, which I placed on a board nailed upon a branch of our tree, and covered with straw to shelter it from the sun and wind. But it was now bedtime, and we deferred our attack on the fortress till next day.

Lesson 38

1. Read chapters 26 and 27 of *Swiss Family Robinson*.
2. Tell someone about what is happening in the book.
3. What do you think is going to happen next? What about in the end of the book?
4. Their donkey returns with another animal. What is it? (Answers)

Chapter 26

I took a long pole, and tried the height from the window I had made; and tied a stone to a string to sound the depth. To my surprise, the pole penetrated without resistance to the very branches where our dwelling was, and the stone went to the roots. It was entirely hollow, and I thought I could easily fix a winding staircase in this wide tunnel. It would seem, that this huge tree, like the willow of our country, is nourished through the bark, for it was flourishing in luxuriant beauty.

We began by cutting a doorway, on the side facing the sea, of the size of the door we had brought from the captain's cabin, with its framework, thus securing ourselves from invasion on that side. We then cleansed, and perfectly smoothed the cavity, fixing in the middle the trunk of a tree about ten feet high, to serve for the axis of the staircase. We had prepared, the evening before, a number of boards from the staves of a large barrel, to form our steps. By the aid of the chisel and mallet, we made deep notches in the inner part of our tree, and corresponding notches in the central pillar; I placed my steps in these notches, riveting them with large nails; I raised myself in this manner step after step, but always turning round the pillar, till we got to the top. We then fixed on the central pillar another trunk of the same height, prepared beforehand, and continued our winding steps. Four times we had to repeat this operation, and, finally, we reached our branches, and terminated the staircase on the level of the floor of our apartment. I cleared the entrance by some strokes of my axe. To render it more solid, I filled up the spaces between the steps with planks, and fastened two strong cords from above, to each side of the staircase, to hold by. Towards different points, I made openings; in which were placed the windows taken from the cabin, which gave light to the interior, and favoured our observations outside.

The construction of this solid and convenient staircase occupied us during a month of patient industry; not that we laboured like slaves, for we had no one to constrain us; we had in this time completed several works of less importance; and many events had amused us amidst our toil.

A few days after we commenced, Flora produced six puppies; but the number being too large for our means of support, I commanded that only a male and female should be preserved, that the breed might be perpetuated; this was done, and the little jackal being placed with the remainder, Flora gave it the same privileges as her own offspring. Our goats also, about this time, gave us two kids; and our sheep some lambs. We saw this increase of our flock with great satisfaction; and for fear these useful animals should take it into their heads to stray from us, as our ass had done, we tied round their necks some small bells we had found on the wreck, intended to propitiate the natives, and which would always put us on the track of the fugitives.

The education of the young buffalo was one of the employments that varied our labour as carpenters. Through the incision in his nostrils, I had passed a small stick, to the ends of which I attached a strap. This formed a kind of bit, after the fashion of those of the Hottentots; and by this I guided him as I chose; though not without much rebellion on his part. It was only after Fritz had broken it in for mounting, that we began to make it carry. It was certainly a remarkable instance of patience and perseverance surmounting difficulties, that we not only made it bear the wallets we usually placed on the ass, but Ernest, Jack, and even little Francis, took lessons in *horsemanship*, by riding him, and, henceforward, would have been able to ride the most spirited horse without fear; for it could not be worse than the buffalo they had assisted to subdue.

In the midst of this, Fritz did not neglect the training of his young eagle. The royal bird began already to pounce very cleverly on the dead game his master brought, and placed before him; sometimes between the horns of the buffalo, sometimes on the back of the great bustard, or the flamingo; sometimes he put it on a board, or on the end of a pole, to accustom it to pounce, like the falcon, on other birds. He taught it to settle on his wrist at a call, or a whistle; but it was some time before he could trust it to fly, without a long string attached to its leg, for fear its wild nature should carry it from us for ever. Even the indolent Ernest was seized with the mania of instructing animals. He undertook the education of his little monkey, who gave him sufficient employment. It was amusing to see the quiet, slow, studious Ernest obliged to make leaps and gambols with his pupil to accomplish his instruction. He wished to accustom Master Knips to carry a pannier, and to climb the cocoa-nut trees with it on his back; Jack and he wove a small light pannier of rushes, and fixed it firmly on his back with three straps. This was intolerable to him at first; he ground his teeth, rolled on the ground, and leaped about in a frantic manner, trying in vain to release himself. They left the pannier on his back night and day, and only allowed him to eat what he had previously put into it. After a little time, he became so accustomed to it, that he rebelled if they wished to remove it, and threw into it everything they gave him to hold. He was very useful to us, but he obeyed only Ernest, who had very properly taught him equally to love and fear him.

Jack was not so successful with his jackal; for, though he gave him the name of *"The Hunter,"* yet, for the first six months, the carnivorous animal chased only for himself, and, if he brought anything to his master, it was only the skin of the animal he had just devoured; but I charged him not to despair, and he continued zealously his instructions.

We then worked at our fountain, a great source of pleasure to my wife and to all of us. We raised, in the upper part of the river, a sort of dam, made with stakes and stones, from whence the water flowed into our channels of the sago-palm, laid down a gentle declivity nearly to our tent, and there it was received into the shell of the turtle, which we had raised on some stones of a convenient height, the hole which the harpoon had made serving to carry off the waste water through a cane that was fitted to it. On two crossed sticks were placed the gourds that served us for pails, and thus we had always the murmuring of the water near us, and a plentiful supply of it, always pure and clean, which the river, troubled by our water-fowl and the refuse of decayed leaves, could not always give us. The only inconvenience of these open channels was, that the water reached us warm and unrefreshing; but this I hoped to remedy in time, by using bamboo pipes buried in the earth. In the mean time, we were grateful for this new acquisition, and gave credit to Fritz, who had suggested the idea.

Chapter 27

One morning, as we were engaged in giving the last finish to our staircase, we were alarmed at hearing at a distance strange, sharp, prolonged sounds, like the roars of a wild beast, but mingled with an unaccountable hissing. Our dogs erected their ears, and prepared for deadly combat. I assembled my family; we then ascended our tree, closing the lower door, loaded our guns, and looked anxiously round, but nothing appeared. I armed my dogs with their porcupine coats of mail and collars, and left them below to take care of our animals.

The horrible howlings seemed to approach nearer to us; at length, Fritz, who was leaning forward to listen as attentively as he could, threw down his gun, and bursting into a loud laugh, cried out, "It is our fugitive, the ass, come back to us, and singing his song of joy on his return!" We listened, and were sure he was right, and could not but feel a little vexation at being put into such a fright by a donkey. Soon after, we had the pleasure of seeing him appear among the trees; and, what was still better, he was accompanied by another animal of his own species, but infinitely more beautiful. I knew it at once to be the donkey, a most important capture, if we could make it; though all naturalists have declared it impossible to tame this elegant creature, yet I determined to make the attempt.

By degrees we advanced softly to them, concealed by the trees; Fritz carrying the lasso, and I the pincers. The donkey, as soon as he got sight of Fritz, who was before me, raised his head, and started back, evidently only in surprise, as it was probably the first man the creature had seen. Fritz remained still, and the animal resumed his browsing. Fritz went up to our old servant, and offered him a handful of oats mixed with salt; the ass came directly to eat its favourite treat; its companion followed, raised its head, snuffed the air, and came so near, that Fritz adroitly threw the noose over its head. The terrified animal attempted to fly, but that drew the cord so tight as almost to stop his respiration, and he lay down, his tongue hanging out. I hastened up and relaxed the cord, lest he should be strangled. I threw the halter of the ass round his neck, and placed the split cane over his nose, tying it firmly below with a string. I subdued this wild animal by the means that blacksmiths use the first time they shoe a horse. I then took off the noose, and tied the halter by two long cords to the roots of two separate trees, and left him to recover himself.

In the mean time, the rest of the family had collected to admire this noble animal, whose graceful and elegant form, so superior to that of the ass, raises it almost to the dignity of a horse. After a while it rose, and stamped furiously with its feet, trying to release itself; but the pain in its nose obliged it to lie down again. Then my eldest son and I, approaching gently, took the two cords, and led or dragged it between two roots very near to each other, to which we tied the cords so short, that it had little power to move, and could not escape. We took care our own donkey should not stray again, by tying his fore-feet loosely, and putting on him a new halter, and left him near the donkey.

I continued, with a patience I had never had in Europe, to use every means I could think of with our new guest, and at the end of a month he was so far subdued, that I ventured to begin his education. This was a long and difficult task. We placed some burdens on his back; but the obedience necessary before we could mount him, it seemed impossible to instill into him. At last, I recollected the method they use in America to tame the wild horses, and I resolved to try it. In spite of the bounds and kicks of the furious animal, I leaped on his back, and seizing one of his long ears between my teeth, I bit it till the blood came. In a moment he reared himself almost erect on his hind-feet, remained for a while stiff and motionless, then came down on his fore-feet slowly, I still holding on his ear. At last I ventured to release him; he made some leaps, but soon subsided into a sort of trot, I having previously placed loose cords on his fore-legs. From that time we were his masters; my sons mounted him one after another; they gave him the name of Lightfoot, and never animal deserved his name better. As a precaution, we kept the cords on his legs for some time; and as he never would submit to the bit, we used a snaffle, by which we obtained power over his head, guiding him by a stick, with which we struck the right or left ear, as we wished him to go.

During this time, our poultry-yard was increased by three broods of chickens. We had at least forty of these little creatures chirping and pecking about, the pride of their good mistress's heart. Part of these were kept at home, to supply the table, and part she allowed to colonize in the woods, where we could find them when we wanted them. "These," she said, "are of more use than your monkeys, jackals, and eagles, who do nothing but eat, and would not be worth eating themselves, if we were in need." However, she allowed there was some use in the buffalo, who carried burdens, and Lightfoot, who carried her sons so well. The fowls, which cost us little for food, would be always ready, she said, either to supply us with eggs or chickens, when the rainy season came on the winter of this climate.

Lesson 39

1. Read chapters 28 and 29 of *Swiss Family Robinson*.
2. What did they find in the grotto (which is a small cave)? (Answers)
3. Tell someone about the chapter.

Chapter 28

The season changed sooner than we expected; the winds raged through the woods, the sea roared, mountains of clouds were piled in the heavens. They soon burst over our heads, and torrents of rain fell night and day, without intermission; the rivers swelled till their waters met, and turned the whole country around us into an immense lake. Happily we had formed our little establishment on a spot rather elevated above the rest of the valley; the waters did not quite reach our tree, but surrounded us about two hundred yards off, leaving us on a sort of island in the midst of the general inundation. We were reluctantly obliged to descend from our aerial abode; the rain entered it on all sides, and the hurricane threatened every moment to carry away the apartment, and all that were in it. We set about our removal, bringing down our hammocks and bedding to the sheltered space under the roots of the trees that we had roofed for the animals. We were painfully crowded in the small space; the stores of provisions, the cooking-utensils, and especially the neighbourhood of the animals, and the various offensive smells, made our retreat almost insupportable. We were choked with smoke if we lighted a fire, and inundated with rain if we opened a door. For the first time since our misfortune, we sighed for the comforts of our native home; but action was necessary, and we set about endeavouring to amend our condition.

The winding staircase was very useful to us; the upper part was crowded with things we did not want, and my wife frequently worked in the lower part, at one of the windows. We crowded our beasts a little more, and gave a current of air to the places they had left. I placed outside the enclosure the animals of the country, which could bear the inclemency of the season; thus I gave a half-liberty to the buffalo and the donkey, tying their legs loosely, to prevent them straying, the boughs of the tree affording them a shelter. We made as few fires as possible, as, fortunately it was never cold, and we had no provisions that required a long process of cookery. We had milk in abundance, smoked meat, and fish, the preserved *ortolans*, and cassava cakes. As we sent out some of our animals in the morning, with bells round their necks, Fritz and I had to seek them and bring them in every evening, when we were invariably wet through. This induced my ingenious Elizabeth to make us a sort of blouse and hood out of old garments of the sailors, which we covered with coatings of the *caoutchouc*, and thus obtained two capital waterproof dresses; all that the exhausted state of our gum permitted us to make.

The care of our animals occupied us a great part of the morning, then we prepared our cassava, and baked our cakes on iron plates. Though we had a glazed door to our hut, the gloominess of the weather, and the obscurity caused by the vast boughs of the tree, made night come on early. We then lighted a candle, fixed in a gourd on the table, round which we were all assembled. The good mother laboured with her needle, mending the clothes; I wrote my journal, which Ernest copied, as he wrote a beautiful hand; while Fritz and Jack taught their young brother to read and write, or amused themselves with drawing the animals or plants they had been struck with. We read the lessons from the Bible in turns, and concluded the evening with devotion. We then retired to rest, content with ourselves and with our innocent and peaceful life. Our kind housekeeper often made us a little feast of a roast chicken, a pigeon, or a duck, and once in four or five days we had fresh butter made in the gourd churn; and the delicious honey which we ate to our cassava bread might have been a treat to European epicures.

The remains of our repast was always divided among our domestic animals. We had four dogs, the jackal, the eagle, and the monkey, who relied on their masters, and were never neglected. But if the buffalo, the donkey, and the sow had not been able to provide for themselves, we must have killed them, for we had no food for them.

We now decided that we would not expose ourselves to another rainy season in such an unsuitable habitation; even my gentle Elizabeth got out of temper with the inconveniences, and begged we would build a better winter house; stipulating, however, that we should return to our tree in summer. We consulted a great deal on this matter; Fritz quoted Robinson Crusoe, who had cut a dwelling out of the rock, which sheltered him in the inclement season; and the idea of making our home at Tent House naturally came into my mind. It would probably be a long and difficult undertaking, but with time, patience, and perseverance, we might work wonders. We resolved, as soon as the weather would allow us, to go and examine the rocks at Tent House.

The last work of the winter was, at my wife's incessant request, a beetle for her flax, and some carding-combs. The beetle was easily made, but the combs cost much trouble. I filed large nails till they were round and pointed, I fixed them, slightly inclined, at equal distances, in a sheet of tin, and raised the edge like a box; I then poured melted lead between the nails and the edge, to fix them more firmly. I nailed this on a board, and the machine was fit for use, and my wife was all anxiety to begin her manufacture.

Chapter 29

I cannot describe our delight when, after long and gloomy weeks, we saw at length the sky clear, and the sun, dispersing the dark clouds of winter, spread its vivifying rays over all nature; the winds were lulled, the waters subsided, and the air became mild and serene. We went out, with shouts of joy, to breathe the balmy air, and gratified our eyes with the sight of the fresh verdure already springing up around us. Nature seemed in her youth again, and amidst the charms that breathed on every side, we forgot our sufferings, and, like the children of Noah coming forth from the ark, we raised a hymn of thanksgiving to the Giver of all good.

All our plantations and seeds had prospered. The corn was springing, and the trees were covered with leaves and blossoms. The air was perfumed with the odour of countless beautiful flowers; and lively with the songs and cries of hundreds of brilliant birds, all busy building their nests. This was really spring in all its glory.

In the mean time we walked over to Tent House to see the state of things, and found that winter had done more damage there than at Falcon's Nest. The storm had overthrown the tent, carried away some of the sailcloth, and injured our provisions so much, that great part was good for nothing, and the rest required to be immediately dried. Fortunately our beautiful pinnace had not suffered much, it was still safe at anchor, and fit for use; but our tub boat was entirely destroyed.

Our most important loss was two barrels of gunpowder, which had been left in the tent, instead of under the shelter of the rock, and which the rain had rendered wholly useless. This made us feel still more strongly the necessity of securing for the future a more suitable shelter than a canvas tent, or a roof of foliage. Still I had small hope from the gigantic plan of Fritz or the boldness of Jack. I could not be blind to the difficulties of the undertaking. The rocks which surrounded Tent House presented an unbroken surface, like a wall without any crevice, and, to all appearance, of so hard a nature as to leave little hopes of success. However, it was necessary to try to contrive some sort of cave, if only for our gunpowder. I made up my mind, and selected the most perpendicular face of the rock as the place to begin our work. It was a much pleasanter situation than our tent, commanding a view of the whole bay, and the two banks of Jackal River, with its picturesque bridge. I marked out with chalk the dimension of the entrance I wished to give to the cave; then my sons and I took our chisels, pickaxes, and heavy miner's hammers, and began boldly to hew the stone.

Our first blows produced very little effect; the rock seemed impenetrable, the sun had so hardened the surface; and the sweat poured off our brows with the hard labour. Nevertheless, the efforts of my young workmen did not relax. Every evening we left our work advanced, perhaps, a few inches; and every morning returned to the task with renewed ardour. At the end of five or six days, when the surface of the rock was removed, we found the stone become easier to work; it then seemed calcarious, and, finally, only a sort of hardened clay, which we could remove with spades; and we began to hope. After a few days' more labour, we found we had advanced about seven feet. Fritz wheeled out the rubbish, and formed a sort of terrace with it before the opening; while I was working at the higher part, Jack, as the least, worked below. One morning he was hammering an iron bar, which he had pointed at the end, into the rock, to loosen the earth, when he suddenly cried out

"Papa! papa! I have pierced through!"

"Not through your hand, child?" asked I.

"No, papa!" cried he; "I have pierced through the mountain! Huzza!"

We had brought from the vessel a box of fireworks, intended for signals; I threw into the cave, by a cord, a quantity of rockets, grenades, &c., and scattered a train of gunpowder from them; to this I applied a long match, and we retired to a little distance. This succeeded well; a great explosion agitated the air, a torrent of the carbonic acid gas rushed through the opening, and was replaced by the pure air; we sent in a few more rockets, which flew round like fiery dragons, disclosing to us the vast extent of the cave. A shower of stars, which concluded our experiment, made us wish the duration had been longer. It seemed as if a crowd of winged genii, carrying each a lamp, were floating about in that enchanted cavern. When they vanished, I threw in some more lighted hay, which blazed in such a lively manner, that I knew all danger was over from the gas; but, for fear of deep pits, or pools of water, I would not venture in without lights. I therefore despatched Jack, on his buffalo, to report this discovery to his mother, and bring all the candles she had made. I purposely sent Jack on the errand, for his lively and poetic turn of mind would, I hoped, invest the grotto with such charms, that his mother would even abandon her wheel to come and see it.

Delighted with his commission, Jack leaped upon his buffalo, and, waving his whip, galloped off with an intrepidity that made my hair stand on end. During his absence, Fritz and I enlarged the opening, to make it easy of access, removed all the rubbish, and swept a road for mamma. We had just finished, when we heard the sound of wheels crossing the bridge, and the cart appeared, drawn by the cow and ass, led by Ernest. Jack rode before on his buffalo, blowing through his hand to imitate a horn, and whipping the lazy cow and ass. He rode up first, and alighted from his huge courser, to help his mother out.

I then lighted our candles, giving one to each, with a spare candle and flint and steel in our pockets. We took our arms, and proceeded in a solemn manner into the rock. I walked first, my sons followed, and their mother came last, with Francis. We had not gone on above a few steps, when we stopped, struck with wonder and admiration; all was glittering around us; we were in a grotto of diamonds! From the height of the lofty vaulted roof hung innumerable crystals, which, uniting with those on the walls, formed colonnades, altars, and every sort of gothic ornament of dazzling lustre, creating a fairy palace, or an illuminated temple.

When we were a little recovered from our first astonishment, we advanced with more confidence. The grotto was spacious, the floor smooth, and covered with a fine dry sand. From the appearance of these crystals, I suspected their nature, and, on breaking off a piece and tasting it, I found, to my great joy, that we were in a grotto of rock salt, which is found in large masses in the earth, usually above a bed of gypsum, and surrounded by fossils. We were charmed with this discovery, of which we could no longer have a doubt. What an advantage this was to our cattle, and to ourselves! We could now procure this precious commodity without care or labour. The acquisition was almost as valuable as this brilliant retreat was in itself, of which we were never tired of admiring the beauty. My wife was struck with our good fortune in opening the rock precisely at the right spot; but I was of opinion, that this mine was of great extent, and that we could not well have missed it.

Some blocks of salt were scattered on the ground, which had apparently fallen from the vaulted roof. I was alarmed; for such an accident might destroy one of my children; but, on examination, I found the mass above too solid to be detached spontaneously, and I concluded that the explosion of the fireworks had given this shock to the subterranean palace, which had not been entered since the creation of the world. I feared there might yet be some pieces loosened; I therefore sent out my wife and younger sons. Fritz and I remained, and, after carefully examining the suspected parts, we fired our guns, and watched the effect; one or two pieces fell, but the rest remained firm, though we struck with long poles as high as we could reach. We were now satisfied of the security of our magnificent abode, and began to plan our arrangements for converting it into a convenient and pleasant habitation. The majority were for coming here immediately, but the wiser heads determined that, for this year, Falcon's Nest was to continue our home. There we went every night, and spent the day at Tent House, contriving and arranging our future winter dwelling.

Lesson 40

1. Read chapters 30 and 31 of *Swiss Family Robinson*.
2. Tell someone about the chapters.

Chapter 30

The last bed of rock, before we reached the cave which Jack had pierced, was so soft, and easy to work, that we had little difficulty in proportioning and opening the place for our door; I hoped that, being now exposed to the heat of the sun, it would soon become as hard as the original surface. The door was that we had used for the staircase at Falcon's Nest; for as we only intended to make a temporary residence of our old tree, there was no necessity for solid fittings; and, besides, I intended to close the entrance of the tree by a door of bark, more effectually to conceal it, in case the natives should visit us. I then laid out the extent of the grotto at pleasure, for we had ample space. We began by dividing it into two parts; that on the right of the entrance was to be our dwelling; on the left were, first, our kitchen, then the workshop and the stables; behind these were the store-rooms and the cellar. In order to give light and air to our apartments, it was necessary to insert in the rock the windows we had brought from the ship; and this cost us many days of labour.

The right-hand portion was subdivided into three rooms: the first our own bedroom; the middle, the common sitting-room, and beyond the boys' room. As we had only three windows, we appropriated one to each bedroom, and the third to the kitchen, contenting ourselves, at present, with a grating in the dining-room. I constructed a sort of chimney in the kitchen, formed of four boards, and conducted the smoke thus, through a hole made in the face of the rock. We made our work-room spacious enough for us to carry on all our manufactures, and it served also for our cart-house. Finally, all the partition-walls were put up, communicating by doors, and completing our commodious habitation. These various labours, the removal of our effects, and arranging them again, all the confusion of a change when it was necessary to be at once workmen and directors, took us a great part of summer; but the recollection of the *vexations* we should escape in the rainy season gave us energy.

We passed nearly all our time at Tent House, the centre of our operations; and, besides the gardens and plantations which surrounded it, we found many advantages which we profited by. Large turtles often came to deposit their eggs in the sand, a pleasant treat for us; but we raised our desires to the possession of the turtles themselves, living, to eat when we chose. As soon as we saw one on the shore, one of my sons ran to cut off its retreat. We then hastened to assist, turned the creature on its back, passed a long cord through its shell, and tied it firmly to a post close to the water. We then placed it on its legs, when of course it made for the water, but could only ramble the length of its cord; it seemed, however, very content, and we had it in readiness when we wanted it. The lobsters, crabs, muscles, and every sort of fish which abounded on the coast, plentifully supplied our table.

At this time I greatly improved my sledge, by placing it on two small wheels belonging to the guns of the ship, making it a light and commodious carriage, and so low, that we could easily place heavy weights on it. Satisfied with our labours, we returned very happy to Falcon's Nest, to spend our Sunday, and to thank God heartily for all the blessings he had given us.

Chapter 31

We went on with our labours but slowly, as many employments diverted us from the great work. We began to plan a boat to replace our tub raft. I wished to try to make one of bark, as these nations do, and I proposed to make an expedition in search of a tree for our purpose. All those in our own neighbourhood were too precious to destroy; some for their fruits, others for their shade. We resolved to search at a distance for trees fit for our purpose, taking in our road a survey of our plantations and fields. Our garden at Tent House produced abundantly continual successions of vegetables in that virgin soil, and in a climate which recognized no change of season. The peas, beans, lentils, and lettuces were flourishing, and only required water, and our channels from the river brought this plentifully to us. We had delicious cucumbers and melons; the maize was already a foot high, the sugar-canes were prospering, and the pine-apples on the high ground promised us a rich treat.

We hoped our distant plantations were going on as well, and all set out one fine morning to Falcon's Nest, to examine the state of things there. We found my wife's corn-fields were luxuriant in appearance, and for the most part ready for cutting. There were barley, wheat, oats, beans, millet, and lentils. We cut such of these as were ready, sufficient to give us seeds for another year. The richest crop was the maize, which suited the soil. But there were a quantity of gatherers more eager to taste these new productions than we were; these were birds of every kind, from the bustard to the quail, and from the various establishments they had formed round, it might be presumed they would not leave much for us.

After our first shock at the sight of these robbers, we used some measures to lessen the number of them. Fritz unhooded his eagle, and pointed out the dispersing bustards. The well-trained bird immediately soared, and pounced on a superb bustard, and laid it at the feet of its master. The jackal, too, who was a capital pointer, brought to his master about a dozen little fat quails, which furnished us with an excellent repast; to which my wife added a liquor of her own invention, made of the green maize crushed in water, and mingled with the juice of the sugar-cane; a most agreeable beverage, white as milk, sweet and refreshing.

We found the bustard, which the eagle had struck down, but slightly wounded; we washed his hurts with a balsam made of wine, butter, and water, and tied him by the leg in the poultry-yard, as a companion to our tame bustard.

We passed the remainder of the day at Falcon's Nest, putting our summer abode into order, and threshing out our grain, to save the precious seed for another year. The Turkey wheat was laid by in sheaves, till we should have time to thresh and winnow it; and then I told Fritz that it would be necessary to put the hand-mill in order, that we had brought from the wreck. Fritz thought we could build a mill ourselves on the river; but this bold scheme was, at present, impracticable.

The next day we set out on an excursion in the neighbourhood. My wife wished to establish colonies of our animals at some distance from Falcon's Nest, at a convenient spot, where they would be secure, and might find subsistence. She selected from her poultry-yard twelve young fowls; I took four young pigs, two couple of sheep, and two goats. These animals were placed in the cart, in which we had previously placed our provisions of every kind, and the tools and utensils we might need, not forgetting the rope ladder and the portable tent; we then harnessed the buffalo, the cow, and the ass, and departed on our tour.

Fritz rode before on Lightfoot, to reconnoitre the ground, that we might not plunge into any difficulties; as, this time, we went in a new direction, exactly in the midst between the rocks and the shore, that we might get acquainted with the whole of the country that stretched to Cape Disappointment. We had the usual difficulty, at first, in getting through the high grass, and the underwood embarrassed our road, till we were compelled to use the axe frequently. I made some trifling discoveries that were useful, while engaged in this labour; amongst others, some roots of trees curved like saddles, and yokes for beasts of draught. I cut away several of these, and placed them on the cart. When we had nearly passed the wood, we were struck with the singular appearance of a little thicket of low bushes, apparently covered with snow. Francis clapped his hands with joy, and begged to get out of the cart that he might make some snowballs. Fritz galloped forward, and returned, bringing me a branch loaded with this beautiful white down, which, to my great joy, I recognized to be cotton. It was a discovery of inestimable value to us, and my wife began immediately to enumerate all the advantages we should derive from it, when I should have constructed for her the machines for spinning and weaving the cotton. We soon gathered as much as filled three bags, intending afterwards to collect the seeds of this marvellous plant, to sow in the neighbourhood of Tent House.

After crossing the plain of the cotton-trees, we reached the summit of a hill, from which the eye rested on a terrestrial paradise. Trees of every sort covered the sides of the hill, and a murmuring stream crossed the plain, adding to its beauty and fertility. The wood we had just crossed formed a shelter against the north winds, and the rich pasture offered food for our cattle. We decided at once that this should be the site of our farm.

We erected our tent, made a fireplace, and set about cooking our dinner. While this was going on, Fritz and I sought a convenient spot for our structure; and we met with a group of beautiful trees, at such a distance one from another, as to form natural pillars for our dwelling; we carried all our tools here; but as the day was far advanced, we delayed commencing our work till next day. We returned to the tent, and found my wife and her boys picking cotton, with which they made some very comfortable beds, and we slept peacefully under our canvass roof.

Lesson 41

1. Read chapter 32.
2. Do you think they will stay on the island forever or will they leave?
3. Tell someone about the chapter.

Vocabulary

1. Review your vocabulary. Go to Lesson 16.

Chapter 32

The trees which I had chosen for my farmhouse were about a foot in diameter in the trunk. They formed a long square; the long side facing the sea. The dimensions of the whole were about twenty-four feet by sixteen. I cut deep mortices in the trees, about ten feet distant from the ground, and again ten feet higher, to form a second story; I then placed in them strong poles: this was the skeleton of my house solid, if not elegant; I placed over this a rude roof of bark, cut in squares, and placed sloping, that the rain might run off. We fastened these with the thorn of the acacia, as our nails were too precious to be lavished.

We continued our work at the house, which occupied us several days. We formed the walls of thin laths interwoven with long pliant reeds for about six feet from the ground; the rest was merely a sort of light trellis-work, to admit light and air. The door opened on the front to the sea. The interior consisted simply of a series of compartments, proportioned to the guests they were to contain. One small apartment was for ourselves, when we chose to visit our colony. On the upper story was a sort of hayloft for the fodder. We projected plastering the walls with clay; but these finishing touches we deferred to a future time, contented that we had provided a shelter for our cattle and fowls. To accustom them to come to this shelter of themselves, we took care to fill their racks with the food they liked best, mingled with salt; and this we proposed to renew at intervals, till the habit of coming to their houses was fixed. We all laboured ardently, but the work proceeded slowly, from our inexperience; and the provisions we had brought were nearly exhausted. I did not wish to return to Falcon's Nest till I had completed my new establishment, and therefore determined to send Fritz and Jack to look after the animals at home, and bring back a fresh stock of provisions. Our two young couriers set out, each on his favourite steed, Fritz leading the ass to bring back the load, and Jack urging the indolent animal forward with his whip.

During their absence, Ernest and I made a little excursion, to add to our provision if we could meet with them, some potatoes and cocoa-nuts. We ascended the stream for some time, which led us to a large marsh, beyond which we discovered a lake abounding with water-fowl. This lake was surrounded by tall, thick grass, with ears of a grain, which I found to be a very good, though small, sort of rice. As to the lake itself, it is only a Swiss, accustomed from his infancy to look on such smooth, tranquil waters, that can comprehend the happiness we felt on looking upon this. We fancied we were once more in Switzerland, our own dear land; but the majestic trees and luxuriant vegetation soon reminded us we were no longer in Europe, and that the ocean separated us from our native home.

We proceeded round the lake, which presented a different scene on every side. This was one of the most lovely and fertile parts we had yet seen of this country. Birds of all kinds abounded; but we were particularly struck with a pair of black swans, sailing majestically on the water. Their plumage was perfectly black and glossy, except the extremity of the wings, which was white. Ernest would have tried his skill again, but I forbade him to disturb the profound tranquillity of this charming region.

But Flora, who probably had not the same taste for the beauties of nature that I had, suddenly darted forward like an arrow, pounced upon a creature that was swimming quietly at the edge of the water, and brought it to us. It was a most curious animal. It resembled an otter in form, but was web-footed, had an erect bushy tail like the squirrel, small head, eyes and ears almost invisible. A long, flat bill, like that of a duck, completed its strange appearance. We were completely puzzled even Ernest, the naturalist, could not give its name. I boldly gave it the name of the beast with a bill. I told Ernest to take it, as I wished to stuff and preserve it.

"It will be," said the little philosopher, "the first natural object for our museum."

"Exactly," replied I; "and, when the establishment is fully arranged, we will appoint you curator."

But, thinking my wife would grow uneasy at our protracted absence, we returned by a direct road to the tent. Our two messengers arrived about the same time, and we all sat down together to a cheerful repast. Every one related his feats. Ernest dwelt on his discoveries, and was very pompous in his descriptions, and I was obliged to promise to take Fritz another time. I learnt, with pleasure, that all was going on well at Falcon's Nest, and that the boys had had the forethought to leave the animals with provisions for ten days. This enabled me to complete my farmhouse. We remained four days longer, in which time I finished the interior, and my wife arranged in our own apartment the cotton mattresses, to be ready for our visits, and put into the houses the fodder and grain for their respective tenants. We then loaded our cart, and began our march. The animals wished to follow us, but Fritz, on Lightfoot, covered our retreat, and kept them at the farm till we were out of sight.

We did not proceed directly, but went towards the wood of monkeys. These mischievous creatures assaulted us with showers of the fir-apples; but a few shots dispersed our assailants.

Fritz collected some of these new fruits they had flung at us, and I recognized them as those of the stone Pine, the kernel of which is good to eat, and produces an excellent oil. We gathered a bag of these, and continued our journey till we reached the neighbourhood of Cape Disappointment. There we ascended a little hill, from the summit of which we looked upon rich plains, rivers, and woods clothed with verdure and brilliant flowers, and gay birds that fluttered among the bushes. "Here, my children," cried I, "here we will build our summer house. This is truly Arcadia." Here we placed our tent, and immediately began to erect a new building, formed in the same manner as the Farm House, but now executed more quickly. We raised the roof in the middle, and made four sloped sides. The interior was divided into eating and sleeping apartments, stables, and a store-room for provisions; the whole was completed and provisioned in ten days; and we had now another mansion for ourselves, and a shelter for new colonies of animals. This new erection received the name of Prospect Hill, to gratify Ernest, who thought it had an English appearance.

However, the end for which our expedition was planned was not yet fulfilled. I had not yet met with a tree likely to suit me for a boat. We returned then to inspect the trees, and I fixed on a sort of oak, the bark of which was closer than that of the European oak, resembling more that of the cork-tree. The trunk was at least five feet in diameter, and I fancied its coating, if I could obtain it whole, would perfectly answer my purpose. I traced a circle at the foot, and with a small saw cut the bark entirely through; Fritz, by means of the rope ladder we had brought with us, and attached to the lower branches of the tree, ascended, and cut a similar circle eighteen feet above mine. We then cut out, perpendicularly, a slip the whole length, and, removing it, we had room to insert the necessary tools, and, with wedges, we finally succeeded in loosening the whole. The first part was easy enough, but there was greater difficulty as we advanced. We sustained it as we proceeded with ropes, and then gently let it down on the grass. I immediately began to form my boat while the bark was fresh and flexible. My sons, in their impatience, thought it would do very well if we nailed a board at each end of the roll; but this would have been merely a heavy trough, inelegant and unserviceable; I wished to have one that would look well by the side of the pinnace; and this idea at once rendered my boys patient and obedient. We began by cutting out at each end of the roll of bark a triangular piece of about five feet long; then, placing the sloping parts one over the other, I united them with pegs and strong glue, and thus finished the ends of my boat in a pointed form. This operation having widened it too much in the middle, we passed strong ropes round it, and drew it into the form we required. We then exposed it to the sun, which dried and fixed it in the proper shape.

As many things were necessary to complete my work, I sent Fritz and Jack to Tent House for the sledge, to convey it there, that we might finish it more conveniently. I had the good fortune to meet with some very hard, crooked wood, the natural curve of which would be admirably suitable for supporting the sides of the boat. We found also a resinous tree, which distilled a sort of pitch, easy to manage, and which soon hardened in the sun. My wife and Francis collected sufficient of it for my work. It was almost night when our two messengers returned. We had only time to sup and retire to our rest.

We were all early at work next morning. We loaded the sledge, placing on it the canoe, the wood for the sides, the pitch, and some young trees, which I had transplanted for our plantation at Tent House, and which we put into the boat. But, before we set out, I wished to erect a sort of fortification at the pass of the rock, for the double purpose of securing us against the attacks of wild beasts or of natives, and for keeping enclosed, in the savannah beyond the rocks, some young pigs, that we wished to multiply there, out of the way of our fields and plantations.

The next morning we returned to Tent House, where we immediately set to work on our canoe with such diligence that it was soon completed. It was solid and elegant, lined through with wood, and furnished with a keel. We provided it with brass rings for the oars, and stays for the mast. Instead of ballast, I laid at the bottom a layer of stones covered with clay, and over this a flooring of boards. The benches for the rowers were laid across, and in the midst the bamboo mast rose majestically, with a triangular sail. Behind I fixed the rudder, worked by a tiller; and I could boast now of having built a capital canoe.

Our fleet was now in good condition. For distant excursions we could take the pinnace, but the canoe would be invaluable for the coasting service.

Our cow had, in the mean time, given us a young male calf, which I undertook to train for service, as I had done the buffalo, beginning by piercing its nostrils; and the calf promised to be docile and useful; and, as each of the other boys had his favourite animal to ride, I bestowed the bull on Francis, and intrusted him with its education, to encourage him to habits of boldness and activity. He was delighted with his new charger, and chose to give him the name of Valiant.

We had still two months before the rainy season, and this time we devoted to completing the comforts of our grotto. We made all the partitions of wood, except those which divided us from the stables, which we built of stone, to exclude any smell from the animals. We soon acquired skill in our works; we had a plentiful supply of beams and planks from the ship; and by practice we became very good plasterers. We covered the floors with a sort of well-beaten mud, smoothed it, and it dried perfectly hard. We then contrived a sort of felt carpet. We first covered the floor with sailcloth; we spread over this wool and goats' hair mixed, and poured over it isinglass dissolved, rolling up the carpet, and beating it well. When this was dry, we repeated the process, and in the end had a felt carpet. We made one of these for each room, to guard against any damp that we might be subject to in the rainy season.

After dinner, our evening occupations commenced; our room was lighted up brilliantly; we did not spare our candles, which were so easily procured, and we enjoyed the reflection in the elegant crystals above us. We had partitioned off a little chapel in one corner of the grotto, which we had left untouched, and nothing could be more magnificent than this chapel lighted up, with its colonnades, portico, and altars. We had divine service here every Sunday. I had erected a sort of pulpit, from which I delivered a short sermon to my congregation, which I endeavoured to render as simple and as instructive as possible.

Jack and Francis had a natural taste for music. I made them instruments from reeds, on which they acquired considerable skill. They accompanied their mother, who had a very good voice; and this music in our lofty grotto had a charming effect.

We had thus made great steps towards civilization; and, though condemned, perhaps, to pass our lives alone on this unknown shore, we might yet be happy. We were placed in the midst of abundance. We were active, industrious, and content; blessed with health, and united by affection, our minds seemed to enlarge and improve every day. We saw around us on every side traces of the Divine wisdom and beneficence; and our hearts overflowed with love and veneration for that Almighty hand which had so miraculously saved, and continued to protect us. I humbly trusted in Him, either to restore us to the world, or send some beings to join us in this beloved island, where for two years we had seen no trace of man. To Him we committed our fate. We were happy and tranquil, looking with resignation to the future.

Lesson 42

1. Read chapter 33 of *Swiss Family Robinson*.
2. Tell someone about the chapter.

Chapter 33

I left the reader at the moment in which I had placed the first part of my journal in the hands of Lieutenant Bell, to deliver to Captain Johnson, of the English vessel the *Adventurer*, expecting him to return the next day with Lieutenant Bell. We separated in this hope, and I thought it necessary to inform my family of this expected visit, which might decide their future lot. My wife and elder sons might wish to seize this only occasion that might occur to revisit their native country to quit their beloved island, which would doubtless cost them much sorrow at the last moment, but was necessary to their future comfort. I could not help feeling distressed at the prospect of my dear children's solitary old age, and I determined, if they did not wish to return with Captain Johnson, to request him to send some colonists out to people our island.

It will be remembered that I had left home alone, and at an early hour, having perceived a vessel from the top of our tree with my telescope. I had set out without breakfast, without giving my sons their tasks, or making any arrangements for the labours of the day. My conference with Lieutenant Bell had been long; it was now past noon, and knowing how prompt my wife was to alarm herself, I was surprised that I did not meet her, nor any of my sons. I began to be uneasy, and on my arrival I hastily mounted the tree, and found my faithful partner extended on her bed, surrounded by her four sons, and apparently in great pain. I demanded, with a cry of grief, what had happened; all wished to speak at once, and it was with some difficulty I learned, that my dear wife, in descending the staircase, had been seized with a giddiness in her head, and had fallen down and injured herself so much, that she was unable to rise without assistance; she was now enduring great pain in her right leg and in her left foot. "Ernest and I," added Fritz, "carried her without delay to her bed, though not without difficulty, for the staircase is so narrow; but she continued to get worse, and we did not know what to do."

Jack. I have rubbed her foot continually, but it swells more and more, as well as her leg, which I dare not touch, it hurts her so much.

Ernest. I remember, father, that of the chests that we brought from the ship there is one unopened, which is marked *"medicines,"* may it not contain something that will relieve mamma?

Father. Perhaps it may, my son. You did well to remember it; we will go to Tent House for it. Fritz, you shall accompany me to assist in bringing it.

I wished to be alone with Fritz, to consult him about the English vessel, and was glad of this opportunity. Before I left my wife, I intended to examine her leg and foot, which were exceedingly painful. When I was preparing to enter the Church, I had studied medicine and practical surgery, in order to be able to administer to the bodily afflictions of my poor parishioners, as well as to their spiritual sorrows. I knew how to bleed, and could replace a dislocated limb. I had often made cures; but since my arrival at the island I had neglected my medical studies, which happily had not been needed. I hoped now, however, to recall as much of my knowledge as would be sufficient to cure my poor wife. I examined her foot first, which I found to be violently sprained. She begged me then to look at her leg, and what was my distress when I saw it was fractured above the ankle; however, the fracture appeared simple, without splinters, and easy to cure. I sent Fritz without delay to procure me two pieces of the bark of a tree, between which I placed the leg, after having, with the assistance of my son, stretched it till the two pieces of broken bone united; I then bound it with bandages of linen, and tied the pieces of bark round the leg, so that it might not be moved. I bound the sprained foot very tightly, till I could procure the balsam which I expected to find in the chest. I felt assured, that the giddiness of the head, which had caused her fall, proceeded from some existing cause, which I suspected, from the pulse and the complexion, must be a fullness of blood; and it appeared to be necessary to take away some ounces, which I persuaded her to allow me to do, when I should have brought my medicine-chest and instruments from Tent House. I left her, with many charges, to the care of my three younger sons, and proceeded to Tent House with Fritz, to whom I now related my morning adventure, and consulted him how we should mention it to his mother. Fritz was astonished. I saw how his mind was employed; he looked round on our fields and plantations, increasing and prospering.

"We must not tell her, father," said he. "I will be at Tent House early in the morning; you must give me some commission to execute; I will await the arrival of the Captain, and tell him that my dear mother is ill, and that he may return as he came."

"You speak rashly, Fritz," answered I. "I have told you that this ship has suffered much from the storm, and needs repairs. Have you not often read the golden rule of our divine Master, *Do unto others as you would have others do unto you?* Our duty is to receive the Captain into our island, and to assist him in repairing and refitting his vessel."

"And he will find," said he, "we know something of that kind of work. Did you show him our beautiful pinnace and canoe? But can such a large vessel enter our Bay of Safety?"

"No," replied I; "I fear there will not be sufficient water; but we will show the captain the large bay at the other end of the island, formed by Cape Disappointment; he will find there a beautiful harbour."

"And he and his officers may live at the farm, and we can go over every day to assist in repairing their vessel," continued Fritz.

"Very well," said I; "and when it is finished, he will, in return, give us a place in it to return to Europe."

"To return to Europe, father!" cried he; "to leave our beautiful winter dwelling, Tent House, and our charming summer residence, Falcon's Nest; our dear, good animals; our crystals of salt; our farms; so much that is our own, and which nobody covets, to return into Europe to poverty, to war, to those wicked soldiers who have banished us! We want nothing. Dear father, can you consent to leave our beloved island?"

"You are right, my dear son," said I. "Would to God we might always remain here happily together; but we are of different ages, and by the law of nature we must one day be separated. Consider, my dear son, if you should survive your brothers, how cheerless it would be to live quite alone on this desert island, without any one to close your eyes. But let us look at these trees; I see they are tamarind-trees; their fruit contains a pulp which is very useful in medicine, and which will suit your mother, I think, as well as the juice of the orange or lemon. We shall find some of the latter at our plantation near Tent House; but, in the mean time, do you climb the tamarind-tree, and gather some of those pods which resemble those of beans, fill one side of the bag with them, the other we will reserve for the oranges and lemons. Not to lose any time, I will go on to Tent House to seek for the two chests, and you can follow me."

Fritz was up the tamarind-tree in a moment. I crossed Family Bridge, and soon reached the grotto. I lighted a candle, which I always kept ready, entered the magazine, and found the two chests, labeled.

They were neither large nor heavy, and, having tied cords round them for the convenience of carrying them, I proceeded to visit the orange and lemon trees, where I found the fruit sufficiently ripe for lemonade. Fritz came to meet me, with a good supply of tamarinds. We filled the other end of his sack with oranges and lemons. He threw it over his shoulder, and, neither of us being overloaded, we pursued our way homewards very quickly, notwithstanding the heat, which was excessively oppressive, though the sun was hidden under the thick clouds, which entirely concealed the sea from us. Nothing was to be seen but the waves breaking against the rocks. Fritz expressed his fears that a storm was coming on, which might prove fatal to the vessel, and wished to take out the pinnace and endeavour to assist Captain Johnson. Delighted as I felt with his fearless humanity, I could not consent; I reminded him of the situation of his mother. "Forgive me, dear father," said he; "I had forgotten everything but the poor vessel. But the captain may do as we did, leave his ship between the rocks, and come, with all in the vessel, to establish themselves here. We will give them up a corner of our islands; and if there should be any ladies amongst them, how pleasant it would be for mamma to have a friend!"

The rain now fell in torrents, and we proceeded with great difficulty. After crossing the bridge, we saw at a distance a very extraordinary figure approaching us; we could not ascertain what species of animal it was. It appeared taller than any of the monkeys we had seen, and much larger, of a black or brown colour. We could not distinguish the head, but it seemed to have two thick and moveable horns before it. We had fortunately taken no gun with us, or Fritz would certainly have fired at this singular animal. But as it rapidly approached us, we soon recognized the step, and the cry of pleasure which hailed us. "It is Jack," we exclaimed; and in fact it was he, who was hurrying to meet us with my large cloak and *waterproof caoutchoucboots*. I had neglected to take them, and my dear little fellow had volunteered to bring them to Tent House. To protect himself on the way, he had put the cloak on, covering his head with the hood, and my boots being too large for him, he had put one on each arm, which he held up to secure the hood. Conceive what a singular figure he made. Notwithstanding our uneasiness, and our wretched condition, for we were wet to the skin, we could not but laugh heartily at him. I would not consent to use the coverings he had brought; neither Fritz nor I could be worse for the distance we had to go, and Jack was younger and more delicate; I obliged him therefore to retain his curious protection; and asked how he had left his mother. "Very uneasy," said he, "about you; else I think she must be much better, for her cheeks are very red, and her eyes very bright, and she talks incessantly. She would have come herself to seek you, but could not rise; and when I told her I would come, she bid me be very quick; but when I was coming down stairs, I heard her call me back for fear of the rain and the thunder; I would not hear her, but ran as fast as I could, hoping to reach Tent House. Why did you come back so soon?"

"To spare you half your journey, my brave little man," said I, hastening on; for Jack's account of his mother made me uneasy. I perceived she must be labouring under fever, and the blood ascending to her head. My children followed me, and we soon reached the foot of our castle in the air.

Lesson 43

1. Read chapter 34 of *Swiss Family Robinson*.
2. His wife is sick and he says that she needs a "bleeding." This was a mistaken medical idea of long ago. They cut patients to drain out the "bad blood" that was making them sick. What happened, though, was that they made people weaker by making them lose blood. It only harmed the patient, but he's doing the best he knows how.
3. Tell someone about the chapter.

Chapter 34

We entered our apartment literally as if we had come out of the sea, and I found my poor Elizabeth much agitated. "Heaven be praised!" said she; "but where is Jack, that rash little fellow?"

"Here I am, mamma," said he, "as dry as when I left you. I have left my dress below, that I might not terrify you; for if Mr. Fritz had had his gun, I might have been shot as a *rhinoceros*, and not been here to tell you my story."

The good mother then turned her thoughts on Fritz and me, and would not suffer us to come near her till we had changed our drenched garments. To oblige her, we retired to a little closet I had contrived between two thick branches at the top of the staircase, which was used to contain our chests of linen, our dresses, and our provisions. Our dress was soon changed; we hung up the wet garments, and I returned to my companion, who was suffering from her foot, but still more from a frightful headache. She had a burning fever. I concluded that bleeding was urgently needed, but commenced by assuaging her thirst with some lemonade. I then opened my box of surgical instruments, and approached the opening to the east which served us for a window, and which we could close by means of a curtain, that was now entirely raised to give air to our dear invalid, and to amuse my children, who were watching the storm. The mighty waves that broke against the rocks, the vivid lightning bursting through the castles of murky clouds, the majestic and incessant rolling of the thunder, formed one of those enchanting spectacles to which they had been from infancy accustomed. As in the Swiss mountains we are liable to frightful storms, to which it is necessary to familiarize oneself, as one cannot avoid them, I had accustomed my wife and children, by my own example, to behold, not only without fear, but even with admiration, these great shocks of the elements, these convulsions of nature.

I had opened the chest, and my children had directed their attention to the instruments it contained; the first were a little rusty, and I handed them to Ernest, who, after examining them, placed them on a table inside the window. I was searching for a lancet in good condition, when a clap of thunder, such as I had never heard in my life, terrified us all so much, that we nearly fell down. This burst of thunder had not been preceded by any lightning, but was accompanied by two immense forked columns of fire, which seemed to stretch from the sky to our very feet. We all cried out, even my poor wife; but the silence of terror succeeded, and seemed to be the silence of death. I flew to the bedside, and found my dear patient in a state of total insensibility. I was convinced that she was dead, and I was dumb with despair. I was roused from my stupor by the voice of my children. I then remembered that I had not lost all: there still remained duties to fulfil, and affection to console me. "My children," cried I, extending my arms to them, "come and comfort your unfortunate father: come and lament with him the best of wives and mothers." Terrified at the appearance of their mother, they surrounded her bed, calling on her in piercing accents. At that moment I saw my little Francis was missing, and my grief was augmented by the fear that he had been killed by the lightning. I hastily turned to the window, expecting to find my child dead, and our dwelling in flames. Fortunately, all was safe; but, in my distraction, I scarcely thanked God for His mercy, at the very moment even when he graciously restored to me my lost treasures.

Francis, frightened by the storm, had hidden himself in his mother's bed, and fallen asleep; awaked by the thunder, he had not dared to move, fearing it announced the arrival of the natives; but at last, the cries of his brothers roused him, and raising his pretty fair head, supposing his mother sleeping, he flung his arms round her neck, saying, "Wake, mamma, we are all here, papa, my brothers, and the storm, too, which is very beautiful, but frightens me. Open your eyes, mamma; look at the bright lightning, and kiss your little Francis." Either his sweet voice, or the cries of her elder children, restored her faculties: she gradually recovered, and called me to her. The excess of my joy threatened to be almost as fatal as my grief. With difficulty I controlled my own feelings and those of my boys; and, after I had sent them from the bed, I ascertained that she was not only really living, but much better. The pulse was calm, and the fever had subsided, leaving only a weakness that was by no means alarming.

I relinquished, joyfully, the intention of bleeding her, the necessity of which I had trembled to contemplate, and contented myself with employing the boys to prepare a cooling mixture, composed of the juice of the lemon, of barley, and tamarinds, which they completed to the great satisfaction of their mother. I then ordered Fritz to descend to the yard, to kill a fowl, pluck and boil it, to make broth, a wholesome and light nourishment for our dear invalid. I told one of his brothers to assist him, and Jack and Francis, frequently employed under their mother, were ready in a moment. Ernest alone remained quietly on his seat, which I attributed to his usual indolence, and tried to make him ashamed of it. "Ernest," said I, "you are not very anxious to oblige your mother; you sit as if the thunderbolt had struck you."

"It has, indeed, rendered me unfit to be of any service to my good mother," said he, quietly; and, drawing his right hand from under his waistcoat, he showed it to me, most frightfully black and burnt.

This dear child, who must have suffered very much, had never uttered a complaint, for fear of alarming his mother; and even now he made a sign to me to be silent, lest she should hear, and discover the truth. She soon, however, fell into a sleep, which enabled me to attend to poor Ernest, and to question him about the accident. I learned that a long and pointed steel instrument, which he was examining near the large window, stooping over it to see it better, had attracted the lightning, which, falling partly on the hand in which he held it, had caused the misfortune. There were traces on his arm of the electric fire, and his hair was burnt on one side. By what miracle the electric fluid had been diverted, and how we, dwelling in a tree, had been preserved from a sudden and general conflagration, I knew not. My son assured me he had seen the fire run along the instrument he held, and from thence fall perpendicularly to the earth, where it seemed to burst with a second explosion. I was impatient to examine this phenomenon, and to see if any other traces were left, except those on the hand of my son, which it was necessary, in the first place, to attend to. I remembered frequently to have applied with success in burns the most simple and easy of remedies, which everybody can command: this is, to bathe the hand affected in cold water, taking care to renew it every eight or ten minutes. I placed Ernest between two tubs of cold water, and, exhorting him to patience and perseverance, I left him to bathe his hand, and approached the opening, to try and discover what had preserved us, by averting the direction of the lightning, which one might have expected would have killed my son, and destroyed our dwelling. I saw only some light traces on the table; but, on looking more attentively, I found that the greater part of the surgical instruments which Ernest had placed upon it were either melted or much damaged. In examining them separately, I remarked one much longer than the rest, which projected beyond the edge of the table, and was much marked by the fire. I could not easily take it up; it had adhered somewhat in melting, and, in endeavouring to disengage it, I saw that the point, which was beyond the opening, touched a thick wire, which seemed to be suspended from the roof of our tent. All was now explained to me; except that I could in no way account for this wire, placed expressly to serve as a conductor for the lightning. It seemed to be the work of magic.

The evening was too far advanced for me to distinguish how it was fastened, and what fixed it below; therefore, enjoining Ernest to call loudly if he needed me, I hastened down. I saw my three cooks very busy, as I passed through, preparing the broth for their mother they assured me it would be excellent. Fritz boasted that he had killed the fowl with all speed, Jack that he had plucked it without tearing it much, and Francis that he had lighted and kept up the fire. They had nothing to employ them just then, and I took them with me to have some one to talk to on the phenomenon of the lightning. Below the window I found a large packet of iron wire, which I had brought from Tent House some days before, intending on some leisure day to make a sort of grating before our poultry-yard. By what chance was it here, and hooked by one end to the roof of our house? Some time before I had replaced our cloth canopy by a sort of roof covered with bark nailed upon laths; the cloth still enclosed the sides and front; all was so inflammable, that, but for the providential conductor, we must have been in flames in an instant. I thanked God for our preservation; and little Francis, seeing me so happy, said

"Is it quite true, papa, that this wire has preserved us?"

"Yes, it is true, my darling; and I wish to know what good genius has placed it there, that I may be thankful," said I.

"Ah! father," said my little fellow, "embrace me, but do not thank me; for I did not know that I was doing good."

Astonished at this information, I requested my boy to tell me why and how he had fixed the wire?

"I wanted to reach some figs," said he, "when you and Fritz were at Tent House, and Jack and Ernest were nursing mamma; I wished to do some good for her. I thought she would like some of our sweet figs; but there were none in my reach, and I had no stick long enough to beat them down. I went below, and found that great roll of wire. I tried to break a piece off, but could not; and I then determined to carry the whole up to our dwelling, and to bend one end into a hook, by which I might catch some of the branches, and bring them near me to gather the figs. I was very successful at first, and secured one or two figs. I had my packet of wire on the table by the window, and stood near it myself. I thought I could reach a branch that hung over our roof, loaded with fruit. I leaned forward, and extended my hook to the branch; I felt I had secured it, and joyfully began to pull. You know, papa, they bend, and don't break; but it remained immovable, as well as my hook, which was held by one of the laths of the roof. I pulled with all my strength, and, in my efforts, I struck my foot against the roll of wire, which fell down to the ground without detaching the hook. You may judge how firm it is, for it is no trifling leap from our house to the ground."

"A good work, indeed, my boy," said I, "is yours, for it has saved us. God has inspired you, and has made use of the hand of a child for our preservation. Your conductor shall remain where you have so happily placed it; we may still have need of it. The sky still looks very threatening; let us return to your mother, and take a light with us."

I had contrived a sort of portable lantern, which lighted us in our offices. Moreover, a calibash pierced with small holes, with a candle inside, was placed at the top of the winding staircase, and lighted it entirely, so that we were able to descend without danger by night as well as by day. I was, however, uneasy about the way we should bring my wife down, if we found it necessary to remove her during her sickness; I named it to Fritz.

"Have no uneasiness, father," said he, "Ernest and I are very strong now, and we can carry mamma like a feather."

"You and I might, my dear boy," said I; "but Ernest cannot be of much assistance to us at present."

I then related his misfortune to them. They were distressed and astonished, not comprehending the cause, which I promised to explain. They wished now, however, to see their brother. Fritz then requested, in a low tone of voice, that he might go to Tent House, to see if the vessel and the captain had arrived. Seeing his brothers listening with curiosity, I thought it best to tell them the affair, requesting them, however, not to name it to their mother at present. Jack, who was now about fourteen years of age, listened with the most intense interest, his eyes sparkling with joy and surprise.

"A vessel! people from Europe! Do you think they have come to seek us? Perhaps they are our relations and friends."

"How glad should I be," said Francis, "if my good grandmamma were there; she loved me so much, and was always giving me sweetmeats." This was the mother of my dear wife, from whom she had parted with extreme regret; I knew that a single word from the child would have revived all her sorrows, and would in her present state be dangerous. I therefore forbade him naming such a thing to his mother, even if we mentioned the vessel.

We ascended, and found our dear patient awake, with Ernest at her side, his hand tied up and I returned with an anxious heart to my invalids.

Lesson 44

1. Read chapters 35 and 36 of *Swiss Family Robinson*.
2. Tell someone about the chapters.

Chapter 35

On entering, I found Francis sitting on his mother's bed, telling her the story of the lightning, of the wire which was called *a conductor*, of the figs that he was going to gather for her, and that papa had called him little Francis *the preserver of the whole family*. She soon was in a sweet slumber; the boys followed her example, and I was left alone with my anxieties; happy, however, to see them at rest after such an evening of agitation. When

Ernest awoke, and heard the tempest so terribly augmented, he was almost distracted; all his selfishness, all his indolence disappeared. He entreated me to allow him to go in search of his brothers who had gone out in search of a plant that might be used as a balm for Ernest's hand, and with difficulty I detained him. To convince him that he was not the sole cause of the danger of Fritz and Jack, I related to him, for the first time, the history of the boat and the vessel, and assured him that the great cause of their anxiety to go over to Tent House, was to search for some traces of the unfortunate seamen and their vessel, exposed to that furious sea.

"And Fritz, also, is exposed to that sea," cried Ernest. "I know it; I am sure that he is at this moment in his canoe, struggling against the waves!"

"And Jack, my poor Jack!" sighed I, infected with his fears.

"No, father," added Ernest; "be composed; Fritz will not be so imprudent; he will have left Jack in our house at the rock; and, probably, seeing the hopelessness of his undertaking, he is returned himself now, and is waiting there till the stream subsides a little; do allow me to go, dear father; you have ordered me cold water for my burnt hand, and it will certainly cure it to get well wet."

I could not consent to expose my third son to the tempest, which was now become frightful; the sailcloth which covered our window was torn into a thousand pieces, and carried away; the rain, like a deluge, forced itself into our dwelling, even to the bed where my wife and child were lying. I could neither make up my mind to leave them myself in this perilous situation, nor to spare my boy, who could not even be of any use to his brothers. I commanded him to remain, succeeded in persuading him of their probable safety, and induced him to lie down to rest. Now, in my terrible solitude, I turned to Him, "who tempers the wind to the shorn lamb;" who forbids us not to address Him in the trials he sends us, to beseech Him to soften them, or to give us strength to bear them. Kneeling down, I dared to supplicate Him to restore me my children, submissively adding, after the example of our blessed Saviour, "Yet, not my will, but thine be done, O Lord."

My prayers appeared to be heard; the storm gradually abated, and the day began to break. I awoke Ernest, and having dressed his wounded hand, he set out for Tent House, in search of his brothers. I followed him with my eyes as far as I could see; the whole country appeared one vast lake, and the road to Tent House was like the bed of a river; but, protected by his good gaiters of buffalo-skin, he proceeded fearlessly, and was soon out of my sight.

I was recalled from the window by the voice of my wife, who was awake, and anxiously inquiring for her sons.

At that moment, the dear and well-known voices were heard under the great window.

"Father, I am bringing back my brothers," cried Ernest.

"Yes, papa, we are all alive, and as wet as fishes," added the sweet voice of Jack.

"But not without having had our troubles," said the manly voice of Fritz.

I rushed down the staircase to meet them, and, embracing them, I led them, trembling with emotion, to the bed of their mother, who could not comprehend the transport of joy I expressed.

"Dear Elizabeth," said I, "here are our sons; God has given them to us a second time."

"Have we then been in any danger of losing them?" said she. "What is the meaning of this?"

They saw their mother was unconscious of their long absence, and assured her it was only the storm which had so completely wetted them, that had alarmed me. I hastened to get them to change their clothes, and go to bed a little while to rest themselves; as, however anxious I was myself, I wished to prepare my wife for their recital, and also to tell her of the vessel. Jack would not go till he had produced his bundle of the karata leaves.

"There is enough for six-and-thirty thunderstorms," said he; "and I will prepare them. I have had some experience with my own, and I know the best method."

He soon divided one of the leaves with his knife, after cutting away the triangular thorn from the end, and applied it to his brother's hand, binding it with his handkerchief. Having completed this dressing, he threw off his clothes, and, jumping into his bed, he and his brothers were sound asleep in ten minutes.

I then sat down by my wife, and began my tale; from my first view of the vessel, and my anxious watching for intercourse with it, in order that we might take the opportunity to return to Europe.

"But why should we return to Europe?" said she; "we want nothing here now, since I have got flax, cotton, and a wheel. Our children lead an active, healthy, and innocent life, and live *with us*, which they might not do in the world. For four years we have been happy here, and what shall we find in Europe to compensate us for what we leave here? poverty, war, and none of those things which we have here abundantly."

"But we should find grandmamma," said little Francis; and stopped, recollecting my prohibition.

He had, however, said sufficient to bring tears to his mother's eyes.

"You are right, my darling," said she, "that is my sole regret; but my dear parent was aged and infirm, in all probability I should no longer find her in this world; and if removed to Heaven, she watches over us in this island, as well as if we were in Europe."

After my dear wife had subdued the agitation this remembrance caused her, I pursued the conversation as follows:

Chapter 36

"I see, my dear wife," said I, "that you, as well as the rest of my family, are contented to remain on this island, where it seems it is the will of God for us to dwell, as it is improbable that in such a tempest Captain Johnson would risk approaching the island, if indeed it has not been already fatal to him. I am impatient to learn if Fritz has any tidings of him; for it was on the shore near Tent House that he and Jack passed the night."

"Well done, my good and courageous boys!" said their mother; "they might at any rate have given assistance to them if wrecked."

"You are more courageous than I am, my dear Elizabeth," answered I; "I have passed the whole night mourning for my children, and you think only of the good they might have done to their fellow-creatures."

My sons were awake by this time, and I eagerly inquired if they had discovered any traces of the vessel. Fritz said they had not; but he feared it would never be able to resist the fury of the tempest.

"No, indeed," said Jack; "those mountains of waves, which were not fixtures like other mountains, came full gallop to swallow up Fritz the great, Jack the little, and their fine canoe."

My wife nearly fainted when she heard they had ventured on that terrible sea; and I reminded Fritz that I had forbidden him to do this.

"But you have often said to me, papa," said he, "do unto others as you would they should do unto you; and what a happiness it would have been to us, when our vessel was wrecked, if we had seen a canoe!"

"With two bold men coming to our assistance," said Jack; "but go on with your story, Fritz."

Fritz continued: "We proceeded first to the rocks, and, with some difficulty, and not until Jack had shed some blood in the cause, we secured the karata-leaves, with their ugly thorns at the end. When our sack was full, we proceeded along the rocks towards Tent House. From this height I tried to discover the ship, but the darkness obscured everything. Once I thought I perceived at a great distance a fixed light, which was neither a star nor the lightning, and which I lost sight of occasionally. We had now arrived at the cascade, which, from the noise, seemed much swollen by the rain; our great stones were quite hidden by a boiling foam. I would have attempted to cross, if I had been alone; but, with Jack on my shoulders, I was afraid of the risk. I therefore prepared to follow the course of the river to Family Bridge. The wet ground continually brought us on our knees, and with great difficulty we reached the bridge. But judge of our consternation! the river had risen so much that the planks were covered, and, as we conceived, the whole was destroyed. I then told Jack to return to Falcon's Nest with the karata-leaves, and I would swim across the river. I returned about a hundred yards up the stream to find a wider and less rapid part, and easily crossed. Judge of my surprise when I saw a human figure approaching to meet me; I had no doubt it was the captain of the vessel, and-"

"And it was Captain Jack," said the bold little fellow. "I was determined not to return home a poltroon who was afraid of the water." When Fritz was gone, I tried the bridge, and soon found there was not sufficient water over it to risk my being drowned. I took off my boots, which might have made me slip, and my cloak, which was too heavy, and, making a dart, I ran with all my strength across, and reached the other side. I put on my boots, which I had in my hands, and advanced to meet Fritz, who called out, as soon as he saw me, "Is it you, captain?" I tried to say, "Yes, certainly," in a deep tone, but my laughter betrayed me.

"To my great regret;" said Fritz, "I should truly have preferred meeting Captain Johnson; but I fear he and his people are at the bottom of the sea. After meeting with Jack, we proceeded to Tent House, where we kindled a good fire, and dried ourselves a little. We then refreshed ourselves with some wine which remained on the table where you had entertained the captain, and proceeded to prepare a signal to inform the vessel we were ready to receive them. We procured a thick bamboo cane from the magazine; I fixed firmly to one end of it the large lantern of the fish's bladder you gave us to take; I filled the lamp with oil, and placed in it a thick cotton-wick, which, when lighted, was very brilliant. Jack and I then placed it on the shore, at the entrance of the bay. We fixed it before the rock, where the land-wind would not reach it, sunk it three or four feet into the ground, steadied it with stones, and then went to rest over our fire, after this long and difficult labour. After drying ourselves a little, we set out on our return, when, looking towards the sea, we were startled by the appearance of the same light we had noticed before; we heard, at the same time, the distant report of a gun, which was repeated three or four times at irregular intervals. We were persuaded that it was the vessel calling to us for aid, and, remembering the command of our Saviour, we thought you would forgive our disobedience if we presented to you in the morning the captain, the lieutenant, and as many as our canoe would contain. We entered it then without any fear, for you know how light and well-balanced it is; and, rowing into the bay, the sail was spread to the wind, and we had no more trouble. I then took the helm; my own signal-light shone clearly on the shore; and, *except* for the rain which fell in torrents, the waves which washed over our canoe, and uneasiness about the ship and about you, and our fear that the wind might carry us into the open sea, we should have had a delightful little maritime excursion. When we got out of the bay, I perceived the wind was driving us towards Shark's Island, which, being directly before the bay, forms two entrances to it. I intended to go round it, and disembark there, if possible, that I might look out for some trace of the ship, but we found this impossible; the sea ran too high; besides, we should have been unable to moor our canoe, the island not affording a single tree or anything we could lash it to, and the waves would soon have carried it away. We had now lost sight of the light, and hearing no more signals, I began to think on your distress when we did not arrive at the hour we promised. I therefore resolved to return by the other side of the bay, carefully avoiding the current, which would have carried us into the open sea. I lowered the sail by means of the ropes you had fixed to it, and we rowed into port. We carefully moored the canoe, and, without returning to Tent House, took the road home. We crossed the bridge as Jack had done, found the waterproof cloak and bag of karata-leaves where he had left them, and soon after met Ernest. As it was daylight, I did not take him for the captain, but knew him immediately, and felt the deepest remorse when I heard from him in what anxiety and anguish you had passed the night. Our enterprise was imprudent, and altogether useless; but we might have saved life, which would have been an ample remuneration. I fear all is hopeless. What do you think, father, of their fate?"

"I hope they are far from this dangerous coast," said I; "but if still in our neighbourhood, we will do all we can to assist them. As soon as the tempest is subsided, we will take the pinnace and sail round the island. You have long urged me to this, Fritz; and who knows but on the opposite side we may find some traces of our own poor sailors, perhaps even meet with them?"

The weather gradually clearing, I called my sons to go out with me. My wife earnestly besought me not to venture on the sea; I assured her it was not sufficiently calm, but we must examine our plantations, to ascertain what damage was done, and at the same time we might look out for some traces of the wreck; besides, our animals were becoming clamorous for food; therefore, leaving Ernest with her, we descended to administer in the first place to their wants.

Lesson 45

1. Read chapter 37 of *Swiss Family Robinson*.
2. Tell someone about what is happening in the book.

Chapter 37

Our animals were impatiently expecting us; they had been neglected during the storm, and were ill-supplied with food, besides being half-sunk in water. The ducks and the flamingo liked it well enough, and were swimming comfortably in the muddy water; but the quadrupeds were complaining aloud, each in his own proper language, and making a frightful confusion of sounds. *Valiant*, especially, the name Francis had bestowed on the calf I had given him to bring up, bleated incessantly for his young master, and could not be quieted till he came. It is wonderful how this child, only twelve years old, had tamed and attached this animal; though sometimes so fierce, with him he was mild as a lamb. The boy rode on his back, guiding him with a little stick, with which he just touched the side of his neck as he wished him to move; but if his brothers had ventured to mount, they would have been certainly thrown off. A pretty sight was our cavalry: Fritz on his handsome donkey, Jack on his huge buffalo, and Francis on his young bull. There was nothing left for Ernest but the donkey, and its slow and peaceful habits suited him very well.

Francis ran up to his favourite, who showed his delight at seeing him as well as he was able, and at the first summons followed his master from the stable. Fritz brought out *Lightfoot*, Jack his buffalo, and I followed with the cow and the ass. We left them to sport about at liberty on the humid earth, till we removed the water from their stable, and supplied them with fresh food. We then drove them in, considering it advisable to pursue our expedition on foot, lest the bridge should still be overflowed. Francis was the superintendent of the fowls, and knew every little chicken by name; he called them out and scattered their food for them, and soon had his beautiful and noisy family fluttering round him.

After having made all our animals comfortable, and given them their breakfast, we began to think of our own. Francis made a fire and warmed some chicken broth for his mother; for ourselves, we were contented with some new milk, some salt herrings, and cold potatoes. I had often searched in my excursions for the precious *bread-fruit* tree, so highly spoken of by modern travellers, which I had hoped might be found in our island, from its favourable situation; but I had hitherto been unsuccessful. We were unable to procure the blessing of *bread*, our ship biscuit had long been exhausted, and though we had sown our European corn, we had not yet reaped any.

After we had together knelt down to thank God for his merciful protection through the terrors of the past night, and besought him to continue it, we prepared to set out. The waves still ran high, though the wind had subsided, and we determined merely to go along the shore, as the roads still continued impassable from the rain, and the sand was easier to walk on than the wet grass; besides, our principal motive for the excursion was to search for any traces of a recent shipwreck. At first we could discover nothing, even with the telescope; but Fritz, mounting a high rock, fancied he discovered something floating towards the island. He besought me to allow him to take the canoe, which was still where he left it the preceding night. As the bridge was now easy to cross, I consented, only insisting on accompanying him to assist in managing it. Jack, who was much afraid of being left behind, was the first to leap in and seize an oar. There was, however, no need of it; I steered my little boat into the current, and we were carried away with such velocity as almost to take our breath. Fritz was at the helm, and appeared to have no fear; I will not say that his father was so tranquil. I held Jack, for fear of accidents, but he only laughed, and observed to his brother that the canoe galloped better than Lightfoot.

We were soon in the open sea, and directed our canoe towards the object we had remarked, and which we still had in sight. We were afraid it was the boat upset, but it proved to be a tolerably large cask, which had probably been thrown overboard to lighten the distressed vessel; we saw several others, but neither mast nor plank to give us any idea that the vessel and boat had perished. Fritz wished much to have made the circuit of the island, to assure ourselves of this, but I would not hear of it; I thought of my wife's terror; besides, the sea was still too rough for our frail bark, and we had, moreover, no provisions. If my canoe had not been well built, it would have run great risk of being overset by the waves, which broke over it. Jack, when he saw one coming, lay down on his face, saying he preferred having them on his back rather than in his mouth; he jumped up as soon as it passed, to help to empty the canoe, till another wave came to fill it again; but, thanks to my out-riggers, we preserved our balance very well, and I consented to go as far as *Cape Disappointment*, which merited the name a second time, for we found no trace here of the vessel, though we mounted the hill, and thus commanded a wide extent of view. As we looked round the country, it appeared completely devastated: trees torn up by the roots, plantations levelled with the ground, water collected into absolute lakes, all announced desolation; and the tempest seemed to be renewing.

The sky was darkened, the wind arose, and was unfavourable for our return; nor could I venture the canoe on the waves, every instant becoming more formidable. We moored our bark to a large palm-tree we found at the foot of the hill, near the shore, and set out by land to our home. We crossed the Gourd Wood and the Wood of Monkeys, and arrived at our farm, which we found, to our great satisfaction, had not suffered much from the storm. The food we had left in the stables was nearly consumed; from which we concluded that the animals we had left here had sheltered themselves during the storm. We refilled the mangers with the hay we had preserved in the loft, and observing the sky getting more and more threatening, we set out without delay for our house, from which we were yet a considerable distance. To avoid *Flamingo Marsh*, which was towards the sea, and *Rice Marsh*, towards the rock, we determined to go through *Cotton Wood*, which would save us from the wind, which was ready to blow us off our feet. I was still uneasy about the ship, which the lieutenant had told me was out of repair; but I indulged a hope that they might have taken refuge in some bay, or found anchorage on some hospitable shore, where they might get their vessel into order.

Jack was alarmed lest they should fall into the hands of the *anthropophagi*, who eat men like hares or sheep, of whom he had read in some book of travels, and excited the ridicule of his brother, who was astonished at his ready belief of travellers' tales, which he asserted were usually false.

"But Robinson Crusoe would not tell a falsehood," said Jack, indignantly; "and there were cannibals came to his island, and were going to eat Friday, if he had not saved him."

"Oh! Robinson could not tell a falsehood," said Fritz, "because he never existed. The whole history is a romance. Is not that the name, father, that is given to works of the imagination?"

"It is," said I; "but we must not call Robinson Crusoe a romance; though Robinson himself, and all the circumstances of his history are probably fictitious, the details are all founded on truth on the adventures and descriptions of voyagers who may be depended on, and unfortunate individuals who have actually been wrecked on unknown shores. If ever our journal should be printed, many may believe that it is only a romance a mere work of the imagination."

My boys hoped we should not have to introduce any natives into our romance, and were astonished that an island so beautiful had not tempted any to inhabit it; in fact, I had often been myself surprised at this circumstance; but I told them many voyagers had noticed islands apparently fertile, and yet uninhabited; besides, the chain of rocks which surrounded this might prevent the approach of natives, unless they had discovered the little *Bay of Safety* where we had landed. Fritz said he anxiously desired to circumnavigate the island, in order to ascertain the size of it, and if there were similar chains of rocks on the opposite side. I promised him, as soon as the stormy weather was past, and his mother well enough to remove to Tent House, we would take our pinnace, and set out on our little voyage.

We now approached the marsh, and he begged me to let him go and cut some canes, as he projected making a sort of carriage for his mother. As we were collecting them, he explained his scheme to me. He wished to weave of these reeds, which were very strong, a large and long sort of pannier, in which his mother might sit or recline, and which might be suspended between two strong bamboo-canes by handles of rope. He then purposed to yoke two of our most gentle animals, the cow and the ass, the one before and the other behind, between these shafts, the leader to be mounted by one of the children as director; the other would follow naturally, and the good mother would thus be carried, as if in a litter, without any danger of jolting. I was pleased with this idea, and we all set to work to load ourselves each with a huge burden of reeds. They requested me not to tell my wife, that they might give her an agreeable surprise. It needed such affection as ours to induce us to the undertaking in such unpropitious weather. It rained in torrents, and the marsh was so soft and wet, that we were in danger of sinking at every step. However, I could not be less courageous than my sons, whom nothing daunted, and we soon made up our bundles, and, placing them on our heads, they formed a sort of umbrella, which was not without its benefits. We soon arrived at Falcon's Nest. Before we reached the tree, I saw a fire shine to such a distance, that I was alarmed; but soon found it was only meant for our benefit by our kind friends at home. When my wife saw the rain falling, she had instructed her little assistant to make a fire in our usual cooking-place, at a little distance from the tree, and protected by a canopy of waterproof cloth from the rain. The young cook had not only kept up a good fire to dry us on our return, but had taken the opportunity of roasting two dozen of those excellent little birds which his mother had preserved in butter, and which, all ranged on the old sword which served us for a spit, were just ready on our arrival, and the fire and feast were equally grateful to the hungry, exhausted, and wet travellers, who sat down to enjoy them.

However, before we sat down to our repast, we went up to see our invalids, whom we found tolerably well, though anxious for our return. I then returned to the fire to dry myself, and to enjoy my repast. Besides the birds, Francis had prepared fresh eggs and potatoes for us. He told me that his mamma had given up her office of cook to him, and assured me that he would perform the duties to our satisfaction, provided he was furnished with materials. Fritz was to hunt, Jack to fish, I was to order dinner, and he would make it ready. "And when we have neither game nor fish," said Jack, "we will attack your poultry-yard." This was not at all to the taste of poor little Francis, who could not bear his favourites to be killed, and who had actually wept over the chicken that was *slaughtered* to make broth for his mother. We were obliged to promise him that, when other resources failed, we would apply to our barrels of salt-fish. He, however, gave us leave to dispose as we liked of the ducks and geese, which were too noisy for him.

After we had concluded our repast, we carried a part of it to our friends above, and proceeded to give them an account of our expedition. I then secured the hammocks somewhat more firmly, to save us from the storm that was still raging, and the hour of rest being at hand, my sons established themselves on mattresses of cotton, made by their kind mother, and in spite of the roaring of the winds, we were soon in profound repose.

Lesson 46

1. Read chapter 38 of *Swiss Family Robinson*.
2. Look for a word in today's reading that you don't know. Guess at its meaning based on the context
3. Look up its definition or ask someone its meaning.

Chapter 38

The storm continued to rage the whole of the following day, and even the day after, with the same violence. Happily our tree stood firm, though several branches were broken; amongst others, that to which Francis's wire was suspended. I replaced it with more care, carried it beyond our roof, and fixed at the extremity the pointed instrument which had attracted the lightning. I then substituted for the hammocks before the window, strong planks, which remained from my building, and which my sons assisted me to raise with pulleys, after having sawed them to the proper length. Through these I made loop-holes, to admit the light and air. In order to carry off the rain, I fixed a sort of spout, made of the wood of a tree I had met with, which was unknown to me, though apparently somewhat like the elder. The whole of the tree, almost to the bark, was filled up with a sort of pith, easily removed. From this tree I made the pipes for our fountain, and the remainder was now useful for these rain-spouts. I employed those days in which I could not go out, in separating the seeds and grain, of which I saw we should have need, and in mending our work-tools; my sons, in the mean time, nestled under the tree among the roots, were incessantly employed in the construction of the carriage for their mother. The karatas had nearly completed the cure of Ernest's hand, and he was able to assist his brothers preparing the canes, which Fritz and Jack wove between the flat wooden wands, with which they had made the frame of their pannier; they succeeded in making it so strong and close, that they might have carried liquids in it. My dear wife's foot and leg were gradually improving; and I took the opportunity of her confinement, to reason with her on her false notion of the dangers of the sea, and to represent to her the gloomy prospect of our sons, if they were left alone in the island. She agreed with me, but could not resolve to leave it; she hoped God would send some vessel to us, which might leave us some society; and after all, if our sons were left, she pointed out to me, that they had our beautiful pinnace, and might at any time, of their own accord, leave the island.

"And why should we anticipate the evils of futurity, my dear friend?" said she. "Let us think only of the present. I am anxious now to know if the storm has spared my fine kitchen-garden."

"You must wait a little," said I. "I am as uneasy as you, for my maize-plantations, my sugar-canes, and my corn-fields."

At last, one night, the storm ceased, the clouds passed away, and the moon showed herself in all her glory. How delighted we were! My wife got me to remove the large planks I had placed before the opening, and the bright moonbeams streamed through the branches of the tree into our room; a gentle breeze refreshed us, and so delighted were we in gazing on that sky of promise, that we could scarcely bear to go to bed, but spent half the night in projects for the morrow; the good mother alone said, that she could not join in our excursions. Jack and Francis smiled at each other, as they thought of their litter, which was now nearly finished.

A bright sun awoke us early next morning. Fritz and Jack had requested me to allow them to finish their carriage; so, leaving Ernest with his mother, I took Francis with me to ascertain the damage done to the garden at Tent House, about which his mother was so anxious. We easily crossed the bridge, but the water had carried away some of the planks; however, my little boy leaped from one plank to another with great agility, though the distance was sometimes considerable. He was so proud of being my sole companion, that he scarcely touched the ground as he ran on before me; but he had a sad shock when he got to the garden; of which we could not find the slightest trace. All was destroyed; the walks, the fine vegetable-beds, the plantations of pines and melons all had vanished. Francis stood like a marble statue, as pale and still; till, bursting into tears, he recovered himself.

"Oh! my good mamma," said he; "what will she say when she hears of this misfortune? But she need not know it, papa," added he, after a pause; "it would distress her too much; and if you and my brothers will help me, we will repair the damage before she can walk. The plants may not be so large; but the earth is moist, and they will grow quickly, and I will work hard to get it into order."

I embraced my dear boy, and promised him this should be our first work. I feared we should have many other disasters to repair; but a child of twelve years old gave me an example of resignation and courage. We agreed to come next day to begin our labour, for the garden was too well situated for me to abandon it. It was on a gentle declivity, at the foot of the rocks, which sheltered it from the north wind, and was conveniently watered from the cascade. I resolved to add a sort of bank, or terrace, to protect it from the violent rains; and Francis was so pleased with the idea, that he began to gather the large stones which were scattered over the garden, and to carry them to the place where I wished to build my terrace. He would have worked all day, if I would have allowed him; but I wanted to look after my young plantations, my sugar-canes, and my fields, and, after the destruction I had just witnessed, I had everything to fear. I proceeded to the avenue of fruit-trees that led to Tent House, and was agreeably surprised. All were half-bowed to the ground, as well as the bamboos that supported them, but few were torn up; and I saw that my sons and I, with the labour of two or three days, could restore them. Some of them had already begun to bear fruit, but all was destroyed for this year. This was, however, a trifling loss, compared with what I had anticipated; for, having no more plants of European fruits, I could not have replaced them. Besides, having resolved to inhabit Tent House at present, entirely, being there defended from storms, it was absolutely necessary to contrive some protection from the heat. My new plantations afforded little shade yet, and I trembled to propose to my wife to come and inhabit these burning rocks. Francis was gathering some of the beautiful unknown flowers of the island for his mother, and when he had formed his bouquet, bringing it to me,

"See, papa," said he, "how the rain has refreshed these flowers. I wish it would rain still, it is so dreadfully hot here. Oh! if we had but a little shade."

"That is just what I was thinking of, my dear," said I; "we shall have shade enough when my trees are grown; but, in the mean time-?"

"In the mean time, papa," said Francis, "I will tell you what you must do. You must make a very long, broad colonnade before our house, covered with cloth, and open before, so that mamma may have air and shade at once."

I was pleased with my son's idea, and promised him to construct a gallery soon, and call it the *Franciade* in honour of him. My little boy was delighted that his suggestion should be thus approved, and begged me not to tell his mamma, as he wished to surprise her, as much as his brothers did with their carriage; and he hoped the *Franciade* might be finished before she visited Tent House. I assured him I would be silent; and we took the road hence, talking about our new colonnade. I projected making it in the most simple and easy way. A row of strong bamboo-canes planted at equal distances along the front of our house, and united by a plank of wood at the top cut into arches between the canes; others I would place sloping from the rock, to which I would fasten them by iron cramps; these were to be covered with sailcloth, prepared with the elastic gum, and well secured to the plank. This building would not take much time, and I anticipated the pleasure of my wife when she found out that it was an invention of her little favourite, who, of a mild and reflecting disposition, was beloved by us all. As we walked along, we saw something approaching, that Francis soon discovered to be his brothers, with their new carriage; and, concluding that his mamma occupied it, he hastened to meet them, lest they should proceed to the garden. But on our approach, we discovered that Ernest was in the litter, which was borne by the cow before, on which Fritz was mounted, and by the ass behind, with Jack on it. Ernest declared the conveyance was so easy and delightful that he should often take his mother's place.

"I like that very much," said Jack; "then I will take care that we will harness the donkey and the buffalo for you, and they will give you a pretty jolting, I promise you. The cow and ass are only for mamma. Look, papa, is it not complete? We wished to try it as soon as we finished it, so we got Ernest to occupy it, while mother was asleep."

Ernest declared it only wanted two cushions, one to sit upon, the other to recline against, to make it perfect; and though I could not help smiling at his love of ease, I encouraged the notion, in order to delay my wife's excursion till our plans were completed. I then put Francis into the carriage beside his brother; and ordering Fritz and Jack to proceed with their equipage to inspect our corn-fields, I returned to my wife, who was still sleeping. On her awaking, I told her the garden and plantations would require a few days' labour to set them in order, and I should leave Ernest, who was not yet in condition to be a labourer, to nurse her and read to her. My sons returned in the evening, and gave me a melancholy account of our corn-fields; the corn was completely destroyed, and we regretted this the more, as we had very little left for seed. We had anticipated a feast of *real bread*, but we were obliged to give up all hope for this year, and to content ourselves with our cakes of cassava, and with potatoes. The maize had suffered less, and might have been a resource for us, but the large, hard grain was so very difficult to reduce to flour fine enough for dough. Fritz often recurred to the necessity of building a mill near the cascade at Tent House; but this was not the work of a moment, and we had time to consider of it; for at present we had no corn to grind. As I found Francis had let his brothers into all our secrets, it was agreed that I, with Fritz, Jack, and Francis, should proceed to Tent House next morning. Francis desired to be of the party, that he might direct the laying out of the garden, he said, with an important air, as he had been his mother's assistant on its formation. We arranged our bag of vegetable-seeds, and having bathed my wife's foot with a simple embrocation, we offered our united prayers, and retired to our beds to prepare ourselves for the toils of the next day.

Lesson 47

1. Read chapter 39 of *Swiss Family Robinson*.
2. Copy part of descriptive sentence. Puts quotation marks around it. Label it with the book title and chapter number.
3. Tell someone about the chapter.

Chapter 39

We rose early; and, after our usual morning duties, we left our invalids for the whole day, taking with us, for our dinner, a goose and some potatoes, made ready the evening before. We harnessed the bull and the buffalo to the cart, and I sent Fritz and Jack to the wood of bamboos, with orders to load the cart with as many as it would contain; and, especially, to select some very thick ones for my colonnade; the rest I intended for props for my young trees; and this I proposed to be my first undertaking. Francis would have preferred beginning with the *Franciade*, or the garden, but he was finally won over by the thoughts of the delicious fruits, which we might lose by our neglect; the peaches, plums, pears, and, above all, the cherries, of which he was very fond. He then consented to assist me in holding the trees whilst I replaced the roots; after which he went to cut the reeds to tie them. Suddenly I heard him cry, "Papa, papa, here is a large chest come for us; come and take it." I ran to him, and saw it was the very chest we had seen floating, and which we had taken for the boat at a distance; the waves had left it in our bay, entangled in the reeds, which grew abundantly here. It was almost buried in the sand. We could not remove it alone, and, notwithstanding our curiosity, we were compelled to wait for the arrival of my sons. We returned to our work, and it was pretty well advanced when the tired and hungry party returned with their cart-load of bamboos. We rested, and sat down to eat our goose. Guavas and sweet acorns, which had escaped the storm, and which my sons brought, completed our repast. Fritz had killed a large bird in the marsh, which I took at first for a young flamingo; but it was a young cassowary, the first I had seen in the island. This bird is remarkable for its extraordinary size, and for its plumage, so short and fine that it seems rather to be hair than feathers. I should have liked to have had it alive to ornament our poultry-yard, and it was so young we might have tamed it; but Fritz's unerring aim had killed it at once. I wished to let my wife see this rare bird, which, if standing on its webbed feet, would have been four feet high; I therefore forbade them to meddle with it.

As we ate, we talked of the chest, and our curiosity being stronger than our hunger, we swallowed our repast hastily, and then ran down to the shore. We were obliged to plunge into the water up to the waist, and then had some difficulty to extricate it from the weed and slime, and to push it on shore. No sooner had we placed it in safety than Fritz, with a strong hatchet, forced it open, and we all eagerly crowded to see the contents. Fritz hoped it would be powder and fire-arms; Jack, who was somewhat fond of dress, and had notions of elegance, declared in favour of clothes, and particularly of linen, finer and whiter than that which his mother wove; if Ernest had been there, books would have been his desire; for my own part, there was nothing I was more anxious for than European seeds, particularly corn; Francis had a lingering wish that the chest might contain some of those gingerbread cakes which his grandmamma used to treat him with in Europe, and which he had often regretted; but he kept this wish to himself, for fear his brothers should call him "little glutton," and assured us that he should like a little pocket-knife, with a small saw, better than anything in the world; and he was the only one who had his wish. The chest was opened, and we saw that it was filled with a number of trifling things likely to tempt these nations, and to become the means of exchange, principally glass and iron ware, coloured beads, pins, needles, looking-glasses, children's toys, constructed as models, such as carts, and tools of every sort; amongst which we found some likely to be useful, such as hatchets, saws, planes, gimlets, etc.; besides a collection of knives, of which Francis had the choice; and scissors, which were reserved for mamma, her own being nearly worn out. I had, moreover, the pleasure of finding a quantity of nails of every size and kind, besides iron hooks, staples, &c, which I needed greatly. After we had examined the contents, and selected what we wanted immediately, we closed up the chest, and conveyed it to our magazine at Tent House. We had spent so much time in our examination, that we had some difficulty to finish propping our trees, and to arrive at home before it was dark. We found my wife somewhat uneasy at our lengthened absence, but our appearance soon calmed her. "Mother," said I, "I have brought back all your chickens to crowd under your wing."

"And we have not come back empty-handed," said Jack. "Look, mamma; here are a beautiful pair of scissors, a large paper of needles, another of pins, and a thimble! How rich you are now! And when you get well, you can make me a pretty waistcoat and a pair of trousers, for I am in great want of them."

"And I, mamma," said Francis, "have brought you a mirror, that you may arrange your cap; you have often been sorry papa did not remember to bring one from the ship. This was intended for the natives, and I will begin with you."

"I believe I rather resemble one now," said my good Elizabeth, arranging the red and yellow silk handkerchief which she usually wore on her head.

"Only, mamma," said Jack, "when you wear the comical pointed bonnet which Ernest made you."

"What matters it," said she, "whether it be pointed or round? It will protect me from the sun, and it is the work of my Ernest, to whom I am much obliged."

Ernest, with great ingenuity and patience, had endeavoured to plait his mother a bonnet of the rice-straw; he had succeeded; but not knowing how to form the round crown, he was obliged to finish it in a point, to the great and incessant diversion of his brothers.

"Mother," said Ernest, in his usual grave and thoughtful tone, "I should not like you to look like a native; therefore, as soon as I regain the use of my hand, my first work shall be to make you a bonnet, which I will take care shall be formed with a round crown, as you will lend me one of your large needles, and I will take, to sew the crown on, the head of either Jack or Francis."

"What do you mean? My head!" said they both together.

"Oh, I don't mean to take it off your shoulders," said he; "it will only be necessary that one of you should kneel down before me, for a day perhaps, while I use your head as a model; and you need not cry out much if I should chance to push my needle in."

This time the philosopher had the laugh on his side, and his tormentors were silenced.

We now explained to my wife where we had found the presents we had brought her. My offerings to her were a light axe, which she could use to cut her fire-wood with, and an iron kettle, smaller and more convenient than the one she had. Fritz had retired, and now came in dragging with difficulty his huge cassowary. "Here, mamma," said he, "I have brought you a little chicken for your dinner;" and the astonishment and laughter again commenced. The rest of the evening was spent in plucking the bird, to prepare part of it for next day. We then retired to rest, that we might begin our labour early next morning. Ernest chose to remain with his books and his mother, for whom he formed with the mattresses a sort of reclining chair, in which she was able to sit up in bed and sew. Thus she endured a confinement of six weeks, without complaint, and in that time got all our clothes put into good order. Francis had nearly betrayed our secret once, by asking his mamma to make him a mason's apron. "A mason's apron!" said she; "are you going to build a house, child?"

"I meant to say a gardener's apron," said he.

His mamma was satisfied, and promised to comply with his request.

In the mean time, my three sons and I laboured assiduously to get the garden into order again, and to raise the terraces, which we hoped might be a defence against future storms. Fritz had also proposed to me to construct a stone conduit, to bring the water to our kitchen-garden from the river, to which we might carry it back, after it had passed round our vegetable-beds. This was a formidable task, but too useful an affair to be neglected; and, aided by the geometrical skill of Fritz, and the ready hands of my two younger boys, the conduit was completed. I took an opportunity, at the same time, to dig a pond above the garden, into which the conduit poured the water; this was always warm with the sun, and, by means of a sluice, we were able to disperse it in little channels to water the garden. The pond would also be useful to preserve small fish and crabs for use. We next proceeded to our embankment. This was intended to protect the garden from any extraordinary overflow of the river, and from the water running from the rocks after heavy rains. We then laid out our garden on the same plan as before, except that I made the walks wider, and not so flat; I carried one directly to our house, which, in the autumn, I intended to plant with shrubs, that my wife might have a shady avenue to approach her garden; where I also planned an arbour, furnished with seats, as a resting-place for her. The rocks were covered with numerous climbing plants, bearing every variety of elegant flower, and I had only to make my selection.

All this work, with the enclosing the garden with palisades of bamboo, occupied us about a fortnight, in which time our invalids made great progress towards their recovery. After the whole was finished, Francis entreated me to begin his gallery. My boys approved of my plan, and Fritz declared that the house was certainly comfortable and commodious, but that it would be wonderfully improved by a colonnade, with a little pavilion at each end, and a fountain in each pavilion.

"I never heard a word of these pavilions," said I.

"No," said Jack, "they are our own invention. The colonnade will be called the *Franciade*; and we wish our little pavilions to be named, the one *Fritzia*, the other *Jackia*, if you please."

I agreed to this reasonable request, and only begged to know how they would procure water for their fountains. Fritz undertook to bring the water, if I would only assist them in completing this little scheme, to give pleasure to their beloved mother. I was charmed to see the zeal and anxiety of my children to oblige their tender mother. Her illness seemed to have strengthened their attachment; they thought only how to console and amuse her. She sometimes told me she really blessed the accident, which had taught her how much she was valued by all around her.

Lesson 48

1. Read chapter 40 of *Swiss Family Robinson*.
2. Tell someone about what happened in this chapter.

Chapter 40

The next day was Sunday, our happy Sabbath for repose and quiet conversation at home. After passing the day in our usual devotions and sober reading, my three elder boys requested my permission to walk towards our farm in the evening. On their return, they informed me it would be necessary to give a few days' labour to our plantations of maize and potatoes. I therefore determined to look to them.

Though I was out early next morning, I found Fritz and Jack had been gone some time, leaving only the ass in the stables, which I secured for my little Francis. I perceived, also, that they had dismounted my cart, and carried away the wheels, from which I concluded that they had met with some tree in their walk the preceding evening, suitable for the pipes for their fountains, and that they had now returned to cut it down, and convey it to Tent House. As I did not know where to meet with them, I proceeded with Francis on the ass to commence his favourite work. I drew my plan on the ground first. At the distance of twelve feet from the rock which formed the front of our house, I marked a straight line of fifty feet, which I divided into ten spaces of five feet each for my colonnade; the two ends were to be reserved for the two pavilions my sons wished to build. I was busy in my calculations, and Francis placing stakes in the places where I wished to dig, when the cart drove up with our two good labourers. They had, as I expected, found the evening before a species of pine, well adapted for their pipes. They had cut down four, of fifteen or twenty feet in length, which they had brought on the wheels of the cart, drawn by the four animals. They had had some difficulty in transporting them to the place; and the greatest still remained the boring the trunks, and then uniting them firmly. I had neither augers nor any tools fit for the purpose. I had, certainly, constructed a little fountain at Falcon's Nest; but the stream was near at hand, and was easily conveyed by cane pipes to our tortoise-shell basin. Here the distance was considerable, the ground unequal, and, to have the water pure and cool, underground pipes were necessary. I thought of large bamboos, but Fritz pointed out the knots, and the difficulty of joining the pieces, and begged me to leave it to him, as he had seen fountains made in Switzerland, and had no fears of success. In the mean time, all hands set to work at the arcade. We selected twelve bamboos of equal height and thickness, and fixed them securely in the earth, at five feet from each other. These formed a pretty colonnade, and were work enough for one day.

We took care to divert all inquiries at night, by discussing the subjects which our invalids had been reading during the day. The little library of our captain was very choice; besides the voyages and travels, which interested them greatly, there was a good collection of historians, and some of the best poets, for which Ernest had no little taste. However, he requested earnestly that he might be of our party next day, and Francis, good-naturedly, offered to stay with mamma, expecting, no doubt, Ernest's congratulations on the forward state of the Franciade. The next morning Ernest and I set out, his brothers having preceded us. Poor Ernest regretted, as we went, that he had no share in these happy schemes for his mother. I reminded him, however, of his dutiful care of her during her sickness, and all his endeavours to amuse her. "And, besides," added I, "did you not make her a straw bonnet?"

"Yes," said he, "and I now remember what a frightful shape it was. I will try to make a better, and will go to-morrow morning to choose my straw."

As we approached Tent House, we heard a most singular noise, echoing at intervals amongst the rocks. We soon discovered the cause; in a hollow of the rocks I saw a very hot fire, which Jack was blowing through a cane, whilst Fritz was turning amidst the embers a bar of iron. When it was red hot, they laid it on an anvil I had brought from the ship, and struck it alternately with hammers to bring it to a point.

"Well done, my young smiths," said I; "we ought to try all things, and keep what is good. Do you expect to succeed in making your auger? I suppose that is what you want."

"Yes, father," said Fritz; "we should succeed well enough if we only had a good pair of bellows; you see we have already got a tolerable point."

Now Fritz could not believe anything was impossible. He had killed a kangaroo the evening before, and skinned it. The flesh made us a dinner; of the skin he determined to make a pair of bellows. He nailed it, with the hair out, not having time to tan it, to two flat pieces of wood, with holes in them; to this he added a reed for the pipe; he then fixed it by means of a long cord and a post, to the side of his fire, and Jack, with his hand or his foot, blew the fire, so that the iron was speedily red hot, and quite malleable. I then showed them how to twist the iron into a screw, rather clumsy, but which would answer the purpose tolerably well. At one end they formed a ring, in which we placed a piece of wood transversely, to enable them to turn the screw. We then made a trial of it. We placed a tree on two props, and Fritz and I managed the auger so well, that we had our tree pierced through in a very little time, working first at one end and then at the other. Jack, in the mean time, collected the shavings we made, which he deposited in the kitchen for his mother's use, to kindle the fire. Ernest, meanwhile, was walking about, making observations, and giving his advice to his brothers on the architecture of their pavilions, till, seeing they were going to bore another tree, he retired into the garden to see the embankment. He returned delighted with the improvements, and much disposed to take some employment. He wanted to assist in boring the tree, but we could not all work at it. I undertook this labour myself, and sent him to blow the bellows, while his brothers laboured at the forge, the work not being too hard for his lame hand.

My young smiths were engaged in flattening the iron to make joints to unite their pipes; they succeeded very well, and then began to dig the ground to lay them. Ernest, knowing something of geometry and land-surveying, was able to give them some useful hints, which enabled them to complete their work successfully. Leaving them to do this, I employed myself in covering in my long colonnade. After I had placed on my columns a plank cut in arches, which united them, and was firmly nailed to them, I extended from it bamboos, placed sloping against the rock, and secured to it by cramps of iron, the work of my young smiths. When my bamboo roof was solidly fixed, the canes as close as possible, I filled the interstices with a clay I found near the river, and poured gum over it; I had thus an impervious and brilliant roof, which appeared to be varnished, and striped green and brown. I then raised the floor a foot, in order that there might be no damp, and paved it with the square stones I had preserved when we cut the rock. It must be understood that all this was the work of many days. I was assisted by Jack and Fritz, and by Ernest and Francis alternately, one always remaining with his mother, who was still unable to walk.

Ernest employed his time, when at home, in making the straw bonnet, without either borrowing his brother's head for a model, or letting any of them know what he was doing. Nevertheless, he assisted his brothers with their pavilions by his really valuable knowledge. They formed them very elegantly, something like a Chinese pagoda. They were exactly square, supported on four columns, and rather higher than the gallery. The roofs terminated in a point, and resembled *a large parasol*. The fountains were in the middle; the basins, breast-high, were formed of the shells of two turtles from our reservoir, which were mercilessly sacrificed for the purpose, and furnished our table abundantly for some days. They succeeded the cassowary, which had supplied us very seasonably: its flesh tasted like beef, and made excellent soup.

But to return to the fountains. Ernest suggested the idea of ornamenting the end of the perpendicular pipe, which brought the water to the basin, with shells; every sort might be collected on the shore, of the most brilliant colours, and curious and varied shapes. He was passionately devoted to natural history, and had made a collection of these, endeavouring to classify them from the descriptions he met with in the books of voyages and travels. Some of these, of the most dazzling beauty, were placed round the pipe, which had been plastered with clay; from thence the water was received into a *volute*, shaped like an antique urn, and again was poured gracefully into the large turtle-shell; a small channel conveyed it then out of the pavilions. The whole was completed in less time than I could have imagined, and greatly surpassed my expectations; conferring an inestimable advantage on our dwelling, by securing us from the heat.

All honour was rendered to Master Francis, the inventor, and *The Franciade* was written in large letters on the middle arch; *Fritzia* and *Jackia* were written in the same way over the pavilions. Ernest alone was not named; and he seemed somewhat affected by it. He had acquired a great taste for rambling and botanizing, and had communicated it also to Fritz, and now that our labours were ended at Tent House, they left us to nurse our invalid, and made long excursions together, which lasted sometimes whole days.

As they generally returned with some game, or some new fruit, we pardoned their absence, and they were always welcome. Sometimes they brought a kangaroo, sometimes an agouti, the flesh of which resembles that of a rabbit, but is richer; sometimes they brought wild ducks, pigeons, and even partridges. These were contributed by Fritz, who never went out without his gun and his dogs. Ernest brought us natural curiosities, which amused us much, stones, crystals, petrifactions, insects, butterflies of rare beauty, and flowers, whose colours and fragrance no one in Europe can form an idea of. Sometimes he brought fruit, which we always administered first to our monkey, as taster: some of them proved very delicious.

Two of his discoveries, especially, were most valuable acquisitions, the guajaraba, on the large leaf of which one may write with a pointed instrument, and the fruit of which, a sort of grape, is very good to eat; also the date-palm, every part of which is so useful, that we were truly thankful to Heaven, and our dear boys, for the discovery. Whilst young, the trunk contains a sort of *marrow*, very delicious. The date-palm is crowned by a head, formed of from forty to eighty leafy branches, which spread round the top. The dates are particularly good about half-dried; and my wife immediately began to preserve them. My sons could only bring the fruit now, but we purposed to transplant some of the trees themselves near our abode. We did not discourage our sons in these profitable expeditions; but they had another aim, which I was yet ignorant of. In the mean time, I usually walked with one of my younger sons towards Tent House, to attend to our garden, and to see if our works continued in good condition to receive mamma, who daily improved; but I insisted on her being completely restored, before she was introduced to them. Our dwelling looked beautiful amongst the picturesque rocks, surrounded by trees of every sort, and facing the smooth and lovely Bay of Safety. The garden was not so forward as I could have wished; but we were obliged to be patient, and hope for the best.

Lesson 49

1. Read chapter 41 of *Swiss Family Robinson*. Do you remember a grotto is a small cave?
2. Tell someone about the chapter.

Chapter 41

One day, having gone over with my younger sons to weed the garden, and survey our possessions, I perceived that the roof of the gallery wanted a little repair, and called Jack to raise for me the rope ladder which I had brought from Falcon's Nest, and which had been very useful while we were constructing the roof; but we sought for it everywhere; it could not be found; and as we were quite free from *robbers* in our island, I could only accuse my elder sons, who had doubtless carried it off to ascend some tall cocoa-nut tree. Obliged to be content, we walked into the garden by the foot of the rocks. Since our arrival, I had been somewhat uneasy at hearing a dull, continued noise, which appeared to proceed from this side. The forge we had passed, now extinguished, and our workmen were absent. Passing along, close to the rocks, the noise became more distinct, and I was truly alarmed. Could it be an earthquake? Or perhaps it announced some volcanic explosion. I stopped before that part of the rock where the noise was loudest; the surface was firm and level; but from time to time, blows and falling stones seemed to strike our ears. I was uncertain what to do; curiosity prompted me to stay, but a sort of terror urged me to remove my child and myself. However, Jack, always daring, was unwilling to go till he had discovered the cause of the phenomenon. "If Francis were here," said he, "he would fancy it was the wicked gnomes, working underground, and he would be in a fine fright. For my part, I believe it is only people come to collect the salt in the rock."

"People!" said I; "you don't know what you are saying, Jack; I could excuse Francis and his *gnomes*, it would be at least a poetic fancy, but yours is quite absurd. Where are the people to come from?"

"But what else can it be?" said he. "Hark! you may hear them strike the rock."

"Be certain, however," said I, "there are no people." At that moment, I distinctly heard human voices, speaking, laughing, and apparently clapping their hands. I could not distinguish any words; I was struck with a mortal terror; but Jack, whom nothing could alarm, clapped his hands also, with joy, that he had guessed right. "What did I say, papa? Was I not right? Are there not people within the rock? friends, I hope." He was approaching the rock, when it appeared to me to be shaking; a stone soon fell down, then another. I seized hold of Jack, to drag him away, lest he should be crushed by the fragments of rock. At that moment another stone fell, and we saw two heads appear through the opening, the heads of Fritz and Ernest. Judge of our surprise and joy! Jack was soon through the opening, and assisting his brothers to enlarge it. As soon as I could enter, I stepped in, and found myself in a real grotto, of a round form, with a vaulted roof, divided by a narrow crevice, which admitted the light and air. It was, however, better lighted by two large gourd lamps. I saw my long ladder of ropes suspended from the opening at the top, and thus comprehended how my sons had penetrated into this recess, which it was impossible to suspect the existence of from the outside. But how had they discovered it? and what were they making of it? These were my two questions. Ernest replied at once to the last. "I wished," said he, "to make a resting-place for my mother, when she came to her garden. My brothers have each built some place for her, and called it by their name. I had a desire that some place in our island might be dedicated to Ernest, and I now present you the *Grotto Ernestine*."

"And after all," said Jack, "it will make a pretty dwelling for the first of us that marries."

"Silence, little giddy-pate," said I; "where do you expect to find a wife in this island? Do you think you shall discover one among the rocks, as your brothers have discovered the grotto? But tell me, Fritz, what directed you here."

"Our good star, father," said he. "Ernest and I were walking round these rocks, and talking of his wish for a resting-place for my mother on her way to the garden. He projected a tent; but the path was too narrow to admit it; and the rock, heated by the sun, was like a stove. We were considering what we should do, when I saw on the summit of the rock a very beautiful little unknown quadruped. From its form I should have taken it for a young chamois, if I had been in Switzerland; but Ernest reminded me that the chamois was peculiar to cold countries, and he thought it was a gazelle or antelope; probably the gazelle of Guinea or Java, called by naturalists the chevrotain. You may suppose I tried to climb the rock on which this little animal remained standing, with one foot raised, and its pretty head turning first to one side and then to the other; but it was useless to attempt it here, where the rock was smooth and perpendicular; besides, I should have put the gazelle to flight, as it is a timid and wild animal. I then remembered there was a place near Tent House where a considerable break occurred in the chain of rocks, and we found that, with a little difficulty, the rock might be scaled by ascending this ravine. Ernest laughed at me, and asked me if I expected the antelope would wait patiently till I got to it? No matter, I determined to try, and I told him to remain; but he soon determined to accompany me, for he fancied that in the fissure of a rock he saw a flower of a beautiful rose-colour, which was unknown to him. My learned botanist thought it must be an *erica*, or heath, and wished to ascertain the fact. One helping the other, we soon got through all difficulties, and arrived at the summit; and here we were amply repaid by the beautiful prospect on every side. We will talk of that afterwards, father; I have formed some idea of the country which these rocks separate us from. But to return to our grotto.

I went along, first looking for my pretty gazelle, which I saw licking a piece of rock, where doubtless she found some salt. I was hardly a hundred yards from her, my gun ready, when I was suddenly stopped by a crevice, which I could not cross, though the opening was not very wide. The pretty quadruped was on the rock opposite to me; but of what use would it have been to shoot it, when I could not secure it. I was obliged to defer it till a better opportunity offered, and turned to examine the opening, which appeared deep; still I could see that the bottom of the cavity was white, like that of our former grotto. I called Ernest, who was behind me, with his plants and stones, to impart to him an idea that suddenly struck me. It was, to make this the retreat for my mother. I told him that I believed the floor of the cave was nearly on a level with the path that led to the garden, and we had only to make an opening in the form of a natural grotto, and it would be exactly what he wished. Ernest was much pleased with the idea, and said he could easily ascertain the level by means of a weight attached to a string; but though he was startled at the difficulty of descending to our labour every day, and returning in the evening, he would not agree to my wish of beginning at the outside of the rock, as we had done in our former grotto, He had several reasons for wishing to work from within. "In the first place," said he, "it will be so much cooler this summer weather; we should be soon unable to go on labouring before the burning rock; then our path is so narrow, that we should not know how to dispose of the rubbish; in the interior, it will serve us to make a bench round the grotto; besides, I should have such pleasure in completing it secretly, and unsuspected, without any assistance or advice except yours, my dear Fritz, which I accept with all my heart; so pray find out some means of descending and ascending readily."

"I immediately recollected your rope ladder, father; it was forty feet long, and we could easily fasten it to the point of the rock. Ernest was delighted and sanguine. We returned with all speed. We took first a roll of cord and some candles; then the rope ladder, which we rolled up as well as we could, but had great difficulty in conveying it up the rock; once or twice, when the ascent was very difficult, we were obliged to fasten a cord to it, and draw it up after us; but determination, courage, and perseverance overcame all obstacles. We arrived at the opening, and, on sounding it, we were glad to find our ladder would be long enough to reach the bottom. We then measured the outside of the rock, and ascertained that the floor of the grotto was near the same level as the ground outside.

"We remembered your lessons, father, and made some experiments to discover if it contained mephitic air. (Hi, it's me again. I don't know what mephitic air is. Do you? But next we'll read that they lit candles which didn't go out. Fire needs oxygen to burn, so it seems they are testing to see if the air was okay to breathe. You won't get all the words, but follow the story.) We first lighted some candles, which were not extinguished; we then kindled a large heap of sticks and dried grass, which-burned well, the smoke passing through the opening like a chimney. Having no uneasiness about this, we deferred our commencement till the next day. Then we lighted the forge, and pointed some iron bars we found in the magazine; these were to be our tools to break open the rock. We secured, also, your chisel, as well as some hammers, and all our tools were thrown down below; we then arranged two gourds to serve us for lamps; and when all was ready, and our ladder firmly fixed, we descended ourselves; and we have nothing more to tell you, except that we were very glad when we heard your voices outside, at the very time when our work was drawing to an end. We were sure, when we distinguished your voices so clearly, that we must be near the external air; we redoubled our efforts, and here we are. Now tell us, father, are you pleased with our idea? and will you forgive us for making a mystery of it?"

I assured them of my forgiveness, and my cordial approbation of their manly and useful enterprise; and made Ernest happy by declaring that it should always be called the *Grotto Ernestine*.

"Thanks to you all, my dear children," said I; "your dear mamma will now prefer Tent House to Falcon's Nest, and will have no occasion to risk breaking a limb in descending the winding staircase. I will assist you to enlarge the opening, and as we will leave it all the simplicity of a natural grotto, it will soon be ready."

We all set to work; Jack carried away the loosened stones and rubbish, and formed benches on each side the grotto. With what had fallen outside, he also made two seats in the front of the rock, and before evening all was complete. Fritz ascended to unfasten the ladder, and to convey it by an easier road to Tent House; he then rejoined us, and we returned to our castle in the air, which was henceforward only to be looked on as a pleasure-house. We resolved, however, to establish here, as we had done at our farm, a colony of our cattle, which increased daily: we had now a number of young cows, which were most useful for our support. We wished, however, for a female buffalo, as the milk of that animal makes excellent cheese. Conversing on our future plans, we soon reached home, and found all well.

Lesson 50

1. Read chapter 42 of *Swiss Family Robinson.*
2. What does the poem tell about his feelings about the island? (Answers)
3. Tell someone about the chapter.

Chapter 42

In a few days we completed the *Grotto Ernestine*. It contained some stalactites; but not so many as our former grotto. We found, however, a beautiful block of salt, which resembled white marble, of which Ernest formed a sort of altar, supported by four pillars, on which he placed a pretty vase of citron-wood, which he had turned himself, and in which he arranged some of the beautiful *erica* which had been the cause of his discovering the grotto. It was one of those occasions when his feelings overcame his natural indolence, when he became for a time the most active of the four, and brought forward all his resources, which were many. This indolence was merely physical; when not excited by any sudden circumstance, or by some fancy which soon assumed the character of a passion, he loved ease, and to enjoy life tranquilly in study. He improved his mind continually, as well by his excellent memory, as by natural talent and application. He reflected, made experiments, and was always successful. He had at last succeeded in making his mother a very pretty bonnet. He had also composed some verses, which were intended to celebrate her visit to Tent House; and this joyful day being at last fixed, the boys all went over, the evening before, to make their preparations. The flowers that the storm had spared were gathered to ornament the fountains, the altar, and the table, on which was placed an excellent cold dinner, entirely prepared by themselves. Fritz supplied and roasted the game, a fine bustard, the flesh of which resembles a turkey, and a brace of partridges. Ernest brought pines, melons, and figs; Jack should have supplied the fish, but was able only to procure oysters, crabs, and turtles' eggs. Francis had the charge of the dessert, which consisted of a dish of strawberries, honeycomb, and the cream of the cocoa-nut. I had contributed a bottle of Canary wine, that we might drink mamma's health. All was arranged on a table in the middle of the *Franciade*, and my sons returned to accompany the expedition next day.

The morning was beautiful, and the sun shone brightly on our emigration. My wife was anxious to set out, expecting she should have to return to her aerial dwelling. Though her leg and foot were better, she still walked feebly, and she begged us to harness the cow and ass to the cart, and to lead them as gently as possible.

"I will only go a little way the first day," said she, "for I am not strong enough to visit Tent House yet."

We felt quite convinced she would change her opinion when once in her litter. I wished to carry her down the staircase; but she declined, and descended very well with the help of my arm. When the door was opened, and she found herself once more in the open air, surrounded by her children, she thanked God, with tears of gratitude, for her recovery, and all his mercies to us. Then the pretty osier carriage arrived. They had harnessed the cow and young bull to it; Francis answering for the docility of Valiant, provided he guided him himself. Accordingly, he was mounted before, his cane in his hand, and his bow and quiver on his back, very proud to be mamma's charioteer. My other three boys mounted on their animals, were ready before, to form the advanced guard, while I proposed to follow, and watch over the whole. My wife was moved even to tears, and could not cease admiring her new carriage, which Fritz and Jack presented to her as their own work. Francis, however, boasted that he had carded the cotton for the soft cushion on which she was to sit, and I, that I had made it. I then lifted her in, and as soon as she was seated Ernest came to put her new bonnet on her head, which greatly delighted her; it was of fine straw, and so thick and firm that it might even defend her from the rain. But what pleased her most was, that it was the shape worn by the Swiss peasants in the Canton of Vaud, where my dear wife had resided some time in her youth. She thanked all her dear children, and felt so easy and comfortable in her new conveyance, that we arrived at Family Bridge without her feeling the least fatigue. Here we stopped.

"Would you like to cross here, my dear?" said I; "and as we are very near, look in at your convenient Tent House, where you will have no staircase to ascend. And we should like to know, too, if you approve of our management of your garden,"

"As you please," said she; "in fact, I am so comfortable in my carriage, that if it were necessary, I could make the tour of the island. I should like to see my house again; but it will be so very hot at this season, that we must not stay long."

"But you must dine there, my dear mother," said Fritz; "it is too late to return to dinner at Falcon's Nest; consider, too, the fatigue it would occasion you."

"I would be very glad, indeed, my dear," said she; "but what are we to dine on? We have prepared no provision, and I fear we shall all be hungry."

"What matter," said Jack, "provided you dine with us? You must take your chance. I will go and get some oysters, that we may not die with hunger;" and off he galloped on his buffalo. Fritz followed him, on some pretence, on Lightfoot. Mamma wished she had brought a vessel to carry some water from the river, for she knew we could get none at Tent House. Francis reminded her we could milk the cow, and she was satisfied, and enjoyed her journey much. At last we arrived before the colonnade. My wife was dumb with wonder for some moments.

"Where am I, and what do I see?" said she, when she could speak.

"You see the *Franciade*, mamma," said her little boy; "this beautiful colonnade was my invention, to protect you from the heat; stay, read what is written above: *Francis to his dear mother. May this colonnade, which is called the Franciade, be to her a temple of happiness.* Now mamma, lean on me, and come and see my brothers' gifts much better than mine;" and he led her to Jack's pavilion, who was standing by the fountain. He held a shell in his hand, which he filled with water, and drank, saying, "To the health of the Queen of the Island; may she have no more accidents, and live as long as her children! Long live Queen Elizabeth, and may she come every day to *Jackia*, to drink her son Jack's health."

I supported my wife, and was almost as much affected as herself. She wept and trembled with joy and surprise. Jack and Ernest then joined their hands, and carried her to the other pavilion, where Fritz was waiting to receive her, and the same scene of tenderness ensued. "Accept this pavilion, dear mother," said he; "and may *Fritzia* ever make you think on Fritz."

The delighted mother embraced them all, and observing Ernest's name was not commemorated by any trophy, thanked him again for her beautiful bonnet. She then drank some of the delicious water of the fountain, and returned to seat herself at the repast, which was another surprise for her. We all made an excellent dinner; and at the dessert, I handed my Canary wine round in shells; and then Ernest rose and sung us very prettily, to a familiar air, some little verses he had composed:

> On this festive happy day,
> Let us pour our grateful lay;
> Since Heaven has hush'd our mother's pain,
> And given her to her sons again.
> Then from this quiet, lovely home
> Never, never, may we roam.
> All we love around us smile:
> Joyful is our desert isle.

When o'er our mother's couch we bent,
Fervent prayers to Heaven we sent,
And God has spared that mother dear,
To bless her happy children here.
Then from this quiet, lovely home,
Never, never, may we roam;
All we love around us smile,
Joyful is our desert isle.

We all joined in the chorus, and none of us thought of the ship, of Europe, or of anything that was passing in the world. The island was our universe, and Tent House was a palace we would not have exchanged for any the world contained. This was one of those happy days that God grants us sometimes on earth, to give us an idea of the bliss of Heaven; and most fervently did we thank Him, at the end of our repast, for all his mercies and blessings to us.

After dinner, I told my wife she must not think of returning to Falcon's Nest, with all its risks of storms and the winding staircase, and she could not better recompense her sons for their labours than by living among them. She was of the same opinion, and was very glad to be so near her kitchen and her stores, and to be able to walk alone with the assistance of a stick in the colonnade, which she could do already; but she made me promise to leave Falcon's Nest as it was. It would be a pretty place to walk to, and besides, this castle in the air was her own invention. We agreed that this very evening she should take possession of her own pretty room, with the good felt carpet, on which she could walk without fear; and that the next day, I should go with my elder sons and the animals to bring the cart, such utensils as we needed, and above all, the poultry. Our dogs always followed their masters, as well as the monkey and jackal, and they were so domesticated, we had no trouble with them.

I then prevailed on my wife to go into her room and rest for an hour, after which we were to visit the garden. She complied, and after her repose found her four sons ready to carry her in her litter as in a sedan-chair. They took care to bring her straight to the grotto, where I was waiting for her. This was a new surprise for the good mother. She could not sufficiently express her astonishment and delight, when Jack and Francis, taking their *flageolets*, accompanied their brothers, who sung the following verse, which Ernest had added to his former attempt.

Dear mother, let this gift be mine,
Accept the Grotto Ernestine.
May all your hours be doubly blest
Within this tranquil place of rest.

Then from this quiet, lovely home
Never, never may we roam;
All we love around us smile.
Joyful is our desert isle!

What cause had we to rejoice in our children! we could not but shed tears to witness their affection and perfect happiness.

Below the vase of flowers, on the block of salt, Ernest had written:

Ernest, assisted by his brother Fritz,
Has prepared this grotto,
As a retreat for his beloved mother,
When she visits her garden.

Ernest then conducted his mother to one of the benches, which he had covered with soft moss, as a seat for her, and there she rested at her ease to hear the history of the discovery of the grotto. It was now my turn to offer my present; the garden, the embankment, the pond, and the arbour. She walked, supported by my arm, to view her little empire, and her delight was extreme; the pond, which enabled her to water her vegetables, particularly pleased her, as well as her shady arbour, under which she found all her gardening tools, ornamented with flowers, and augmented by two light*watering-pans,* constructed by Jack and Francis, from two gourds. They had canes for spouts, with the gourd bottles at the end, pierced with holes, through which the water came in the manner of a watering-pan. The embankment was also a great surprise; she proposed to place plants of pines and melon on it, and I agreed to it. Truly did she rejoice at the appearance of the vegetables, which promised us some excellent European provision, a great comfort to her. After expressing her grateful feelings, she returned to the grotto, and seating herself in her sedan-chair, returned to Tent House, to enjoy the repose she needed, after such a day of excitement. We did not, however, lie down before we had together thanked God for the manifold blessings he had given us, and for the pleasure of that day.

"If I had been in Europe," said my dear wife, "on the festival of my recovery, I should have received a bouquet of flowers, a ribbon, or some trinket; here I have had presented a carriage, a colonnade, pavilions, ornamental fountains, a large grotto, a garden, a pond, an arbour, and a straw bonnet!"

Lesson 51

1. Read chapter 43 of *Swiss Family Robinson.*
2. Tell someone what happened in this chapter.

3. A mill is for grinding grain. Two large flat rocks turn against each other to grind the grain into flour. Who's planning to build one? (Answers)

Chapter 43

The next and following days were spent in removing our furniture and property, particularly our poultry, which had multiplied greatly. We also constructed a poultry-yard, at a sufficient distance from our house to save our sleep from disturbance, and still so near that we could easily tend them. We made it as a continuation of the colonnade, and on the same plan, but enclosed in the front by a sort of wire trellis-work, which Fritz and Jack made wonderfully well. Fritz, who had a turn for architecture and mechanics, gave me some good hints, especially one, which we put into execution. This was to carry the water from the basin of the fountain through the poultry-yard, which enabled us also to have a little pond for our ducks. The pigeons had their abode above the hen-roosts, in some pretty baskets, which Ernest and Francis made, similar to those made by the natives of the Friendly Isles, of which they had seen engravings in Cook's Voyages. When all was finished, my wife was delighted to think that even in the rainy season she could attend to her feathered family and collect their eggs.

"What a difference," said she, admiring the elegance of our buildings, "what a difference between this Tent House and the original dwelling that suggested the name to us, and which was our only shelter four years ago. What a surprising progress luxury has made with us in that time! Do you remember, my dear, the barrel which served us for a table, and the oyster-shells for spoons, the tent where we slept, crowded together on dried leaves, and without undressing, and the river half a mile off, where we were obliged to go to drink if we were thirsty? Compared to what we were then, we are now great *lords.*"

"Kings, you mean, mamma," said Jack, "for all this island is ours, and it is quite like a kingdom."

"And how many millions of subjects does Prince Jack reckon in the kingdom of his august father?" said I.

Prince Jack declared he had not yet counted the parrots, kangaroos, *agoutis*, and monkeys. The laughter of his brothers stopped him. I then agreed with my wife that our luxuries had increased; but I explained to her that this was the result of our industry. All civilized nations have commenced as we did; necessity has developed the intellect which God has given to man alone, and by degrees the arts have progressed, and knowledge has extended more perhaps than is conducive to happiness. What appeared luxury to us now was still simplicity compared with the luxury of towns, or even villages, among civilized nations. My wife declared she had everything she wished for, and should not know what more to ask for, as we now had only to rest and enjoy our happiness.

I declared against spending our time in rest and indolence, as the sure means of ending our pleasure; and I well knew my dear wife was, like myself, an enemy to idleness; but she dreaded any more laborious undertakings.

"But, mamma," said Fritz, "you must let me make a mill under the cascade; it will be so useful when our corn grows, and even now for the maize. I also think of making an oven in the kitchen, which will be very useful for you to bake your bread in."

"These would indeed be useful labours," said the good mother, smiling; "but can you accomplish them?"

"I hope so," said Fritz, "with the help of God and that of my dear brothers."

Ernest promised his best aid, in return for his brother's kind services in forming his grotto, only requesting occasional leisure for his natural history collections. His mother did not see the utility of these collections, but, willing to indulge her kind and attentive Ernest, she offered, till she could walk well, to assist him in arranging and labelling his plants, which were yet in disorder, and he gratefully consented. In procuring her some paper for the purpose, of which I had brought a large quantity from the vessel, I brought out an unopened packet, amongst which was a piece of some fabric, neither paper nor stuff apparently. We examined it together, and at length remembered it was a piece of stuff made at Otaheite, which our captain had bought of a native at an island where we had touched on our voyage. Fritz appearing much interested in examining this cloth, Ernest said gravely, "I can teach you how to make it;" and immediately bringing *Cook's Voyages*, where a detailed description is given, he proceeded to read it. Fritz was disappointed to find it could only be made of the bark of three trees of these our island produced only one. These trees were the mulberry-tree, the bread fruit, and the wild fig. We had the last in abundance, but of the two former we had not yet discovered a single plant.

Fritz was not, however, discouraged. "They ought to be here," said he, "since they are found in all the South-Sea Islands. Perhaps we may find them on the other side of the rocks, where I saw some superb unknown trees from the height where we discovered the grotto; and who knows but I may find my pretty gazelle there again. The rogue can leap better than I can over those rocks. I had a great wish to descend them, but found it impossible; some are very high and perpendicular; others have overhanging summits; I might, however, get round as you did by the pass, between the torrent and the rocks at the Great Bay."

Jack offered to be his guide, even with his eyes shut, into that rich country where he conquered and captured his buffalo; and Ernest begged to be of the party. As this was an expedition I had long projected, I agreed to accompany them next day, their mother being content to have Francis left with her as a protector. I cautioned Fritz not to fire off his gun when we approached the buffaloes, as any show of hostility might render them furious; otherwise the animals, unaccustomed to man, have no fear of him, and will not harm him. "In general," added I, "I cannot sufficiently recommend to you to be careful of your powder; we have not more than will last us a year, and there may be a necessity to have recourse to it for our defence."

"I have a plan for making it," said Fritz, who never saw a difficulty in anything. "I know it is composed of charcoal, saltpetre, and sulphur and we ought to find all these materials in the island. It is only necessary to combine them, and to form it into little round grains. This is my only difficulty; but I will consider it over; and I have my mill to think on first. I have a confused recollection of a powder manufactory at Berne: there was some machinery which went by water; this machinery moved some hammers, which pounded and mixed the ingredients was not this the case, father?"

"Something like it," said I; "but we have many things to do before making powder. First, we must go to sleep; we must set out before daybreak, if we intend to return to-morrow evening." We did indeed rise before the sun, which would not rise for us. The sky was very cloudy, and shortly we had an abundant and incessant rain, which obliged us to defer our journey, and put us all in bad humour, but my wife, who was not sorry to keep us with her, and who declared this gracious rain would water her garden, and bring it forward. Fritz was the first who consoled himself; he thought on nothing but building mills, and manufacturing gunpowder. He begged me to draw him a mill; this was very easy, so far as regards the exterior, that is, the wheel, and the waterfall that sets it in motion; but the interior, the disposition of the wheels, the stones to bruise the grain, the sieve, or bolter, to separate the flour from the bran; all this complicated machinery was difficult to explain; but he comprehended all, adding his usual expression, "I will try, and I shall succeed." Not to lose any time, and to profit by this rainy day, he began by making sieves of different materials, which he fastened to a circle of pliant wood, and tried by passing through them the flour of the cassava; he made some with sailcloth, others with the hair of the donkey, which is very long and strong, and some of the fibres of bark. His mother admired his work, which he continued to improve more and more; she assured him the sieve would be sufficient for her; it was useless to have the trouble of building a mill.

"But how shall we bruise the grain, mamma?" said he; "it would be tedious and hard work."

"And you think there will be no hard work in building your mill?" said Jack. "I am curious to see how you will contrive to form that huge stone, which is called the millstone."

"You shall see," said Fritz; "only find me the stone, and it shall soon be done. Do you think, father, that of our rock would be suitable?"

I told him I thought it would be hard enough, but it would be difficult to cut from the rock a piece large enough for the purpose. He made his usual reply, "*I will try*. Ernest and Jack will assist me; and perhaps you, papa."

I declared my willingness, but named him the *master-mason;* we must only be his workmen. Francis was impatient to see the mill in operation. "Oh!" said Jack, "you shall soon have that pleasure. It is a mere trifle; we only want stone, wood, tools, and science."

At the word "*science*," Ernest, who was reading in a corner, without listening to us, raised his head suddenly, saying, "What science are you in need of?"

"Of one you know nothing of, Mr. Philosopher," said Jack. "Come, tell us, do you know how to build a mill?"

"A mill?" answered Ernest; "of what description? There are many sorts. I was just looking in my dictionary for it. There are corn-mills, and powder-mills, oil-mills, wind-mills, water-mills, hand-mills, and saw-mills; which do you want?"

Fritz would have liked them all.

"You remind me," said I, "that we brought from the vessel a hand-mill and a saw-mill, taken to pieces, to be sure, but numbered and labelled, so that they could be easily united: they should be in the magazine, where you found the anvil and iron bars; I had forgotten them."

"Let us go and examine them," said Fritz, lighting his lantern; "I shall get some ideas from them."

"Rather," said his mother, "they will spare you the trouble of thinking and labouring."

I sent them all four to seek these treasures, which, heaped in an obscure corner of the store-room, had escaped my recollection. When we were alone, I seriously besought my wife not to oppose any occupations our children might plan, however they might seem beyond their power; the great point being, to keep them continually occupied, so that no evil or dangerous fancies might fill their minds. "Let them," I said, "cut stone, fell trees, or dig fountains, and bless God that their thoughts are so innocently directed." She understood me, and promised not to discourage them, only fearing the excessive fatigue of these undertakings.

Lesson 52

1. Read chapter 44 of *Swiss Family Robinson*.
2. Find a word in today's reading that you don't know. Guess its meaning based on the context.

3. Look up its definition or ask someone its meaning.
4. Tell someone about the chapter.

Chapter 44

Fritz struck his forehead, and, seizing Ernest by the arm "Brother," said he, "what fools we have been!"

Ernest inquired what folly they had been guilty of.

"Why did we not," said Fritz, "when we were working within our grotto, attempt to make the opening on the other side? We should not have had much difficulty, I am persuaded, and if our tools had not been sufficient, a little powder would have opened us a door on the other side. Only consider, father, the convenience of bringing the cart loaded with the trees we wanted through our grotto, and to be able to go a-hunting without having I don't know how many miles to go."

"Well, we can still do that," said Ernest, in his usual calm, grave manner; "if we do not find another passage, we will make one through the Grotto Ernestine, with mamma's permission, as it is her property."

This idea of my son appeared good. It was quite certain, from our experience at Tent House and in the grotto, that the cavity in the rocks was of very great extent, and it did not appear difficult to pierce through to the other side; but some other chain of rocks, some gigantic tree, some hill, at the end of our tunnel, might render all our labour useless. I proposed that we should defer our work till we had examined the nature of the ground on the other side; my sons agreed, and we proceeded with renewed courage, when we were suddenly checked by the sight of the sea beating against a perpendicular rock of terrific height, which terminated our island on this side, and did not give us a chance of going on. I saw the rock did not extend far; but how to get round it, I could not devise. I did not conceive we could get the pinnace round, as the coast seemed surrounded by reefs; masses of rock stood up in the sea, and the breakers showed that more were hidden. After much consideration and many plans, Ernest proposed that we should swim out to the uncovered rocks, and endeavour to pass round. Fritz objected, on account of his arms and ammunition; but Ernest suggested that the powder should be secured in the pockets of his clothes, which he might carry on his head, holding his gun above the water.

With some difficulty we arranged our incumbrances, and succeeded in reaching the range of outer rocks, without swimming, as the water was not above our shoulders. We rested here awhile, and, putting on some of our clothes, we commenced our walk over sharp stones, which wounded our feet. In many places, where the rocks lay low, we were up to the waist in the water. Ernest, the proposer of the plan, encouraged us, and led the way for some time; but at last he fell behind, and remained so long, that I became alarmed, and calling aloud, for I had lost sight of him, he answered me, and at last I discovered him stretched on the rock, endeavouring to separate a piece from it with his knife.

"Father," said he, "I am now certain that this bed of rocks, over which we are walking, and which we fancied was formed of stone or flints, is nothing but the work of those remarkable *zoophytes*, called coral insects, which form coral and many other extraordinary things; they can even make whole islands. Look at these little points and hollows, and these stars of every colour and every form; I would give all the world to have a specimen of each kind."

He succeeded in breaking off a piece, which was of a deep orange-colour inside; he collected also, and deposited in his bag, some other pieces, of various forms and colours. These greatly enriched his collection; and, idle as he was, he did not complain of any difficulty in obtaining them. He had given his gun to Jack, who complained much of the ruggedness of our road. Our march was truly painful, and I repented more than once of having yielded to the idea; besides the misery of walking along these shelly rocks, which presented points like the sharp teeth of a saw, tearing our shoes and even our skin, the sea, in some of the lower places, was so high as to bar our passage, and we were obliged, in the interval between two waves, to rush across, with the water to our chins. We had some difficulty to avoid being carried away. I trembled especially for Jack; though small and light, he preferred facing the wave to avoiding it. I was several times obliged to catch hold of him, and narrowly escaped destruction along with him. Happily, our march was not above half a mile, and we gained the shore at last without any serious accident, but much fatigued and foot-sore; and we made a resolution never more to cross the coral reefs.

The island was much narrower here, and instead of the wide plain, crossed by a river, divided by delightful woods, giving an idea of paradise on earth; we were journeying through a contracted valley, lying between the rocky wall which divided the island, and a chain of sandy hills, which hid the sea and sheltered the valley from the wind. Fritz and I ascended one of these hills. Any navigators, sailing along these shores, would pronounce the island inaccessible and entirely barren. This is not the fact; the grass is very thick, and the trees of noble growth; we found many unknown to us, some loaded with fruit. I should never finish, if I were to try and name all the plants found in this shady valley, which might be called the botanic garden of Nature. Ernest was in ecstasies; he wished to carry away everything, but he did not know how to dispose of them.

"Ah!" said he, "if only our grotto were open to this side!"

At this moment Fritz came running out of breath, crying out, "The bread-fruit tree! I have found the bread-fruit tree! Here is the fruit, excellent, delicious bread. Taste it, father;

here, Ernest; here, Jack;" and he gave us each a part of an oval fruit, about the size of an ordinary melon, which really seemed very good and nourishing.

"There are many of these trees," continued he, "loaded with fruit. Would that we had our grotto opened, that we might collect a store of them, now that they are ripe."

My boys pointed out to me exactly the situation of the grotto, judging from the rock above, and longed for their tools, that they might commence the opening directly. We proceeded to make our way through a border of trees and bushes, that separated us from the rock, that we might examine it, and judge of the difficulties of our undertaking. Jack preceded us, as usual, after giving Ernest his gun; Fritz followed him, and suddenly turning to me, said,

"I believe kind Nature has saved us much trouble; the rock appears to be divided from top to bottom; at the foot I see a sort of cave, or grotto, already made."

There was a gentle stream, gushing from a perpendicular rock; then forming a graceful bend, it took its course towards the great bay, and fell in a cascade into the sea. We remained some time here to fill our gourds, drinking moderately, and taking a bath, which refreshed us all greatly.

The evening was approaching, and we began to fear we should not reach home before night. I had warned my wife that there was a possibility that we might be delayed, though I could not then anticipate the cause of our delay. We endeavoured, however, by walking as quickly as we could, and resting no more, to reach our farm at any rate. We followed the course of the river, on the opposite shore of which rose a wide plain, where we saw the herd of buffaloes quietly grazing, ruminating, and drinking, without paying the slightest attention to us. We thought we distinguished some other quadrupeds amongst them, which Fritz was certain were zebras or donkeys; but certainly not his dear gazelle, for which he had incessantly looked round. Jack was in despair that the river separated us from the buffaloes, so that he could not cast his lasso round the legs of one of them, as he had promised Ernest. He even wished to swim across the stream, to have a hunt; but I forbade him, encouraging him to hope that perhaps a single buffalo might cross to our side, and throw itself in the way of his lasso. I was far from wishing such a thing myself, for we had no time to lose, nor any means to secure and lead it home, should we succeed in capturing one, not having any cords with us; and moreover, intending to return from the bay in the canoe.

When we arrived at the bay, the night, which comes on rapidly in equinoctial countries, had almost closed. We were scarcely able to see, without terror, the changes that the late storm had occasioned; the narrow pass which led from the other side of the island, between the river and a deep stream that flowed from the rocks, was entirely obstructed with rocks and earth fallen upon it; and to render our passage practicable, it was necessary to undertake a labour that the darkness now prevented, and which would at any time be attended by danger. We were obliged then to spend the night in the open air, and separated from our dear and anxious friends at Tent House. Fortunately, Fritz had collected a store of bread-fruit for his mother, with which he had filled his own pockets and those of his brothers. These, with water from the river, formed our supper; for we had nothing but the bone of our leg of mutton left. We turned back a little way, to establish ourselves under a clump of trees, where we were in greater safety; we loaded our muskets, we kindled a large fire of dry branches, and recommending ourselves to the protection of God, we lay ourselves down on the soft moss to wait for the first rays of light.

With the exception of Jack, who from the first slept as if he had been in his bed, we none of us could rest. The night was beautiful; a multitude of stars shone over our heads in the ethereal vault. Ernest was never tired of gazing on them. After some questions and suppositions on the plurality of worlds, their courses and their distances, he quitted us to wander on the borders of the river, which reflected them in all their brilliancy. From this night his passion for astronomy commenced, a passion which he carried beyond all others. This became his favourite and continual study, nor did he fall far short of Duval, whose history he had read. Whilst he was engaged in contemplation, Fritz and I conversed on our projects for tunnelling to the grotto, and on the utility of such a passage, as this side of the island was quite lost to us, from the difficulty in reaching it. "And yet," said I, "it is to this difficulty we owe the safety we have enjoyed. Who can say that the bears and the buffaloes may not find the way through the grotto? I confess I am not desirous of their visits, nor even of those of the donkeys. Who knows but they might persuade your favourite Lightfoot to return and live amongst them? Liberty has many charms. Till now, we have been very happy on our side of the island, without the productions of this. My dear boy, there is a proverb, 'Let *well* alone,' Let us not have too much ambition, it has ruined greater states than ours."

Fritz seemed grieved to give up his plan, and suggested that he could forge some strong bars of iron to place before the opening, which could be removed at will.

"But," said I, "they will not prevent the snakes from passing underneath. I have noticed some with terror, as they are animals I have a great antipathy to; and if your mother saw one crawl into her grotto, she would never enter it again; even if she did not die of fright."

"Well, we must give it up," said Fritz; "but it is a pity. Do you think, father, there are more bears in the island than those we killed?"

"In all probability," said I; "it is scarcely to be supposed that there should only be two. I cannot well account for their being here. They can swim very well, and perhaps the abundance of fruit in this part of the island may have attracted them." I then gave my son a short account of their manners and habits, from the best works on the history of these animals.

Lesson 53

1. Read chapter 46 of *Swiss Family Robinson.* (Because of pages missing from the book, chapter 45 is combined in with chapter 44.)
2. Tell someone what happens in the chapter.

Chapter 46

Whilst we continued to talk and to admire the beauty of the stars, they at length began to fade away before the first light of morning. Ernest returned to us, and we awoke Jack, who had slept uninterruptedly, and was quite unconscious where he was. We returned to the pass, which now, by the light of day, seemed to us in a more hopeless state than in the dusk of evening. I was struck with consternation: it appeared to me that we were entirely enclosed at this side; and I shuddered to think of crossing the island again, to pass round at the other end, of the risk we should run of meeting wild beasts, and of the painful and perilous passage along the coral reefs. At that moment I would gladly have consented to open a passage through the grotto, at the hazard of any visitors, in order to get through myself, that I might relieve the anxious feelings of my dear wife and boy. The thoughts of their agony unnerved me, and took away all courage for the commencement of a labour which seemed impossible, our only utensils being a small saw, and a little dibble for taking up plants, which Ernest had been unwilling to leave behind us. The path by which Jack and I had passed was covered with rocks and masses of soil, which obstructed even the course of the stream; we could not discover the place we had forded, the river had opened itself a wider course, far beyond its former one.

"It is impossible," said Fritz, gazing on the ruins, "that we can remove all these immense stones without proper tools; but, perhaps, with a little courage, we may cross over them, the rivulet being widened cannot be very deep. At all events, it cannot be worse than the coral reefs."

"Let us try; but I fear it will be impossible, at least for *him*," said I, pointing to Jack.

"*Him*, indeed, papa, and why not?" said the bold fellow; "*he* is perhaps as strong, and more active, than some of *them*; ask Fritz what he thinks of his workman. Shall I go the first to show you the way?"

And he was advancing boldly, but I checked him, and said, that before we undertook to scale these masses of rock, absolutely bare, where we had nothing to support us, or to hold by, it would be as well to examine if, by descending lower, we could not find a less dangerous road. We descended to the narrow pass, and found our drawbridge, plantation, all our fortification that my boys were so proud of, and where, at Fritz's request, I had even planted a small cannon, all, all destroyed; the cannon swallowed up with the rest. My boys deplored their disappointment; but I showed them how useless such a defence must ever be. Nature had provided us with a better fortification than we could construct, as we just now bitterly experienced.

We had descended several yards lower with incredible difficulty, plunged in a wet, heavy soil, and obliged to step across immense stones, when Fritz, who went first, cried out, joyfully

"The roof, papa! the roof of our *chalet*! it is quite whole; it will be a bridge for us if we can only get to it."

"What roof? What chalet?" said I, in astonishment.

"The roof of our little hermitage," said he, "which we had covered so well with stones, like the Swiss *chalets*."

I then recollected that I had made this little hut, after the fashion of the Swiss chalet, of bark, with a roof nearly flat and covered with stones, to secure it against the winds. It was this circumstance, and its situation, that had saved it in the storm. I had placed it opposite the cascade, that we might see the fall in all its beauty, and, consequently, a little on one side of the passage filled up by the fall of the rocks. Some fragments reached the roof of the hut, and we certainly could not have entered it; but the chalet was supported by this means, and the roof was still standing and perfectly secure. We contrived to slide along the rock which sustained it; Jack was the first to stand on the roof and sing victory. It was very easy to descend on the other side, holding by the poles and pieces of bark, and we soon found ourselves safe in our *own* island. Ernest had lost his gun in the passage: not being willing to resign his bag of curiosities, he had dropped the gun into the abyss.

"You may take the gun I left in the canoe," said Fritz; "but, another time, throw away your stones, and keep your gun you will find it a good friend in need."

"Let us embark in our canoe," cried Jack. "The sea! the sea! Long live the waves! they are not so hard as the stones."

I was very glad to have the opportunity of conveying my canoe back to the port of Tent House; our important occupations had prevented me till now, and everything favoured the plan: the sea was calm, the wind favourable, and we should arrive at home sooner, and with less fatigue, than by land. We skirted the great Bay to the Cabbage-palm Wood. I had moored the canoe so firmly to one of the palms, that I felt secure of it being there. We arrived at the place, and no canoe was there! The mark of the cord which fastened it was still to be seen round the tree, but the canoe had entirely disappeared. Struck with astonishment, we looked at each other with terror, and without being able to articulate a word. What was become of it?

"Some animal, the jackals; a monkey, perhaps, might have detached it," said Jack; "but they could not have eaten the canoe." And we could not find a trace of it, any more than of the gun Fritz had left in it.

This extraordinary circumstance gave me a great deal of thought. Natives, surely, had landed on our island, and carried off our canoe. We could no longer doubt it when we discovered on the sands the print of naked feet! It is easy to believe how uneasy and agitated I was. I hastened to take the road to Tent House, from which we were now more than three leagues distant. I forbade my sons to mention this event, or our suspicions, to their mother, as I knew it would rob her of all peace of mind. I tried to console myself. It was possible that chance had conducted them to the Bay, that they had seen our pretty canoe, and that, satisfied with their prize, and seeing no inhabitants, they might not return. Perhaps, on the contrary, these islanders might prove kind and humane, and become our friends. There was no trace of their proceedings further than the shore.

We called at *The Farm*, on purpose to examine. All appeared in order; and certainly, if they had reached here, there was much to tempt them: our cotton mattresses, our osier seats, and some household utensils that my wife had left here. Our geese and fowls did not appear to have been alarmed, but were pecking about as usual for worms and insects. I began to hope that we might get off with the loss of our canoe, a loss which might be repaired. We were a sufficient number, being well armed, not to be afraid of a few natives, even if they penetrated further into the island, and showed hostile intentions. I exhorted my sons to do nothing to irritate them; on the contrary, to meet them with kindness and attention, and to commit no violence against them unless called on to defend their lives. I also recommended them to select from the wrecked chest, some articles likely to please the natives, and to carry them always about with them. "And I beseech you, once more," added I, "not to alarm your mother." They promised me; and we continued our road unmolested to Falcon's Nest. Jack preceded us, delighted, he said, to see our castle again, which he hoped the natives had not carried away. Suddenly, we saw him return, running, with terror painted on his countenance.

"They are there!" said he; "they have taken possession of it; our dwelling is full of them. Oh! how frightful they are! What a blessing mamma is not there; she would have died of fright to see them enter."

I confess I was much agitated; but, not wishing to expose my children to danger before I had done all in my power to prevent it, I ordered them to remain behind till I called them. I broke a branch from a tree hastily, which I held in one hand, and in the other some long nails, which I found by chance in the bottom of my pocket; and I advanced thus to my Tree-Castle. I expected to have found the door of my staircase torn open and broken, and our new guests ascending and descending; but I saw at once it was closed as I had left it; being of bark, it was not easily distinguished. How had these natives reached the dwelling, forty feet from the ground? I had placed planks before the great opening; they were no longer there; the greater part of them had been hurled down to the ground, and I heard such a noise in our house, that I could not doubt Jack's report. I advanced timidly, holding up in the air the branch and my offerings, when I discovered, all at once, that I was offering them to a troop of monkeys, lodged in the fortress, which they were amusing themselves by destroying. We had numbers of them in the island; some large and mischievous, against whom we had some difficulty in defending ourselves when crossing the woods, where they principally dwelt. The frequent report of fire-arms round our dwelling had kept them aloof till now, when, emboldened by our absence, and enticed by the figs on our tree, they had come in crowds. These vexatious animals had got through the roof, and, once in, had thrown down the planks that covered the opening; they made the most frightful grimaces, throwing down everything they could seize.

Although this devastation caused me much vexation, I could not help laughing at their antics, and at the humble and submissive manner in which I had advanced to pay homage to them. I called my sons, who laughed heartily, and rallied "*the prince of the monkeys*" without mercy, for not knowing his own subjects. Fritz wished much to discharge his gun amongst them, but I forbade him. I was too anxious to reach Tent House, to be able to turn my thoughts on these depredators just now.

We continued our journey but I pause here; my heart is oppressed. My feelings when I reached home require another chapter to describe them, and I must summon courage for the task.

Lesson 54

1. Read chapter 47 of *Swiss Family Robinson*.
2. Copy the beginning of a sentence that transitions. (Finally…The next day…)
3. Who's missing? (Answer)

Chapter 47

We soon arrived at Family Bridge, where I had some hopes of meeting Francis, and perhaps his mother, who was beginning to walk very well; but I was disappointed they were not there. Yet I was not uneasy, for they were neither certain of the hour of our return, nor of the way we might take. I expected, however, to find them in the colonnade;

they were not there. I hastily entered the house; I called aloud, "Elizabeth! Francis! where are you?" No one answered. A mortal terror seized me and for a moment I could not move.

"They will be in the grotto," said Ernest.

"Or in the garden," said Fritz.

"Perhaps on the shore," cried Jack; "my mother likes to watch the waves, and Francis may be gathering shells."

These were possibilities. My sons flew in all directions in search of their mother and brother. I found it impossible to move, and was obliged to sit down. I trembled, and my heart beat till I could scarcely breathe. I did not venture to dwell on the extent of my fears, or, rather, I had no distinct notion of them. I tried to recover myself. I murmured, "Yes at the grotto, or the garden; they will return directly." Still, I could not compose myself. I was overwhelmed with a sad presentiment of the misfortune which impended over me. It was but too soon realized. My sons returned in fear and consternation. They had no occasion to tell me the result of their search; I saw it at once, and, sinking down motionless, I cried, "Alas! they are not there!"

Jack returned the last, and in the most frightful state; he had been at the sea-shore, and, throwing himself into my arms, he sobbed out, "The natives have been here, and carried away my mother and Francis; perhaps they have devoured them; I have seen the marks of their horrible feet on the sands, and the print of dear Francis's boots."

This account at once recalled me to strength and action.

"Come, my children, let us fly to save them. God will pity our sorrow, and assist us. He will restore them. Come, come!"

They were ready in a moment. But a distracting thought seized me. Had they carried off the pinnace? If so, every hope was gone. Jack, in his distress, had never thought of remarking this; but, the instant I named it, Fritz and he ran to ascertain the important circumstance, Ernest, in the mean time, supporting me, and endeavouring to calm me.

"Perhaps," said he, "they are still in the island. Perhaps they may have fled to hide themselves in some wood, or amongst the reeds. Even if the pinnace be left, it would be prudent to search the island from end to end before we leave it. Trust Fritz and me, we will do this; and, even if we find them in the hands of the enemy, we will recover them. Whilst we are off on this expedition, you can be preparing for our voyage, and we will search the world from one end to the other, every country and every sea, but we will find them. And we shall succeed. Let us put our whole trust in God. He is our Father, he will not try us beyond our strength."

I embraced my child, and a flood of tears relieved my overcharged heart. My eyes and hands were raised to Heaven; my silent prayers winged their flight to the Almighty, to him who tries us and consoles us. A ray of hope seemed to visit my mind, when I heard my boys cry out, as they approached

"The pinnace is here! They have not carried that away!"

I fervently thanked God it was a kind of miracle; for this pretty vessel was more tempting than the canoe. Perhaps, as it was hidden in a little creek between the rocks, it had escaped their observation; perhaps they might not know how to manage it; or they might not be numerous enough. No matter, it was there, and might be the means of our recovering the beloved objects those barbarians had torn from us. How gracious is God, to give us hope to sustain us in our afflictions! Without hope, we could not live; it restores and revives us, and, even if never realized below, accompanies us to the end of our life, and beyond the grave!

I imparted to my eldest son the idea of his brother, that they might be concealed in some part of the island; but I dared not rely on this sweet hope. Finally, as we ought not to run the risk of abandoning them, if they were still here, and perhaps in the power of the natives, I consented that my two eldest sons should go to ascertain the fact. Besides, however impatient I was, I felt that a voyage such as we were undertaking into unknown seas might be of long duration, and it was necessary to make some preparations I must think on food, water, arms, and many other things. There are situations in life which seize the heart and soul, rendering us insensible to the wants of the body this we now experienced.

We had just come from a painful journey, on foot, of twenty-four hours, during which we had had little rest, and no sleep. Since morning we had eaten nothing but some morsels of the bread-fruit; it was natural that we should be overcome with fatigue and hunger. But we none of us had even thought of our own state we were supported, if I may use the expression, by our despair. At the moment that my sons were going to set out, the remembrance of their need of refreshment suddenly occurred to me, and I besought them to rest a little, and take something; but they were too much agitated to consent. I gave Fritz a bottle of Canary, and some slices of roast mutton I met with, which he put in his pocket. They had each a loaded musket, and they set out, taking the road along the rocks, where the most hidden retreats and most impenetrable woods lay; they promised me to fire off their pieces frequently to let their mother know they were there, if she was hidden among the rocks they took also one of the dogs. Flora we could not find, which made us conclude she had followed her mistress, to whom she was much attached.

As soon as my eldest sons had left us, I made Jack conduct me to the shore where he had seen the footmarks, that I might examine them, to judge of their number and direction. I found many very distinct, but so mingled, I could come to no positive conclusion. Some were near the sea, with the foot pointing to the shore; and amongst these Jack thought he could distinguish the boot-mark of Francis. My wife wore very light boots also, which I had made for her; they rendered stockings unnecessary, and strengthened her ankles. I could not find the trace of these; but I soon discovered that my poor Elizabeth had been here, from a piece torn from an apron she wore, made of her own cotton, and dyed red. I had now not the least doubt that she was in the canoe with her son. It was a sort of consolation to think they were together; but how many mortal fears accompanied this consolation! Oh! was I ever to see again these objects of my tenderest affection!

Certain now that they were not in the island, I was impatient for the return of my sons, and I made every preparation for our departure. The first thing I thought of was the wrecked chest, which would furnish me with means to conciliate the natives, and to ransom my loved ones. I added to it everything likely to tempt them; utensils, stuffs, trinkets; I even took with me gold and silver coin, which was thrown on one side as useless, but might be of service to us on this occasion. I wished my riches were three times as much as they were, that I might give all in exchange for the life and liberty of my wife and son. I then turned my thoughts on those remaining to me: I took, in bags and gourds, all that we had left of cassava-bread, manioc-roots, and potatoes; a barrel of salt-fish, two bottles of rum, and several jars of fresh water. Jack wept as he filled them at his fountain, which he perhaps might never see again, any more than his dear Valiant, whom I set at liberty, as well as the cow, ass, buffalo, and the beautiful donkey. These docile animals were accustomed to us and our attentions, and they remained in their places, surprised that they were neither harnessed nor mounted. We opened the poultry-yard and pigeon-cote. The flamingo would not leave us, it went and came with us from the house to the pinnace. We took also oil, candles, fuel, and a large iron pot to cook our provisions in. For our defense, I took two more guns, and a small barrel of powder, all we had left. I added besides some changes of linen, not forgetting some for my dear wife, which I hoped might be needed. The time fled rapidly while we were thus employed; night came on, and my sons returned not. My grief was inconceivable; the island was so large and woody, that they might have lost themselves, or the natives might have returned and encountered them. After twenty hours of frightful terror, I heard the report of a gun alas! only *one* report! it was the signal agreed on if they returned alone; *two* if they brought their mother; *three* if Francis also accompanied them; but I expected they would return alone, and I was still grateful. I ran to meet them; they were overcome with fatigue and vexation.

They begged to set out immediately, not to lose one precious moment; they were now sure the island did not contain those they lamented, and they hoped I would not return without discovering them, for what would the island be to us without our loved ones?

Fritz, at that moment, saw his dear Lightfoot capering round him, and could not help sighing as he caressed him, and took leave of him.

"May I find thee here," said he, "where I leave thee in such sorrow; and I will bring back thy young master," added he, turning to the bull, who was also approaching him.

He then begged me again to set out, as the moon was just rising in all her majesty.

"The queen of night," said Ernest; "will guide us to the queen of our island, who is perhaps now looking up to her, and calling on us to help her."

"Most assuredly," said I, "she is thinking on us; but it is on God she is calling for help. Let us join her in prayer, my dear children, for herself and our dear Francis."

They fell on their knees with me, and I uttered the most fervent and earnest prayer that ever human heart poured forth; and I rose with confidence that our prayers were heard. I proceeded with new courage to the creek that contained our pinnace, where Jack arranged all we had brought; we rowed out of the creek, and when we were in the bay, we held a council to consider on which side we were to commence our search. I thought of returning to the great bay, from whence our canoe had been taken; my sons, on the contrary, thought that these islanders, content with their acquisition, had been returning homewards, coasting along the island, when an unhappy chance had led their mother and brother to the shore, where the natives had seen them, and carried them off. At the most, they could but be a day before us; but that was long enough to fill us with dreadful anticipations. I yielded to the opinion of my sons, which had a great deal of reason on its side, besides the wind was favourable in that direction; and, abandoning ourselves in full confidence to Almighty God, we spread our sails, and were soon in the open sea.

Lesson 55

1. Read chapter 48 of *Swiss Family Robinson*.
2. Copy the beginning of a sentence that transitions. (Next…The following morning…)
3. Tell someone about the chapter.

Chapter 48

A gentle wind swelled our sails, and the current carried us rapidly into the open sea. I then seated myself at the helm, and employed the little knowledge I had gained during our voyage from Europe in directing our bark, so that we might avoid the rocks and coral banks that surrounded our island. My two oldest sons, overcome with fatigue, had no sooner seated themselves on a bench, than they fell into a profound sleep, notwithstanding their sorrows. Jack held out the best; his love of the sea kept him awake, and I surrendered the helm to him till I took a momentary slumber, my head resting against the stern. A happy dream placed me in the midst of my family in our dear island; but a shout from Ernest awoke me, he was calling on Jack to leave the helm, as he was contriving to run the vessel among the breakers on the coast. I seized the helm, and soon set all right, determined not to trust my giddy son again.

Jack, of all my sons, was the one who evinced most taste for the sea; but being so young when we made our voyage, his knowledge of nautical affairs was very scanty. My elder sons had learnt more. Ernest, who had a great thirst for knowledge of every kind, had questioned the pilot on all he had seen him do. He had learned a great deal in theory, but of practical knowledge he had none. The mechanical genius of Fritz had drawn conclusions from what he saw; this would have induced me to place much trust in him in case of that danger which I prayed Heaven might be averted. What a situation was mine for a father! Wandering through unknown and dangerous seas with my three sons, my only hope, in search of a fourth, and of my beloved helpmate; utterly ignorant which way we should direct our course, or where to find a trace of those we sought. How often do we allay the happiness granted us below by vain wishes! I had at one time regretted that we had no means of leaving our island; now we had left it, and our sole wish was to recover those we had lost, to bring them back to it, and never to leave it more. I sometimes regretted that I had led my sons into this danger. I might have ventured alone; but I reflected that I could not have left them, for Fritz had said, "If the natives had carried off the pinnace, I would have swum from isle to isle till I had found them." My boys all endeavoured to encourage and console me. Fritz placed himself at the rudder, observing that the pinnace was new and well built, and likely to resist a tempest. Ernest stood on the deck silently watching the stars, only breaking his silence by telling me he should be able by them to supply the want of the compass, and point out how we should direct our course. Jack climbed dexterously up the mast to let me see his skill; we called him the cabin-boy, Fritz was the pilot, Ernest the astronomer, and I was the captain and commander of the expedition. Daybreak showed us we had passed far from our island, which now only appeared a dark speck. I, as well as Fritz and Jack, was of opinion that it would be advisable to go round it, and try our fortune on the opposite coast; but Ernest, who had not forgotten his telescope, was certain he saw land in a direction he pointed out to us. We took the glass, and were soon convinced he was right. As day advanced, we saw the land plainly, and did not hesitate to sail towards it.

As this appeared the land nearest to our island, we supposed the natives might have conveyed their captives there. But more trials awaited us before we arrived there. It being necessary to shift the sail, in order to reach the coast in view, my poor cabin-boy, Jack, ran up the mast, holding by the ropes; but before he reached the sail, the rope which he held broke suddenly; he was precipitated into the sea, and disappeared in a moment; but he soon rose to the surface, trying to swim, and mingling his cries with ours. Fritz, who was the first to see the accident, was in the water almost as soon as Jack, and seizing him by the hair, swam with the other hand, calling on him to try and keep afloat, and hold by him. When I saw my two sons thus struggling with the waves, that were very strong from a land wind, I should, in my despair, have leaped in after them; but Ernest held me, and implored me to remain to assist in getting them into the pinnace. He had thrown ropes to them, and a bench which he had torn up with the strength of despair. Fritz had contrived to catch one of the ropes and fasten it round Jack, who still swam, but feebly, as if nearly exhausted. Fritz had been considered an excellent swimmer in Switzerland; he preserved all his presence of mind, calling to us to draw the rope gently, while he supported the poor boy, and pushed him towards the pinnace. At last I was able to reach and draw him up; and when I saw him extended, nearly lifeless, at the bottom of the pinnace, I fell down senseless beside him. How precious to us now was the composed mind of Ernest! In the midst of such a scene, he was calm and collected; promptly disengaging the rope from the body of Jack, he flung it back to Fritz, to help him in reaching the pinnace, attaching the other end firmly to the mast. This done, quicker than I can write it, he approached us, raised his brother so that he might relieve himself from the quantity of water he had swallowed; then turning to me, restored me to my senses by administering to me some drops of rum, and by saying, "Courage, father! you have saved Jack, and I will save Fritz. He has hold of the rope; he is swimming strongly; he is coming; he is here!"

He left me to assist his brother, who was soon in the vessel, and in my arms. Jack, perfectly recovered, joined him; and fervently did I thank God for granting me, in the midst of my trials, such a moment of happiness. We could not help fancying this happy preservation was an augury of our success in our anxious search, and that we should bring back the lost ones to our island.

"Oh, how terrified mamma would have been," said Jack, "to see me sink! I thought I was going, like a stone, to the bottom of the sea; but I pushed out my arms and legs with all my strength, and up I rose."

He as well as Fritz was quite wet. I had by chance brought some changes of clothes, which I made them put on, after giving each a little rum. They were so much fatigued, and I was so overcome by my agitation, that we were obliged to relinquish rowing, most unwillingly, as the skies threatened a storm. We gradually began to distinguish clearly the island we wished to approach; and the land-birds, which came to rest on our sails, gave us hopes that we should reach it before night; but, suddenly, such a thick fog arose, that it hid every object from us, even the sea itself, and we seemed to be sailing among the clouds. I thought it prudent to drop our anchor, as, fortunately, we had a tolerably strong one; but there appeared so little water, that I feared we were near the breakers, and I watched anxiously for the fog to dissipate, and permit us to see the coast. It finally changed into a heavy rain, which we could with difficulty protect ourselves from; there was, however, a half-deck to the pinnace, under which we crept, and sheltered ourselves. Here, crowded close together, we talked over the late accident. Fritz assured me he was never in any danger, and that he would plunge again into the sea that moment, if he had the least hope that it would lead him to find his mother and Francis. We all said the same; though Jack confessed that his friends, the waves, had not received his visit very politely, but had even beat him very rudely.

"But I would bear twice as much," said he, "to see mamma and dear Francis again. Do you think, papa, that the natives could ever hurt them? Mamma is so good, and Francis is so pretty! and then, poor mamma is so lame yet; I hope they would pity her, and carry her."

Alas! I could not hope as my boy did; I feared that they would force her to walk. I tried to conceal other horrible fears, that almost threw me into despair. I recalled all the cruelties of the cannibal nations, and shuddered to think that my Elizabeth and my darling child were perhaps in their ferocious hands. Prayer and confidence in God were the only means, not to console, but to support me, and teach me to endure my heavy affliction with resignation. I looked on my three sons, and endeavoured, for their sakes, to hope and submit. The darkness rapidly increased, till it became total; we concluded it was night. The rain having ceased, I went out to strike a light, as I wished to hang the lighted lantern to the mast, when Ernest, who was on deck, called out loudly, "Father! brothers! come! the sea is on fire!" And, indeed, as far as the eye could reach, the surface of the water appeared in flames; this light, of the most brilliant, fiery red, reached even to the vessel, and we were surrounded by it. It was a sight at once beautiful, and almost terrific. Jack seriously inquired, if there was not a volcano at the bottom of the sea; and I astonished him much by telling him, that this light was caused by a kind of marine animals, which in form resembled plants so much, that they were formerly considered such; but naturalists and modern voyagers have entirely destroyed this error, and furnished proofs that they are organized beings, having all the spontaneous movements peculiar to animals. They feel when they are touched, seek for food, seize and devour it; they are of various kinds and colours, and are known under the general name of *zoophytes*.

"And this which glitters in such beautiful colours on the sea, is called *pyrosoma*," said Ernest. "See, here are some I have caught in my hat; you may see them move. How they change colour orange, green, blue, like the rainbow; and when you touch them, the flame appears still more brilliant; now they are pale yellow."

They amused themselves some time with these bright and beautiful creatures, which appear to have but a half-life. They occupied a large space on the water, and their astonishing radiance, in the midst of the darkness of the atmosphere, had such a striking and magnificent effect, that for a few moments we were diverted from our own sad thoughts; but an observation from Jack soon recalled them.

"If Francis passed this way," said he, "how he would be amused with these funny creatures, which look like fire, but do not burn; but I know he would be afraid to touch them; and how much afraid mamma would be, as she likes no animals she does not know. Ah! how glad I shall be to tell her all about our voyage, and my excursion into the sea, and how Fritz dragged me by the hair, and what they call these fiery fishes; tell me again, Ernest; py- py- "

"Pyrosoma, Mr. Peron calls them," said Ernest. "The description of them is very interesting in his voyage, which I have read to mamma; and as she would recollect it, she would not be afraid."

"I pray to God," replied I, "that she may have nothing more to fear than the pyrosoma, and that we may soon see them again, with her and Francis."

We all said Amen; and, the day breaking, we decided to weigh the anchor, and endeavour to find a passage through the reefs to reach the island, which we now distinctly saw, and which seemed an uncultivated and rocky coast. I resumed my place at the helm, my sons took the oars, and we advanced cautiously, sounding every minute. What would have become of us if our pinnace had been injured! The sea was perfectly calm, and, after prayer to God, and a slight refreshment, we proceeded forward, looking carefully round for any canoe of the natives it might be, even our own; but, no! we were not fortunate enough to discover any trace of our beloved friends, nor any symptom of the isle being inhabited; however, as it was our only point of hope, we did not wish to abandon it. By dint of searching, we found a small bay, which reminded us of our own. It was formed by a river, broad and deep enough for our pinnace to enter. We rowed in; and having placed our vessel in a creek, where it appeared to be secure, we began to consider the means of exploring the whole island.

Lesson 56

1. Read chapter 49 of *Swiss Family Robinson*.
2. Copy the beginning of a sentence that transitions. (Next…The following morning…)
3. Tell someone about the chapter.

Chapter 49

I did not disembark on this unknown shore without great emotion: it might be inhabited by a barbarous and cruel race, and I almost doubted the prudence of thus risking my three remaining children in the hazardous and uncertain search after our dear lost ones. I think I could have borne my bereavement with Christian resignation, if I had seen my wife and child die in my arms; I should then have been certain they were happy in the bosom of their God; but to think of them in the power of ferocious and idolatrous natives, who might subject them to cruel tortures and death, chilled my very blood. I demanded of my sons, if they felt courage to pursue the difficult and perilous enterprise we had commenced. They all declared they would rather die than not find their mother and brother. Fritz even besought me, with Ernest and Jack, to return to the island, in case the wanderers should come back, and be terrified to find it deserted; and to leave him the arms, and the means of trafficking with the natives, without any uneasiness about his prudence and discretion.

I assured him I did not distrust his courage and prudence, but I showed him the futility of hoping that the natives would voluntarily carry back their victims, or that they could escape alone. And should he meet with them here, and succeed, how could he carry his recovered treasures to the island?

"No, my children," said I, "we will all search, in the confidence that God will bless our efforts."

"And perhaps sooner than we think," said Ernest. "Perhaps they are in this island."

Jack was running off immediately to search, but I called my little madcap back, till we arranged our plans. I advised that two of us should remain to watch the coast, while the other two penetrated into the interior. The first thing necessary to ascertain was if the island was inhabited, which might easily be done, by climbing some tree that overlooked the country, and remarking if there were any traces of the natives, any huts, or fires lighted, &c. Those who made any discovery were immediately to inform the rest, that we might go in a body to recover our own. If nothing announced that the island was inhabited, we were to leave it immediately, to search elsewhere. All wished to be of the party of discovery. At length, Ernest agreed to remain with me, and watch for any arrivals by sea. Before we parted, we all knelt to invoke the blessing of God on our endeavours. Fritz and Jack, as the most active, were to visit the interior of the island, and to return with information as soon as possible. To be prepared for any chance, I gave them a game-bag filled with toys, trinkets, and pieces of money, to please the natives; I also made them take some food. Fritz took his gun, after promising me he would not fire it, except to defend his life, lest he should alarm the natives, and induce them to remove their captives. Jack took his lasso, and they set out with our benedictions, accompanied by the brave Turk, on whom I depended much to discover his mistress and his companion Flora, if she was still with her friends.

As soon as they were out of sight, Ernest and I set to work to conceal as much as possible our pinnace from discovery. We lowered the masts, and hid with great care under the deck the precious chest with our treasure, provisions, and powder. We got our pinnace with great difficulty, the water being low, behind a rock, which completely concealed it on the land-side, but it was still visible from the sea. Ernest suggested that we should entirely cover it with branches of trees, so that it might appear like a heap of bushes; and we began to cut them immediately with two hatchets we found in the chest, and which we speedily fitted with handles. We found also a large iron staple, which Ernest succeeded, with a hammer and pieces of wood, in fixing in the rock to moor the pinnace to. We had some difficulty in finding branches within our reach; there were many trees on the shore, but their trunks were bare. We found, at last, at some distance, an extensive thicket, composed of a beautiful shrub, which Ernest recognized to be a species of mimosa. The trunk of this plant is knotty and stunted, about three or four feet high, and spreads its branches horizontally, clothed with beautiful foliage, and so thickly interwoven, that the little quadrupeds who make their dwellings in these thickets are obliged to open covered roads out of the entangled mass of vegetation.

At the first blow of the hatchet, a number of beautiful little creatures poured forth on all sides. They resembled the kangaroos of our island, but were smaller, more elegant, and remarkable for the beauty of their skin, which was striped like that of the zebra.

"It is the striped kangaroo," cried Ernest, "described in the voyages of Peron. How I long to have one. The female should have a pouch to contain her young ones."

He lay down very still at the entrance of the thicket, and soon had the satisfaction of seizing two, which leaped out almost into his arms. This animal is timid as the hare of our country. They endeavoured to escape, but Ernest held them fast. One was a female, which had her young one in her pouch, which my son took out very cautiously. It was an elegant little creature, with a skin like its mother, only more brilliant it was full of graceful antics. The poor mother no longer wished to escape; all her desire seemed to be to recover her offspring, and to replace it in its nest. At last, she succeeded in seizing and placing it carefully in security. Then her desire to escape was so strong, that Ernest could scarcely hold her. He wished much to keep and tame her, and asked my permission to empty one of the chests for a dwelling for her, and to carry her off in the pinnace; but I refused him decidedly. I explained to him the uncertainty of our return to the island, and the imprudence of adding to our cares, and, "certainly," added I, "you would not wish this poor mother to perish from famine and confinement, when your own mother is herself a prisoner?"

His eyes filled with tears, and he declared he would not be such a savage as to keep a poor mother in captivity. "Go, pretty creature," said he, releasing her, "and may my mother be as fortunate as you." She soon profited by his permission, and skipped off with her treasure.

We continued to cut down the branches of the mimosa; but they were so entangled, and the foliage so light, that we agreed to extend our search for some thicker branches.

As we left the shore, the country appeared more fertile: we found many unknown trees, which bore no fruit; but some covered with delicious flowers. Ernest was in his element, he wanted to collect and examine all, to endeavour to discover their names, either from analogy to other plants, or from descriptions he had read. He thought he recognized the *melaleuca*, several kinds of *mimosa*, and the Virginian pine, which has the largest and thickest branches. We loaded ourselves with as much as we could carry, and, in two or three journeys, we had collected sufficient to cover the vessel, and to make a shelter for ourselves, if we were obliged to pass the night on shore. I had given orders to my sons that both were to return before night, at all events; and if the least hope appeared, one was to run with all speed to tell us. All my fear was that they might lose their way in this unknown country: they might meet with lakes, marshes, or perplexing forests; every moment I was alarmed with the idea of some new danger, and never did any day seem so long. Ernest endeavoured, by every means in his power, to comfort and encourage me; but the buoyancy of spirit, peculiar to youth, prevented him dwelling long on one painful thought. He amused his mind by turning to search for the marine productions with which the rocks were covered: sea-weed, mosses of the most brilliant colours, *zoophytes* of various kinds, occupied his attention. He brought them to me, regretting that he could not preserve them.

"Oh! if my dear mother could see them," said he, "or if Fritz could paint them, how they would amuse Francis!"

This recalled our sorrows, and my uneasiness increased.

Lesson 57

1. Read chapter 50 of *Swiss Family Robinson*.
2. Tell someone about the chapter.
3. This is a long chapter. What happened to Jack? (Answers)

Chapter 50

All was so still around us, and our pinnace was so completely hidden with its canopy of verdure, that I could not help regretting that I had not accompanied my sons. It was now too late, but my steps involuntarily turned to the road I had seen them take, Ernest remaining on the rocks in search of natural curiosities; but I was suddenly recalled by a cry from Ernest

"Father, a canoe! a canoe!"

"Alas! is it not ours?" I said, rushing to the shore, where, indeed, I saw beyond the reefs a canoe, floating lightly, apparently filled with the islanders, easy to distinguish from their dark complexion. This canoe did not resemble ours; it was longer, narrower, and seemed to be composed of long strips of bark, quite rough, tied together at each end, which gave somewhat of a graceful form to it, though it evidently belonged to the infancy of the art of navigation. It is almost inconceivable how these frail barks resist the slightest storm; but these islanders swim so well, that even if the canoe fills, they jump out, empty it, and take their places again. When landed, one or two men take up the canoe and carry it to their habitation. This, however, appeared to be provided with out-riggers, to preserve the equilibrium, and six natives, with a sort of oars, made it fly like the wind. When it passed the part of the island where we were, we hailed it as loudly as we could; the natives answered by frightful cries, but showed no intention of approaching us or entering the bay; on the contrary, they went on with great rapidity, continuing their cries. I followed them with my eyes as far as I could in speechless emotion; for either my fancy deceived me, or I faintly distinguished a form of fairer complexion than the dark-hued beings who surrounded him features or dress I could not see; on the whole, it was a vague impression, that I trembled alike to believe or to doubt. Ernest, more active than I, had climbed a sand-bank, and, with his telescope, had commanded a better view of the canoe. He watched it round a point of land, and then came down almost as much agitated as myself. I ran to him and said,

"Ernest, was it your mother?"

"No, papa; I am certain it was not my mother," said he. "Neither was it Francis."

Here he was silent: a cold shuddering came over me.

"Why are you silent?" said I; "what do you think?"

"Indeed, papa, I could distinguish nothing," said he, "even with the telescope, they passed so quickly. Would that it were my mother and brother, we should then be sure they were living, and might follow them. We can go quicker than they with the sail; we shall overtake them behind the cape, and then we shall at least be satisfied."

I hesitated, lest my sons should come back. I would have given worlds to see them arrive before our departure, and to know they were safe. I often left off my work to take a glance into the interior of the island, hoping to see them. Frequently I mistook the trees in the twilight, which was now coming on, for moving objects. At last, I was not deceived, I saw distinctly a figure walking rapidly.

"They are here!" I cried, running forward, followed by Ernest; and we soon saw a dark-coloured figure approaching. I concluded it was a native, and, though disappointed, was not alarmed, as he was alone. I stopped, and begged Ernest to recollect all the words he had met with in his books, of the language of the natives. The black man approached; and conceive my surprise when I heard him cry, in my own language

"Don't be alarmed, father, it is I, your son Fritz."

"Is it possible," said I; "can I believe it? and Jack? What have you done with my Jack? Where is he? Speak...."

Ernest did not ask. Alas! he knew too well; he had seen with his telescope that it was his dear brother Jack that was in the canoe with the natives; but he had not dared to tell me. I was in agony. Fritz, harassed with fatigue, and overwhelmed with grief, sunk down on the ground.

"Oh father!" said he, sobbing, "I dread to appear before you without my brother! I have lost him. Can you ever forgive your unfortunate Fritz?"

"Oh yes, yes; we are all equally unfortunate," cried I, sinking down beside my son, while Ernest seated himself on the other side to support me. I then besought Fritz to tell me if the natives had murdered my dear boy. He assured me that he was not killed, but carried off by the natives; still he hoped he was safe. Ernest then told me he had seen him seated in the canoe, apparently without clothes, but not stained black as Fritz was.

"I earnestly wish he had been," said Fritz; "to that I attribute my escape. But I am truly thankful to God that you have seen him, Ernest. Which way have the monsters gone?"

Ernest pointed out the cape, and Fritz was anxious that we should embark without delay, and endeavour to snatch him from them.

"And have you learned nothing of your mother and Francis?" said I.

"Alas! nothing," said he; "though I think I recognized a handkerchief, belonging to dear mamma, on the head of a native. I will tell you all my adventure as we go. You forgive me, dear father?"

"Yes, my dear son," said I; "I forgive and pity you." After recommending ourselves to the protection of God, I desired Fritz to commence his melancholy recital.

"It will be melancholy, indeed," said the poor boy, weeping; "if we do not find my dear Jack, I shall never forgive myself for not having stained his skin before my own; then he should have been with you now "

"But I have you, my dear son, to console your father," said I. "I can do nothing myself, in my sorrow. I depend on you, my two eldest, to restore to me what I have lost. Go on, Fritz."

"We went on," continued he, "with courage and hope; and as we proceeded, we felt that you were right in saying we ought not to judge of the island by the borders. You can form no idea of the fertility of the island, or of the beauty of the trees and shrubs we met with at every step, quite unknown to me; some were covered with fragrant flowers, others with tempting fruits; which, however, we did not venture to taste, as we had not Knips to try them."

"Did you see any monkeys?" asked Ernest.

"Not one," replied his brother, "to the great vexation of Jack; but we saw parrots, and all sorts of birds of the most splendid plumage. Whilst we were remarking these creatures, I did not neglect to look carefully about for any trace that might aid our search. I saw no hut, no sort of dwelling, nor anything that could indicate that the island was inhabited, and not the slightest appearance of fresh water; and we should have been tormented with thirst if we had not found some cocoa-nuts containing milk. But if we found no dwellings, we often discovered traces of the natives, extinguished fires, remains of kangaroos and of fish, cocoa-nut shells, and even entire nuts, which we secured for ourselves; we remarked, also, footmarks on the sand. We both wished anxiously to meet with a native, that we might endeavour to make him comprehend, by signs, whom we were in search of, hoping that natural affection might have some influence even with these untaught creatures. I was only fearful that my dress and the colour of my skin might terrify them. In the mean time, Jack, with his usual rashness, had climbed to the summit of one of the tallest trees, and suddenly cried out, 'Fritz, prepare your signs, the natives are landing. Oh! what black ugly creatures they are, and nearly naked! you ought to dress yourself like them, to make friends with them. You can stain your skin with these,' throwing me down branches of a sort of fruit of a dark purple colour, large as a plum, with a skin like the mulberry. 'I have been tasting them, they are very nauseous, and they have stained my fingers black; rub yourself well with the juice of this fruit, and you will be a perfect native,'

"I agreed immediately. He descended from the tree while I undressed, and with his assistance I stained myself from head to foot, as you see me; but don't be alarmed, a single dip in the sea will make me a European again. The good-natured Jack then helped to dress me in a sort of tunic made of large leaves, and laughed heartily when he looked at me. I then wished to disguise him in the same way, but he would not consent; he declared that, when he met with mamma and Francis, he should fly to embrace them, and that he should alarm and disgust them in such a costume. He said I could protect him if the natives wished to devour him: they were now at hand, and we went forward, Jack following me with my bundle of clothes under his arm. I had slung my kangaroo-skin bag of powder and provision on my shoulders, and I was glad to see that most of the natives wore the skin of that animal, for the most part spread out like a mantle over their shoulders; few of them had other clothes, excepting one, who appeared to be the chief, and had a tunic of green rushes, neatly woven. I tried to recollect all the words of native language I could, but very few occurred to me. But, alas! they did not appear to understand my words. The chief thought I wished to rob him of his handkerchief, and repelled me roughly. I then wished to retire, and I told Jack to follow me; but four islanders seized him, opened his waistcoat and shirt, and cried out together, '*Alea tea tata.*' In an instant he was stripped, and his clothes and mine were put on in a strange fashion by the natives. Jack, mimicking all their contortions, recovered his shirt from one of them, put it on, and began to dance, calling on me to do the same, and, in a tone as if singing, repeated, 'Make your escape, Fritz, while I am amusing them; I will then run off and join you very soon,' As if I could for a moment think of leaving him in the hands of these barbarians! However, I recollected at that moment the bag you had given me of toys and trinkets; we had thoughtlessly left it under the great tree where I had undressed. I told Jack, in the same tone, I would fetch it, if he could amuse the natives till I returned, which he might be certain would be very soon. I ran off with all speed, and without opposition arrived at the tree, found my bag well guarded, indeed, father; for what was my surprise to find our two faithful dogs, Turk and Flora, sitting over it."

"Flora!" cried I, "she accompanied my dear wife and child into their captivity; they must be in this island why have we left it!"

"My dear father," continued Fritz, "depend on it, they are not there; but I feel convinced that the wretches who have carried off Jack, hold dear mamma and Francis in captivity; therefore we must, at all events, pursue them. The meeting between Flora and me was truly joyful, for I was now convinced that my mother and Francis were not far off, though certainly not on the same island, or their attached friend would not have quitted them. I concluded that the chief who had taken my mamma's handkerchief had also taken her dog, and brought her on this excursion, and that she had here met with her friend Turk, who had rambled from us.

"After caressing Flora, and taking up my bag, I ran off full speed to the spot where my dear Jack was trying to divert the barbarians. As I approached, I heard cries, not the noisy laughter of the natives, but cries of distress from my beloved brother, cries for help, addressed to me. I did not walk I flew till I reached the spot, and I then saw him bound with a sort of strong cord, made of gut; his hands were fastened behind his back, his legs tied together, and these cruel men were carrying him towards their canoe, while he was crying out, 'Fritz, Fritz, where are you?' I threw myself desperately on the six men who were bearing him off. In the struggle, my gun, which I held in my hand, caught something, and accidentally went off, and O, father, it was my own dear Jack that I wounded! I cannot tell how I survived his cry of 'You have killed me!' And when I saw his blood flow, my senses forsook me, and I fainted. When I recovered, I was alone; they had carried him off. I rose, and following the traces of his blood, arrived fortunately at the shore just as they were embarking. God permitted me to see him again, supported by one of the natives, and even to hear his feeble voice cry, 'Console yourself, Fritz, I am not dead; I am only wounded in the shoulder; it is not your fault; go, my kind brother, as quick as possible to papa, and you will both' the canoe sailed away so swiftly, that I heard no more; but I understood the rest *'you will both come and rescue me.'* But will there be time? Will they dress his wound? Oh! father, what have I done! Can you forgive me?"

Overwhelmed with grief, I could only hold out my hand to my poor boy, and assure him I could not possibly blame him for this distressing accident.

Ernest, though greatly afflicted, endeavoured to console his brother; he told him a wound in the shoulder was not dangerous, and the natives certainly intended to dress his wound, or they would have left him to die. Fritz, somewhat comforted, begged me to allow him to bathe, to divest himself of the colouring, which was now become odious to him, as being that of these ruthless barbarians. I was reluctant to consent; I thought it might still be useful, in gaining access to the natives; but he was certain they would recognize him in that disguise as the bearer of *the thunder*, and would distrust him. I now recollected to ask what had become of his gun, and was sorry to learn that they had carried it off whilst he lay insensible; he himself considered that it would be useless to them, as they had fortunately left him the bag of ammunition. Ernest, however, regretted the loss to ourselves, this being the third we had lost the one we had left in the canoe being also in the possession of the natives. The dogs we missed, too, and Fritz could give no account of them; we concluded they had either followed the natives, or were still in the island. This was another severe sorrow; it seemed as if every sort of misfortune was poured out upon us. I rested on the shoulder of Ernest in my anguish. Fritz took advantage of my silence, and leaped out of the pinnace to have a bath. I was alarmed at first; but he was such an excellent swimmer, and the sea was so calm, that I soon abandoned my fears for him.

Lesson 58

1. Read chapter 51 of *Swiss Family Robinson*.
2. Copy the beginning of a sentence that transitions.
3. Tell someone about the chapter.

Chapter 51

Fritz was now swimming far before us, and appeared to have no idea of turning, so that I was at once certain he projected swimming on to the point where we had lost sight of the natives, to be the first to discover and aid his brother. Although he was an excellent swimmer, yet the distance was so great, that I was much alarmed; and especially for his arrival by night in the midst of the natives. This fear was much increased by a very extraordinary sound, which we now heard gradually approaching us; it was a sort of submarine tempest. The weather was beautiful; there was no wind, the moon shone in a cloudless sky, yet the waves were swoln as if by a storm, and threatened to swallow us; we heard at the same time a noise like violent rain. Terrified at these phenomena, I cried out aloud for Fritz to return; and though it was almost impossible my voice could reach him, we saw him swimming towards us with all his strength. Ernest and I used all our power in rowing to meet him, so that we soon got to him. The moment he leaped in, he uttered in a stifled voice, pointing to the mountains of waves, "They are enormous marine monsters! whales, I believe! such an immense shoal! They will swallow us up!"

"No," said Ernest, quietly; "don't be alarmed; the whale is a gentle and harmless animal, when not attacked. I am very glad to see them so near. We shall pass as quietly through the midst of these colossal creatures, as we did through the shining *zoophytes*: doubtless the whales are searching for them, for they constitute a principal article of their food."

They were now very near us, sporting on the surface of the water, or plunging into its abysses, and forcing out columns of water through their nostrils to a great height, which occasionally fell on us, and wetted us. Sometimes they raised themselves on their huge tail, and looked like giants ready to fall on us and crush us; then they went down again into the water, which foamed under their immense weight. Then they seemed to be going through some military evolutions, advancing in a single line, like a body of regular troops, one after another swimming with grave dignity; still more frequently they were in lines of two and two. This wonderful sight partly diverted us from our own melancholy thoughts. Fritz had, however, seized his oar, without giving himself time to dress, whilst I, at the rudder, steered as well as I could through these monsters, who are, notwithstanding their appearance, the mildest animals that exist.

They allowed us to pass so closely, that we were wetted with the water they spouted up, and might have touched them; and with the power to overturn us with a stroke of their tail, they never noticed us; they seemed to be satisfied with each other's society. We were truly sorry to see their mortal enemy appear amongst them, the sword-fish of the south, armed with its long saw, remarkable for a sort of *fringe* of nine or ten inches long, which distinguishes it from the sword-fish of the north. They are both terrible enemies to the whale, and next to man, who wages an eternal war with them, its most formidable foes.

The whales in our South Seas had only the sword-fish to dread; as soon as they saw him approach, they dispersed, or dived into the depths of the ocean. One only, very near us, did not succeed in escaping, and we witnessed a combat, of which, however, we could not see the event. These two monsters attacked each other with equal ferocity; but as they took an opposite direction to that we were going, we soon lost sight of them, but we shall never forget our meeting with these wonderful giants of the deep.

We happily doubled the promontory behind which the canoe had passed, and found ourselves in an extensive gulf, which narrowed as it entered the land, and resembled the mouth of a river. We did not hesitate to follow its course. We went round the bay, but found no traces of man, but numerous herds of the amphibious animal, called sometimes the sea-lion, the sea-dog, or the sea-elephant, or trunked *phoca*: modern voyagers give it the last name. These animals, though of enormous size, are gentle and peaceful, unless roused by the cruelty of man. They were in such numbers on this desert coast, that they would have prevented our approach if we had intended it. They actually covered the beach and the rocks, opening their huge mouths, armed with very sharp teeth, more frightful than dangerous. As it was night when we entered the bay, they were all sleeping, but they produced a most deafening noise with their breathing. We left them to their noisy slumber; for us, alas! no such comfort remained. The continual anxiety attending an affliction like ours destroys all repose, and for three days we had not slept an hour. Since the new misfortune of Jack's captivity, we were all kept up by a kind of fever. Fritz was in a most incredible state of excitement, and declared he would never sleep till he had rescued his beloved brother. His bath had partially removed the colouring from his skin, but he was still dark enough to pass for a native, when arrayed like them. The shores of the strait we were navigating were very steep, and we had yet not met with any place where we could land; however, my sons persisted in thinking the natives could have taken no other route, as they had lost sight of their canoe round the promontory. As the strait was narrow and shallow, I consented that Fritz should throw off the clothes he had on, and swim to reconnoitre a place which seemed to be an opening in the rocks or hills that obstructed our passage, and we soon had the pleasure of seeing him standing on the shore, motioning for us to approach. The strait was now so confined, that we could not have proceeded any further with the pinnace; we could not even bring it to the shore. Ernest and I were obliged to step into the water up to the waist; but we took the precaution to tie a long and strong rope to the prow, and when we were aided by the vigorous arm of Fritz, we soon drew the pinnace near enough to fix it by means of the anchor.

There were neither trees nor rocks on that desert shore to which we could fasten the pinnace; but, to our great delight and encouragement, we found, at a short distance from our landing-place, a bark canoe, which my sons were certain was that in which Jack had been carried off. We entered it, but at first saw only the oars; at last, however, Ernest discovered, in the water which half filled the canoe, part of a handkerchief, stained with blood, which they recognized as belonging to Jack. This discovery, which relieved our doubts, caused Fritz to shed tears of joy. We were certainly on the track of the robbers, and might trust that they had not proceeded farther with their barbarity. We found on the sand, and in the boat, some cocoa-nut shells and fish-bones, which satisfied us of the nature of their repasts. We resolved to continue our search into the interior of the country, following the traces of the steps of the natives. We could not find any traces of Jack's foot, which would have alarmed us, if Fritz had not suggested that they had carried him, on account of his wound. We were about to set out, when the thoughts of the pinnace came over us; it was more than ever necessary for us to preserve this, our only means of return, and which moreover contained our goods for ransom, our ammunition, and our provisions, still untouched, for some bread-fruit Fritz had gathered, some muscles, and small, but excellent, oysters, had been sufficient for us. It was fortunate that we had brought some gourds of water with us, for we had not met with any. We decided that it would be necessary to leave one of our party to guard the precious pinnace, though this would be but an insufficient and dangerous defence, in case of the approach of the natives. My recent bereavements made me tremble at the idea of leaving either of my sons. I cannot yet reflect on the agony of that moment without horror yet it was the sole means to secure our vessel; there was not a creek or a tree to hide it, and the situation of the canoe made it certain the natives must return there to embark. My children knew my thoughts, by the distracted glances with which I alternately regarded them and the pinnace, and, after consulting each other's looks, Ernest said

"The pinnace must not remain here unguarded, father, to be taken, or, at any rate, pillaged by the natives, who will return for their canoe. Either we must all wait till they come, or you must leave me to defend it. I see, Fritz, that you could not endure to remain here."

In fact, Fritz impatiently stamped with his foot, saying

"I confess, I cannot remain here; Jack may be dying of his wound, and every moment is precious. I will seek him find him and save him! I have a presentiment I shall; and if I discover him, as I expect, in the hands of the natives, I know the way to release him, and to prevent them carrying off our pinnace."

I saw that the daring youth, in the heat of his exasperation, exposed alone to the horde of barbarians, might also become their victim. I saw that my presence was necessary to restrain and aid him; and I decided, with a heavy heart, to leave Ernest alone to protect the vessel. His calm and cool manner made it less dangerous for him to meet the natives. He knew several words of their language, and had read of the mode of addressing and conciliating them. He promised me to be prudent, which his elder brother could not be. We took the bag of toys which Fritz had brought, and left those in the chest, to use if necessary; and, praying for the blessing of Heaven on my son, we left him. My sorrow was great; but he was no longer a child, and his character encouraged me. Fritz embraced his brother, and promised him to bring Jack back in safety.

Lesson 59

1. Read the first part of chapter 52 of *Swiss Family Robinson*.
2. Copy the beginning of a sentence that transitions and tell someone about the chapter.

Chapter 52

After having traversed for some time a desert, sandy plain without meeting a living creature, we arrived at a thick wood, where we lost the traces we had carefully followed. We were obliged to direct our course by chance, keeping no fixed road, but advancing as the interwoven branches permitted us. The wood was alive with the most beautiful birds of brilliant and varied plumage; but, in our anxious and distressed state, we should have been more interested in seeing a native than a bird. We passed at last through these verdant groves, and reached an arid plain extending to the shore. We again discovered numerous footsteps; and, whilst we were observing them, we saw a large canoe pass rapidly, filled with islanders: and this time I thought that, in spite of the distance, I could recognize the canoe we had built, and which they had robbed us of. Fritz wished to swim after them, and was beginning to undress himself, and I only stopped him by declaring that if he did, I must follow him, as I had decided not to be separated from him. I even proposed that we should return to Ernest, as I was of opinion that the natives would stop at the place where we had disembarked, to take away the boat they had left, and we might then, by means of the words Ernest had acquired, learn from them what had become of my wife and children. Fritz agreed to this, though he still persisted that the easiest and quickest mode of return would have been by swimming. We were endeavouring to retrace our road, when, to our great astonishment, we saw, at a few yards' distance, a man clothed in a long black robe advancing towards us, whom we immediately recognized as a European.

"Either I am greatly deceived," said I, "or this is a missionary, a worthy servant of God, come into these remote regions to make Him known to the wretched idolators."

We hastened to him. I was not wrong. He was one of those zealous and courageous Christians who devote their energies and their lives to the instruction and eternal salvation of men born in another hemisphere, of another colour, uncivilized, but not less our brothers. I had quitted Europe with the same intention, but Providence had ordered it otherwise; yet I met with joy one of my Christian brethren, and, unable to speak from emotion, I silently embraced him. He spoke to me in English a language I had fortunately learned myself, and taught to my children and his words fell on my soul like the message of the angel to Abraham, commanding him to spare his son.

"You are the person I am seeking," said he, in a mild and tender tone, "and I thank Heaven that I have met with you. This youth is Fritz, your eldest son, I conclude; but where have you left your second son, Ernest?"

"Reverend man," cried Fritz, seizing his hands, "you have seen my brother Jack. Perhaps my mother? You know where they are. Oh! are they living?"

"Yes, they are living, and well taken care of," said the missionary; "come, and I will lead you to them."

It was, indeed, necessary to lead me; I was so overcome with joy, that I should have fainted, but the good missionary made me inhale some volatile salts which he had about him; and supported by him and my son, I managed to walk. My first words were a thanksgiving to God for his mercy; then I implored my good friend to tell me if I should indeed see my wife and children again. He assured me that an hour's walk would bring me to them; but I suddenly recollected Ernest, and refused to present myself before the beloved ones while he was still in danger. The missionary smiled, as he told me he expected this delay, and wished to know where we had left Ernest. I recounted to him our arrival in the island, and the purpose for which we had left Ernest; with our intention of returning to him as soon as we saw the canoe pass, hoping to obtain some intelligence from the natives.

"But how could you have made yourselves understood?" said he; "are you acquainted with their language?"

I told him Ernest had studied the vocabulary of the South Sea islanders.

"Doubtless that of Tahiti, or the Friendly Islands," said he; "but the dialect of these islanders differs much from theirs. I have resided here more than a year, and have studied it, so may be of use to you; let us go. Which way did you come?"

"Through that thick wood," replied I; "where we wandered a long time; and I fear we shall have some difficulty in finding our way back."

"You should have taken the precaution to notch the trees as you came," said our worthy friend; "without that precaution, you were in danger of being lost; but we will find my marks, which will lead us to the brook, and following its course we shall be safe."

"We saw no brook," remarked Fritz.

"There is a brook of excellent water, which you have missed in crossing the forest; if you had ascended the course of the stream, you would have reached the hut which contains your dear friends; the brook runs before it."

Fritz struck his forehead with vexation.

"God orders all for the best," said I to the good priest; "we might not have met with you; we should have been without Ernest; you might have sought us all day in vain. Ah! good man, it is under your holy auspices that our family ought to meet, in order to increase our happiness. Now please to tell me"

"But first," interrupted Fritz, "pray tell me how Jack is? He was wounded, and-"

"Be composed, young man," said the calm man of God; "the wound, which he confesses he owes to his own imprudence, will have no evil consequences; the natives had applied some healing herbs to it, but it was necessary to extract a small ball, an operation which I performed yesterday evening. Since then he suffers less; and will be soon well, when his anxiety about you is relieved."

Fritz embraced the kind missionary, entreating his pardon for his rashness, and adding, "Did my brother talk to you of us, sir?"

"He did," answered his friend; "but I was acquainted with you before; your mother talked continually of her husband and children. What mingled pain and delight she felt yesterday evening when the natives brought to her dear Jack, wounded! I was fortunately in the hut to comfort her, and assist her beloved boy."

"And dear Francis," said I, "how rejoiced he would be to see his brother again!"

"Francis," said the missionary, smiling, "will be the protector of you all. He is the idol of the natives now; an idolatry permitted by Christianity."

We proceeded through the wood as we conversed, and at last reached the brook. I had a thousand questions to ask, and was very anxious to know how my wife and Francis had been brought to this island, and how they met with the missionary. The five or six days we had been separated seemed to me five or six months. We walked too quickly for me to get much information. The English minister said little, and referred me to my wife and son for all details. On the subject of his own noble mission he was less reserved.

"Thank God," said he, "I have already succeeded in giving this people some notions of humanity. They love their *black friend*, as they call me, and willingly listen to my preaching, and the singing of some hymns. When your little Francis was taken, he had his reed flageolet in his pocket, and his playing and graceful manners have so captivated them that I fear they will with reluctance resign him. The king is anxious to adopt him. But do not alarm yourself, brother; I hope to arrange all happily, with the divine assistance. I have gained some power over them, and I will avail myself of it. A year ago, I could not have answered for the life of the prisoners; now I believe them to be in safety. But how much is there yet to teach these simple children of nature, who listen only to her voice, and yield to every impression! Their first impulse is good, but they are so unsteady that affection may suddenly change to hatred; they are inclined to theft, violent in their anger, yet generous and affectionate. You will see an instance of this in the abode where a woman, more unfortunate than your wife, since she has lost her husband, has found an asylum."

He was silent, and I did not question him farther on this subject. We were approaching the arm of the sea where we had left our pinnace, and my heart, at ease about the rest, became now anxious solely for Ernest. Sometimes the hills concealed the water from us; Fritz climbed them, anxious to discover his brother, at last I heard him suddenly cry out "Ernest, Ernest...."

He was answered by shouts, or rather howls, amongst which I could not distinguish the voice of my son. Terror seized me.

"These are the islanders," said I to the missionary; "and these frightful cries...."

"Are cries of joy," said he, "which will be increased when they see you. This path will conduct us to the shore. Call Fritz; but I do not see him; he will, doubtless, have descended the hill, and joined them. Have no fears; recommend your sons to be prudent. The *black friend* will speak to his black friends, and they will hear him."

We proceeded towards the shore, when, at some distance, I perceived my two sons on the deck of the pinnace, which was covered with the islanders, to whom they were distributing the treasures of the chest, at least those we had put apart in the bag; they had not been so imprudent as to open the chest itself, which would soon have been emptied; it remained snugly below the deck, with the powder-barrel. At every new acquisition, the natives uttered cries of joy, repeating *moña, moña* signifying *beautiful*. The mirrors were at first received with the most delight, but this soon changed into terror; they evidently conceived there was something magical about them, and flung them all into the sea. The coloured glass beads had then the preference, but the distribution caused many disputes. Those who had not obtained any, wished to deprive the rest of them by force. The clamour and quarrelling were increasing, when the voice of the missionary was heard, and calmed them as if by enchantment. All left the pinnace, and crowded round him; he harangued them in their own language, and pointed me out to them, naming me, *me touatane*, that is, *father*, which they repeated in their turn. Some approached me, and rubbed their noses against mine, which, the pastor had informed me, was a mark of respect. In the mean time, Fritz had informed Ernest that his mother and brothers were found, and that the man who accompanied us was a European. Ernest received the intelligence with a calm joy; it was only by the tears in his eyes you could discover how much his heart was affected; he leaped from the pinnace and came to thank the missionary. I had my share of his gratitude too, for coming to seek him, before I had seen the dear lost ones.

We had now to think of joining them. We unanimously decided to proceed by water; in the first place, that we might bring our pinnace as near as possible to my dear Elizabeth, who was still suffering from her fall, her forced voyage, and, above all, from her anxiety; besides, I confess that I felt a little fatigue, and should have reluctantly set out to cross the wood a third time; but, in addition to this, I was assured that it was the promptest mode of reaching our friends, and this alone would have decided me. The pinnace was then loosened, the sail set, and we entered with thankfulness. Dreading the agitation of my wife if she saw us suddenly, I entreated our new friend to precede us, and prepare her. He consented; but, as he was coming on board, he was suddenly stopped by the natives, and one of them addressed him for some time. The missionary listened till he had concluded, with calmness and dignity; then, turning to me, he said

"You must answer for me, brother, the request which *Parabery* makes: he wishes me, in the name of the whole, to wait a few moments for their chief, to whom they give the title of king. *Bara-ourou*, as he is called, has assembled them here for a ceremony, at which all his warriors must assist. I have been anxious to attend, fearing it might be a sacrifice to their idols, which I have always strongly opposed, and wishing to seize this occasion to declare to them the one true God."

Lesson 60

1. Read the second part of chapter 52 of *Swiss Family Robinson*.
2. Tell someone about the chapter.
3. Who was reunited with the father? (Answer)

Chapter 52 continued

"Bara-ourou is not wicked, and I hope to succeed in touching his heart, enlightening his mind, and converting him to Christianity; his example would certainly be followed by the greatest part of his subjects, who are much attached to him. Your presence, and the name of God uttered by you, with the fervour and in the attitude of profound veneration and devotion, may aid this work of charity and love. Have you sufficient self-command to delay, for perhaps a few hours, the meeting with your family? Your wife and children, not expecting you, will not suffer from suspense. If you do not agree to this, I will conduct you to them, and return, I hope in time, to fulfil my duty. I wait your decision to reply to

Parabery, who is already sufficiently acquainted with the truth, to desire that his king and his brethren should know it also."

Such were the words of this true servant of God; but I cannot do justice to the expression of his heavenly countenance. Mr. Willis, for such was his name, was forty-five or fifty years of age, tall and thin; the labours and fatigues of his divine vocation had, more than years, left their traces on his noble figure and countenance; he stooped a little, his open and elevated forehead was slightly wrinkled, and his thin hair was prematurely grey; his clear blue eyes were full of intelligence and kindness, reading your thoughts, and showing you all his own. He usually kept his arms folded over his breast, and was very calm in speaking; but when his extended hand pointed to heaven, the effect was irresistible; one might have thought he saw the very glory he spoke of. His simple words to me seemed a message from God, and it would have been impossible to resist him. It was indeed a sacrifice; but I made it without hesitation. I glanced at my sons, who had their eyes cast down; but I saw Fritz knitting his brows. "I shall stay with you, father," said I, "happy if I can assist you in fulfilling your sacred duties."

"And you, young people," said he, "are you of the same opinion?"

Fritz came forward, and frankly said, "Sir, it was, unfortunately, I who wounded my brother Jack; he has been generous enough to conceal this; you extracted the ball which I discharged into his shoulder; I owe his life to you, and mine is at your disposal; I can refuse you nothing; and, however impatient, I must remain with you."

"I repeat the same," said Ernest; "you protected our mother and brothers, and, by God's permission, you restore them to us. We will all remain with you; you shall fix the time of our meeting, which will not, I trust, be long delayed."

I signified my approbation, and the missionary gave them his hand, assuring them that their joy on meeting their friends would be greatly increased by the consciousness of this virtuous self-denial.

We soon experienced this. Mr. Willis learned from Parabery, that they were going to fetch their king in our pretty canoe when we saw it pass. The royal habitation was situated on the other side of the promontory, and we soon heard a joyful cry, that they saw the canoe coming. While the natives were engaged in preparing to meet their chief, I entered the pinnace, and descending beneath the deck, I took from the chest what I judged most fitting to present to his majesty. I chose an axe, a saw, a pretty, small, ornamented sabre, which could not do much harm, a packet of nails, and one of glass-beads. I had scarcely put aside these articles, when my sons rushed to me in great excitement.

"Oh! father," cried they, at once, "look! look! summon all your fortitude; see! there is Francis himself in the canoe; oh! how curiously he is dressed!"

I looked, and saw, at some distance, our canoe ascending the strait; it was decorated with green branches, which the natives, who formed the king's guard, held in their hand; others were rowing vigorously; and the chief, wearing a red and yellow handkerchief, which had belonged to my wife, as a turban, was seated at the stern, and a pretty, little, blooming, flaxen-haired boy was placed on his right shoulder. With what delight did I recognize my child. He was naked above the waist, and wore a little tunic of woven leaves, which reached to his knees, a necklace and bracelets of shells, and a variety of coloured feathers mingled with his bright curls; one of these fell over his face, and doubtless prevented him from seeing us. The chief seemed much engaged with him, and continually took some ornament from his own dress to decorate him. "It is my child!" said I, in great terror, to Mr. Willis, "my dearest and youngest! They have taken him from his mother. What must be her grief! He is her Benjamin the child of her love. Why have they taken him? Why have they adorned him in this manner? Why have they brought him here?"

"Have no fear," said the missionary; "they will do him no harm. I promise you they shall restore him, and you shall take him back to his mother. Place yourselves at my side, with these branches in your hands."

He took some from Parabery, who held a bundle of them, and gave us each one; each of the natives took one also. They were from a tree which had slender, elegant leaves, and rich scarlet flowers species of *mimosa*; the Indians call it the tree of peace. They carry a branch of it when they have no hostile intentions; in all their assemblies, when war is proclaimed, they make a fire of these branches, and if all are consumed, it is considered an omen of victory.

While Mr. Willis was explaining this to us, the canoe approached. Two natives took Francis on their shoulders, two others took the king in the same way, and advanced gravely towards us. What difficulty I had to restrain myself from snatching my child from his bearers, and embracing him! My sons were equally agitated; Fritz was darting forward, but the missionary restrained him. Francis, somewhat alarmed at his position, had his eyes cast down, and had not yet seen us. When the king was within twenty yards of us, they stopped, and all the natives prostrated themselves before him; we alone remained standing. Then Francis saw us, and uttered a piercing cry, calling out, "Papa! dear brothers!" He struggled to quit the shoulders of his bearers, but they held him too firmly. It was impossible to restrain ourselves longer; we all cried out, and mingled our tears and lamentations. I said to the good missionary, a little too harshly, perhaps, "Ah! if you were a father!"

"I am," said he, "the father of all this flock, and your children are mine; I am answerable for all. Command your sons to be silent; request the child to be composed, and leave the rest to me."

I immediately took advantage of the permission to speak. "Dear Francis," said I, holding out my arms, "we are come to seek you and your mother; after all our dangers, we shall soon meet again, to part no more. But be composed, my child, and do not risk the happiness of that moment by any impatience. Trust in God, and in this good friend that He has given us, and who has restored to me the treasures without which I could not live." We then waved our hands to him, and he remained still, but wept quietly, murmuring our names: "Papa, Fritz, Ernest, tell me about mamma," said he, at last, in an inquiring tone.

"She does not know we are so near her," said I. "How did you leave her?"

"Very much grieved," said he, "that they brought me away; but they have not done me any harm, they are so kind; and we shall soon all go back to her. Oh! what joy for her and our friends!"

"One word about Jack," said Fritz; "how does his wound go on?"

"Oh, pretty well," answered he; "he has no pain now, and Sophia nurses him and amuses him. How little Matilda would weep when the natives carried me off! If you knew, papa, how kind and good she is!"

I had no time to ask who Sophia and Matilda were. They had allowed me to speak to my son to tranquillize him, but the king now commanded silence, and, still elevated on the shoulders of his people, began to harangue the assembly. He was a middle-aged man, with striking features; his thick lips, his hair tinged with red paint, his dark brown face, which, as well as his body, was tattooed with white, gave him a formidable aspect; yet his countenance was not unpleasant, and announced no ferocity. In general, these natives have enormous mouths, with long white teeth; they wear a tunic of reeds or leaves from the waist to the knees. My wife's handkerchief, which I had recognized at first, was gracefully twisted round the head of the king; his hair was fastened up high, and ornamented with feathers, but he had nearly removed them all to deck my boy. He placed him at his side, and frequently pointed him out during his speech. I was on thorns. As soon as he had concluded, the natives shouted, clapped their hands, and surrounded my child, dancing, and presenting him fruit, flowers, and shells, crying out, *Ouraki!* a cry in which the king, who was now standing, joined also.

"What does the word *Ouraki* mean?" said I to the missionary.

"It is the new name of your son," answered he; "or rather of the son of *Bara-ourou*, who has just adopted him."

"Never!" cried I, darting forward. "Boys, let us rescue your brother from these barbarians!" We all three rushed towards Francis, who, weeping, extended his arms to us. The natives attempted to repulse us; but at that moment the missionary pronounced some words in a loud voice; they immediately prostrated themselves on their faces, and we had no difficulty in securing the child. We brought him to our protector, who still remained in the same attitude in which he had spoken, with his eyes and his right hand raised towards heaven. He made a sign for the natives to rise, and afterwards spoke for some time to them. What would I have given to have understood him! But I formed some idea from the effect of his words. He frequently pointed to us, pronouncing the word *eroue*, and particularly addressed the king, who listened motionless to him. At the conclusion of his speech, Bara-ourou approached, and attempted to take hold of Francis, who threw himself into my arms, where I firmly held him.

"Let him now go," said Mr. Willis, "and fear nothing."

I released the child; the king lifted him up, pressed his own nose to his; then, placing him on the ground, took away the feathers and necklace with which he had decked him, and replaced him in my arms, rubbing my nose also, and repeating several words. In my first emotion, I threw myself on my knees, and was imitated by my two sons.

"It is well!" cried the missionary, again raising his eyes and hands. "Thus should you offer thanks to heaven. The king, convinced it is the will of God, restores your child, and wishes to become your friend: he is worthy to be so, for he adores and fears your God. May he soon learn to know and believe all the truths of Christianity! Let us pray together that the time may come when, on these shores, where paternal love has triumphed, I may see a temple rise to the Father of all, the God of peace and love."

He kneeled down, and the king and all his people followed his example. Without understanding the words of his prayer, I joined in the spirit of it with all my heart and soul.

I then presented my offerings to the king, increasing them considerably. I would willingly have given all my treasures in exchange for him he had restored to me. My sons also gave something to each of the natives, who incessantly cried *tayo, tayo*. I begged Mr. Willis to tell the king I gave him my canoe, and hoped he would use it to visit us in our island, to which we were returning. He appeared pleased, and wished to accompany us in our pinnace, which he seemed greatly to admire; some of his people followed him on board to row, the rest placed themselves in the canoes. We soon entered the sea again, and, doubling the second point, we came to an arm of the sea much wider, and deep enough for our pinnace, and which conducted us to the object of our dearest hopes.

Lesson 61

1. Read chapter 53 of *Swiss Family Robinson*.
2. Tell someone about what's happening.

Chapter 53

We were never weary with caressing our dear Francis. We were very anxious to learn from him all the particulars of the arrival of the natives in our island, the seizure of his mother and himself, their voyage, and their residence here, and who were the friends they had met with: but it was impossible, his tawny majesty never left us for a moment, and played with the boy as if he had been a child himself. Francis showed him all the toys from our chest; he was extremely amused with the small mirrors, and the dolls. A painted carriage, driven by a coachman who raised his whip when the wheels turned, appeared miraculous to him. He uttered screams of delight as he pointed it out to his followers. The ticking of my watch also charmed him; and as I had several more, I gave him it, showing him how to wind it up. But the first time he tried to do it, he broke the spring, and when it was silent he cared no longer for it, but threw it on one side. However, as the gold was very glittering, he took it up again, and suspending it from the handkerchief that was wound round his head, it hung over his nose, and formed a striking ornament. Francis showed him his face in a mirror, which royal amusement made him laugh heartily. He asked the missionary if it was the invisible and Almighty God who had made all these wonderful things. Mr. Willis replied, that it was he who gave men the power to make them. I do not know whether Bara-ourou comprehended this, but he remained for some time in deep thought. I profited by this to ask the missionary what were the words which had terrified them so when they wished to keep my son from me, and which had compelled them to surrender him?

"I told them," answered he, "that the Almighty and unseen God, of whom I spoke to them daily, ordered them, by my voice, to restore a son to his father; I threatened them with his anger if they refused, and promised them his mercy if they obeyed; and they did obey. The first step is gained, they know the duty of adoring and obeying God; every other truth proceeds from this, and I have no doubt that my natives will one day become good Christians. My method of instruction is suited to their limited capacity. I prove to them that their wooden idols, made by their own hands, could neither create, hear them, nor protect them. I have shown them God in his works, have declared him to be as good as he is powerful, hating evil, cruelty, murder, and cannibalism, and they have renounced all these. In their late wars they have either released or adopted their prisoners. If they carried off your wife and son, they intended it for a good action, as you will soon understand."

I could not ask Francis any questions, as Bara-ourou continued playing with him, so turning to Ernest, I asked him what passed when the natives joined him?

"When you left me," said he, "I amused myself by searching for shells, plants, and *zoophytes*, with which the rocks abound, and I have added a good deal to my collection. I was at some distance from the pinnace, when I heard a confused sound of voices, and concluded that the natives were coming; in fact, ten or a dozen issued from the road you had entered, and I cannot comprehend how you missed meeting them. Fearing they would attempt to take possession of my pinnace, I returned speedily, and seized a loaded musket, though I determined to use it only to defend my own life, or the pinnace. I stood on the deck in an attitude as bold and imposing as I could command; but I did not succeed in intimidating them. They leaped, one after the other, on deck, and surrounded me, uttering loud cries. I could not discover whether they were cries of joy or of fury; but I showed no fear, and addressed them in a friendly tone, in some words from Capt. Cook's vocabulary; but they did not seem to comprehend me, neither could I understand any of theirs except *écroue* (father), which they frequently repeated, and *tara-tauo* (woman). One of them had Fritz's gun, from which I concluded they were of the party that had carried off Jack. I took it, and showing him mine, endeavoured to make him understand that it also belonged to me. He thought I wished to exchange, and readily offered to return it, and take mine. This would not have suited me; Fritz's gun was discharged, and I could not let them have mine loaded. To prevent accident, surrounded as I was, I decided to give them a fright, and seeing a bird flying above us, I took aim so correctly, that my shot brought down the bird, a blue pigeon.

They were for a moment stupified with terror; then immediately all left the pinnace, except Parabery; he seemed to be pleased with me, often pointing to the sky, saying *mete*, which means *good*, I believe. His comrades were examining the dead bird. Some touched their own shoulders, to try if they were wounded as well as the bird and Jack had been, which convinced me they had carried him off. I tried to make Parabery understand my suspicion, and I think I succeeded, for he made me an affirmative sign, pointing to the interior of the island, and touching his shoulder with an air of pity. I took several things from the chest, and gave them to him, making signs that he should show them to the others, and induce them to return to me. He comprehended me very well, and complied with my wishes. I was soon surrounded by the whole party, begging of me. I was busy distributing beads, mirrors, and small knives when you came, and we are now excellent friends. Two or three of them returned to the wood, and brought me cocoa-nuts and bananas. But we must be careful to hide our guns, of which they have a holy horror. And now, dear father, I think we ought not to call these people *savages*. They have the simplicity of childhood; a trifle irritates them, a trifle appeases them; they are grateful and affectionate. I find them neither cruel nor barbarous. They have done me no harm, when they might easily have killed me, thrown me into the sea, or carried me away."

"We must not," said I, "judge of all native people by these, who have had the benefit of a virtuous teacher. Mr. Willis has already cast into their hearts the seeds of that divine religion, which commands us to do unto others as we would they should do unto us, and to pardon and love our enemies."

While we were discoursing, we arrived at a spot where the canoes had already landed; we were about to do the same, but the king did not seem inclined to quit the pinnace, but continued speaking to the missionary. I was still fearful that he wished to keep Francis, to whom he seemed to be more and more attached, holding him constantly on his knee; but at last, to my great joy, he placed him in my arms.

"He keeps his word with you," said Mr. Willis. "You may carry him to his mother; but, in return, he wishes you to permit him to go in your pinnace to his abode on the other side of the strait, that he may show it to the women, and he promises to bring it back; perhaps there would be danger in refusing him."

I agreed with him; but still there was a difficulty in granting this request. If he chose to keep it, how should we return? Besides, it contained our only barrel of powder, and all our articles of traffic, and how could we expect it would escape pillage?

Mr. Willis confessed he had not yet been able to cure their fondness for theft, and suggested, as the only means of security, that I should accompany the king, and bring the pinnace back, which was then to be committed to the charge of Parabery, for whose honesty he would be responsible.

Here was another delay; the day was so far advanced, that I might not, perhaps, be able to return before night. Besides, though my wife did not know we were so near her, she knew they had carried away Francis, and she would certainly be very uneasy about him. Bara-ourou looked very impatient, and as it was necessary to answer him, I decided at once; I resigned Francis to the missionary, entreating him to take him to his mother, to prepare her for our approach, and to relate the cause of our delay.

I went on board my pinnace, and, conducted by the good Parabery, we took our way to that part of the coast where the dear ones resided whom I so anxiously desired to see. Some of the natives accompanied us in their own canoe; we should have preferred having only our friend Parabery, but we were not the masters.

Favoured by the wind, we soon reached the shore we had formerly quitted, and found our excellent missionary waiting for us.

"Come," said he, "you are now going to receive your reward. Your wife and children impatiently expect you; they would have come to meet you, but your wife is still weak, and Jack suffering your presence will soon cure them."

I was too much affected to answer. Fritz gave me his arm, as much to support me as to restrain himself from rushing on before. Ernest did the same with Mr. Willis; his mildness pleased the good man, who also saw his taste for study, and tried to encourage it. After half an hour's walk, the missionary told us we were now near our good friends. I saw no sign of a habitation, nothing but trees and rocks; at last I saw a light smoke among the trees, and at that moment Francis, who had been watching, ran to meet us.

"Mamma is expecting you," said he, showing us the way through a grove of shrubs, thick enough to hide entirely the entrance into a kind of grotto; we had to stoop to pass into it. It resembled much the entrance of the bear's den, which we found in the remote part of our island. A mat of rushes covered the opening, yet permitted the light to penetrate it. Francis removed the matting, calling

"Mamma, here we are!"

A lady, apparently about twenty-seven years of age, of mild and pleasing appearance, came forward to meet me. She a clothed in a robe mad of palm-leaves tied together, which reached from her throat to her feet, leaving her beautiful arms uncovered. Her light hair was braided and fastened up round her head.

"You are welcome," said she, taking my hand; "you will be my poor friend's best physician."

We entered, and saw my dear wife seated on a bed of moss and leaves; she wept abundantly, pointing out to me our dear boy by her side. A little nymph of eleven or twelve years old was endeavouring to raise him.

"Here are your papa and brothers, Jack," said she; "you are very happy in having what I have not: but your papa will be mine, and you shall be my brother."

Jack thanked her affectionately. Fritz and Ernest, kneeling beside the couch, embraced their mother. Fritz begged her to forgive him for hurting his brother; and then tenderly inquired of Jack after his wound. For me, I cannot describe my gratitude and agitation; I could scarce utter a word to my dear wife, who, on her part, sunk down quite overcome on her bed. The lady, who was, I understood, named Madame Hirtel, approached to assist her. When she recovered, she presented to me Madame Hirtel and her two daughters. The eldest, Sophia, was attending on Jack; Matilda, who was about ten or eleven years of age, was playing with Francis; while the good missionary, on his knees, thanked God for having re-united us.

"And for life," cried my dear wife. "My dear husband, I well knew you would set out to seek me; but how could I anticipate that you would ever succeed in finding me? We will now separate no more; this beloved friend has agreed to accompany us to the Happy Island, as I intend to call it, if I ever have the happiness to reach it again with all I love in the world. How graciously God permits us to derive blessings from our sorrows. See what my trial has produced me: a friend and two dear daughters, for henceforward we are only one family."

We were mutually delighted with this arrangement, and entreated Mr. Willis to visit us often, and to come and live in the Happy Island when his mission was completed.

"I will consent," said he, "if you will come and assist me in my duties; for which purpose you and your sons must acquire the language of these islanders. We are much nearer your island than you think, for you took a very circuitous course, and Parabery, who knows it, declares it is only a day's voyage with a fair wind. And, moreover, he tells me, that he is so much delighted with you and your sons, that he cannot part with you, and wishes me to obtain your permission to accompany you, and remain with you. He will be exceedingly useful to you: will teach the language to you all, and will be a ready means of communication between us."

I gladly agreed to take Parabery with us as a friend; but it was no time yet to think of departing, as Mr. Willis wished to have Jack some days longer under his care; we therefore arranged that I and my two sons should become his guests, as his hut was but a short distance off. We had many things to hear; but, as my wife was yet too weak to relate her adventures, we resolved first to have the history of Madame Hirtel. Night coming on, the missionary lighted a gourd lamp, and, after a light collation of bread-fruit, Madame Hirtel began her story.

Lesson 62

1. Read chapter 54 of *Swiss Family Robinson*.
2. Tell someone about the chapter.
3. Who is story teller now? Who is "I?" (Answers)

Vocabulary

1. Review your vocabulary in Lesson 16 and practice the words.

Chapter 54

"My life," she began, "passed without any remarkable events, till the misfortune occurred which brought me to this island. I was married, when very young, to Mr. Hirtel, a merchant at Hamburg, an excellent man, whose loss I have deeply felt. I was very happy in this union, arranged by my parents, and sanctioned by reason. We had three children, a son and two daughters, in the first three years of our marriage; and M. Hirtel, seeing his family increase so rapidly, wished to increase his income. An advantageous establishment was offered him in the Canary Islands; he accepted it, and prevailed on me to settle there, with my family, for some years. My parents were dead, I had no tie to detain me in Europe. I was going to see new regions, those fortunate isles I had heard so much of, and I set out joyfully with my husband and children, little foreseeing the misfortunes before me.

"Our voyage was favourable; the children, like myself, were delighted with the novelties of it. I was then twenty-three years old; Sophia, seven; Matilda, six; and Alfred, our pretty, gentle boy, not yet five. Poor child! he was the darling and the plaything of all the crew."

She wept bitterly for a few moments, and then resumed her narration.

"He was as fair as your own Francis, and greatly resembled him. We proceeded first to Bourdeaux, where my husband had a correspondent, with whom he had large dealings; by his means my husband was enabled to raise large sums for his new undertaking. We carried with us, in fact, nearly his whole fortune. We re-embarked under the most favourable auspices; the weather delightful, and the wind fair; but we very soon had a change; we were met by a terrible storm and hurricane, such as the sailors had never witnessed. For a week our ship was tossed about by contrary winds, driven into unknown seas, lost all its rigging, and was at last so broken, that the water poured in on all sides. All was lost, apparently; but, in this extremity, my husband made a last attempt to save us. He tied my daughters and myself firmly to a plank, taking the charge of my boy himself, as he feared the additional weight would be too much for our raft. His intention was to tie himself to another plank, to fasten this to ours, and, taking his son in his arms, to give us a chance of being carried to the shore, which did not appear far off. Whilst he was occupied in placing us, he gave Alfred to the care of a sailor who was particularly attached to him. I heard the man say, 'Leave him with me, I will take care to save him.' On this, M. Hirtel insisted on his restoring him, and I cried out that he should be given to me. At that moment the ship, which was already fallen on its side, filled rapidly with water, plunged, and disappeared with all on board. The plank on which I and my daughters were fixed alone floated, and I saw nothing but death and desolation round me."

Madame Hirtel paused, almost suffocated by the remembrance of that awful moment.

"Poor woman!" said my wife, weeping, "it is five years since this misfortune. It was at the same time as our shipwreck, and was doubtless caused by the same storm. But how much more fortunate was I! I lost none that were dear to me, and we even had the vessel left for our use. But, my dear, unfortunate friend, by what miracle were you saved?"

"It was He who only can work miracles," said the missionary, "who cares for the widow and the orphan, and without whose word not a hair of the head can perish, who at that moment gave courage to the Christian mother."

"My strength," continued she, "was nearly exhausted, when, after being tossed about by the furious waves, I found myself thrown upon what I supposed to be a sand-bank with my two children. I envied the state of my husband and son. If I had not been a mother, I should have wished to have followed them; but my two girls lay senseless at my side, and I was anxious, as I perceived they still breathed, to recover them. At the moment M. Hirtel pushed the raft into the water, he threw upon it a box bound with iron, which I grasped mechanically, and still held, when we were left on shore. It was not locked, yet it was with some difficulty, in my confined position, that I succeeded in opening it. It contained a quantity of gold and bank-notes, which I looked upon with contempt, and regret. The wind was still blowing, but the clouds began to break, and the sun appeared, which dried and warmed us.

"My poor children opened their eyes, and knew me, and I felt I was not utterly comfortless; but their first words were to ask for their father and brother. I could not tell them they were no more. I tried to deceive myself, to support my strength, by a feeble and delusive hope. M. Hirtel swam well, the sailor still better; and the last words I had heard still rung in my ears 'Do not be uneasy, I will save the child.' If I saw anything floating at a distance, my heart began to beat, and I ran towards the water; but I saw it was only wreck, which I could not even reach. Some pieces were, however, thrown on shore, and with these and our own raft I was enabled to make a sort of shelter, by resting them against a rock. My poor children, by crouching under this, sheltered themselves from the rain, or from the rays of the sun. I had the good fortune to preserve a large beaver hat, which I wore at the time, and this protected me; but these resources gave me little consolation; my children were complaining of hunger, and I felt only how much we were in want of. I had seen a shell-fish on the shore, resembling the oyster, or muscle. I collected some, and, opening them with my knife, we made a repast on them, which sufficed for the first day. Night came. My children offered up their evening prayer, and I earnestly besought the succour of the Almighty. I then lay down beside my babes on our raft, as conveniently as we could, and they soon slept. The fearful thoughts of the past, and dreadful anticipations of the future, prevented me from sleeping. My situation was indeed melancholy; but I felt, as a mother, I ought not to wish for death.

"As soon as day broke, I went close to the shore, to seek some shell-fish for our breakfast. In crossing the sand, I nearly plunged my foot into a hole, and fancied I heard a crash. I stooped, and putting my hand into the opening, found it was full of eggs; I had broken two or three, which I tasted, and thought very good. From the colour, form, and taste, I knew them to be turtle's eggs; there were at least sixty, so I had no more care about food. I carried away in my apron as many as I could preserve from the rays of the sun: this I endeavoured to effect by burying them in the sand, and covering them with one end of our plank, and succeeded very well. Besides these, there were as many to be found on the shore as we required; I have sometimes found as many as ninety together. These were our sole support while we remained there: my children liked them very much. I forgot to add, that I was fortunate enough to discover a stream of fresh water, running into the sea; it was the same which runs past this house, and which conducted me here. The first day we suffered greatly from thirst, but on the second we met with the stream which saved us. I will not tire you by relating day by day our sad life; every one was the same, and took away by degrees every hope from me. As long as I dared to indulge any, I could not bear to leave the shore; but at last it became insupportable to me. I was worn out with gazing continually on that boundless horizon, and that moving crystal which had swallowed up my hopes. I pined for the verdure and shade of trees.

"Although I had contrived to make for my daughters little hats of a marine rush, they suffered much from the extreme heat, the burning rays of a tropical sun. I decided at last to abandon that sandy shore; to penetrate, at all risks, into the country, in order to seek a shady and cooler abode, and to escape from the view of that sea which was so painful to me. I resolved not to quit the stream which was so precious to us, for, not having any vessel to contain water, I could not carry it with us. Sophia, who is naturally quick, formed, from a large leaf, a sort of goblet, which served us to drink from; and I filled my pockets with turtles' eggs, as provision for a few days. I then set off with my two children, after praying the God of all mercy to watch over us; and, taking leave of the vast tomb which held my husband and my son, I never lost sight of the stream; if any obstacle obliged me to turn a little way from it, I soon recovered my path.

"My eldest daughter, who was very strong and robust, followed me stoutly, as I took care not to walk too far without resting; but I was often compelled to carry my little Matilda on my shoulders. Both were delighted with the shade of the woods, and were so amused with the delightful birds that inhabited them, and a pretty little sportive green monkey, that they became as playful as ever. They sang and prattled; but often asked me if papa and Alfred would not soon return to see these pretty creatures, and if we were going to seek them. These words rent my heart, and I thought it best then to tell them they would meet no more on earth, and that they were both gone to heaven, to that good God to whom they prayed morning and evening. Sophia was very thoughtful, and the tears ran down her cheeks: 'I will pray to God more than ever,' said she, 'that he may make them happy, and send them back to us,' 'Mamma,' said Matilda, 'have we left the sea to go to heaven? Shall we soon be there? And shall we see beautiful birds like these?'

"We walked on very slowly, making frequent rests, till night drew on, and it was necessary to find a place for repose. I fixed on a sort of thick grove, which I could only enter by stooping; it was formed of one tree, whose branches, reaching the ground, take root there, and soon produce other stems, which follow the same course, and become, in time, an almost impenetrable thicket. Here I found a place for us to lie down, which appeared sheltered from wild beasts or natives, whom I equally dreaded. We had still some eggs, which we ate; but I saw with fear that the time approached when we must have more food, which I knew not where to find. I saw, indeed, some fruits on the trees, but I did not know them, and feared to give them to my children, who wished to have them. I saw also cocoa-nuts, but quite out of my reach; and even if I could have got them, I did not know how to open them. The tree under whose branches we had found protection was, I conjectured, an American fig-tree; it bore a quantity of fruit, very small and red, and like the European fig. I ventured to taste them, and found them inferior to ours, insipid and soft, but, I thought, quite harmless. I remarked that the little green monkeys ate them greedily, so I had no more fear, and allowed my children to regale themselves. I was much more afraid of wild beasts during the night; however, I had seen nothing worse than some little quadrupeds resembling the rabbit or squirrel, which came in numbers to shelter themselves during the night under our tree. The children wished to catch one, but I could not undertake to increase my charge. We had a quiet night, and were early awaked by the songs of the birds. How delighted I was to have escaped the noise of the waves, and to feel the freshness of the woods, and the perfume of the flowers, with which my children made garlands, to decorate my head and their own! These ornaments, during this time of mourning and bereavement, affected me painfully, and I was weak enough to forbid them this innocent pleasure; I tore away my garland, and threw it into the rivulet. "Gather flowers," said I, "but do not dress yourselves in them; they are no fitting ornaments for us; your father and Alfred cannot see them." They were silent and sad, and threw their garlands into the water, as I had done.

"We followed the stream, and passed two more nights under the trees. We had the good fortune to find more figs; but they did not satisfy us, and our eggs were exhausted. In my distress I almost decided to return to the shore, where we might at least meet with that nourishment. As I sat by the stream, reflecting mournfully on our situation, the children, who had been throwing stones into the water, cried out, "Look, mamma, what pretty fishes!" I saw, indeed, a quantity of small salmon-trout in the river; but how could I take them? I tried to seize them with my hands, but could not catch them; necessity, however, is the mother of invention. I cut a number of branches with my knife, and wove them together to make a kind of light hurdle, the breadth of the stream, which was very narrow just here. I made two of these; my daughters assisted me, and were soon very skillful. We then undressed ourselves, and took a bath, which refreshed us much. I placed one of my hurdles upright across the rivulet, and the second a little lower. The fishes who remained between attempted to pass, but the hurdles were woven too close. We watched for them attempting the other passage; many escaped us, but we captured sufficient for our dinner. We threw them out upon the grass, at a distance from the stream, so that they could not leap back. My daughters had taken more than I; but the sensible Sophia threw back those we did not require, to give them pleasure, she said, and Matilda did the same, to see them leap. We then removed our hurdles, dressed ourselves, and I began to consider how I should cook my fish; for I had no fire, and had never kindled one myself. I tried to strike a light, and after some difficulty succeeded. I collected the fragments of the branches used for the hurdles, the children gathered some dry leaves, and I had soon a bright, lively fire, which I was delighted to see, notwithstanding the heat of the climate. I scraped the scales from the fish with my knife, washed them in the rivulet, and then placed them on the fire to broil; this was my apprenticeship in the art of cookery. I thought how useful it would be to give young ladies some knowledge of the useful arts; for who can foresee what they may need? Our European dinner delighted us as much as the bath and the fishing which had preceded it. I decided to fix our residence at the side of the rivulet, and beneath the fig-trees. My children would early learn to bear privations, to content themselves with a simple and frugal life, and to labour for their own support. I might teach them all that I knew would be useful to them in future, and above all, impress upon their young minds the great truths of our holy religion. By bringing this constantly before their unsophisticated understanding, I might hope they would draw from it the necessary virtues of resignation and contentment. I was only twenty-three years of age, and might hope, by God's mercy, to be spared to them some time, and in the course of years who knew what might happen? Besides we were not so far from the sea but that I might visit it sometimes, if it were only to seek for turtles' eggs. I remained then under our fig-tree at night, and by day on the borders of the stream."

"It was under a fig-tree, also," said my wife, "that I have spent four happy years of my life. Unknown to each other, our fate has been similar; but henceforward I hope we shall not be separated."

Madame Hirtel embraced her kind friend, and observing that the evening was advanced, and that my wife, after such agitation, needed repose, we agreed to defer till next day the conclusion of the interesting narrative. My elder sons and myself followed the missionary to his hut, which resembled the king's *palace*, though it was smaller; it was constructed of bamboos, bound together, and the intervals filled with moss and clay; it was covered in the same way, and was tolerably solid. A mat in one corner, without any covering, formed his bed; but he brought out a bear's skin, which he used in winter, and which he now spread on the ground for us. I had observed a similar one in the grotto, and he told us we should hear the history of these skins next day, in the continuation of the story of Emily, or *Mimi*, as she was affectionately called by all. We retired to our couch, after a prayer from Mr. Willis; and for the first time since my dear wife was taken from me, I slept in peace.

Lesson 63

1. Read chapter 55 of *Swiss Family Robinson.*
2. Tell someone about the chapter.

Chapter 55

We went to the grotto early in the morning, and found our two invalids much improved: my wife had slept better, and Mr. Willis found Jack's wound going on well. Madame *Mimi* told her daughters to prepare breakfast: they went out and soon returned, with a native woman and a boy of four or five years old, carrying newly-made rush baskets filled with all sorts of fruit: figs, guavas, strawberries, cocoa-nuts, and the bread-fruit.

"I must introduce you," said Emily, "to the rest of my family: this is Canda, the wife of your friend Parabery, and this is their son, *Minou-minou,* whom I regard as my own. Your Elizabeth is already attached to them, and bespeaks your friendship for them. They will follow us to the Happy Island."

"Oh, if you knew," said Francis, "what a well-behaved boy *Minou* is! He can climb trees, run, and leap, though he is less than I am. He must be my friend."

"And Canda," said Elizabeth, "shall be our assistant and friend."   `

She gave her hand to Canda, I did the same, and caressed the boy, who seemed delighted with me, and, to my great surprise, spoke to me in very good German the mother, too, knew several words of the language. They busied themselves with our breakfast: opened the cocoa-nuts, and poured the milk into the shells, after separating the kernel; they arranged the fruits on the trunk of a tree, which served for a table, and did great credit to the talent of their instructress.

"I should have liked to have offered you coffee," said Madame Hirtel, "which grows in this island, but having no utensils for roasting, grinding, or preparing it, it has been useless to me, and I have not even gathered it."

"Do you think, my dear, that it would grow in our island?" said my wife to me, in some anxiety.

I then recollected, for the first time, how fond my wife was of coffee, which, in Europe, had always been her favourite breakfast. There would certainly be in the ship some bags, which I might have brought away; but I had never thought of it, and my unselfish wife, not seeing it, had never named it, except once wishing we had some to plant in the garden. Now that there was a probability of obtaining it, she confessed that coffee and bread were the only luxuries she regretted. I promised to try and cultivate it in our island; foreseeing, however, that it would probably not be of the best quality, I told her she must not expect Mocha; but her long privation from this delicious beverage had made her less fastidious, and she assured me it would be a treat to her. After breakfast, we begged Madame Hirtel to resume her interesting narrative. She continued:

"After the reflections on my situation, which I told you of last night, I determined only to return to the sea-shore, when our food failed us in the woods; but I acquired other means of procuring it. Encouraged by the success of my fishing, I made a sort of net from the filaments of the bark of a tree and a plant resembling hemp. With these I succeeded in catching some birds: one, resembling our thrush, was very fat, and of delicious flavour. I had the greatest difficulty in overcoming my repugnance to taking away their life; nothing but the obligation of preserving our own could have reconciled me to it. My children plucked them; I then spitted them on a slender branch and roasted them before the fire. I also found some nests of eggs, which I concluded were those of the wild ducks which frequented our stream. I made myself acquainted with all the fruits which the monkeys and parroquets eat, and which were not out of my reach. I found a sort of acorn which had the flavour of a nut. The children also discovered plenty of large strawberries, a delicious repast; and I found a quantity of honeycomb in the hollow of a tree, which I obtained by stupifying the bees with a smoking brand.

"I took care to mark down every day on the blank leaves of my pocket-book. I had now marked thirty days of my wandering life on the border of the river, for I never strayed beyond the sound of its waters. Still I kept continually advancing towards the interior of the island. I had yet met with nothing alarming, and the weather had been most favourable; but we were not long to enjoy this comfort. The rainy season came on: and one night, to my great distress, I heard it descend in torrents. We were no longer under our fig-tree, which would have sheltered us for a considerable time. The tree under which we now were had tempted me by having several cavities between the roots, filled with soft moss, which formed natural couches, but the foliage was very thin, and we were soon drenched completely. I crept near my poor children to protect them a little, but in vain; our little bed was soon filled with water, and we were compelled to leave it. Our clothes were so heavy with the rain that we could scarcely stand; and the night was so dark that we could see no road, and ran the risk of falling, or striking against some tree, if we moved. My children wept, and I trembled for their health, and for my own, which was so necessary to them. This was one of the most terrible nights of my pilgrimage. My children and I knelt down, and I prayed to our Heavenly Father for strength to bear this trial, if it was his will to continue it. I felt consolation and strength from my prayers, and rose with courage and confidence; and though the rain continued unabated, I waited with resignation the pleasure of the Almighty. I reconciled my children to our situation; and Sophia told me she had asked her father, who was near the gracious God, to entreat Him to send no more rain, but let the sun come back. I assured them God would not forget them; they began to be accustomed to the rain, only Sophia begged they might take off their clothes, and then it would be like a bath in the brook. I consented to this, thinking they would be less liable to suffer than by wearing their wet garments.

"The day began to break, and I determined to walk on without stopping, in order to warm ourselves by the motion; and to try to find some cave, some hollow tree, or some tree with thick foliage, to shelter us the next night.

"I undressed the children, and made a bundle of their clothes, which I would have carried myself, but I found they would not be too heavy for them, and I judged it best to accustom them early to the difficulties, fatigue, and labour, which would be their lot; and to attend entirely on themselves; I, therefore, divided the clothes into two unequal bundles, proportioned to their strength, and having made a knot in each, I passed a slender branch through it, and showed them how to carry it on their shoulders.

"When I saw them walking before me in this native fashion, with their little white bodies exposed to the storm, I could not refrain from tears. I blamed myself for condemning them to such an existence, and thought of returning to the shore, where some vessel might rescue us; but we were now too far off to set about it. I continued to proceed with much more difficulty than my children, who had nothing on but their shoes and large hats. I carried the valuable box, in which I had placed the remains of our last night's supper, an act of necessary prudence, as there was neither fishing nor hunting now.

"As the day advanced, the rain diminished, and even the sun appeared above the horizon.

"'Look, my darlings,' said I, 'God has heard us, and sent his sun to warm and cheer us. Let us thank him,'

"'Papa has begged it of him!' said Matilda. 'Oh! mamma, let us pray him to send Alfred back!'

"My poor little girl bitterly regretted the loss of her brother. Even now she can scarcely hear his name without tears. When the natives brought Francis to us, she at first took him for her brother. 'Oh, how you have grown in heaven!' cried she; and, after she discovered he was not her brother, she often said to him, 'How I wish your name was Alfred!'

"Forgive me for dwelling so long on the details of my wretched journey, which was not without its comforts, in the pleasure I took in the development of my children's minds, and in forming plans for their future education. Though anything relating to science, or the usual accomplishments, would be useless to them, I did not wish to bring them up like young natives; I hoped to be able to communicate much useful knowledge to them, and to give them juster ideas of this world and that to come.

"As soon as the sun had dried them, I made them put on their dresses, and we continued our walk by the brook, till we arrived at the grove which is before this rock. I removed the branches to pass through it, and saw beyond them the entrance to this grotto. It was very low and narrow; but I could not help uttering a cry of joy, for this was the only sort of retreat that could securely shelter us. I was going to enter it without thought, not reflecting there might be in it some ferocious animal, when I was arrested by a plaintive cry, more like that of a child than a wild beast; I advanced with more caution, and tried to find out what sort of an inhabitant the cave contained. It was indeed a human being! an infant, whose age I could not discover; but it seemed too young to walk, and was, besides, tied up in leaves and moss, enclosed in a piece of bark, which was much torn and rent. The poor infant uttered the most piteous cries, and I did not hesitate a moment to enter the cave, and to take the innocent little creature in my arms; it ceased its cries as soon as it felt the warmth of my cheek; but it was evidently in want of food, and I had nothing to give it but some figs, of which I pressed the juice into its mouth; this seemed to satisfy it, and, rocking it in my arms, it soon went to sleep. I had then time to examine it, and to look round the cave. From the size and form of the face, I concluded it might be older than I had first thought; and I recollected to have read that the natives carried their children swaddled up in this way, even till they could walk. The complexion of the child was a pale olive, which I have since discovered is the natural complexion of the natives, before the exposure to the heat of the sun gives them the bronze hue you have seen; the features were good, except that the lips were thicker and the mouth larger than those of the Europeans. My two girls were charmed with it, and caressed it with great joy. I left them to rock it gently in its cradle of bark, till I went round this cave, which I intended for my palace, and which I have never quitted. You see it. The form is not changed; but, since Heaven has sent me a friend," looking at the missionary, "it is adorned with furniture and utensils which have completed my comforts. But to return.

"The grotto was spacious, and irregular in form. In a hollow I found, with surprise, a sort of bed, carefully arranged with moss, dry leaves, and small twigs. I was alarmed. Was this grotto inhabited by men or by wild beasts? In either case, it was dangerous to remain here. I encouraged a hope, however, that, from the infant being here, the mother must be the inhabitant, and that, on her return, finding me nursing her child, she might be induced to share her asylum with us. I could not, however, reconcile this hope with the circumstance of the child being abandoned in this open cave.

"As I was considering whether I ought to remain, or leave the cave, I heard strange cries at a distance, mingled with the screams of my children, who came running to me for protection, bringing with them the young native, who fortunately was only half awaked, and soon went to sleep again, sucking a fig. I laid him gently on the bed of leaves, and told my daughters to remain near him in a dark corner; then, stepping cautiously, I ventured to look out to discover what was passing, without being seen. The noise approached nearer, to my great alarm, and I could perceive, through the trees, a crowd of men armed with long pointed lances, clubs, and stones; they appeared furious, and the idea that they might enter the cave froze me with terror. I had an idea of taking the little native babe, and holding it in my arms, as my best shield; but this time my fears were groundless. The whole troop passed outside the wood, without even looking on the same side as the grotto; they appeared to follow some traces they were looking out for on the ground. I heard their shouts for some time, but they died away, and I recovered from my fears. Still, the dread of meeting them overcame even hunger. I had nothing left in my box but some figs, which I kept for the infant, who was satisfied with them, and I told my daughters we must go to bed without supper. The sleeping infant amused them so much, that they readily consented to give up the figs. He awoke smiling, and they gave him the figs to suck. In the mean time, I prepared to release him from his bondage to make him more comfortable; and I then saw that the outer covering of bark was torn by the teeth of some animal, and even the skin of the child slightly grazed. I ventured to carry him to the brook, into which I plunged him two or three times, which seemed to give him great pleasure.

"I ran back to the cave, which is, you see, not more than twenty yards distant, and found Sophia and Matilda very much delighted at a treasure they had found under the dry leaves in a corner. This was a great quantity of fruits of various kinds, roots of some unknown plant, and a good supply of beautiful honey, on which the little gluttons were already feasting. They came directly to give some on their fingers to their little doll, as they called the babe. This discovery made me very thoughtful. Was it possible that we were in a bear's den! I had read that they sometimes carried off infants and that they were very fond of fruits and of honey, of which they generally had a hoard. I remarked on the earth, and especially at the entrance, where the rain had made it soft, the impression of large paws which left me no doubt. The animal would certainly return to his den, and we were in the greatest danger; but where could we go? The sky, dark with clouds, threatened a return of the storm; and the troop of natives might still be wandering about the island. I had not courage, just as night set in, to depart with my children; nor could I leave the poor infant, who was now sleeping peacefully, after his honey and figs. His two nurses soon followed his example; but for me there was no rest; the noise of the wind among the trees, and of the rain pattering on the leaves, the murmur of the brook, the light bounds of the kangaroo, all made my heart beat with fear and terror; I fancied it was the bear returning to devour us. I had cut and broken some branches to place before the entrance; but these were but a weak defence against a furious and probably famished animal; and if he even did no other harm to my children, I was sure their terror at the sight of him would kill them. I paced backwards and forwards, from the entrance to the bed, in the darkness, envying the dear sleepers their calm and fearless rest; the dark-skinned baby slept soundly, nestled warmly between my daughters, till day broke at last, without anything terrible occurring. Then my little people awoke, and cried out with hunger. We ate of the fruits and honey brought us by our unknown friend, feeding, also, our little charge, to whom my daughters gave the pet name of *Minou*, which he still keeps.

Lesson 64

1. Read chapter 56 of *Swiss Family Robinson*.
2. Tell someone about the chapter.

Vocabulary

1. Go to Lesson 13 to review the words.

Chapter 56

"We had been more than an hour under the tree, when I heard cries again; but this time I was not alarmed, for I distinguished the voice of the disconsolate mother, and I knew that I could comfort her. Her grief brought her back to the spot where she thought her child had been devoured; she wished, as she afterwards told us, when we could understand her, to search for some remains of him, his hair, his bones, or even a piece of the bark that bound him; and here he was, full of life and health. She advanced slowly, sobbing, and her eyes turned to the ground. She was so absorbed in her search, that she did not see us when we were but twenty yards from her. Suddenly, Sophia darted like an arrow to her, took her hand, and said, '*Come, Minou is here.*'

"Canda neither knew what she saw nor what she heard; she took my daughter for something supernatural, and made no resistance, but followed her to the fig-tree. Even then she did not recognize the little creature, released from his bonds, half-clothed, covered with flowers, and surrounded by three divinities, for she took us for such, and wished to prostrate herself before us. She was still more convinced of it when I took up her son, and placed him in her arms: she recognized him, and the poor little infant held out his arms to her. I can never express to you the transport of the mother; she screamed, clasped her child till he was half-suffocated, rapidly repeating words which we could not understand, wept, laughed, and was in a delirium of delight that terrified *Minou*. He began to cry, and held out his arms to Sophia, who, as well as Matilda, was weeping at the sight. Canda looked at them with astonishment; she soothed the child, and put him to her breast, which he rejected at first, but finally seized it, and his mother was happy. I took the opportunity to try and make her comprehend, that the great animal had brought him here; that we had found him, and taken care of him; and I made signs for her to follow me, which she did without hesitation, till we reached the grotto, when, without entering, she fled away with her infant with such rapidity, that it was impossible to overtake her, and was soon out of sight.

"I had some difficulty in consoling my daughters for the loss of *Minou*; they thought they should see him no more, and that his mother was very ungrateful to carry him off, without even letting them take leave of him. They were still weeping and complaining, when we saw the objects of our anxiety approaching; but Canda was now accompanied by a man, who was carrying the child. They entered the grotto, and prostrated themselves before us. You know Parabery; his countenance pleased and tranquillized us. As a relation of the king, he was distinguished by wearing a short tunic of leaves; his body was tattooed and stained with various colours; but not his face, which expressed kindness and gratitude, united with great intelligence. He comprehended most of my signs. I did not succeed so well in understanding him; but saw he meant kindly. In the mean time my daughters had a more intelligible conversation with Canda and *Minou*; they half-devoured the latter with caresses, fed him with figs and honey, and amused him so much, that he would scarcely leave them. Canda was not jealous of this preference, but seemed delighted with it; she, in her turn, caressed my daughters, admired their glossy hair and fair skin, and pointed them out to her husband; she repeated *Minou* after them, but always added another *Minou*, and appeared to think this name beautiful. After some words with Parabery, she placed *Minou-Minou* in Sophia's arms, and they both departed, making signs that they would return; but we did not see them for some time after. Sophia and Matilda had their full enjoyment of their favourite; they wished to teach him to walk and to speak, and they assured me he was making great progress. They were beginning to hope his parents had left him entirely, when they came in sight, Parabery bending under the weight of two bear-skins, and a beautiful piece of matting to close the entrance to my grotto; Canda carried a basket on her head filled with fine fruit; the cocoa, the bread-fruit (which they call *rima*), pine-apples, figs, and, finally, a piece of bear's flesh, roasted at the fire, which I did not like; but I enjoyed the fruits and the milk of the cocoa-nut, of which *Minou-Minou* had a good share. They spread the bear-skins in the midst of the grotto; Parabery,

Canda, and the infant, between them, took possession of one without ceremony, and motioned to us to make our bed of the other. But the bears having only been killed the evening before, these skins had an intolerable smell. I made them comprehend this, and Parabery immediately carried them off and placed them in the brook, secured by stones. He brought us in exchange a heap of moss and leaves, on which we slept very well.

"From this moment we became one family. Canda remained with us, and repaid to my daughters all the care and affection they bestowed on *Minou-Minou*. There never was a child had more indulgence; but he deserved it, for his quickness and docility. At the end of a few months he began to lisp a few words of German, as well as his mother, of whom I was the teacher, and who made rapid progress. Parabery was very little with us, but he undertook to be our purveyor, and furnished us abundantly with everything necessary for our subsistence. Canda taught my daughter to make beautiful baskets, some, of a flat form, served for our plates and dishes. Parabery made us knives from sharp stones. My daughters, in return, taught Canda to sew. At the time of our shipwreck we had, each of us, in her pocket, a morocco housewife, with a store of needles and thread. By means of these we had mended our linen, and we now made dresses of palm-leaves. The bear-skins, washed in the stream, and thoroughly dried in the burning sun, have been very useful to us in the cold and rainy season. Now that we had guides, we made, in the fine season, excursions to different parts of the island. *Minou-Minou* soon learned to walk, and being strong, like all these islanders, would always accompany us. We went one day to the sea-shore. I shuddered at the sight, and Canda, who knew that my husband and child had perished in the sea, wept with me. We now spoke each other's language well enough to converse. She told me that a *black friend* (Emily bowed to Mr. Willis) had arrived in a neighbouring island, to announce to them that there was a Being, almighty and all-merciful, who lived in Heaven, and heard all they said. Her comprehension of this truth was very confused, and I endeavoured to make it more clear and positive.

"'I see very well,' said she, 'that you know him. Is it to Him that you speak every morning and evening, kneeling as we do before our king Bara-ourou?'

"'Yes, Canda,' said I, 'it is before Him who is the King of Kings, who gave us our life, who preserves it, and bestows on us all good, and who promises us still more when this life is past.'

"'Was it he who charged you to take care of *Minou-Minou*, and to restore him to me?' asked she.

"'Yes, Canda; all that you or I do that is good, is put into our hearts by Him.'

"I thus tried to prepare the simple mind of Canda for the great truths that Mr. Willis was to teach her."

"You left me little to do," said Mr. Willis. "I found Parabery and Canda prepared to believe, with sincere faith, the holy religion I came to teach. The God of the white people was the only one they adored. I knew Parabery, he had come to hunt seals in the island where I was established, and I was struck by his appearance. What was my astonishment to find, that when I spoke to him of the one true God, he was no stranger to the subject. He had even some ideas of a Saviour, and of future rewards and punishments.

"'It was the white lady,' said he, 'who taught me this; she teaches Canda and *Minou-minou*, whose life she saved, and whom she is bringing up to be good like herself.'

"I had a great desire," continued Mr. Willis, "to become acquainted with my powerful assistant in the great work of my mission. I told Parabery this, who offered to bring me here in his canoe; I came and found, in a miserable cave, or rather in a bear's den, all the virtues of mature age united to the charms of youth; a resigned and pious mother, bringing up her children, as women should be brought up, in simplicity, forbearance, and love of industry; teaching them, as the best knowledge, to love God with all their heart, and their neighbour as themselves. Under the inspection of their mother, they were educating the son of Parabery. This child, then four years and a half old, spoke German well, and knew his alphabet, which Madame Hirtel traced on the floor of the grotto; in this way she taught her daughters to read; they taught *Minou-minou*, who, in his turn, teaches his parents. Parabery often brings his friends to the grotto, and Madame Hirtel, having acquired the language, casts into their hearts the good seed, which I venture to hope will not be unfruitful.

"Finding these people in such a good state, and wishing to enjoy the society of a family, like myself, banished to a remote region, I decided to take up my abode in this island.

"Parabery soon built me a hut in the neighbourhood of the grotto; Madame Hirtel compelled me to take one of her bear-skins. I have by degrees formed my establishment, dividing with my worthy neighbour the few useful articles I brought from Europe, and we live a tranquil and happy life.

"And now comes the time that brought about our meeting. Some of our islanders, in a fishing expedition, were driven by the wind on your island. At the entrance of a large bay, they found a small canoe of bark, carefully moored to a tree. Either their innate propensity for theft, or the notion that it had no owner, prevailed over them, and they brought it away. I was informed of this, and was curious to see it; I recognized at once that it was made by Europeans: the careful finish, the neat form, the oars, rudder, mast, and triangular sail, all showed that it had not been made by natives. The seats of the rowers were made of planks, and were painted, and what further convinced me was, that I found in it a capital gun, loaded, and a horn of powder in a hole under one of the seats. I then made particular inquiries about the island from whence they had brought the canoe; and all their answers confirmed my idea that it must be inhabited by a European, from whom they had perhaps taken his only means of leaving it.

"Restless about this fancy, I tried to persuade them to return and discover if the island was inhabited. I could not prevail on them to restore the canoe; but, seeing me much agitated, they resolved secretly to procure me a great pleasure as they thought, by returning to the island and bringing away any one they could meet with, whether he would or not. Parabery, always the leader in perilous enterprises, and who was so attached to me, would not be left out in one which was to produce me such pleasure. They set out, and you know the result of their expedition. I leave it to your wife to tell you how she was brought away, and pass on to the time of their arrival. My people brought them to me in triumph, and were vexed that they had only found one woman and a child, whom I might give to the white lady. This I did promptly. Your wife was ill and distressed, and I carried her immediately to the grotto. There she found a companion who welcomed her with joy; Francis replaced her own lost Alfred, and the two good mothers were soon intimate friends. But, notwithstanding this solace, your Elizabeth was inconsolable at the separation from her husband and children, and terrified at the danger to which you would expose yourself in searching for her. We were even afraid she would lose her reason, when the king came to take away Francis. He had seen him on his arrival, and was much taken with his appearance; he came again to see him, and resolved to adopt him as his son. You know what passed on this subject; and now you are once more united to all those who are dear to you.

"Bless God, brother, who knows how to produce good from what we think evil, and acknowledge the wisdom of his ways. You must return all together to your island; I am too much interested in the happiness of Emily to wish to detain her; and if God permits me, when my missions are completed, I will come to end my days with you, and to bless your rising colony."

I suppress all our reflections on this interesting history, and our gratitude for the termination of our trials, and hasten to the recital, which, at my particular entreaty, my wife proceeded to give us.

Lesson 65

1. Read the first part of chapter 57.
2. Tell someone about the chapter.

Chapter 57

"My story," she began, "will not be long. I might make it in two words, *you have lost me, and you have found me*. I have every reason to thank Heaven for a circumstance, which has proved to me how dear I am to you, and has given me the happiness of gaining a friend and two dear daughters. Can one complain of an event which has produced such consequences, even though it was attended with some violence? But I ought to do the natives justice, this violence was as gentle as it could be. I need only tell you Parabery was there, to convince you I was well treated, and it was solely the sorrow of being parted from you that affected my health. I shall be well now, and as soon as Jack can walk, I shall be ready to embark for our happy island. I will now tell you how I was brought away.

"When you and our three sons left, to make the tour of the island, I was very comfortable; you had told me you might return late, or probably not till next day, and when the evening passed away without seeing you, I was not uneasy. Francis was constantly with me; we went together to water the garden, and rested in the Grotto Ernestine; then I returned to the house, took my wheel, and placed myself in my favourite colonnade, where I should be the first to see your return. Francis, seeing me at work, asked if he might go as far as the bridge to meet you; to which I readily consented. He set out, and I was sitting, thinking of the pleasure I should have in seeing you again, and hearing you relate your voyage, when I saw Francis running, crying out, 'Mamma! mamma! there is a canoe on the sea; I know it is ours; it is full of men, perhaps natives.'

"'Silly little fellow!' said I, 'it is your father and brothers; if they are in the canoe, there can be no doubt of it. Your father told me he would bring it, and they would return by water; I had forgotten this when I let you go. Now you can go and meet them on the shore; give me your arm, and I will go too,' and we set off very joyfully to meet our captors. I soon, alas! saw my error; it was, indeed, our canoe, but, instead of my dear ones, there were in it six half-naked natives, with terrible countenances, who landed and surrounded us. My blood froze with fright, and if I had wished to flee, I was unable. I fell on the shore, nearly insensible; still, I heard the cries of my dear Francis, who clung to me, and held me with all his strength; at last my senses quite failed me, and I only recovered to find myself lying at the bottom of the canoe. My son, weeping over me, was trying to recover me, assisted by one of the natives, of less repulsive appearance than his companions, and who seemed the chief; this was Parabery. He made me swallow a few drops of a detestable fermented liquor, which, however, restored me. I felt, as I recovered, the extent of my disaster, and your grief, my dears, when you should find me missing. I should have been wholly disconsolate, but that Francis was left to me, and he was continually praying me to live for his sake. I received some comfort from a vague notion that as this was our canoe, the natives had already carried you off, and were taking us to you.

"I was confirmed in this hope, when I saw that the natives, instead of making to sea, continued to coast the island, till they came to the Great Bay. I had then no doubt but that we should meet with you; but this hope was soon destroyed. Two or three more of the natives were waiting there on the shore; they spoke to their friends in the canoe; and I understood from their gestures, that they were saying they could not find anybody there. I have since learnt from Canda, that part of them landed at the Great Bay, with instructions to search that side of the island for inhabitants, whilst the rest proceeded with the canoe to examine the other side, and had succeeded but too well. The night came on, and they were anxious to return, which, doubtless, prevented them pillaging our house. I believe, moreover, that none of them could have reached Tent House, defended by our strong palisade, and hidden by the rocks amidst which it is built; and the other party, finding us on the shore, would not penetrate further.

"When all had entered the canoe, they pushed off, by the light of the stars, into the open sea. I think I must have sunk under my sorrow, but for Francis, and, I must confess it, my dear dog Flora, who had never left me. Francis told me, that she had tried to defend me, and flew at the natives; but one of them took my apron, tore it, and tied it over her mouth like a muzzle, bound her legs, and then threw her into the canoe, where the poor creature lay at my feet, moaning piteously. She arrived with us in this island, but I have not seen her since; I have often inquired of Parabery, but he could not tell me what had become of her."

"But I know," said Fritz, "and have seen her. We brought Turk with us, and the natives had carried Flora to that desert part of the island, from whence Jack was carried off; so the two dogs met. When I had the misfortune to wound Jack, I quite forgot them; they were rambling off, in chase of kangaroos; we left them, and no doubt they are there still. But we must not abandon the poor beasts; if my father will permit me, I will go and seek them in Parabery's canoe."

As we were obliged to wait a few days for Jack's recovery, I consented, on condition that Parabery accompanied them, and the next day was fixed for the expedition. Ernest begged to be of the party, that he might see the beautiful trees and flowers they had described. I then requested the narration might be continued, which had been interrupted by this episode of the two dogs. Francis resumed it where his mother had left off.

"We had a favourable passage. The sea was calm, and the boat went so smoothly, that both mamma and I went to sleep. You must have come a much longer round than necessary, papa, as your voyage lasted three days, and we arrived here the day after our departure. Mamma was then awake, and wept constantly, believing she should never more see you or my brothers. Parabery seemed very sorry for her, and tried to console her; at last, he addressed to her two or three words of German, pointing to heaven. His words were very plain *Almighty God, good*; and then *black friend*, and *white lady*; adding the words *Canda, bear*, and *Minou-minou*. We did not understand what he meant; but he seemed so pleased at speaking these words, that we could not but be pleased too; and to hear him name God in German gave us confidence, though we could not comprehend where or how he had learnt the words. 'Perhaps,' said mamma, 'he has seen your papa and brothers,' I thought so too; still, it appeared strange that, in so short a time, he could acquire and remember these words. However it might be, mamma was delighted to have him near her, and taught him to pronounce the words *father, mother*, and *son*, which did not seem strange to him, and he soon knew them. She pointed to me and to herself, as she pronounced the words, and he readily comprehended them, and said to us, with bursts of laughter, showing his large ivory teeth, *Canda, mother; Minou-minou, son; Parabery, father; white lady, mother*. Mamma thought he referred to her, but it was to Madame Emily. He tried to pronounce this name and two others, but could not succeed; at last, he said, *girls, girls*, and almost convinced us he must know some Europeans, which was a great comfort to us.

"When I saw mamma more composed, I took out my flageolet to amuse her, and played the air to Ernest's verses. This made her weep again very much, and she begged me to desist; the natives, however, wished me to continue, and I did not know whom to obey. I changed the air, playing the merriest I knew. They were in ecstasies; they took me in their arms one after the other, saying, *Bara-ourou, Bara-ourou*. I repeated the word after them, and they were still more delighted. But mamma was so uneasy to see me in their arms, that I broke from them, and returned to her.

"At last we landed. They carried mamma, who was too weak to walk. About a hundred yards from the shore, we saw a large building of wood and reeds, before which there was a crowd of natives. One who was very tall came to receive us. He was dressed in a short tunic, much ornamented, and wore a necklace of pierced shells. He was a little disfigured by a white bone passed through his nostrils. But you saw him, papa, when he wanted to adopt me; it was Bara-ourou, the king of the island. I was presented to him, and he was pleased with me, touched the end of my nose with his, and admired my hair very much. My conductors ordered me to play on the flageolet. I played some lively German airs, which made them dance and leap, till the king fell down with fatigue, and made a sign for me to desist. He then spoke for some time to the natives, who stood in a circle round him. He looked at mamma, who was seated in a corner, near her protector Parabery. He called the latter, who obliged mamma to rise, and presented her to the king. Bara-ourou looked only at the red and yellow India handkerchief which she wore on her head; he took it off, very unceremoniously, and put it on his own head, saying, *miti*, which means beautiful. He then made us re-embark in the canoe with him, amusing himself with me and my flageolet, which he attempted to play by blowing it through his nose, but did not succeed. After turning round a point which seemed to divide the island into two, we landed on a sandy beach. Parabery and another native proceeded into the interior, carrying my mother, and we followed. We arrived at a hut similar to the king's, but not so large. There we were received by Mr. Willis, whom we judged to be the *black friend*, and from that time we had no more fears. He took us under his protection, first speaking to the king and to Parabery in their own language. He then addressed mamma in German, mixed with a few English words, which we understood very well. He knew nothing of you and my brothers; but, from what mamma told him, he promised to have you sought for, and brought as soon as possible to the island. In the mean time, he offered to lead us to a friend who would take care of us, and nurse poor mamma, who looked very ill. She was obliged to be carried to the grotto; but, after that, her cares were over, and her pleasure without alloy; for the *black friend* had promised to seek you. The *white lady* received us like old friends, and Sophia and Matilda took me at first for their own brother, and still love me as if I was. We only wished for you all. Madame Mimi made mamma lie down on the bear-skin, and prepared her a pleasant beverage from the milk of the cocoa-nut. Sophia and Matilda took me to gather strawberries, and figs, and beautiful flowers; and we caught fish in the brook, between two osier hurdles. We amused ourselves very well with *Minou-minou*, while Canda and Madame Emily amused mamma.

"The king came the next day to see his little favourite; he wished me to go with him to another part of the island, where he often went to hunt; but I would not leave mamma and my new friends. I was wrong, papa; for you were there, and my brothers; it was there Jack was wounded and brought away. I might have prevented all that, and you would then have returned to us. How sorry I have been for my obstinacy! It was I, more than Fritz, who was the cause of his being wounded.

"Bara-ourou returned in the evening to the grotto; and think, papa, of our surprise, our delight, and our distress, when he brought us poor Jack, wounded and in great pain, but still all joy at finding us again! The king told Mr. Willis he was sure Jack was my brother, and he made us a present of him, adding, that he gave him in exchange for mamma's handkerchief. Mamma thanked him earnestly, and placed Jack beside her. From him she learned all you had done to discover us. He informed Mr. Willis where he had left you, and he promised to seek and bring you to us. He then examined the wound, which Jack wished him to think he had himself caused with Fritz's gun; but this was not probable, as the ball had entered behind, and lodged in the shoulder. Mr. Willis extracted it with some difficulty, and poor Jack suffered a good deal; but all is now going on well. What a large party we shall be, papa, when we are all settled in our island; Sophia and Matilda, *Minou-Minou*, Canda, Parabery, you, papa, and two mammas, and Mr. Willis!"

My wife smiled as the little orator concluded. Mr. Willis then dressed Jack's wound, and thought he might be removed in five or six days.

"Now, my dear Jack," said I, "it is your turn to relate your history. Your brother left off where you were entertaining the natives with your buffooneries; and certainly they were never better introduced. But how did they suddenly think of carrying you away?"

"Parabery told me," said Jack, "that they were struck with my resemblance to Francis as soon as I took my flageolet. After I had played a minute or two, the native who wore mamma's handkerchief, whom I now know to be the king, interrupted me by crying out and clapping his hands. He spoke earnestly to the others, pointing to my face, and to my flageolet, which he had taken; he looked also at my jacket of blue cotton, which one of them had tied round his shoulders like a mantle; and doubtless he then gave orders for me to be carried to the canoe. They seized upon me; I screamed like a madman, kicked them and scratched them; but what could I do against seven or eight great natives? They tied my legs together, and my hands behind me, and carried me like a parcel. I could then do nothing but cry out for Fritz; and the knight of the gun came rather too soon. In attempting to defend me, some way or other, off went his gun, and the ball took up its abode in my shoulder. I can assure you an unpleasant visitor is that same ball; but here he is, the scoundrel! Father Willis pulled him out by the same door as that by which he went in; and since his departure, all goes on well.

"Now for my story. When poor Fritz saw that I was wounded, he fell down as if he had been shot at the same time. The natives, thinking he was dead, took away his gun, and carried me into the canoe. I was in despair more for the death of my brother than from my wound, which I almost forgot, and was wishing they would throw me into the sea, when I saw Fritz running at full speed to the shore; but we pushed off, and I could only call out some words of consolation. The natives were very kind to me, and one of them held me up seated on the out-rigger; they washed my wound with sea-water, sucked it, tore my pocket-handkerchief to make a bandage, and as soon as we landed, squeezed the juice of some herb into it. We sailed very quickly, and passed the place where we had landed in the morning. I knew it again, and could see Ernest standing on a sand-bank; he was watching us, and I held out my arms to him. I thought I also saw you, papa, and heard you call; but the natives yelled, and though I cried with all my strength, it was in vain. I little thought they were taking me to mamma. As soon as we had disembarked, they brought me to this grotto; and I thought I must have died of surprise and joy when I was met by mamma and Francis, and then by Sophia, Matilda, mamma Emily, and Mr. Willis, who is a second father to me. This is the end of my story. And a very pretty end it is, that brings us all together. What matters it to have had a little vexation for all this pleasure? I owe it all to you, Fritz; if you had let me sink to the bottom of the sea, instead of dragging me out by the hair, I should not have been here so happy as I am; I am obliged to the gun, too; thanks to it, I was the first to reach mamma, and see our new friends."

Lesson 66

1. Read the conclusion of *Swiss Family Robinson*.
2. How does the book end?

Chapter 57 continued

The next day, Fritz and Ernest set out on their expedition with Parabery, in his canoe, to seek our two valued dogs. The good islander carried his canoe on his back to the shore. I saw them set off, but not without some dread, in such a frail bark, into which the water leaked through every seam. But my boys could swim well; and the kind, skilful, and bold Parabery undertook to answer for their safety. I therefore recommended them to God, and returned to the grotto, to tranquillize my wife's fears. Jack was inconsolable that he could not form one of the party; but Sophia scolded him for wishing to leave them, to go upon the sea, which had swallowed up poor Alfred.

In the evening we had the pleasure of seeing our brave dogs enter the grotto. They leaped on us in a way that terrified the poor little girls at first, who took them for bears; but they were soon reconciled to them when they saw them fawn round us, lick our hands, and pass from one to the other to be caressed. My sons had had no difficulty in finding them; they had run to them at the first call, and seemed delighted to see their masters again.

The poor animals had subsisted on the remains of the kangaroos, but apparently had met with no fresh water, for they seemed dying with thirst, and rushed to the brook as soon as they discovered it, and returned again and again. Then they followed us to the hut of the good missionary, who had been engaged all day in visiting the dwellings of the natives, and teaching them the truths of religion. I had accompanied him, but, from ignorance of the language, could not aid him. I was, however, delighted with the simple and earnest manner in which he spoke, and the eagerness with which they heard him. He finished by a prayer, kneeling, and they all imitated him, lifting up their hands and eyes to heaven. He told me he was trying to make them celebrate the Sunday. He assembled them in his tent, which he wished to make a temple for the worship of the true God. He intended to consecrate it for this purpose, and to live in the grotto, after our departure.

The day arrived at last. Jack's shoulder was nearly healed, and my wife, along with her happiness, recovered her strength. The pinnace had been so well guarded by Parabery and his friends that it suffered no injury. I distributed among the islanders everything I had that could please them, and made Parabery invite them to come and see us in our island, requesting we might live on friendly terms. Mr. Willis wished much to see it, and to complete our happiness he promised to accompany and spend some days with us; and Parabery said he would take him back when he wished it.

We embarked, then, after taking leave of Bara-ourou, who was very liberal in his presents, giving us, besides fruits of every kind, a whole hog roasted, which was excellent.

We were fourteen in number; sixteen, reckoning the two dogs. The missionary accompanied us, and a young islander, whom Parabery had procured to be his servant, as he was too old and too much occupied with his mission to attend to his own wants. This youth was of a good disposition and much attached to him. Parabery took him to assist in rowing when he returned.

Emily could not but feel rather affected at leaving the grotto, where she had passed four tranquil, if not happy years, fulfilling the duties of a mother. Neither could she avoid a painful sensation when she once more saw the sea that had been so fatal to her husband and son; she could scarcely subdue the fear she had of trusting all she had left to that treacherous element. She held her daughters in her arms, and prayed for the protection of Heaven. Mr. Willis and I spoke to her of the goodness of God, and pointed out to her the calmness of the water, the security of the pinnace, and the favourable state of the wind. My wife described to her our establishment, and promised her a far more beautiful grotto than the one she had left, and at last she became more reconciled.

After seven or eight hours' voyage, we arrived at Cape Disappointment, and we agreed the bay should henceforth be called the Bay of the Happy Return.

The distance to Tent House from hence was much too great for the ladies and children to go on foot. My intention was to take them by water to the other end of the island near our house; but my elder sons had begged to be landed at the bay, to seek their live stock, and take them home. I left them there with Parabery; Jack recommended his buffalo to them, and Francis his bull, and all were found. We coasted the island, arrived at Safety Bay, and were soon at Tent House, where we found all, as we had left it, in good condition.

Notwithstanding the description my wife had given them, our new guests found our establishment far beyond their expectation. With what delight Jack and Francis ran up and down the colonnade with their young friends! What stories they had to tell of all the surprises they had prepared for their mother! They showed them *Fritzia, Jackia,* the *Franciade*, and gave their friends water from their beautiful fountain. Absence seemed to have improved everything; and I must confess I had some difficulty to refrain from demonstrating my joy as wildly as my children. *Minou-minou*, Parabery, and Canda, were lost in admiration, calling out continually, *miti*! beautiful! My wife was busied in arranging a temporary lodging for our guests. The work-room was given up to Mr. Willis; my wife and Madame Emily had our apartment, the two little girls being with them, to whom the hammocks of the elder boys were appropriated. Canda, who knew nothing about beds, was wonderfully, comfortable on the carpet. Fritz, Ernest, and the two natives, stowed themselves wherever they wished, in the colonnade, or in the kitchen; all was alike to them. I slept on moss and cotton in Mr. Willis's room, with my two younger sons. Every one was content, waiting till our ulterior arrangements were completed.

Chapter 58

I must conclude my journal here. We can scarcely be more happy than we are, and I feel no cares about my children. Fritz is so fond of the chase and of mechanics, and Ernest of study, that they will not wish to marry; but I please myself by hoping at some time to see my dear Jack and Francis happily united to Sophia and Matilda. What remains for me to tell? The details of happiness, however sweet in enjoyment, are often tedious in recital.

I will only add, that after passing a few days with us, Mr. Willis returned to his charge, promising to visit us, and eventually to join us. The Grotto Ernestine, fitted up by Fritz and Parabery, made a pretty abode for Madame Hirtel and her daughters, and the two islanders. *Minou-minou* did not leave his young mammas, and was very useful to them. I must state, also, that my son Ernest, without abandoning the study of natural history, applied himself to astronomy, and mounted the large telescope belonging to the ship; he acquired considerable knowledge of this sublime science, which his mother, however, considered somewhat useless. The course of the other planets did not interest her, so long as all went on well in that which she inhabited; and nothing now was wanting to her happiness, surrounded as she was by friends.

The following year we had a visit from a Russian vessel, the *Neva*, commanded by Captain Krusenstern, a countryman and distant relation of mine. The celebrated Horner, of Zurich, accompanied him as astronomer. Having read the first part of our journal, sent into Europe by Captain Johnson, he had come purposely to see us. Delighted with our establishment, he did not advise us to quit it. Captain Krusenstern invited us to take a passage in his vessel; we declined his offer; but my wife, though she renounced her country for ever, was glad of the opportunity of making inquiries about her relations and friends. As she had concluded, her good mother had died some years before, blessing her absent children. My wife shed some tears, but was consoled by the certainty of her mother's eternal felicity, and the hope of their meeting in futurity.

One of her brothers was also dead; he had left a daughter, to whom my wife had always been attached, though she was very young when we left. Henrietta Bodmer was now sixteen, and, Mr. Horner assured us, a most amiable girl. My wife wished much to have her with us.

Ernest would not leave Mr. Horner a moment, he was so delighted to meet with one so eminently skilful in his favourite science. Astronomy made them such friends, that Mr. Horner petitioned me to allow him to take my son to Europe, promising to bring him back himself in a few years. This was a great trial to us, but I felt that his taste for science required a larger field than our island. His mother was reluctant to part with him, but consoled herself with a notion, that he might bring his cousin Henrietta back with him.

Many tears were shed at our parting; indeed, the grief of his mother was so intense, that my son seemed almost inclined to give up his inclination; but Mr. Horner made some observations about the transit of Venus, so interesting that Ernest could not resist. He left us, promising to bring us back everything we wished for. In the mean time Captain Krusenstern left us a good supply of powder, provisions, seeds, and some capital tools, to the great delight of Fritz and Jack. They regretted their brother greatly, but diverted their minds from sorrow by application to mechanics, assisted by the intelligent Parabery. They have already succeeded in constructing, near the cascade, a corn-mill and a saw-mill, and have built a very good oven.

We miss Ernest very much. Though his taste for study withdrew him a good deal from us, and he was not so useful as his brothers, we found his calm and considerate advice often of value, and his mildness always spread a charm over our circle, in joy or in trouble.

Except this little affliction, we are very happy. Our labours are divided regularly. Fritz and Jack manage the Board of Works. They have opened a passage through the rock which divided us from the other side of the island; thus doubling our domain and our riches. At the same time, they formed a dwelling for Madame Hirtel near our own, from the same excavation in the rock. Fritz took great pains with it; the windows are made of oiled paper instead of glass; but we usually assemble in our large work-room, which is very well lighted.

Francis has the charge of our flocks and of the poultry, all greatly increased. For me, I preside over the grand work of agriculture. The two mothers, their two daughters, and Canda, manage the garden, spin, weave, take care of our clothes, and attend to household matters. Thus we all work, and everything prospers. Several families of the natives, pupils of Mr. Willis, have obtained leave, through him, to join us, and are settled at Falcon's Nest, and at the Farm. These people assist us in the cultivation of our ground, and our dear missionary in the cultivation of our souls. Nothing is wanting to complete our happiness but the return of dear Ernest.

Lesson 67 (Materials, optional: shoe box, newspaper, flour, paint, twigs, rocks, dirt/sand)

1. **Build a diorama of a scene from the island.** Use paper mache in your shoe box to build the land. Build the land today and then let it dry. You may need to finish on another day. **OR**
2. Design an invention you could have made on the island (with what was available to them)–a tool or a game or something else. Draw a picture of it.

Lesson 68

1. Finish your diorama and take a picture of it diorama for your portfolio or include your drawing with a title and a little explanation of what it is.
2. Read a chapter of *The Peterkin Papers*. This is a collection of stories about an unusual family. We're jumping into a story from the middle, but we will get to them all.
3. Tell someone the story.

AT DINNER.

ANOTHER little incident occurred in the Peterkin family. This was at dinner-time.

They sat down to a dish of boiled ham. Now it was a peculiarity of the children of the family, that half of them liked fat, and half liked lean. Mr. Peterkin sat down to cut the ham. But the ham turned out to be a very remarkable one. The fat and the lean came in separate slices,–first one of lean, then one of fat, then two slices of lean, and so on. Mr.

 Peterkin began as usual by helping the children first, according to their age. Now Agamemnon, who liked lean, got a fat slice; and Elizabeth Eliza, who preferred fat, had a lean slice. Solomon John, who could eat nothing but lean, was helped to fat, and so on. Nobody had what he could eat.

It was a rule of the Peterkin family, that no one should eat any of the vegetables without some of the meat; so now, although the children saw upon their plates apple-sauce and squash and tomato and sweet potato and sour potato, not one of them could eat a mouthful, because not one was satisfied with the meat. Mr. and Mrs. Peterkin, however, liked both fat and lean, and were making a very good meal, when they looked up and saw the children all sitting eating nothing, and looking dissatisfied into their plates.

"What is the matter now?" said Mr. Peterkin.

But the children were taught not to speak at table. Agamemnon, however, made a sign of disgust at his fat, and Elizabeth Eliza at her lean, and so on, and they presently discovered what was the difficulty.

"What shall be done now?" said Mrs. Peterkin.

They all sat and thought for a little while.

At last said Mrs. Peterkin, rather uncertainly, "Suppose we ask the lady from Philadelphia what is best to be done."

But Mr. Peterkin said he didn't like to go to her for everything; let the children try and eat their dinner as it was.

And they all tried, but they couldn't. "Very well, then." said Mr. Peterkin, "let them go and ask the lady from Philadelphia."

"All of us?" cried one of the little boys, in the excitement of the moment.

"Yes," said Mrs. Peterkin, "only put on your India-rubber boots." And they hurried out of the house.

The lady from Philadelphia was just going in to her dinner; but she kindly stopped in the entry to hear what the trouble was. Agamemnon and Elizabeth Eliza told her all the difficulty, and the lady from Philadelphia said, "But why don't you give the slices of fat to those who like the fat, and the slices of lean to those who like the lean?"

They looked at one another. Agamemnon looked at Elizabeth Eliza, and Solomon John looked at the little boys. "Why didn't we think of that?" said they, and ran home to tell their mother.

Lesson 69

1. Read chapter 2 of *The Peterkin Papers*.
2. Tell someone the story.

ABOUT ELIZABETH ELIZA'S PIANO.

ELIZABETH ELIZA had a present of a piano, and she was to take lessons of the postmaster's daughter.

They decided to have the piano set across the window in the parlor, and the carters brought it in, and went away.

After they had gone the family all came in to look at the piano; but they found the carters had placed it with its back turned towards the middle of the room, standing close against the window.

How could Elizabeth Eliza open it? How could she reach the keys to play upon it?

Solomon John proposed that they should open the window, which Agamemnon could do with his long arms. Then Elizabeth Eliza should go round upon the piazza, and open the piano. Then she could have her music-stool on the piazza, and play upon the piano there.

So they tried this; and they all thought it was a very pretty sight to see Elizabeth Eliza playing on the piano, while she sat on the piazza, with the honeysuckle vines behind her.

It was very pleasant, too, moonlight evenings. Mr. Peterkin liked to take a doze on his sofa in the room; but the rest of the family liked to sit on the piazza. So did Elizabeth Eliza, only she had to have her back to the moon.

All this did very well through the summer; but, when the fall came, Mr. Peterkin thought the air was too cold from the open window, and the family did not want to sit out on the piazza.

Elizabeth Eliza practiced in the mornings with her cloak on; but she was obliged to give up her music in the evenings the family shivered so.

One day, when she was talking with the lady from Philadelphia, she spoke of this trouble.

The lady from Philadelphia looked surprised, and then said, "But why don't you turn the piano round?"

One of the little boys pertly said, "It is a square piano."

But Elizabeth Eliza went home directly, and, with the help of Agamemnon and Solomon John, turned the piano round.

"Why did we not think of that before?" said Mrs. Peterkin. "What shall we do when the lady from Philadelphia goes home again?"

Lesson 70

1. Read chapter 3 of *The Peterkin Papers*.
2. Tell someone about the story.

THE PETERKINS TRY TO BECOME WISE.

THEY were sitting round the breakfast-table, and wondering what they should do because the lady from Philadelphia had gone away. "If," said Mrs. Peterkin, "we could only be more wise as a family!" How could they manage it? Agamemnon had been to college, and the children all went to school; but still as a family they were not wise. "It comes from books," said one of the family. "People who have a great many books are very wise." Then they counted up that there were very few books in the house,–a few school-books and Mrs. Peterkin's cook-book were all.

"That's the thing!" said Agamemnon. "We want a library."

"We want a library!" said Solomon John. And all of them exclaimed, "We want a library!"

"Let us think how we shall get one," said Mrs. Peterkin. "I have observed that other people think a great deal of thinking."

So they all sat and thought a great while.

Then said Agamemnon, "I will make a library. There are some boards in the wood-shed, and I have a hammer and some nails , and perhaps we can borrow some hinges, and there we have our library!"

They were all very much pleased at the idea.

"That's the book-case part," said Elizabeth Eliza; "but where are the books?"

So they sat and thought a little while, when Solomon John exclaimed, "I will make a book!"

They all looked at him in wonder.

"Yes," said Solomon John, "books will make us wise, but first I must make a book."

So they went into the parlor, and sat down to make a book. But there was no ink. What should he do for ink? Elizabeth Eliza said she had heard that nutgalls and vinegar made very good ink. So they decided to make some. The little boys said they could find some nutgalls up in the woods. So they all agreed to set out and pick some. Mrs. Peterkins put on her cape-bonnet, and the little boys got into their india-rubber boots, and off they went.

The nutgalls were hard to find. There was almost everything else in the woods,–chestnuts, and walnuts, and small hazel-nuts, and a great many squirrels; and they had to walk a great way before they found any nutgalls. At last they came home with a large basket and two nutgalls in it. Then came the question of the vinegar. Mrs. Peterkin had used her very last on some beets they had the day before. "Suppose we go and ask the minister's wife," said Elizabeth Eliza. So they all went to the minister's wife. She said if they wanted some good vinegar they had better set a barrel of cider down in the cellar, and in a year or two it would make very nice vinegar. But they said they wanted it that very afternoon. When the minister's wife heard this, she said she should be very glad to let them have some vinegar, and gave them a cupful to carry home.

So they stirred in the nutgalls, and by the time evening came they had very good ink.

Then Solomon John wanted a pen. Agamemnon had a steel one, but Solomon John said, "Poets always used quills." Elizabeth Eliza suggested that they should go out to the poultry-yard and get a quill. But it was already dark. They had, however, two lanterns, and the little boys borrowed the neighbors'. They set out in procession for the poultry-yard. When they got there, the fowls were all at roost, so they could look at them quietly.

But there were no geese! There were Shanghais and Cochin-Chinas, and Guinea hens, and Barbary hens, and speckled hens, and Poland roosters, and bantams, and ducks, and turkeys, but not one goose! "No geese but ourselves," said Mrs. Peterkin, wittily, as they returned to the house. The sight of this procession roused up the village. "A torchlight procession!" cried all the boys of the town; and they gathered round the house, shouting for the flag; and Mr. Peterkin had to invite them in, and give them cider and gingerbread, before he could explain to them that it was only his family visiting his hens.

After the crowd had dispersed, Solomon John sat down to think of his writing again. Agamemnon agreed to go over to the bookstore to get a quill. They all went over with him. The bookseller was just shutting up his shop. However, he agreed to go in and get a quill, which he did, and they hurried home.

So Solomon John sat down again, but there was no paper. And now the bookstore was shut up. Mr. Peterkin suggested that the mail was about in, and perhaps he should have a letter, and then they could use the envelope to write upon. So they all went to the post-office, and the little boys had their india-rubber boots on, and they all shouted when they found Mr. Peterkin had a letter. The postmaster inquired what they were shouting about; and when they told him, he said he would give Solomon John a whole sheet of paper for his book. And they all went back rejoicing.

So Solomon John sat down, and the family all sat round the table looking at him. He had his pen, his ink, and his paper. He dipped his pen into the ink and held it over the paper, and thought a minute, and then said, "But I haven't got anything to say."

Lesson 71

1. Read chapter 4 of *The Peterkin Papers.*
2. Tell someone about the story.

MRS. PETERKIN WISHES TO GO TO DRIVE.

ONE morning Mrs. Peterkin was feeling very tired, as she had been having a great many things to think of, and she said to Mr. Peterkin, "I believe I shall take a ride this morning!"

And the little boys cried out, "Oh, may we go too?"

Mrs. Peterkin said that Elizabeth Eliza and the little boys might go.

So Mr. Peterkin had the horse put into the carryall, and he and Agamemnon went off to their business, and Solomon John to school; and Mrs. Peterkin began to get ready for her ride.

She had some currants she wanted to carry to old Mrs. Twomly, and some gooseberries for somebody else, and Elizabeth Eliza wanted to pick some flowers to take to the minister's wife, so it took them a long time to prepare.

The little boys went out to pick the currants and the gooseberries, and Elizabeth Eliza went out for her flowers, and Mrs. Peterkin put on her cape-bonnet, and in time they were all ready. The little boys were in their india-rubber boots, and they got into the carriage.

Elizabeth Eliza was to drive; so she sat on the front seat, and took up the reins, and the horse started off merrily, and then suddenly stopped, and would not go any farther.

Elizabeth Eliza shook the reins, and pulled them, and then she clucked to the horse; and Mrs. Peterkin clucked; and the little boys whistled and shouted; but still the horse would not go.

"We shall have to whip him," said Elizabeth Eliza.

Now Mrs. Peterkin never liked to use the whip; but, as the horse would not go, she said she would get out and turn her head the other way, while Elizabeth Eliza whipped the horse, and when he began to go she would hurry and get in.

So they tried this, but the horse would not stir.

"Perhaps we have too heavy a load," said Mrs. Peterkin, as she got in.

So they took out the currants and the gooseberries and the flowers, but still the horse would not go.

One of the neighbors, from the opposite house, looking out just then, called out to them to try the whip. There was a high wind, and they could not hear exactly what she said.

"I have tried the whip," said Elizabeth Eliza.

"She says 'whips,' such as you eat," said one of the little boys.

"We might make those," said Mrs. Peterkin, thoughtfully.

"We have got plenty of cream," said Elizabeth Eliza.

"Yes, let us have some whips," cried the little boys, getting out.

And the opposite neighbor cried out something about whips; and the wind was very high.

So they went into the kitchen, and whipped up the cream, and made some very delicious whips; and the little boys tasted all round, and they all thought they were very nice.

They carried some out to the horse, who swallowed it down very quickly.

"That is just what he wanted," said Mrs. Peterkin; "now he will certainly go!"

So they all got into the carriage again, and put in the currants and the gooseberries and the flowers; and Elizabeth Eliza shook the reins, and they all clucked; but still the horse would not go!

"We must either give up our ride," said Mrs. Peterkin, mournfully, "or else send over to the lady from Philadelphia, and see what she will say."

The little boys jumped out as quickly as they could; they were eager to go and ask the lady from Philadelphia. Elizabeth Eliza went with them, while her mother took the reins.

They found that the lady from Philadelphia was very ill that day, and was in her bed. But when she was told what the trouble was, she very kindly said they might draw up the curtain from the window at the foot of the bed, and open the blinds, and she would see. Then she asked for her opera-glass, and looked through it, across the way, up the street, to Mrs. Peterkin's door.

After she had looked through the glass, she laid it down, leaned her head back against the pillow, for she was very tired, and then said, "Why don't you unchain the horse from the horse-post?"

Elizabeth Eliza and the little boys looked at one another, and then hurried back to the house and told their mother. The horse was untied, and they all went to ride.

Lesson 72

1. Read the first part of chapter one of *The Railway Children*.
2. Draw a picture of their home (inside or out or both).
3. What does it mean that their home had "every modern convenience?" What do you think was modern in a home more than 100 years ago?
4. Who is the book about? What do you know so far?

They were not railway children to begin with. I don't suppose they had ever thought about railways except as a means of getting to Maskelyne and Cook's, the Pantomime, Zoological Gardens, and Madame Tussaud's. They were just ordinary suburban children, and they lived with their Father and Mother in an ordinary red-brick-fronted villa, with coloured glass in the front door, a tiled passage that was called a hall, a bath-room with hot and cold water, electric bells, French windows, and a good deal of white paint, and 'every modern convenience', as the house-agents say.

There were three of them. Roberta was the eldest. Of course, Mothers never have favourites, but if their Mother *had* had a favourite, it might have been Roberta. Next came Peter, who wished to be an Engineer when he grew up; and the youngest was Phyllis, who meant extremely well.

Mother did not spend all her time in paying dull calls to dull ladies, and sitting dully at home waiting for dull ladies to pay calls to her. She was almost always there, ready to play with the children, and read to them, and help them to do their home-lessons. Besides this she used to write stories for them while they were at school, and read them aloud after tea, and she always made up funny pieces of poetry for their birthdays and for other great occasions, such as the christening of the new kittens, or the refurnishing of the doll's house, or the time when they were getting over the mumps.

These three lucky children always had everything they needed: pretty clothes, good fires, a lovely nursery with heaps of toys, and a Mother Goose wall-paper. They had a kind and merry nursemaid, and a dog who was called James, and who was their very own. They also had a Father who was just perfect--never cross, never unjust, and always ready for a game--at least, if at any time he was *not* ready, he always had an excellent reason for it, and explained the reason to the children so interestingly and funnily that they felt sure he couldn't help himself.

You will think that they ought to have been very happy. And so they were, but they did not know *how* happy till the pretty life in the Red Villa was over and done with, and they had to live a very different life indeed.

The dreadful change came quite suddenly.

Peter had a birthday--his tenth. Among his other presents was a model engine more perfect than you could ever have dreamed of. The other presents were full of charm, but the Engine was fuller of charm than any of the others were.

Its charm lasted in its full perfection for exactly three days. Then, owing either to Peter's inexperience or Phyllis's good intentions, which had been rather pressing, or to some other cause, the Engine suddenly went off with a bang. James was so frightened that he went out and did not come back all day. All the Noah's Ark people who were in the tender were broken to bits, but nothing else was hurt except the poor little engine and the feelings of Peter. The others said he cried over it--but of course boys of ten do not cry, however terrible the tragedies may be which darken their lot. He said that his eyes were red because he had a cold. This turned out to be true, though Peter did not know it was when he said it, the next day he had to go to bed and stay there. Mother began to be afraid that he might be sickening for measles, when suddenly he sat up in bed and said:

"I hate gruel--I hate barley water--I hate bread and milk. I want to get up and have something *real* to eat."

"What would you like?" Mother asked.

"A pigeon-pie," said Peter, eagerly, "a large pigeon-pie. A very large one."

So Mother asked the Cook to make a large pigeon-pie. The pie was made. And when the pie was made, it was cooked. And when it was cooked, Peter ate some of it. After that his cold was better. Mother made a piece of poetry to amuse him while the pie was being made. It began by saying what an unfortunate but worthy boy Peter was, then it went on:

> He had an engine that he loved
>   With all his heart and soul,
> And if he had a wish on earth
>   It was to keep it whole.
>
> One day--my friends, prepare your minds;
>   I'm coming to the worst--
> Quite suddenly a screw went mad,
>   And then the boiler burst!
>
> With gloomy face he picked it up
>   And took it to his Mother,
> Though even he could not suppose
>   That she could make another;

For those who perished on the line
  He did not seem to care,
His engine being more to him
  Than all the people there.

And now you see the reason why
  Our Peter has been ill:
He soothes his soul with pigeon-pie
  His gnawing grief to kill.

He wraps himself in blankets warm
  And sleeps in bed till late,
Determined thus to overcome
  His miserable fate.

And if his eyes are rather red,
  His cold must just excuse it:
Offer him pie; you may be sure
  He never will refuse it.

Father had been away in the country for three or four days. All Peter's hopes for the curing of his afflicted Engine were now fixed on his Father, for Father was most wonderfully clever with his fingers. He could mend all sorts of things. He had often acted as veterinary surgeon to the wooden rocking-horse; once he had saved its life when all human aid was despaired of, and the poor creature was given up for lost, and even the carpenter said he didn't see his way to do anything. And it was Father who mended the doll's cradle when no one else could; and with a little glue and some bits of wood and a pen-knife made all the Noah's Ark beasts as strong on their pins as ever they were, if not stronger.

Peter, with heroic unselfishness, did not say anything about his Engine till after Father had had his dinner and his after-dinner cigar. The unselfishness was Mother's idea--but it was Peter who carried it out. And needed a good deal of patience, too.

At last Mother said to Father, "Now, dear, if you're quite rested, and quite comfy, we want to tell you about the great railway accident, and ask your advice."

"All right," said Father, "fire away!"

So then Peter told the sad tale, and fetched what was left of the Engine.

"Hum," said Father, when he had looked the Engine over very carefully.

The children held their breaths.

"Is there *no* hope?" said Peter, in a low, unsteady voice.

"Hope? Rather! Tons of it," said Father, cheerfully; "but it'll want something besides hope--a bit of brazing say, or some solder, and a new valve. I think we'd better keep it for a rainy day. In other words, I'll give up Saturday afternoon to it, and you shall all help me."

"*Can* girls help to mend engines?" Peter asked doubtfully.

"Of course they can. Girls are just as clever as boys, and don't you forget it! How would you like to be an engine-driver, Phil?"

"My face would be always dirty, wouldn't it?" said Phyllis, in unenthusiastic tones, "and I expect I should break something."

"I should just love it," said Roberta--"do you think I could when I'm grown up, Daddy? Or even a stoker?"

"You mean a fireman," said Daddy, pulling and twisting at the engine. "Well, if you still wish it, when you're grown up, we'll see about making you a fire-woman. I remember when I was a boy--"

Just then there was a knock at the front door.

"Who on earth!" said Father. "An Englishman's house is his castle, of course, but I do wish they built semi-detached villas with moats and drawbridges."

Ruth--she was the parlour-maid and had red hair--came in and said that two gentlemen wanted to see the master.

"I've shown them into the Library, Sir," said she.

"I expect it's the subscription to the Vicar's testimonial," said Mother, "or else it's the choir holiday fund. Get rid of them quickly, dear. It does break up an evening so, and it's nearly the children's bedtime."

But Father did not seem to be able to get rid of the gentlemen at all quickly.

"I wish we *had* got a moat and drawbridge," said Roberta; "then, when we didn't want people, we could just pull up the drawbridge and no one else could get in. I expect Father will have forgotten about when he was a boy if they stay much longer."

Mother tried to make the time pass by telling them a new fairy story about a Princess with green eyes, but it was difficult because they could hear the voices of Father and the gentlemen in the Library, and Father's voice sounded louder and different to the voice he generally used to people who came about testimonials and holiday funds.

Then the Library bell rang, and everyone heaved a breath of relief.

"They're going now," said Phyllis; "he's rung to have them shown out."

But instead of showing anybody out, Ruth showed herself in, and she looked queer, the children thought.

"Please'm," she said, "the Master wants you to just step into the study. He looks like the dead, mum; I think he's had bad news. You'd best prepare yourself for the worst, 'm--p'raps it's a death in the family or a bank busted or--"

"That'll do, Ruth," said Mother gently; "you can go."

Then Mother went into the Library. There was more talking. Then the bell rang again, and Ruth fetched a cab. The children heard boots go out and down the steps. The cab drove away, and the front door shut. Then Mother came in. Her dear face was as white as her lace collar, and her eyes looked very big and shining. Her mouth looked like just a line of pale red--her lips were thin and not their proper shape at all.

"It's bedtime," she said. "Ruth will put you to bed."

"But you promised we should sit up late tonight because Father's come home," said Phyllis.

"Father's been called away--on business," said Mother. "Come, darlings, go at once."

They kissed her and went. Roberta lingered to give Mother an extra hug and to whisper:

"It wasn't bad news, Mammy, was it? Is anyone dead--or--"

"Nobody's dead--no," said Mother, and she almost seemed to push Roberta away. "I can't tell you anything tonight, my pet. Go, dear, go *now*."

So Roberta went.

Ruth brushed the girls' hair and helped them to undress. (Mother almost always did this herself.) When she had turned down the gas and left them she found Peter, still dressed, waiting on the stairs.

"I say, Ruth, what's up?" he asked.

"Don't ask me no questions and I won't tell you no lies," the red- headed Ruth replied. "You'll know soon enough."

Late that night Mother came up and kissed all three children as they lay asleep. But Roberta was the only one whom the kiss woke, and she lay mousey-still, and said nothing.

"If Mother doesn't want us to know she's been crying," she said to herself as she heard through the dark the catching of her Mother's breath, "we *won't* know it. That's all."

When they came down to breakfast the next morning, Mother had already gone out.

"To London," Ruth said, and left them to their breakfast.

"There's something awful the matter," said Peter, breaking his egg. "Ruth told me last night we should know soon enough."

"Did you *ask* her?" said Roberta, with scorn.

"Yes, I did!" said Peter, angrily. "If you could go to bed without caring whether Mother was worried or not, I couldn't. So there."

"I don't think we ought to ask the servants things Mother doesn't tell us," said Roberta.

"That's right, Miss Goody-goody," said Peter, "preach away."

"*I'm* not goody," said Phyllis, "but I think Bobbie's right this time."

"Of course. She always is. In her own opinion," said Peter.

"Oh, *don't*!" cried Roberta, putting down her egg-spoon; "don't let's be horrid to each other. I'm sure some dire calamity is happening. Don't let's make it worse!"

"Who began, I should like to know?" said Peter.

Roberta made an effort, and answered:--

"I did, I suppose, but--"

"Well, then," said Peter, triumphantly. But before he went to school he thumped his sister between the shoulders and told her to cheer up.

Lesson 73

1. Read the rest of chapter 1 of *The Railway Children*.
2. Draw a picture of their new home, inside or outside.
3. Just so you know: their father was arrested.
4. Tell someone about chapter 1.

The children came home to one o'clock dinner, but Mother was not there. And she was not there at tea-time.

It was nearly seven before she came in, looking so ill and tired that the children felt they could not ask her any questions. She sank into an arm-chair. Phyllis took the long pins out of her hat, while Roberta took off her gloves, and Peter unfastened her walking- shoes and fetched her soft velvety slippers for her.

When she had had a cup of tea, and Roberta had put eau-de-Cologne on her poor head that ached, Mother said:--

"Now, my darlings, I want to tell you something. Those men last night did bring very bad news, and Father will be away for some time. I am very worried about it, and I want you all to help me, and not to make things harder for me."

"As if we would!" said Roberta, holding Mother's hand against her face.

"You can help me very much," said Mother, "by being good and happy and not quarrelling when I'm away"--Roberta and Peter exchanged guilty glances--"for I shall have to be away a good deal."

"We won't quarrel. Indeed we won't," said everybody. And meant it, too.

"Then," Mother went on, "I want you not to ask me any questions about this trouble; and not to ask anybody else any questions."

Peter cringed and shuffled his boots on the carpet.

"You'll promise this, too, won't you?" said Mother.

"I did ask Ruth," said Peter, suddenly. "I'm very sorry, but I did."

"And what did she say?"

"She said I should know soon enough."

"It isn't necessary for you to know anything about it," said Mother; "it's about business, and you never do understand business, do you?"

"No," said Roberta; "is it something to do with Government?" For Father was in a Government Office.

"Yes," said Mother. "Now it's bed-time, my darlings. And don't *you* worry. It'll all come right in the end."

"Then don't *you* worry either, Mother," said Phyllis, "and we'll all be as good as gold."

Mother sighed and kissed them.

"We'll begin being good the first thing tomorrow morning," said Peter, as they went upstairs.

"Why not *now*?" said Roberta.

"There's nothing to be good *about* now, silly," said Peter.

"We might begin to try to *feel* good," said Phyllis, "and not call names."

"Who's calling names?" said Peter. "Bobbie knows right enough that when I say 'silly', it's just the same as if I said Bobbie."

"*Well*," said Roberta.

"No, I don't mean what you mean. I mean it's just a--what is it Father calls it?--a germ of endearment! Good night."

The girls folded up their clothes with more than usual neatness-- which was the only way of being good that they could think of.

"I say," said Phyllis, smoothing out her pinafore, "you used to say it was so dull--nothing happening, like in books. Now something *has* happened."

"I never wanted things to happen to make Mother unhappy," said Roberta. "Everything's perfectly horrid."

Everything continued to be perfectly horrid for some weeks.

Mother was nearly always out. Meals were dull and dirty. The between-maid was sent away, and Aunt Emma came on a visit. Aunt Emma was much older than Mother. She was going abroad to be a governess. She was very busy getting her clothes ready, and they were very ugly, dingy clothes, and she had them always littering about, and the sewing-machine seemed to whir--on and on all day and most of the night. Aunt Emma believed in keeping children in their proper places. And they more than returned the compliment. Their idea of Aunt Emma's proper place was anywhere where they were not. So they saw very little of her. They preferred the company of the servants, who were more amusing. Cook, if in a good temper, could sing comic songs, and the housemaid, if she happened not to be offended with you, could imitate a hen that has laid an egg, a bottle of champagne being opened, and could mew like two cats fighting. The servants never told the children what the bad news was that the gentlemen had brought to Father. But they kept hinting that they could tell a great deal if they chose--and this was not comfortable.

One day when Peter had made a booby trap over the bath-room door, and it had acted beautifully as Ruth passed through, that red-haired parlour-maid caught him and boxed his ears.

"You'll come to a bad end," she said furiously, "you nasty little limb, you! If you don't mend your ways, you'll go where your precious Father's gone, so I tell you straight!"

Roberta repeated this to her Mother, and next day Ruth was sent away.

Then came the time when Mother came home and went to bed and stayed there two days and the Doctor came, and the children crept wretchedly about the house and wondered if the world was coming to an end.

Mother came down one morning to breakfast, very pale and with lines on her face that used not to be there. And she smiled, as well as she could, and said:--

"Now, my pets, everything is settled. We're going to leave this house, and go and live in the country. Such a ducky dear little white house. I know you'll love it."

A whirling week of packing followed--not just packing clothes, like when you go to the seaside, but packing chairs and tables, covering their tops with sacking and their legs with straw.

All sorts of things were packed that you don't pack when you go to the seaside. Crockery, blankets, candlesticks, carpets, bedsteads, saucepans, and even fenders and fire-irons.

The house was like a furniture warehouse. I think the children enjoyed it very much. Mother was very busy, but not too busy now to talk to them, and read to them, and even to make a bit of poetry for Phyllis to cheer her up when she fell down with a screwdriver and ran it into her hand.

"Aren't you going to pack this, Mother?" Roberta asked, pointing to the beautiful cabinet inlaid with red turtleshell and brass.

"We can't take everything," said Mother.

"But we seem to be taking all the ugly things," said Roberta.

"We're taking the useful ones," said Mother; "we've got to play at being Poor for a bit, my chickabiddy."

When all the ugly useful things had been packed up and taken away in a van by men in green-baize aprons, the two girls and Mother and Aunt Emma slept in the two spare rooms where the furniture was all pretty. All their beds had gone. A bed was made up for Peter on the drawing-room sofa.

"I say, this is larks," he said, wriggling joyously, as Mother tucked him up. "I do like moving! I wish we moved once a month."

Mother laughed.

"I don't!" she said. "Good night, Peterkin."

As she turned away Roberta saw her face. She never forgot it.

"Oh, Mother," she whispered all to herself as she got into bed, "how brave you are! How I love you! Fancy being brave enough to laugh when you're feeling like *that*!"

Next day boxes were filled, and boxes and more boxes; and then late in the afternoon a cab came to take them to the station.

Aunt Emma saw them off. They felt that *they* were seeing *her* off, and they were glad of it.

"But, oh, those poor little foreign children that she's going to governess!" whispered Phyllis. "I wouldn't be them for anything!"

At first they enjoyed looking out of the window, but when it grew dusk they grew sleepier and sleepier, and no one knew how long they had been in the train when they were roused by Mother's shaking them gently and saying:--

"Wake up, dears. We're there."

They woke up, cold and melancholy, and stood shivering on the draughty platform while the baggage was taken out of the train. Then the engine, puffing and blowing, set to work again, and dragged the train away. The children watched the tail-lights of the guard's van disappear into the darkness.

This was the first train the children saw on that railway which was in time to become so very dear to them. They did not guess then how they would grow to love the railway, and how soon it would become the centre of their new life, nor what wonders and changes it would bring to them. They only shivered and sneezed and hoped the walk to the new house would not be long. Peter's nose was colder than he ever remembered it to have been before. Roberta's hat was crooked, and the elastic seemed tighter than usual. Phyllis's shoe-laces had come undone.

"Come," said Mother, "we've got to walk. There aren't any cabs here."

The walk was dark and muddy. The children stumbled a little on the rough road, and once Phyllis absently fell into a puddle, and was picked up damp and unhappy. There were no gas-lamps on the road, and the road was uphill. The cart went at a foot's pace, and they followed the gritty crunch of its wheels. As their eyes got used to the darkness, they could see the mound of boxes swaying dimly in front of them.

A long gate had to be opened for the cart to pass through, and after that the road seemed to go across fields--and now it went down hill. Presently a great dark lumpish thing showed over to the right.

"There's the house," said Mother. "I wonder why she's shut the shutters."

"Who's *she*?" asked Roberta.

"The woman I engaged to clean the place, and put the furniture straight and get supper."

There was a low wall, and trees inside.

"That's the garden," said Mother.

"It looks more like a dripping-pan full of black cabbages," said Peter.

The cart went on along by the garden wall, and round to the back of the house, and here it clattered into a cobble-stoned yard and stopped at the back door.

There was no light in any of the windows.

Everyone hammered at the door, but no one came.

The man who drove the cart said he expected Mrs. Viney had gone home.

"You see your train was that late," said he.

"But she's got the key," said Mother. "What are we to do?"

"Oh, she'll have left that under the doorstep," said the cart man; "folks do hereabouts." He took the lantern off his cart and stooped.

"Ay, here it is, right enough," he said.

He unlocked the door and went in and set his lantern on the table.

"Got e'er a candle?" said he.

"I don't know where anything is." Mother spoke rather less cheerfully than usual.

He struck a match. There was a candle on the table, and he lighted it. By its thin little glimmer the children saw a large bare kitchen with a stone floor. There were no curtains, no hearth-rug. The kitchen table from home stood in the middle of the room. The chairs were in one corner, and the pots, pans, brooms, and crockery in another. There was no fire, and the black grate showed cold, dead ashes.

As the cart man turned to go out after he had brought in the boxes, there was a rustling, scampering sound that seemed to come from inside the walls of the house.

"Oh, what's that?" cried the girls.

"It's only the rats," said the cart man. And he went away and shut the door, and the sudden draught of it blew out the candle.

"Oh, dear," said Phyllis, "I wish we hadn't come!" and she knocked a chair over.

"*Only* the rats!" said Peter, in the dark.

Lesson 74

1. Read the first part of chapter two of *The Railway Children*.
2. Tell about what's happening.

"What fun!" said Mother, in the dark, feeling for the matches on the table. "How frightened the poor mice were--I don't believe they were rats at all."

She struck a match and relighted the candle and everyone looked at each other by its winky, blinky light.

"Well," she said, "you've often wanted something to happen and now it has. This is quite an adventure, isn't it? I told Mrs. Viney to get us some bread and butter, and meat and things, and to have supper ready. I suppose she's laid it in the dining-room. So let's go and see."

The dining-room opened out of the kitchen. It looked much darker than the kitchen when they went in with the one candle. Because the kitchen was whitewashed, but the dining-room was dark wood from floor to ceiling, and across the ceiling there were heavy black beams. There was a muddled maze of dusty furniture--the breakfast- room furniture from the old home where they had lived all their lives. It seemed a very long time ago, and a very long way off.

There was the table certainly, and there were chairs, but there was no supper.

"Let's look in the other rooms," said Mother; and they looked. And in each room was the same kind of blundering half-arrangement of furniture, and fire-irons and crockery, and all sorts of odd things on the floor, but there was nothing to eat; even in the pantry there were only a rusty cake-tin and a broken plate with whitening mixed in it.

"What a horrid old woman!" said Mother; "she's just walked off with the money and not got us anything to eat at all."

"Then shan't we have any supper at all?" asked Phyllis, dismayed, stepping back on to a soap-dish that cracked responsively.

"Oh, yes," said Mother, "only it'll mean unpacking one of those big cases that we put in the cellar. Phil, do mind where you're walking to, there's a dear. Peter, hold the light."

The cellar door opened out of the kitchen. There were five wooden steps leading down. It wasn't a proper cellar at all, the children thought, because its ceiling went up as high as the kitchen's. A bacon-rack hung under its ceiling. There was wood in it, and coal. Also the big cases.

Peter held the candle, all on one side, while Mother tried to open the great packing-case. It was very securely nailed down.

"Where's the hammer?" asked Peter.

"That's just it," said Mother. "I'm afraid it's inside the box. But there's a coal-shovel--and there's the kitchen poker."

And with these she tried to get the case open.

"Let me do it," said Peter, thinking he could do it better himself. Everyone thinks this when he sees another person stirring a fire, or opening a box, or untying a knot in a bit of string.

"You'll hurt your hands, Mammy," said Roberta; "let me."

"I wish Father was here," said Phyllis; "he'd get it open in two shakes. What are you kicking me for, Bobbie?"

"I wasn't," said Roberta.

Just then the first of the long nails in the packing-case began to come out with a scrunch. Then a lath was raised and then another, till all four stood up with the long nails in them shining fiercely like iron teeth in the candle-light.

"Hooray!" said Mother; "here are some candles--the very first thing! You girls go and light them. You'll find some saucers and things. Just drop a little candle-grease in the saucer and stick the candle upright in it."

"How many shall we light?"

"As many as ever you like," said Mother, gaily. "The great thing is to be cheerful. Nobody can be cheerful in the dark except owls and dormice."

So the girls lighted candles. The head of the first match flew off and stuck to Phyllis's finger; but, as Roberta said, it was only a little burn, and she might have had to be a Roman martyr and be burned whole if she had happened to live in the days when those things were fashionable.

Then, when the dining-room was lighted by fourteen candles, Roberta fetched coal and wood and lighted a fire.

"It's very cold for May," she said, feeling what a grown-up thing it was to say.

The fire-light and the candle-light made the dining-room look very different, for now you could see that the dark walls were of wood, carved here and there into little wreaths and loops.

The girls hastily 'tidied' the room, which meant putting the chairs against the wall, and piling all the odds and ends into a corner and partly hiding them with the big leather arm-chair that Father used to sit in after dinner.

"Bravo!" cried Mother, coming in with a tray full of things. "This is something like! I'll just get a tablecloth and then--"

The tablecloth was in a box with a proper lock that was opened with a key and not with a shovel, and when the cloth was spread on the table, a real feast was laid out on it.

Everyone was very, very tired, but everyone cheered up at the sight of the funny and delightful supper. There were biscuits, the Marie and the plain kind, sardines, preserved ginger, cooking raisins, and candied peel and marmalade.

"What a good thing Aunt Emma packed up all the odds and ends out of the Store cupboard," said Mother. "Now, Phil, *don't* put the marmalade spoon in among the sardines."

"No, I won't, Mother," said Phyllis, and put it down among the Marie biscuits.

"Let's drink Aunt Emma's health," said Roberta, suddenly; "what should we have done if she hadn't packed up these things? Here's to Aunt Emma!"

And the toast was drunk in ginger wine and water, out of willow- patterned tea-cups, because the glasses couldn't be found.

They all felt that they had been a little hard on Aunt Emma. She wasn't a nice cuddly person like Mother, but after all it was she who had thought of packing up the odds and ends of things to eat.

It was Aunt Emma, too, who had aired all the sheets ready; and the men who had moved the furniture had put the bedsteads together, so the beds were soon made.

"Good night, chickies," said Mother. "I'm sure there aren't any rats. But I'll leave my door open, and then if a mouse comes, you need only scream, and I'll come and tell it exactly what I think of it."

Then she went to her own room. Roberta woke to hear the little travelling clock chime two. It sounded like a church clock ever so far away, she always thought. And she heard, too, Mother still moving about in her room.

Next morning Roberta woke Phyllis by pulling her hair gently, but quite enough for her purpose.

"Wassermarrer?" asked Phyllis, still almost wholly asleep.

"Wake up! wake up!" said Roberta. "We're in the new house--don't you remember? No servants or anything. Let's get up and begin to be useful. We'll just creep down mouse-quietly, and have everything beautiful before Mother gets up. I've woke Peter. He'll be dressed as soon as we are."

So they dressed quietly and quickly. Of course, there was no water in their room, so when they got down they washed as much as they thought was necessary under the spout of the pump in the yard. One pumped and the other washed. It was splashy but interesting.

"It's much more fun than basin washing," said Roberta. "How sparkly the weeds are between the stones, and the moss on the roof--oh, and the flowers!"

The roof of the back kitchen sloped down quite low. It was made of thatch and it had moss on it, and house-leeks and stonecrop and wallflowers, and even a clump of purple flag-flowers, at the far corner.

"This is far, far, far and away prettier than Edgecombe Villa," said Phyllis. "I wonder what the garden's like."

"We mustn't think of the garden yet," said Roberta, with earnest energy. "Let's go in and begin to work."

They lighted the fire and put the kettle on, and they arranged the crockery for breakfast; they could not find all the right things, but a glass ash-tray made an excellent salt-cellar, and a newish baking-tin seemed as if it would do to put bread on, if they had any.

When there seemed to be nothing more that they could do, they went out again into the fresh bright morning.

"We'll go into the garden now," said Peter. But somehow they couldn't find the garden. They went round the house and round the house. The yard occupied the back, and across it were stables and outbuildings. On the other three sides the house stood simply in a field, without a yard of garden to divide it from the short smooth turf. And yet they had certainly seen the garden wall the night before.

It was a hilly country. Down below they could see the line of the railway, and the black yawning mouth of a tunnel. The station was out of sight. There was a great bridge with tall arches running across one end of the valley.

"Never mind the garden," said Peter; "let's go down and look at the railway. There might be trains passing."

"We can see them from here," said Roberta, slowly; "let's sit down a bit."

So they all sat down on a great flat grey stone that had pushed itself up out of the grass; it was one of many that lay about on the hillside, and when Mother came out to look for them at eight o'clock, she found them deeply asleep in a contented, sun-warmed bunch.

They had made an excellent fire, and had set the kettle on it at about half-past five. So that by eight the fire had been out for some time, the water had all boiled away, and the bottom was burned out of the kettle. Also they had not thought of washing the crockery before they set the table.

"But it doesn't matter--the cups and saucers, I mean," said Mother. "Because I've found another room--I'd quite forgotten there was one. And it's magic! And I've boiled the water for tea in a saucepan."

The forgotten room opened out of the kitchen. In the agitation and half darkness the night before its door had been mistaken for a cupboard's. It was a little square room, and on its table, all nicely set out, was a joint of cold roast beef, with bread, butter, cheese, and a pie.

"Pie for breakfast!" cried Peter; "how perfectly ripping!"

"It isn't pigeon-pie," said Mother; "it's only apple. Well, this is the supper we ought to have had last night. And there was a note from Mrs. Viney. Her son-in-law has broken his arm, and she had to get home early. She's coming this morning at ten."

That was a wonderful breakfast. It is unusual to begin the day with cold apple pie, but the children all said they would rather have it than meat.

"You see it's more like dinner than breakfast to us," said Peter, passing his plate for more, "because we were up so early."

The day passed in helping Mother to unpack and arrange things. Six small legs quite ached with running about while their owners carried clothes and crockery and all sorts of things to their proper places. It was not till quite late in the afternoon that Mother said:--

"There! That'll do for to-day. I'll lie down for an hour, so as to be as fresh as a lark by supper-time."

Then they all looked at each other. Each of the three expressive countenances expressed the same thought. That thought was double, and consisted, like the bits of information in the Child's Guide to Knowledge, of a question and an answer.

Q. Where shall we go?

A. To the railway.

So to the railway they went, and as soon as they started for the railway they saw where the garden had hidden itself. It was right behind the stables, and it had a high wall all round.

"Oh, never mind about the garden now!" cried Peter. "Mother told me this morning where it was. It'll keep till to-morrow. Let's get to the railway."

The way to the railway was all down hill over smooth, short turf with here and there furze bushes and grey and yellow rocks sticking out like candied peel from the top of a cake.

The way ended in a steep run and a wooden fence--and there was the railway with the shining metals and the telegraph wires and posts and signals.

They all climbed on to the top of the fence, and then suddenly there was a rumbling sound that made them look along the line to the right, where the dark mouth of a tunnel opened itself in the face of a rocky cliff; next moment a train had rushed out of the tunnel with a shriek and a snort, and had slid noisily past them. They felt the rush of its passing, and the pebbles on the line jumped and rattled under it as it went by.

"Oh!" said Roberta, drawing a long breath; "it was like a great dragon tearing by. Did you feel it fan us with its hot wings?"

"I suppose a dragon's lair might look very like that tunnel from the outside," said Phyllis.

But Peter said:--

"I never thought we should ever get as near to a train as this. It's the most ripping sport!"

"Better than toy-engines, isn't it?" said Roberta.

(I am tired of calling Roberta by her name. I don't see why I should. No one else did. Everyone else called her Bobbie, and I don't see why I shouldn't.)

"I don't know; it's different," said Peter. "It seems so odd to see *all* of a train. It's awfully tall, isn't it?"

"We've always seen them cut in half by platforms," said Phyllis.

"I wonder if that train was going to London," Bobbie said. "London's where Father is."

"Let's go down to the station and find out," said Peter.

So they went.

They walked along the edge of the line, and heard the telegraph wires humming over their heads. When you are in the train, it seems such a little way between post and post, and one after another the posts seem to catch up the wires almost more quickly than you can count them. But when you have to walk, the posts seem few and far between.

But the children got to the station at last.

Lesson 75

1.   Read the second part of chapter two of *The Railway Children*.
2.   What does mother say they are too poor to afford? (Answers)
3.   What does it mean to "nick" something? (Answers)
4.   Tell someone about the chapter.

Never before had any of them been at a station, except for the purpose of catching trains-- or perhaps waiting for them--and always with grown-ups in attendance, grown-ups who were not themselves interested in stations, except as places from which they wished to get away.

Never before had they passed close enough to a signal-box to be able to notice the wires, and to hear the mysterious 'ping, ping,' followed by the strong, firm clicking of machinery.

The very sleepers on which the rails lay were a delightful path to travel by--just far enough apart to serve as the stepping-stones in a game of foaming torrents hastily organised by Bobbie.

Then to arrive at the station, not through the booking office, but in a freebooting sort of way by the sloping end of the platform. This in itself was joy.

Joy, too, it was to peep into the porters' room, where the lamps are, and the Railway almanac on the wall, and one porter half asleep behind a paper.

There were a great many crossing lines at the station; some of them just ran into a yard and stopped short, as though they were tired of business and meant to retire for good. Trucks stood on the rails here, and on one side was a great heap of coal--not a loose heap, such as you see in your coal cellar, but a sort of solid building of coals with large square blocks of coal outside used just as though they were bricks, and built up till the heap looked like the picture of the Cities of the Plain in 'Bible Stories for Infants.' There was a line of whitewash near the top of the coaly wall.

When presently the Porter lounged out of his room at the twice- repeated tingling thrill of a gong over the station door, Peter said, "How do you do?" in his best manner, and hastened to ask what the white mark was on the coal for.

"To mark how much coal there be," said the Porter, "so as we'll know if anyone nicks it. So don't you go off with none in your pockets, young gentleman!"

This seemed, at the time but a merry jest, and Peter felt at once that the Porter was a friendly sort with no nonsense about him. But later the words came back to Peter with a new meaning.

Have you ever gone into a farmhouse kitchen on a baking day, and seen the great crock of dough set by the fire to rise? If you have, and if you were at that time still young enough to be interested in everything you saw, you will remember that you found yourself quite unable to resist the temptation to poke your finger into the soft round of dough that curved inside the pan like a giant mushroom. And you will remember that your finger made a dent in the dough, and that slowly, but quite surely, the dent disappeared, and the dough looked quite the same as it did before you touched it. Unless, of course, your hand was extra dirty, in which case, naturally, there would be a little black mark.

Well, it was just like that with the sorrow the children had felt at Father's going away, and at Mother's being so unhappy. It made a deep impression, but the impression did not last long.

They soon got used to being without Father, though they did not forget him; and they got used to not going to school, and to seeing very little of Mother, who was now almost all day shut up in her upstairs room writing, writing, writing. She used to come down at tea-time and read aloud the stories she had written. They were lovely stories.

The rocks and hills and valleys and trees, the canal, and above all, the railway, were so new and so perfectly pleasing that the remembrance of the old life in the villa grew to seem almost like a dream.

Mother had told them more than once that they were 'quite poor now,' but this did not seem to be anything but a way of speaking. Grown- up people, even Mothers, often make remarks that don't seem to mean anything in particular, just for the sake of saying something, seemingly. There was always enough to eat, and they wore the same kind of nice clothes they had always worn.

But in June came three wet days; the rain came down, straight as lances, and it was very, very cold. Nobody could go out, and everybody shivered. They all went up to the door of Mother's room and knocked.

"Well, what is it?" asked Mother from inside.

"Mother," said Bobbie, "mayn't I light a fire? I do know how."

And Mother said: "No, my ducky-love. We mustn't have fires in June--coal is so dear. If you're cold, go and have a good romp in the attic. That'll warm you."

"But, Mother, it only takes such a very little coal to make a fire."

"It's more than we can afford, chickeny-love," said Mother, cheerfully. "Now run away, there's darlings--I'm madly busy!"

"Mother's always busy now," said Phyllis, in a whisper to Peter. Peter did not answer. He shrugged his shoulders. He was thinking.

Thought, however, could not long keep itself from the suitable furnishing of a bandit's lair in the attic. Peter was the bandit, of course. Bobbie was his lieutenant, his band of trusty robbers, and, in due course, the parent of Phyllis, who was the captured maiden for whom a magnificent ransom--in horse-beans--was unhesitatingly paid.

They all went down to tea flushed and joyous as any mountain brigands.

But when Phyllis was going to add jam to her bread and butter, Mother said:--

"Jam *or* butter, dear--not jam *and* butter. We can't afford that sort of reckless luxury nowadays."

Phyllis finished the slice of bread and butter in silence, and followed it up by bread and jam. Peter mingled thought and weak tea.

After tea they went back to the attic and he said to his sisters:--

"I have an idea."

"What's that?" they asked politely.

"I shan't tell you," was Peter's unexpected rejoinder.

"Oh, very well," said Bobbie; and Phil said, "Don't, then."

"Girls," said Peter, "are always so hasty tempered."

"I should like to know what boys are?" said Bobbie, with fine disdain. "I don't want to know about your silly ideas."

"You'll know some day," said Peter, keeping his own temper by what looked exactly like a miracle; "if you hadn't been so keen on a row, I might have told you about it being only noble-heartedness that made me not tell you my idea. But now I shan't tell you anything at all about it--so there!"

And it was, indeed, some time before he could be induced to say anything, and when he did it wasn't much. He said:--

"The only reason why I won't tell you my idea that I'm going to do is because it *may* be wrong, and I don't want to drag you into it."

"Don't you do it if it's wrong, Peter," said Bobbie; "let me do it." But Phyllis said:--

"*I* should like to do wrong if *you're* going to!"

"No," said Peter, rather touched by this devotion; "it's a forlorn hope, and I'm going to lead it. All I ask is that if Mother asks where I am, you won't blab."

"We haven't got anything *to* blab," said Bobbie, indignantly.

"Oh, yes, you have!" said Peter, dropping horse-beans through his fingers. "I've trusted you to the death. You know I'm going to do a lone adventure--and some people might think it wrong--I don't. And if Mother asks where I am, say I'm playing at mines."

"What sort of mines?"

"You just say mines."

"You might tell *us*, Pete."

"Well, then, *coal*-mines. But don't you let the word pass your lips on pain of torture."

"You needn't threaten," said Bobbie, "and I do think you might let us help."

"If I find a coal-mine, you shall help cart the coal," Peter condescended to promise.

"Keep your secret if you like," said Phyllis.

"Keep it if you *can*," said Bobbie.

"I'll keep it, right enough," said Peter.

Between tea and supper there is an interval even in the most greedily regulated families. At this time Mother was usually writing, and Mrs. Viney had gone home.

Two nights after the dawning of Peter's idea he beckoned the girls mysteriously at the twilight hour.

"Come hither with me," he said, "and bring the Roman Chariot."

The Roman Chariot was a very old perambulator that had spent years of retirement in the loft over the coach-house. The children had oiled its works till it glided noiseless as a pneumatic bicycle, and answered to the helm as it had probably done in its best days.

"Follow your dauntless leader," said Peter, and led the way down the hill towards the station.

Just above the station many rocks have pushed their heads out through the turf as though they, like the children, were interested in the railway.

In a little hollow between three rocks lay a heap of dried brambles and heather.

Peter halted, turned over the brushwood with a well-scarred boot, and said:--

"Here's the first coal from the St. Peter's Mine. We'll take it home in the chariot. Punctuality and despatch. All orders carefully attended to. Any shaped lump cut to suit regular customers."

The chariot was packed full of coal. And when it was packed it had to be unpacked again because it was so heavy that it couldn't be got up the hill by the three children, not even when Peter harnessed himself to the handle with his braces, and firmly grasping his waistband in one hand pulled while the girls pushed behind.

Three journeys had to be made before the coal from Peter's mine was added to the heap of Mother's coal in the cellar.

Afterwards Peter went out alone, and came back very black and mysterious.

"I've been to my coal-mine," he said; "to-morrow evening we'll bring home the black diamonds in the chariot."

It was a week later that Mrs. Viney remarked to Mother how well this last lot of coal was holding out.

The children hugged themselves and each other in complicated wriggles of silent laughter as they listened on the stairs. They had all forgotten by now that there had ever been any doubt in Peter's mind as to whether coal-mining was wrong.

But there came a dreadful night when the Station Master put on a pair of old sand shoes that he had worn at the seaside in his summer holiday, and crept out very quietly to the yard where the Sodom and Gomorrah heap of coal was, with the whitewashed line round it. He crept out there, and he waited like a cat by a mousehole. On the top of the heap something small and dark was scrabbling and rattling furtively among the coal.

The Station Master concealed himself in the shadow of a brake-van that had a little tin chimney and was labelled:--

G. N. and S. R.

34576

Return at once to

White Heather Sidings

and in this concealment he lurked till the small thing on the top of the heap ceased to scrabble and rattle, came to the edge of the heap, cautiously let itself down, and lifted something after it. Then the arm of the Station Master was raised, the hand of the Station Master fell on a collar, and there was Peter firmly held by the jacket, with an old carpenter's bag full of coal in his trembling clutch.

"So I've caught you at last, have I, you young thief?" said the Station Master.

"I'm not a thief," said Peter, as firmly as he could. "I'm a coal- miner."

"Tell that to the Marines," said the Station Master.

"It would be just as true whoever I told it to," said Peter.

"You're right there," said the man, who held him. "Stow your jaw, you young rip, and come along to the station."

"Oh, no," cried in the darkness an agonised voice that was not Peter's.

"Not the *police* station!" said another voice from the darkness.

"Not yet," said the Station Master. "The Railway Station first. Why, it's a regular gang. Any more of you?"

"Only us," said Bobbie and Phyllis, coming out of the shadow of another truck labelled Staveley Colliery, and bearing on it the legend in white chalk: 'Wanted in No. 1 Road.'

"What do you mean by spying on a fellow like this?" said Peter, angrily.

"Time someone did spy on you, *I* think," said the Station Master. "Come along to the station."

"Oh, *don't*!" said Bobbie. "Can't you decide *now* what you'll do to us? It's our fault just as much as Peter's. We helped to carry the coal away--and we knew where he got it."

"No, you didn't," said Peter.

"Yes, we did," said Bobbie. "We knew all the time. We only pretended we didn't just to humour you."

Peter's cup was full. He had mined for coal, he had struck coal, he had been caught, and now he learned that his sisters had 'humoured' him.

"Don't hold me!" he said. "I won't run away."

The Station Master loosed Peter's collar, struck a match and looked at them by its flickering light.

"Why," said he, "you're the children from the Three Chimneys up yonder. So nicely dressed, too. Tell me now, what made you do such a thing? Haven't you ever been to church or learned your catechism or anything, not to know it's wicked to steal?" He spoke much more gently now, and Peter said:--

"I didn't think it was stealing. I was almost sure it wasn't. I thought if I took it from the outside part of the heap, perhaps it would be. But in the middle I thought I could fairly count it only mining. It'll take thousands of years for you to burn up all that coal and get to the middle parts."

"Not quite. But did you do it for a lark or what?"

"Not much lark carting that beastly heavy stuff up the hill," said Peter, indignantly.

"Then why did you?" The Station Master's voice was so much kinder now that Peter replied:--

"You know that wet day? Well, Mother said we were too poor to have a fire. We always had fires when it was cold at our other house, and--"

"*Don't*!" interrupted Bobbie, in a whisper.

"Well," said the Station Master, rubbing his chin thoughtfully, "I'll tell you what I'll do. I'll look over it this once. But you remember, young gentleman, stealing is stealing, and what's mine isn't yours, whether you call it mining or whether you don't. Run along home."

"Do you mean you aren't going to do anything to us? Well, you are a brick," said Peter, with enthusiasm.

"You're a dear," said Bobbie.

"You're a darling," said Phyllis.

"That's all right," said the Station Master.

And on this they parted.

"Don't speak to me," said Peter, as the three went up the hill. "You're spies and traitors--that's what you are."

But the girls were too glad to have Peter between them, safe and free, and on the way to Three Chimneys and not to the Police Station, to mind much what he said.

"We *did* say it was us as much as you," said Bobbie, gently.

"Well--and it wasn't."

"It would have come to the same thing in Courts with judges," said Phyllis. "Don't be snarky, Peter. It isn't our fault your secrets are so jolly easy to find out." She took his arm, and he let her.

"There's an awful lot of coal in the cellar, anyhow," he went on.

"Oh, don't!" said Bobbie. "I don't think we ought to be glad about *that*."

"I don't know," said Peter, plucking up a spirit. "I'm not at all sure, even now, that mining is a crime."

But the girls were quite sure. And they were also quite sure that he was quite sure, however little he cared to own it.

Lesson 76

1. Read the first part of chapter three of *The Railway Children*.
2. Why does Peter feel better? (Answers)
3. Tell someone what's happening in the story.

After the adventure of Peter's Coal-mine, it seemed well to the children to keep away from the station--but they did not, they could not, keep away from the railway. They had lived all their lives in a street where cabs and omnibuses rumbled by at all hours, and the carts of butchers and bakers and candlestick makers (I never saw a candlestick-maker's cart; did you?) might occur at any moment. Here in the deep silence of the sleeping country the only things that went by were the trains. They seemed to be all that was left to link the children to the old life that had once been theirs. Straight down the hill in front of Three Chimneys the daily passage of their six feet began to mark a path across the crisp, short turf. They began to know the hours when certain trains passed, and they gave names to them. The 9.15 up was called the Green Dragon. The 10.7 down was the Worm of Wantley. The midnight town express, whose shrieking rush they sometimes woke from their dreams to hear, was the Fearsome Fly-by-night. Peter got up once, in chill starshine, and, peeping at it through his curtains, named it on the spot.

It was by the Green Dragon that the old gentleman travelled. He was a very nice-looking old gentleman, and he looked as if he were nice, too, which is not at all the same thing. He had a fresh-coloured, clean-shaven face and white hair, and he wore rather odd-shaped collars and a top-hat that wasn't exactly the same kind as other people's. Of course the children didn't see all this at first. In fact the first thing they noticed about the old gentleman was his hand.

It was one morning as they sat on the fence waiting for the Green Dragon, which was three and a quarter minutes late by Peter's Waterbury watch that he had had given him on his last birthday.

"The Green Dragon's going where Father is," said Phyllis; "if it were a really real dragon, we could stop it and ask it to take our love to Father."

"Dragons don't carry people's love," said Peter; "they'd be above it."

"Yes, they do, if you tame them thoroughly first. They fetch and carry like pet spaniels," said Phyllis, "and feed out of your hand. I wonder why Father never writes to us."

"Mother says he's been too busy," said Bobbie; "but he'll write soon, she says."

"I say," Phyllis suggested, "let's all wave to the Green Dragon as it goes by. If it's a magic dragon, it'll understand and take our loves to Father. And if it isn't, three waves aren't much. We shall never miss them."

So when the Green Dragon tore shrieking out of the mouth of its dark lair, which was the tunnel, all three children stood on the railing and waved their pocket-handkerchiefs without stopping to think whether they were clean handkerchiefs or the reverse. They were, as a matter of fact, very much the reverse.

And out of a first-class carriage a hand waved back. A quite clean hand. It held a newspaper. It was the old gentleman's hand.

After this it became the custom for waves to be exchanged between the children and the 9.15.

And the children, especially the girls, liked to think that perhaps the old gentleman knew Father, and would meet him 'in business,' wherever that shady retreat might be, and tell him how his three children stood on a rail far away in the green country and waved their love to him every morning, wet or fine.

For they were now able to go out in all sorts of weather such as they would never have been allowed to go out in when they lived in their villa house. This was Aunt Emma's doing, and the children felt more and more that they had not been quite fair to this unattractive aunt, when they found how useful were the long gaiters and waterproof coats that they had laughed at her for buying for them.

Mother, all this time, was very busy with her writing. She used to send off a good many long blue envelopes with stories in them--and large envelopes of different sizes and colours used to come to her. Sometimes she would sigh when she opened them and say:--

"Another story come home to roost. Oh, dear, Oh, dear!" and then the children would be very sorry.

But sometimes she would wave the envelope in the air and say:-- "Hooray, hooray. Here's a sensible Editor. He's taken my story and this is the proof of it."

At first the children thought 'the Proof' meant the letter the sensible Editor had written, but they presently got to know that the proof was long slips of paper with the story printed on them.

Whenever an Editor was sensible there were buns for tea.

One day Peter was going down to the village to get buns to celebrate the sensibleness of the Editor of the Children's Globe, when he met the Station Master.

Peter felt very uncomfortable, for he had now had time to think over the affair of the coal-mine. He did not like to say "Good morning" to the Station Master, as you usually do to anyone you meet on a lonely road, because he had a hot feeling, which spread even to his ears, that the Station Master might not care to speak to a person who had stolen coals. 'Stolen' is a nasty word, but Peter felt it was the right one. So he looked down, and said Nothing.

It was the Station Master who said "Good morning" as he passed by. And Peter answered, "Good morning." Then he thought:--

"Perhaps he doesn't know who I am by daylight, or he wouldn't be so polite."

And he did not like the feeling which thinking this gave him. And then before he knew what he was going to do he ran after the Station Master, who stopped when he heard Peter's hasty boots crunching the road, and coming up with him very breathless and with his ears now quite magenta-coloured, he said:--

"I don't want you to be polite to me if you don't know me when you see me."

"Eh?" said the Station Master.

"I thought perhaps you didn't know it was me that took the coals," Peter went on, "when you said 'Good morning.' But it was, and I'm sorry. There."

"Why," said the Station Master, "I wasn't thinking anything at all about the precious coals. Let bygones be bygones. And where were you off to in such a hurry?"

"I'm going to buy buns for tea," said Peter.

"I thought you were all so poor," said the Station Master.

"So we are," said Peter, confidentially, "but we always have three pennyworth of halfpennies for tea whenever Mother sells a story or a poem or anything."

"Oh," said the Station Master, "so your Mother writes stories, does she?"

"The beautifulest you ever read," said Peter.

"You ought to be very proud to have such a clever Mother."

"Yes," said Peter, "but she used to play with us more before she had to be so clever."

"Well," said the Station Master, "I must be getting along. You give us a look in at the Station whenever you feel so inclined. And as to coals, it's a word that--well--oh, no, we never mention it, eh?"

"Thank you," said Peter. "I'm very glad it's all straightened out between us." And he went on across the canal bridge to the village to get the buns, feeling more comfortable in his mind than he had felt since the hand of the Station Master had fastened on his collar that night among the coals.

Next day when they had sent the threefold wave of greeting to Father by the Green Dragon, and the old gentleman had waved back as usual, Peter proudly led the way to the station.

"But ought we?" said Bobbie.

"After the coals, she means," Phyllis explained.

"I met the Station Master yesterday," said Peter, in an offhand way, and he pretended not to hear what Phyllis had said; "he expresspecially invited us to go down any time we liked."

"After the coals?" repeated Phyllis. "Stop a minute--my bootlace is undone again."

"It always *is* undone again," said Peter, "and the Station Master was more of a gentleman than you'll ever be, Phil--throwing coal at a chap's head like that."

Phyllis did up her bootlace and went on in silence, but her shoulders shook, and presently a fat tear fell off her nose and splashed on the metal of the railway line. Bobbie saw it.

"Why, what's the matter, darling?" she said, stopping short and putting her arm round the heaving shoulders.

"He called me un-un-ungentlemanly," sobbed Phyllis. "I didn't never call him unladylike, not even when he tied my Clorinda to the firewood bundle and burned her at the stake for a martyr."

Peter had indeed perpetrated this outrage a year or two before.

"Well, you began, you know," said Bobbie, honestly, "about coals and all that. Don't you think you'd better both unsay everything since the wave, and let honour be satisfied?"

"I will if Peter will," said Phyllis, sniffling.

"All right," said Peter; "honour is satisfied. Here, use my hankie, Phil, for goodness' sake, if you've lost yours as usual. I wonder what you do with them."

"You had my last one," said Phyllis, indignantly, "to tie up the rabbit-hutch door with. But you're very ungrateful. It's quite right what it says in the poetry book about sharper than a serpent it is to have a toothless child--but it means ungrateful when it says toothless. Miss Lowe told me so."

"All right," said Peter, impatiently, "I'm sorry. *There*! Now will you come on?"

They reached the station and spent a joyous two hours with the Porter. He was a worthy man and seemed never tired of answering the questions that begin with "Why--" which many people in higher ranks of life often seem weary of.

He told them many things that they had not known before--as, for instance, that the things that hook carriages together are called couplings, and that the pipes like great serpents that hang over the couplings are meant to stop the train with.

"If you could get a holt of one o' them when the train is going and pull 'em apart," said he, "she'd stop dead off with a jerk."

"Who's she?" said Phyllis.

"The train, of course," said the Porter. After that the train was never again 'It' to the children.

"And you know the thing in the carriages where it says on it, 'Five pounds' fine for improper use.' If you was to improperly use that, the train 'ud stop."

"And if you used it properly?" said Roberta.

"It 'ud stop just the same, I suppose," said he, "but it isn't proper use unless you're being murdered. There was an old lady once--someone kidded her on it was a refreshment-room bell, and she used it improper, not being in danger of her life, though hungry, and when the train stopped and the guard came along expecting to find someone weltering in their last moments, she says, "Oh, please, Mister, I'll take a glass of stout and a bath bun," she says. And the train was seven minutes behind her time as it was."

"What did the guard say to the old lady?"

"*I* dunno," replied the Porter, "but I lay she didn't forget it in a hurry, whatever it was."

In such delightful conversation the time went by all too quickly.

The Station Master came out once or twice from that sacred inner temple behind the place where the hole is that they sell you tickets through, and was most jolly with them all.

"Just as if coal had never been discovered," Phyllis whispered to her sister.

He gave them each an orange, and promised to take them up into the signal-box one of these days, when he wasn't so busy.

Several trains went through the station, and Peter noticed for the first time that engines have numbers on them, like cabs.

"Yes," said the Porter, "I knowed a young gent as used to take down the numbers of every single one he seed; in a green note-book with silver corners it was, owing to his father being very well-to-do in the wholesale stationery."

Peter felt that he could take down numbers, too, even if he was not the son of a wholesale stationer. As he did not happen to have a green leather note-book with silver corners, the Porter gave him a yellow envelope and on it he noted:--

    379, 663

and felt that this was the beginning of what would be a most interesting collection.

That night at tea he asked Mother if she had a green leather note- book with silver corners. She had not; but when she heard what he wanted it for she gave him a little black one.

"It has a few pages torn out," said she; "but it will hold quite a lot of numbers, and when it's full I'll give you another. I'm so glad you like the railway. Only, please, you mustn't walk on the line."

"Not if we face the way the train's coming?" asked Peter, after a gloomy pause, in which glances of despair were exchanged.

"No--really not," said Mother.

Then Phyllis said, "Mother, didn't *you* ever walk on the railway lines when you were little?"

Mother was an honest and honourable Mother, so she had to say, "Yes."

"Well, then," said Phyllis.

"But, darlings, you don't know how fond I am of you. What should I do if you got hurt?"

Lesson 77

1. Read the second part of chapter three of *The Railway Children*.
2. Draw a picture of what you think the station looks like.

"Are you fonder of us than Granny was of you when you were little?" Phyllis asked. Bobbie made signs to her to stop, but Phyllis never did see signs, no matter how plain they might be.

Mother did not answer for a minute. She got up to put more water in the teapot.

"No one," she said at last, "ever loved anyone more than my mother loved me."

Then she was quiet again, and Bobbie kicked Phyllis hard under the table, because Bobbie understood a little bit the thoughts that were making Mother so quiet--the thoughts of the time when Mother was a little girl and was all the world to *her* mother. It seems so easy and natural to run to Mother when one is in trouble. Bobbie understood a little how people do not leave off running to their mothers when they are in trouble even when they are grown up, and she thought she knew a little what it must be to be sad, and have no mother to run to any more.

So she kicked Phyllis, who said:--

"What are you kicking me like that for, Bob?"

And then Mother laughed a little and sighed and said:--

"Very well, then. Only let me be sure you do know which way the trains come--and don't walk on the line near the tunnel or near corners."

"Trains keep to the left like carriages," said Peter, "so if we keep to the right, we're bound to see them coming."

"Very well," said Mother, and I dare say you think that she ought not to have said it. But she remembered about when she was a little girl herself, and she did say it--and neither her own children nor you nor any other children in the world could ever understand exactly what it cost her to do it. Only some few of you, like Bobbie, may understand a very little bit.

It was the very next day that Mother had to stay in bed because her head ached so. Her hands were burning hot, and she would not eat anything, and her throat was very sore.

"If I was you, Mum," said Mrs. Viney, "I should take and send for the doctor. There's a lot of catchy complaints a-going about just now. My sister's eldest--she took a chill and it went to her inside, two years ago come Christmas, and she's never been the same gell since."

Mother wouldn't at first, but in the evening she felt so much worse that Peter was sent to the house in the village that had three laburnum trees by the gate, and on the gate a brass plate with W. W. Forrest, M.D., on it.

W. W. Forrest, M.D., came at once. He talked to Peter on the way back. He seemed a most charming and sensible man, interested in railways, and rabbits, and really important things.

When he had seen Mother, he said it was influenza.

"Now, Lady Grave-airs," he said in the hall to Bobbie, "I suppose you'll want to be head-nurse."

"Of course," said she.

"Well, then, I'll send down some medicine. Keep up a good fire. Have some strong beef tea made ready to give her as soon as the fever goes down. She can have grapes now, and beef essence--and soda-water and milk, and you'd better get in a bottle of brandy. The best brandy. Cheap brandy is worse than poison."

She asked him to write it all down, and he did.

When Bobbie showed Mother the list he had written, Mother laughed. It *was* a laugh, Bobbie decided, though it was rather odd and feeble.

"Nonsense," said Mother, laying in bed with eyes as bright as beads. "I can't afford all that rubbish. Tell Mrs. Viney to boil two pounds of scrag-end of the neck for your dinners to-morrow, and I can have some of the broth. Yes, I should like some more water now, love. And will you get a basin and sponge my hands?"

Roberta obeyed. When she had done everything she could to make Mother less uncomfortable, she went down to the others. Her cheeks were very red, her lips set tight, and her eyes almost as bright as Mother's.

She told them what the Doctor had said, and what Mother had said.

"And now," said she, when she had told all, "there's no one but us to do anything, and we've got to do it. I've got the shilling for the mutton."

"We can do without the beastly mutton," said Peter; "bread and butter will support life. People have lived on less on desert islands many a time."

"Of course," said his sister. And Mrs. Viney was sent to the village to get as much brandy and soda-water and beef tea as she could buy for a shilling.

"But even if we never have anything to eat at all," said Phyllis, "you can't get all those other things with our dinner money."

"No," said Bobbie, frowning, "we must find out some other way. Now *think*, everybody, just as hard as ever you can."

They did think. And presently they talked. And later, when Bobbie had gone up to sit with Mother in case she wanted anything, the other two were very busy with scissors and a white sheet, and a paint brush, and the pot of Brunswick black that Mrs. Viney used for grates and fenders. They did not manage to do what they wished, exactly, with the first sheet, so they took another out of the linen cupboard. It did not occur to them that they were spoiling good sheets which cost good money. They only knew that they were making a good--but what they were making comes later.

Bobbie's bed had been moved into Mother's room, and several times in the night she got up to mend the fire, and to give her mother milk and soda-water. Mother talked to herself a good deal, but it did not seem to mean anything. And once she woke up suddenly and called out: "Mamma, mamma!" and Bobbie knew she was calling for Granny, and that she had forgotten that it was no use calling, because Granny was dead.

In the early morning Bobbie heard her name and jumped out of bed and ran to Mother's bedside.

"Oh--ah, yes--I think I was asleep," said Mother. "My poor little duck, how tired you'll be--I do hate to give you all this trouble."

"Trouble!" said Bobbie.

"Ah, don't cry, sweet," Mother said; "I shall be all right in a day or two."

And Bobbie said, "Yes," and tried to smile.

When you are used to ten hours of solid sleep, to get up three or four times in your sleep-time makes you feel as though you had been up all night. Bobbie felt quite stupid and her eyes were sore and stiff, but she tidied the room, and arranged everything neatly before the Doctor came.

This was at half-past eight.

"Everything going on all right, little Nurse?" he said at the front door. "Did you get the brandy?"

"I've got the brandy," said Bobbie, "in a little flat bottle."

"I didn't see the grapes or the beef tea, though," said he.

"No," said Bobbie, firmly, "but you will to-morrow. And there's some beef stewing in the oven for beef tea."

"Who told you to do that?" he asked.

"I noticed what Mother did when Phil had mumps."

"Right," said the Doctor. "Now you get your old woman to sit with your mother, and then you eat a good breakfast, and go straight to bed and sleep till dinner-time. We can't afford to have the head- nurse ill."

He was really quite a nice doctor.

When the 9.15 came out of the tunnel that morning the old gentleman in the first-class carriage put down his newspaper, and got ready to wave his hand to the three children on the fence. But this morning there were not three. There was only one. And that was Peter.

Peter was not on the railings either, as usual. He was standing in front of them in an attitude like that of a show-man showing off the animals in a menagerie, or of the kind clergyman when he points with a wand at the 'Scenes from Palestine,' when there is a magic-lantern and he is explaining it.

Peter was pointing, too. And what he was pointing at was a large white sheet nailed against the fence. On the sheet there were thick black letters more than a foot long.

Some of them had run a little, because of Phyllis having put the Brunswick black on too eagerly, but the words were quite easy to read.

And this what the old gentleman and several other people in the train read in the large black letters on the white sheet:--

LOOK OUT AT THE STATION.

A good many people did look out at the station and were disappointed, for they saw nothing unusual. The old gentleman looked out, too, and at first he too saw nothing more unusual than the gravelled platform and the sunshine and the wallflowers and forget-me-nots in the station borders. It was only just as the train was beginning to puff and pull itself together to start again that he saw Phyllis. She was quite out of breath with running.

"Oh," she said, "I thought I'd missed you. My bootlaces would keep coming down and I fell over them twice. Here, take it."

She thrust a warm, dampish letter into his hand as the train moved.

He leaned back in his corner and opened the letter. This is what he read:--

"Dear Mr. We do not know your name.

Mother is ill and the doctor says to give her the things at the end of the letter, but she says she can't aford it, and to get mutton for us and she will have the broth. We do not know anybody here but you, because Father is away and we do not know the address. Father will pay you, or if he has lost all his money, or anything, Peter will pay you when he is a man. We promise it on our honer. I.O.U. for all the things Mother wants.

"sined Peter.

"Will you give the parsel to the Station Master, because of us not knowing what train you come down by? Say it is for Peter that was sorry about the coals and he will know all right.

"Roberta.

"Phyllis.

"Peter."

Then came the list of things the Doctor had ordered.

The old gentleman read it through once, and his eyebrows went up. He read it twice and smiled a little. When he had read it thrice, he put it in his pocket and went on reading The Times.

At about six that evening there was a knock at the back door. The three children rushed to open it, and there stood the friendly Porter, who had told them so many interesting things about railways. He dumped down a big hamper on the kitchen flags.

"Old gent," he said; "he asked me to fetch it up straight away."

"Thank you very much," said Peter, and then, as the Porter lingered, he added:--

"I'm most awfully sorry I haven't got twopence to give you like Father does, but--"

"You drop it if you please," said the Porter, indignantly. "I wasn't thinking about no tuppences. I only wanted to say I was sorry your Mamma wasn't so well, and to ask how she finds herself this evening--and I've fetched her along a bit of sweetbrier, very sweet to smell it is. Twopence indeed," said he, and produced a bunch of sweetbrier from his hat, "just like a conjurer," as Phyllis remarked afterwards.

"Thank you very much," said Peter, "and I beg your pardon about the twopence."

"No offence," said the Porter, untruly but politely, and went.

Then the children undid the hamper. First there was straw, and then there were fine shavings, and then came all the things they had asked for, and plenty of them, and then a good many things they had not asked for; among others peaches and port wine and two chickens, a cardboard box of big red roses with long stalks, and a tall thin green bottle of lavender water, and three smaller fatter bottles of eau-de-Cologne. There was a letter, too.

"Dear Roberta and Phyllis and Peter," it said; "here are the things you want. Your mother will want to know where they came from. Tell her they were sent by a friend who heard she was ill. When she is well again you must tell her all about it, of course. And if she says you ought not to have asked for the things, tell her that I say you were quite right, and that I hope she will forgive me for taking the liberty of allowing myself a very great pleasure."

The letter was signed G. P. something that the children couldn't read.

"I think we *were* right," said Phyllis.

"Right? Of course we were right," said Bobbie.

"All the same," said Peter, with his hands in his pockets, "I don't exactly look forward to telling Mother the whole truth about it."

"We're not to do it till she's well," said Bobbie, "and when she's well we shall be so happy we shan't mind a little fuss like that. Oh, just look at the roses! I must take them up to her."

"And the sweetbrier," said Phyllis, sniffing it loudly; "don't forget the sweetbrier."

"As if I should!" said Roberta. "Mother told me the other day there was a thick hedge of it at her mother's house when she was a little girl."

Lesson 78

1. Read the first part of chapter four of *The Railway Children*.
2. An aqueduct carries water (a picture follows).

What was left of the second sheet and the Brunswick black came in very nicely to make a banner bearing the legend

SHE IS NEARLY WELL THANK YOU

and this was displayed to the Green Dragon about a fortnight after the arrival of the wonderful hamper. The old gentleman saw it, and waved a cheerful response from the train. And when this had been done the children saw that now was the time when they must tell Mother what they had done when she was ill. And it did not seem nearly so easy as they had thought it would be. But it had to be done. And it was done. Mother was extremely angry. She was seldom angry, and now she was angrier than they had ever known her. This was horrible. But it was much worse when she suddenly began to cry. Crying is catching, I believe, like measles and whooping-cough. At any rate, everyone at once found itself taking part in a crying-party.

Mother stopped first. She dried her eyes and then she said:--

"I'm sorry I was so angry, darlings, because I know you didn't understand."

"We didn't mean to be naughty, Mammy," sobbed Bobbie, and Peter and Phyllis sniffed.

"Now, listen," said Mother; "it's quite true that we're poor, but we have enough to live on. You mustn't go telling everyone about our affairs--it's not right. And you must never, never, never ask strangers to give you things. Now always remember that--won't you?"

They all hugged her and rubbed their damp cheeks against hers and promised that they would.

"And I'll write a letter to your old gentleman, and I shall tell him that I didn't approve--oh, of course I shall thank him, too, for his kindness. It's *you* I don't approve of, my darlings, not the old gentleman. He was as kind as ever he could be. And you can give the letter to the Station Master to give him--and we won't say any more about it."

Afterwards, when the children were alone, Bobbie said:--

"Isn't Mother splendid? You catch any other grown-up saying they were sorry they had been angry."

"Yes," said Peter, "she *is* splendid; but it's rather awful when she's angry."

"She's like Avenging and Bright in the song," said Phyllis. "I should like to look at her if it wasn't so awful. She looks so beautiful when she's really downright furious."

They took the letter down to the Station Master.

"I thought you said you hadn't got any friends except in London," said he.

"We've made him since," said Peter.

"But he doesn't live hereabouts?"

"No--we just know him on the railway."

Then the Station Master retired to that sacred inner temple behind the little window where the tickets are sold, and the children went down to the Porters' room and talked to the Porter. They learned several interesting things from him--among others that his name was Perks, that he was married and had three children, that the lamps in front of engines are called head-lights and the ones at the back tail-lights.

"And that just shows," whispered Phyllis, "that trains really *are* dragons in disguise, with proper heads and tails."

It was on this day that the children first noticed that all engines are not alike.

"Alike?" said the Porter, whose name was Perks, "lor, love you, no, Miss. No more alike nor what you an' me are. That little 'un without a tender as went by just now all on her own, that was a tank, that was--she's off to do some shunting t'other side o' Maidbridge. That's as it might be you, Miss. Then there's goods engines, great, strong things with three wheels each side--joined with rods to strengthen 'em--as it might be me. Then there's main- line engines as it might be this 'ere young gentleman when he grows up and wins all the races at 'is school--so he will. The main-line engine she's built for speed as well as power. That's one to the 9.15 up."

"The Green Dragon," said Phyllis.

"We calls her the Snail, Miss, among ourselves," said the Porter. "She's oftener be'ind'and nor any train on the line."

"But the engine's green," said Phyllis.

"Yes, Miss," said Perks, "so's a snail some seasons o' the year."

The children agreed as they went home to dinner that the Porter was most delightful company.

Next day was Roberta's birthday. In the afternoon she was politely but firmly requested to get out of the way and keep there till tea- time.

"You aren't to see what we're going to do till it's done; it's a glorious surprise," said Phyllis.

And Roberta went out into the garden all alone. She tried to be grateful, but she felt she would much rather have helped in whatever it was than have to spend her birthday afternoon by herself, no matter how glorious the surprise might be.

Now that she was alone, she had time to think, and one of the things she thought of most was what mother had said in one of those feverish nights when her hands were so hot and her eyes so bright.

The words were: "Oh, what a doctor's bill there'll be for this!"

She walked round and round the garden among the rose-bushes that hadn't any roses yet, only buds, and the lilac bushes and syringas and American currants, and the more she thought of the doctor's bill, the less she liked the thought of it.

And presently she made up her mind. She went out through the side door of the garden and climbed up the steep field to where the road runs along by the canal. She walked along until she came to the bridge that crosses the canal and leads to the village, and here she waited. It was very pleasant in the sunshine to lean one's elbows on the warm stone of the bridge and look down at the blue water of the canal. Bobbie had never seen any other canal, except the Regent's Canal, and the water of that is not at all a pretty colour. And she had never seen any river at all except the Thames, which also would be all the better if its face was washed.

Perhaps the children would have loved the canal as much as the railway, but for two things. One was that they had found the railway *first*--on that first, wonderful morning when the house and the country and the moors and rocks and great hills were all new to them. They had not found the canal till some days later. The other reason was that everyone on the railway had been kind to them--the Station Master, the Porter, and the old gentleman who waved. And the people on the canal were anything but kind.

The people on the canal were, of course, the bargees, who steered the slow barges up and down, or walked beside the old horses that trampled up the mud of the towing-path, and strained at the long tow-ropes.

Peter had once asked one of the bargees the time, and had been told to "get out of that," in a tone so fierce that he did not stop to say anything about his having just as much right on the towing-path as the man himself. Indeed, he did not even think of saying it till some time later.

Then another day when the children thought they would like to fish in the canal, a boy in a barge threw lumps of coal at them, and one of these hit Phyllis on the back of the neck. She was just stooping down to tie up her bootlace--and though the coal hardly hurt at all it made her not care very much about going on fishing.

On the bridge, however, Roberta felt quite safe, because she could look down on the canal, and if any boy showed signs of meaning to throw coal, she could duck behind the parapet.

Presently there was a sound of wheels, which was just what she expected.

The wheels were the wheels of the Doctor's dogcart, and in the cart, of course, was the Doctor.

He pulled up, and called out:--

"Hullo, head nurse! Want a lift?"

"I wanted to see you," said Bobbie.

"Your mother's not worse, I hope?" said the Doctor.

"No--but--"

"Well, skip in, then, and we'll go for a drive."

Roberta climbed in and the brown horse was made to turn round--which it did not like at all, for it was looking forward to its tea--I mean its oats.

"This *is* jolly," said Bobbie, as the dogcart flew along the road by the canal.

"We could throw a stone down any one of your three chimneys," said the Doctor, as they passed the house.

"Yes," said Bobbie, "but you'd have to be a jolly good shot."

"How do you know I'm not?" said the Doctor. "Now, then, what's the trouble?"

Bobbie fidgeted with the hook of the driving apron.

"Come, out with it," said the Doctor.

"It's rather hard, you see," said Bobbie, "to out with it; because of what Mother said."

"What *did* Mother say?"

"She said I wasn't to go telling everyone that we're poor. But you aren't everyone, are you?"

"Not at all," said the Doctor, cheerfully. "Well?"

"Well, I know doctors are very extravagant--I mean expensive, and Mrs. Viney told me that her doctoring only cost her twopence a week because she belonged to a Club."

"Yes?"

"You see she told me what a good doctor you were, and I asked her how she could afford you, because she's much poorer than we are. I've been in her house and I know. And then she told me about the Club, and I thought I'd ask you--and--oh, I don't want Mother to be worried! Can't we be in the Club, too, the same as Mrs. Viney?"

The Doctor was silent. He was rather poor himself, and he had been pleased at getting a new family to attend. So I think his feelings at that minute were rather mixed.

"You aren't cross with me, are you?" said Bobbie, in a very small voice.

The Doctor roused himself.

"Cross? How could I be? You're a very sensible little woman. Now look here, don't you worry. I'll make it all right with your Mother, even if I have to make a special brand-new Club all for her. Look here, this is where the Aqueduct begins."

"What's an Aque--what's its name?" asked Bobbie.

"A water bridge," said the Doctor. "Look."

The road rose to a bridge over the canal. To the left was a steep rocky cliff with trees and shrubs growing in the cracks of the rock. And the canal here left off running along the top of the hill and started to run on a bridge of its own--a great bridge with tall arches that went right across the valley.

Bobbie drew a long breath.

"It *is* grand, isn't it?" she said. "It's like pictures in the History of Rome."

"Right!" said the Doctor, "that's just exactly what it *is* like. The Romans were dead nuts on aqueducts. It's a splendid piece of engineering."

"I thought engineering was making engines."

"Ah, there are different sorts of engineering--making road and bridges and tunnels is one kind. And making fortifications is another. Well, we must be turning back. And, remember, you aren't to worry about doctor's bills or you'll be ill yourself, and then I'll send you in a bill as long as the aqueduct."

When Bobbie had parted from the Doctor at the top of the field that ran down from the road to Three Chimneys, she could not feel that she had done wrong. She knew that Mother would perhaps think differently. But Bobbie felt that for once she was the one who was right, and she scrambled down the rocky slope with a really happy feeling.

Phyllis and Peter met her at the back door. They were unnaturally clean and neat, and Phyllis had a red bow in her hair. There was only just time for Bobbie to make herself tidy and tie up her hair with a blue bow before a little bell rang.

"There!" said Phyllis, "that's to show the surprise is ready. Now you wait till the bell rings again and then you may come into the dining-room."

So Bobbie waited.

"Tinkle, tinkle," said the little bell, and Bobbie went into the dining-room, feeling rather shy. Directly she opened the door she found herself, as it seemed, in a new world of light and flowers and singing. Mother and Peter and Phyllis were standing in a row at the end of the table. The shutters were shut and there were twelve candles on the table, one for each of Roberta's years. The table was covered with a sort of pattern of flowers, and at Roberta's place was a thick wreath of forget-me-nots and several most interesting little packages. And Mother and Phyllis and Peter were singing--to the first part of the tune of St. Patrick's Day. Roberta knew that Mother had written the words on purpose for her birthday. It was a little way of Mother's on birthdays. It had begun on Bobbie's fourth birthday when Phyllis was a baby. Bobbie remembered learning the verses to say to Father 'for a surprise.' She wondered if Mother had remembered, too. The four-year-old verse had been:--

> Daddy dear, I'm only four
> And I'd rather not be more.
>
> Four's the nicest age to be,
> Two and two and one and three.
>
> What I love is two and two,
> Mother, Peter, Phil, and you.
>
>
> What you love is one and three,
> Mother, Peter, Phil, and me.
>
> Give your little girl a kiss
> Because she learned and told you this.

The song the others were singing now went like this:--

> Our darling Roberta,
> No sorrow shall hurt her
> If we can prevent it
> Her whole life long.
>
> Her birthday's our fete day,
> We'll make it our great day,
> And give her our presents
> And sing her our song.
>
> May pleasures attend her
> And may the Fates send her
> The happiest journey
> Along her life's way.

With skies bright above her
And dear ones to love her!
Dear Bob! Many happy
Returns of the day!

When they had finished singing they cried, "Three cheers for our Bobbie!" and gave them very loudly. Bobbie felt exactly as though she were going to cry--you know that odd feeling in the bridge of your nose and the pricking in your eyelids? But before she had time to begin they were all kissing and hugging her.

Lesson 79

1.   Read the second part of chapter four of *The Railway Children*.
2.   In a steam engine, the coal feeds the fire, which heats the water, which turns it into steam, which pushes the piston, causing the wheels to turn.

"Now," said Mother, "look at your presents."

They were very nice presents. There was a green and red needle-book that Phyllis had made herself in secret moments. There was a darling little silver brooch of Mother's shaped like a buttercup, which Bobbie had known and loved for years, but which she had never, never thought would come to be her very own. There was also a pair of blue glass vases from Mrs. Viney. Roberta had seen and admired them in the village shop. And there were three birthday cards with pretty pictures and wishes.

Mother fitted the forget-me-not crown on Bobbie's brown head.

"And now look at the table," she said.

There was a cake on the table covered with white sugar, with 'Dear Bobbie' on it in pink sweets, and there were buns and jam; but the nicest thing was that the big table was almost covered with flowers--wallflowers were laid all round the tea-tray--there was a ring of forget-me-nots round each plate. The cake had a wreath of white lilac round it, and in the middle was something that looked like a pattern all done with single blooms of lilac or wallflower or laburnum.

"It's a map--a map of the railway!" cried Peter. "Look--those lilac lines are the metals--and there's the station done in brown wallflowers. The laburnum is the train, and there are the signal-boxes, and the road up to here--and those fat red daisies are us three waving to the old gentleman--that's him, the pansy in the laburnum train."

"And there's 'Three Chimneys' done in the purple primroses," said Phyllis. "And that little tiny rose-bud is Mother looking out for us when we're late for tea. Peter invented it all, and we got all the flowers from the station. We thought you'd like it better."

"That's my present," said Peter, suddenly dumping down his adored steam-engine on the table in front of her. Its tender had been lined with fresh white paper, and was full of sweets.

"Oh, Peter!" cried Bobbie, quite overcome by this munificence, "not your own dear little engine that you're so fond of?"

"Oh, no," said Peter, very promptly, "not the engine. Only the sweets."

Bobbie couldn't help her face changing a little--not so much because she was disappointed at not getting the engine, as because she had thought it so very noble of Peter, and now she felt she had been silly to think it. Also she felt she must have seemed greedy to expect the engine as well as the sweets. So her face changed. Peter saw it. He hesitated a minute; then his face changed, too, and he said: "I mean not *all* the engine. I'll let you go halves if you like."

"You're a brick," cried Bobbie; "it's a splendid present." She said no more aloud, but to herself she said:--

"That was awfully jolly decent of Peter because I know he didn't mean to. Well, the broken half shall be my half of the engine, and I'll get it mended and give it back to Peter for his birthday."-- "Yes, Mother dear, I should like to cut the cake," she added, and tea began.

It was a delightful birthday. After tea Mother played games with them--any game they liked--and of course their first choice was blindman's-buff, in the course of which Bobbie's forget-me-not wreath twisted itself crookedly over one of her ears and stayed there. Then, when it was near bed-time and time to calm down, Mother had a lovely new story to read to them.

"You won't sit up late working, will you, Mother?" Bobbie asked as they said good night.

And Mother said no, she wouldn't--she would only just write to Father and then go to bed.

But when Bobbie crept down later to bring up her presents--for she felt she really could not be separated from them all night--Mother was not writing, but leaning her head on her arms and her arms on the table. I think it was rather good of Bobbie to slip quietly away, saying over and over, "She doesn't want me to know she's unhappy, and I won't know; I won't know." But it made a sad end to the birthday.

*   *   *   *   *   *

The very next morning Bobbie began to watch her opportunity to get Peter's engine mended secretly. And the opportunity came the very next afternoon.

Mother went by train to the nearest town to do shopping. When she went there, she always went to the Post-office. Perhaps to post her letters to Father, for she never gave them to the children or Mrs. Viney to post, and she never went to the village herself. Peter and Phyllis went with her. Bobbie wanted an excuse not to go, but try as she would she couldn't think of a good one. And just when she felt that all was lost, her frock caught on a big nail by the kitchen door and there was a great criss-cross tear all along the front of the skirt. I assure you this was really an accident. So the others pitied her and went without her, for there was no time for her to change, because they were rather late already and had to hurry to the station to catch the train.

When they had gone, Bobbie put on her everyday frock, and went down to the railway. She did not go into the station, but she went along the line to the end of the platform where the engine is when the down train is alongside the platform--the place where there are a water tank and a long, limp, leather hose, like an elephant's trunk. She hid behind a bush on the other side of the railway. She had the toy engine done up in brown paper, and she waited patiently with it under her arm.

Then when the next train came in and stopped, Bobbie went across the metals of the up-line and stood beside the engine. She had never been so close to an engine before. It looked much larger and harder than she had expected, and it made her feel very small indeed, and, somehow, very soft--as if she could very, very easily be hurt rather badly.

"I know what silk-worms feel like now," said Bobbie to herself.

The engine-driver and fireman did not see her. They were leaning out on the other side, telling the Porter a tale about a dog and a leg of mutton.

"If you please," said Roberta--but the engine was blowing off steam and no one heard her.

"If you please, Mr. Engineer," she spoke a little louder, but the Engine happened to speak at the same moment, and of course Roberta's soft little voice hadn't a chance.

It seemed to her that the only way would be to climb on to the engine and pull at their coats. The step was high, but she got her knee on it, and clambered into the cab; she stumbled and fell on hands and knees on the base of the great heap of coals that led up to the square opening in the tender. The engine was not above the weaknesses of its fellows; it was making a great deal more noise than there was the slightest need for. And just as Roberta fell on the coals, the engine-driver, who had turned without seeing her, started the engine, and when Bobbie had picked herself up, the train was moving--not fast, but much too fast for her to get off.

All sorts of dreadful thoughts came to her all together in one horrible flash. There were such things as express trains that went on, she supposed, for hundreds of miles without stopping. Suppose this should be one of them? How would she get home again? She had no money to pay for the return journey.

"And I've no business here. I'm an engine-burglar--that's what I am," she thought. "I shouldn't wonder if they could lock me up for this." And the train was going faster and faster.

There was something in her throat that made it impossible for her to speak. She tried twice. The men had their backs to her. They were doing something to things that looked like taps.

Suddenly she put out her hand and caught hold of the nearest sleeve. The man turned with a start, and he and Roberta stood for a minute looking at each other in silence. Then the silence was broken by them both.

The man said, "Here's a bloomin' go!" and Roberta burst into tears.

The other man said he was blooming well blest--or something like it--but though naturally surprised they were not exactly unkind.

"You're a naughty little gell, that's what you are," said the fireman, and the engine-driver said:--

"Daring little piece, I call her," but they made her sit down on an iron seat in the cab and told her to stop crying and tell them what she meant by it.

She did stop, as soon as she could. One thing that helped her was the thought that Peter would give almost his ears to be in her place--on a real engine--really going. The children had often wondered whether any engine-driver could be found noble enough to take them for a ride on an engine--and now there she was. She dried her eyes and sniffed earnestly.

"Now, then," said the fireman, "out with it. What do you mean by it, eh?"

"Oh, please," sniffed Bobbie.

"Try again," said the engine-driver, encouragingly.

Bobbie tried again.

"Please, Mr. Engineer," she said, "I did call out to you from the line, but you didn't hear me--and I just climbed up to touch you on the arm--quite gently I meant to do it--and then I fell into the coals--and I am so sorry if I frightened you. Oh, don't be cross--oh, please don't!" She sniffed again.

"We ain't so much *cross*," said the fireman, "as interested like. It ain't every day a little gell tumbles into our coal bunker outer the sky, is it, Bill? What did you *do* it for--eh?"

"That's the point," agreed the engine-driver; "what did you do it *for*?"

Bobbie found that she had not quite stopped crying. The engine-driver patted her on the back and said: "Here, cheer up, Mate. It ain't so bad as all that 'ere, I'll be bound."

"I wanted," said Bobbie, much cheered to find herself addressed as 'Mate'--"I only wanted to ask you if you'd be so kind as to mend this." She picked up the brown-paper parcel from among the coals and undid the string with hot, red fingers that trembled.

Her feet and legs felt the scorch of the engine fire, but her shoulders felt the wild chill rush of the air. The engine lurched and shook and rattled, and as they shot under a bridge the engine seemed to shout in her ears.

The fireman shovelled on coals.

Bobbie unrolled the brown paper and disclosed the toy engine.

"I thought," she said wistfully, "that perhaps you'd mend this for me--because you're an engineer, you know."

The engine-driver said he was blowed if he wasn't blest.

"I'm blest if I ain't blowed," remarked the fireman.

But the engine-driver took the little engine and looked at it--and the fireman ceased for an instant to shovel coal, and looked, too.

"It's like your precious cheek," said the engine-driver--"whatever made you think we'd be bothered tinkering penny toys?"

"I didn't mean it for precious cheek," said Bobbie; "only everybody that has anything to do with railways is so kind and good, I didn't think you'd mind. You don't really--do you?" she added, for she had seen a not unkindly wink pass between the two.

"My trade's driving of an engine, not mending her, especially such a hout-size in engines as this 'ere," said Bill. "An' 'ow are we a-goin' to get you back to your sorrowing friends and relations, and all be forgiven and forgotten?"

"If you'll put me down next time you stop," said Bobbie, firmly, though her heart beat fiercely against her arm as she clasped her hands, "and lend me the money for a third-class ticket, I'll pay you back--honour bright. I'm not a confidence trick like in the newspapers--really, I'm not."

"You're a little lady, every inch," said Bill, relenting suddenly and completely. "We'll see you gets home safe. An' about this engine--Jim--ain't you got ne'er a pal as can use a soldering iron? Seems to me that's about all the little bounder wants doing to it."

"That's what Father said," Bobbie explained eagerly. "What's that for?"

She pointed to a little brass wheel that he had turned as he spoke.

"That's the injector."

"In--what?"

"Injector to fill up the boiler."

"Oh," said Bobbie, mentally registering the fact to tell the others; "that *is* interesting."

"This 'ere's the automatic brake," Bill went on, flattered by her enthusiasm. "You just move this 'ere little handle--do it with one finger, you can--and the train jolly soon stops. That's what they call the Power of Science in the newspapers."

He showed her two little dials, like clock faces, and told her how one showed how much steam was going, and the other showed if the brake was working properly.

By the time she had seen him shut off steam with a big shining steel handle, Bobbie knew more about the inside working of an engine than she had ever thought there was to know, and Jim had promised that his second cousin's wife's brother should solder the toy engine, or Jim would know the reason why. Besides all the knowledge she had gained Bobbie felt that she and Bill and Jim were now friends for life, and that they had wholly and forever forgiven her for stumbling uninvited among the sacred coals of their tender.

At Stacklepoole Junction she parted from them with warm expressions of mutual regard. They handed her over to the guard of a returning train--a friend of theirs--and she had the joy of knowing what guards do in their secret fastnesses, and understood how, when you pull the communication cord in railway carriages, a wheel goes round under the guard's nose and a loud bell rings in his ears. She asked the guard why his van smelt so fishy, and learned that he had to carry a lot of fish every day, and that the wetness in the hollows of the corrugated floor had all drained out of boxes full of plaice and cod and mackerel and soles and smelts.

Bobbie got home in time for tea, and she felt as though her mind would burst with all that had been put into it since she parted from the others. How she blessed the nail that had torn her frock!

"Where have you been?" asked the others.

"To the station, of course," said Roberta. But she would not tell a word of her adventures till the day appointed, when she mysteriously led them to the station at the hour of the 3.19's transit, and proudly introduced them to her friends, Bill and Jim. Jim's second cousin's wife's brother had not been unworthy of the sacred trust reposed in him. The toy engine was, literally, as good as new.

"Good-bye--oh, good-bye," said Bobbie, just before the engine screamed *its* good-bye. "I shall always, always love you--and Jim's second cousin's wife's brother as well!"

And as the three children went home up the hill, Peter hugging the engine, now quite its own self again, Bobbie told, with joyous leaps of the heart, the story of how she had been an Engine-burglar.

Lesson 80

1. Read the first part of chapter five of *The Railway Children*.
2. Write a summary in one sentence.

Vocabulary

1. Write an antonym, or word with the opposite meaning, for each of these words: content, lazy, discourage, helpful, prepared, thoughtful, humble, knowledge, colorful, dread (Answers)
2. How did you use suffixes and prefixes to change the meaning of the words?

It was one day when Mother had gone to Maidbridge. She had gone alone, but the children were to go to the station to meet her. And, loving the station as they did, it was only natural that they should be there a good hour before there was any chance of Mother's train arriving, even if the train were punctual, which was most unlikely. No doubt they would have been just as early, even if it had been a fine day, and all the delights of woods and fields and rocks and rivers had been open to them. But it happened to be a very wet day and, for July, very cold. There was a wild wind that drove flocks of dark purple clouds across the sky "like herds of dream-elephants," as Phyllis said. And the rain stung sharply, so that the way to the station was finished at a run. Then the rain fell faster and harder, and beat slantwise against the windows of the booking office and of the chill place that had General Waiting Room on its door.

"It's like being in a besieged castle," Phyllis said; "look at the arrows of the foe striking against the battlements!"

"It's much more like a great garden-squirt," said Peter.

They decided to wait on the up side, for the down platform looked very wet indeed, and the rain was driving right into the little bleak shelter where down-passengers have to wait for their trains.

The hour would be full of incident and of interest, for there would be two up trains and one down to look at before the one that should bring Mother back.

"Perhaps it'll have stopped raining by then," said Bobbie; "anyhow, I'm glad I brought Mother's waterproof and umbrella."

They went into the desert spot labelled General Waiting Room, and the time passed pleasantly enough in a game of advertisements. You know the game, of course? It is something like dumb Crambo. The players take it in turns to go out, and then come back and look as like some advertisement as they can, and the others have to guess what advertisement it is meant to be. Bobbie came in and sat down under Mother's umbrella and made a sharp face, and everyone knew she was the fox who sits under the umbrella in the advertisement. Phyllis tried to make a Magic Carpet of Mother's waterproof, but it would not stand out stiff and raft-like as a Magic Carpet should, and nobody could guess it. Everyone thought Peter was carrying things a little too far when he blacked his face all over with coal-dust and struck a spidery attitude and said he was the blot that advertises somebody's Blue Black Writing Fluid.

It was Phyllis's turn again, and she was trying to look like the Sphinx that advertises What's-his-name's Personally Conducted Tours up the Nile when the sharp ting of the signal announced the up train. The children rushed out to see it pass. On its engine were the particular driver and fireman who were now numbered among the children's dearest friends. Courtesies passed between them. Jim asked after the toy engine, and Bobbie pressed on his acceptance a moist, greasy package of toffee that she had made herself.

Charmed by this attention, the engine-driver consented to consider her request that some day he would take Peter for a ride on the engine.

"Stand back, Mates," cried the engine-driver, suddenly, "and horf she goes."

And sure enough, off the train went. The children watched the tail-lights of the train till it disappeared round the curve of the line, and then turned to go back to the dusty freedom of the General Waiting Room and the joys of the advertisement game.

They expected to see just one or two people, the end of the procession of passengers who had given up their tickets and gone away. Instead, the platform round the door of the station had a dark blot round it, and the dark blot was a crowd of people.

"Oh!" cried Peter, with a thrill of joyous excitement, "something's happened! Come on!"

They ran down the platform. When they got to the crowd, they could, of course, see nothing but the damp backs and elbows of the people on the crowd's outside. Everybody was talking at once. It was evident that something had happened.

"It's my belief he's nothing worse than a natural," said a farmerish-looking person. Peter saw his red, clean-shaven face as he spoke.

"If you ask me, I should say it was a Police Court case," said a young man with a black bag.

"Not it; the Infirmary more like--"

Then the voice of the Station Master was heard, firm and official:--

"Now, then--move along there. I'll attend to this, if *you* please."

But the crowd did not move. And then came a voice that thrilled the children through and through. For it spoke in a foreign language. And, what is more, it was a language that they had never heard. They had heard French spoken and German. Aunt Emma knew German, and used to sing a song about bedeuten and zeiten and bin and sin. Nor was it Latin. Peter had been in Latin for four terms.

It was some comfort, anyhow, to find that none of the crowd understood the foreign language any better than the children did.

"What's that he's saying?" asked the farmer, heavily.

"Sounds like French to me," said the Station Master, who had once been to Boulogne for the day.

"It isn't French!" cried Peter.

"What is it, then?" asked more than one voice. The crowd fell back a little to see who had spoken, and Peter pressed forward, so that when the crowd closed up again he was in the front rank.

"I don't know what it is," said Peter, "but it isn't French. I know that." Then he saw what it was that the crowd had for its centre. It was a man--the man, Peter did not doubt, who had spoken in that strange tongue. A man with long hair and wild eyes, with shabby clothes of a cut Peter had not seen before--a man whose hands and lips trembled, and who spoke again as his eyes fell on Peter.

"No, it's not French," said Peter.

"Try him with French if you know so much about it," said the farmer-man.

"Parlay voo Frongsay?" began Peter, boldly, and the next moment the crowd recoiled again, for the man with the wild eyes had left leaning against the wall, and had sprung forward and caught Peter's hands, and begun to pour forth a flood of words which, though he could not understand a word of them, Peter knew the sound of.

"There!" said he, and turned, his hands still clasped in the hands of the strange shabby figure, to throw a glance of triumph at the crowd; "there; *that's* French."

"What does he say?"

"I don't know." Peter was obliged to own it.

"Here," said the Station Master again; "you move on if you please. *I'll* deal with this case."

A few of the more timid or less inquisitive travellers moved slowly and reluctantly away. And Phyllis and Bobbie got near to Peter. All three had been *taught* French at school. How deeply they now wished that they had *learned* it! Peter shook his head at the stranger, but he also shook his hands as warmly and looked at him as kindly as he could. A person in the crowd, after some hesitation, said suddenly, "No comprenny!" and then, blushing deeply, backed out of the press and went away.

"Take him into your room," whispered Bobbie to the Station Master. "Mother can talk French. She'll be here by the next train from Maidbridge."

The Station Master took the arm of the stranger, suddenly but not unkindly. But the man wrenched his arm away, and cowered back coughing and trembling and trying to push the Station Master away.

"Oh, don't!" said Bobbie; "don't you see how frightened he is? He thinks you're going to shut him up. I know he does--look at his eyes!"

"They're like a fox's eyes when the beast's in a trap," said the farmer.

"Oh, let me try!" Bobbie went on; "I do really know one or two French words if I could only think of them."

Sometimes, in moments of great need, we can do wonderful things--things that in ordinary life we could hardly even dream of doing. Bobbie had never been anywhere near the top of her French class, but she must have learned something without knowing it, for now, looking at those wild, hunted eyes, she actually remembered and, what is more, spoke, some French words. She said:--

"Vous attendre. Ma mere parlez Francais. Nous--what's the French for 'being kind'?"

Nobody knew.

"Bong is 'good,'" said Phyllis.

"Nous etre bong pour vous."

I do not know whether the man understood her words, but he understood the touch of the hand she thrust into his, and the kindness of the other hand that stroked his shabby sleeve.

She pulled him gently towards the inmost sanctuary of the Station Master. The other children followed, and the Station Master shut the door in the face of the crowd, which stood a little while in the booking office talking and looking at the fast closed yellow door, and then by ones and twos went its way, grumbling.

Inside the Station Master's room Bobbie still held the stranger's hand and stroked his sleeve.

"Here's a go," said the Station Master; "no ticket--doesn't even know where he wants to go. I'm not sure now but what I ought to send for the police."

"Oh, *don't*!" all the children pleaded at once. And suddenly Bobbie got between the others and the stranger, for she had seen that he was crying.

By a most unusual piece of good fortune she had a handkerchief in her pocket. By a still more uncommon accident the handkerchief was moderately clean. Standing in front of the stranger, she got out the handkerchief and passed it to him so that the others did not see.

"Wait till Mother comes," Phyllis was saying; "she does speak French beautifully. You'd just love to hear her."

"I'm sure he hasn't done anything like you're sent to prison for," said Peter.

"Looks like without visible means to me," said the Station Master. "Well, I don't mind giving him the benefit of the doubt till your Mamma comes. I *should* like to know what nation's got the credit of *him*, that I should."

Then Peter had an idea. He pulled an envelope out of his pocket, and showed that it was half full of foreign stamps.

"Look here," he said, "let's show him these--"

Bobbie looked and saw that the stranger had dried his eyes with her handkerchief. So she said: "All right."

They showed him an Italian stamp, and pointed from him to it and back again, and made signs of question with their eyebrows. He shook his head. Then they showed him a Norwegian stamp--the common blue kind it was--and again he signed No. Then they showed him a Spanish one, and at that he took the envelope from Peter's hand and searched among the stamps with a hand that trembled. The hand that he reached out at last, with a gesture as of one answering a question, contained a *Russian* stamp.

Lesson 81

1. Read the second part of chapter five of *The Railway Children*.
2. Tell someone about the chapter.
3. "The man who was" is a short story by a famous author, Kipling. The "man who was" had been a British officer and then something happened and he became a "nobody" but still held onto his pride and loyalty.

"He's Russian," cried Peter, "or else he's like 'the man who was'-- in Kipling, you know."

The train from Maidbridge was signalled.

"I'll stay with him till you bring Mother in," said Bobbie.

"You're not afraid, Missie?"

"Oh, no," said Bobbie, looking at the stranger, as she might have looked at a strange dog of doubtful temper. "You wouldn't hurt me, would you?"

She smiled at him, and he smiled back, a queer crooked smile. And then he coughed again. And the heavy rattling swish of the incoming train swept past, and the Station Master and Peter and Phyllis went out to meet it. Bobbie was still holding the stranger's hand when they came back with Mother.

The Russian rose and bowed very ceremoniously.

Then Mother spoke in French, and he replied, haltingly at first, but presently in longer and longer sentences.

The children, watching his face and Mother's, knew that he was telling her things that made her angry and pitying, and sorry and indignant all at once.

"Well, Mum, what's it all about?" The Station Master could not restrain his curiosity any longer.

"Oh," said Mother, "it's all right. He's a Russian, and he's lost his ticket. And I'm afraid he's very ill. If you don't mind, I'll take him home with me now. He's really quite worn out. I'll run down and tell you all about him to-morrow."

"I hope you won't find you're taking home a frozen viper," said the Station Master, doubtfully.

"Oh, no," Mother said brightly, and she smiled; "I'm quite sure I'm not. Why, he's a great man in his own country, writes books-- beautiful books--I've read some of them; but I'll tell you all about it to-morrow."

She spoke again in French to the Russian, and everyone could see the surprise and pleasure and gratitude in his eyes. He got up and politely bowed to the Station Master, and offered his arm most ceremoniously to Mother. She took it, but anybody could have seen that she was helping him along, and not he her.

"You girls run home and light a fire in the sitting-room," Mother said, "and Peter had better go for the Doctor."

But it was Bobbie who went for the Doctor.

"I hate to tell you," she said breathlessly when she came upon him in his shirt sleeves, weeding his pansy-bed, "but Mother's got a very shabby Russian, and I'm sure he'll have to belong to your Club. I'm certain he hasn't got any money. We found him at the station."

"Found him! Was he lost, then?" asked the Doctor, reaching for his coat.

"Yes," said Bobbie, unexpectedly, "that's just what he was. He's been telling Mother the sad, sweet story of his life in French; and she said would you be kind enough to come directly if you were at home. He has a dreadful cough, and he's been crying."

The Doctor smiled.

"Oh, don't," said Bobbie; "please don't. You wouldn't if you'd seen him. I never saw a man cry before. You don't know what it's like."

Dr. Forrest wished then that he hadn't smiled.

When Bobbie and the Doctor got to Three Chimneys, the Russian was sitting in the arm-chair that had been Father's, stretching his feet to the blaze of a bright wood fire, and sipping the tea Mother had made him.

"The man seems worn out, mind and body," was what the Doctor said; "the cough's bad, but there's nothing that can't be cured. He ought to go straight to bed, though--and let him have a fire at night."

"I'll make one in my room; it's the only one with a fireplace," said Mother. She did, and presently the Doctor helped the stranger to bed.

There was a big black trunk in Mother's room that none of the children had ever seen unlocked. Now, when she had lighted the fire, she unlocked it and took some clothes out--men's clothes--and set them to air by the newly lighted fire. Bobbie, coming in with more wood for the fire, saw the mark on the night-shirt, and looked over to the open trunk. All the things she could see were men's clothes. And the name marked on the shirt was Father's name. Then Father hadn't taken his clothes with him. And that night-shirt was one of Father's new ones. Bobbie remembered its being made, just before Peter's birthday. Why hadn't Father taken his clothes? Bobbie slipped from the room. As she went she heard the key turned in the lock of the trunk. Her heart was beating horribly. *Why* hadn't Father taken his clothes? When Mother came out of the room, Bobbie flung tightly clasping arms round her waist, and whispered:--

"Mother--Daddy isn't--isn't *dead*, is he?"

"My darling, no! What made you think of anything so horrible?"

"I--I don't know," said Bobbie, angry with herself, but still clinging to that resolution of hers, not to see anything that Mother didn't mean her to see.

Mother gave her a hurried hug. "Daddy was quite, *quite* well when I heard from him last," she said, "and he'll come back to us some day. Don't fancy such horrible things, darling!"

Later on, when the Russian stranger had been made comfortable for the night, Mother came into the girls' room. She was to sleep there in Phyllis's bed, and Phyllis was to have a mattress on the floor, a most amusing adventure for Phyllis. Directly Mother came in, two white figures started up, and two eager voices called:--

"Now, Mother, tell us all about the Russian gentleman."

A white shape hopped into the room. It was Peter, dragging his quilt behind him like the tail of a white peacock.

"We have been patient," he said, "and I had to bite my tongue not to go to sleep, and I just nearly went to sleep and I bit too hard, and it hurts ever so. *Do* tell us. Make a nice long story of it."

"I can't make a long story of it to-night," said Mother; "I'm very tired."

Bobbie knew by her voice that Mother had been crying, but the others didn't know.

"Well, make it as long as you can," said Phil, and Bobbie got her arms round Mother's waist and snuggled close to her.

"Well, it's a story long enough to make a whole book of. He's a writer; he's written beautiful books. In Russia at the time of the Czar one dared not say anything about the rich people doing wrong, or about the things that ought to be done to make poor people better and happier. If one did one was sent to prison."

"But they *can't*," said Peter; "people only go to prison when they've done wrong."

"Or when the Judges *think* they've done wrong," said Mother. "Yes, that's so in England. But in Russia it was different. And he wrote a beautiful book about poor people and how to help them. I've read it. There's nothing in it but goodness and kindness. And they sent him to prison for it. He was three years in a horrible dungeon, with hardly any light, and all damp and dreadful. In prison all alone for three years."

Mother's voice trembled a little and stopped suddenly.

"But, Mother," said Peter, "that can't be true *now*. It sounds like something out of a history book--the Inquisition, or something."

"It *was* true," said Mother; "it's all horribly true. Well, then they took him out and sent him to Siberia, a convict chained to other convicts--wicked men who'd done all sorts of crimes--a long chain of them, and they walked, and walked, and walked, for days and weeks, till he thought they'd never stop walking. And overseers went behind them with whips--yes, whips--to beat them if they got tired. And some of them went lame, and some fell down, and when they couldn't get up and go on, they beat them, and then left them to die. Oh, it's all too terrible! And at last he got to the mines, and he was condemned to stay there for life--for life, just for writing a good, noble, splendid book."

"How did he get away?"

"When the war came, some of the Russian prisoners were allowed to volunteer as soldiers. And he volunteered. But he deserted at the first chance he got and--"

"But that's very cowardly, isn't it"--said Peter--"to desert? Especially when it's war."

"Do you think he owed anything to a country that had done *that* to him? If he did, he owed more to his wife and children. He didn't know what had become of them."

"Oh," cried Bobbie, "he had *them* to think about and be miserable about *too*, then, all the time he was in prison?"

"Yes, he had them to think about and be miserable about all the time he was in prison. For anything he knew they might have been sent to prison, too. They did those things in Russia. But while he was in the mines some friends managed to get a message to him that his wife and children had escaped and come to England. So when he deserted he came here to look for them."

"Had he got their address?" said practical Peter.

"No; just England. He was going to London, and he thought he had to change at our station, and then he found he'd lost his ticket and his purse."

"Oh, *do* you think he'll find them?--I mean his wife and children, not the ticket and things."

"I hope so. Oh, I hope and pray that he'll find his wife and children again."

Even Phyllis now perceived that mother's voice was very unsteady.

"Why, Mother," she said, "how very sorry you seem to be for him!"

Mother didn't answer for a minute. Then she just said, "Yes," and then she seemed to be thinking. The children were quiet.

Presently she said, "Dears, when you say your prayers, I think you might ask God to show His pity upon all prisoners and captives."

"To show His pity," Bobbie repeated slowly, "upon all prisoners and captives. Is that right, Mother?"

"Yes," said Mother, "upon all prisoners and captives. All prisoners and captives."

Lesson 82

1. Read the first part of chapter six of *The Railway Children*.
2. Tell someone about what's happening in the chapter.

The Russian gentleman was better the next day, and the day after that better still, and on the third day he was well enough to come into the garden. A basket chair was put for him and he sat there, dressed in clothes of Father's which were too big for him. But when Mother had hemmed up the ends of the sleeves and the trousers, the clothes did well enough. His was a kind face now that it was no longer tired and frightened, and he smiled at the children whenever he saw them. They wished very much that he could speak English. Mother wrote several letters to people she thought might know whereabouts in England a Russian gentleman's wife and family might possibly be; not to the people she used to know before she came to live at Three Chimneys--she never wrote to any of them--but strange people-- Members of Parliament and Editors of papers, and Secretaries of Societies.

And she did not do much of her story-writing, only corrected proofs as she sat in the sun near the Russian, and talked to him every now and then.

The children wanted very much to show how kindly they felt to this man who had been sent to prison and to Siberia just for writing a beautiful book about poor people. They could smile at him, of course; they could and they did. But if you smile too constantly, the smile is apt to get fixed like the smile of the hyaena. And then it no longer looks friendly, but simply silly. So they tried other ways, and brought him flowers till the place where he sat was surrounded by little fading bunches of clover and roses and Canterbury bells.

And then Phyllis had an idea. She beckoned mysteriously to the others and drew them into the back yard, and there, in a concealed spot, between the pump and the water-butt, she said:--

"You remember Perks promising me the very first strawberries out of his own garden?" Perks, you will recollect, was the Porter. "Well, I should think they're ripe now. Let's go down and see."

Mother had been down as she had promised to tell the Station Master the story of the Russian Prisoner. But even the charms of the railway had been unable to tear the children away from the neighbourhood of the interesting stranger. So they had not been to the station for three days.

They went now.

And, to their surprise and distress, were very coldly received by Perks.

"'Ighly honoured, I'm sure," he said when they peeped in at the door of the Porters' room. And he went on reading his newspaper.

There was an uncomfortable silence.

"Oh, dear," said Bobbie, with a sigh, "I do believe you're *cross*."

"What, me? Not me!" said Perks loftily; "it ain't nothing to me."

"What *ain't* nothing to you?" said Peter, too anxious and alarmed to change the form of words.

"Nothing ain't nothing. What 'appens either 'ere or elsewhere," said Perks; "if you likes to 'ave your secrets, 'ave 'em and welcome. That's what I say."

The secret-chamber of each heart was rapidly examined during the pause that followed. Three heads were shaken.

"We haven't got any secrets from *you*," said Bobbie at last.

"Maybe you 'ave, and maybe you 'aven't," said Perks; "it ain't nothing to me. And I wish you all a very good afternoon." He held up the paper between him and them and went on reading.

"Oh, *don't*!" said Phyllis, in despair; "this is truly dreadful! Whatever it is, do tell us."

"We didn't mean to do it whatever it was."

No answer. The paper was refolded and Perks began on another column.

"Look here," said Peter, suddenly, "it's not fair. Even people who do crimes aren't punished without being told what it's for--as once they were in Russia."

"I don't know nothing about Russia."

"Oh, yes, you do, when Mother came down on purpose to tell you and Mr. Gills all about *our* Russian."

"Can't you fancy it?" said Perks, indignantly; "don't you see 'im a- asking of me to step into 'is room and take a chair and listen to what 'er Ladyship 'as to say?"

"Do you mean to say you've not heard?"

"Not so much as a breath. I did go so far as to put a question. And he shuts me up like a rat-trap. 'Affairs of State, Perks,' says he. But I did think one o' you would 'a' nipped down to tell me--you're here sharp enough when you want to get anything out of old Perks"-- Phyllis flushed purple as she thought of the strawberries--"information about locomotives or signals or the likes," said Perks.

"We didn't know you didn't know."

"We thought Mother had told you."

"Wewantedtotellyouonlywethoughtitwouldbestalenews."

The three spoke all at once.

Perks said it was all very well, and still held up the paper. Then Phyllis suddenly snatched it away, and threw her arms round his neck.

"Oh, let's kiss and be friends," she said; "we'll say we're sorry first, if you like, but we didn't really know that you didn't know."

"We are so sorry," said the others.

And Perks at last consented to accept their apologies.

Then they got him to come out and sit in the sun on the green Railway Bank, where the grass was quite hot to touch, and there, sometimes speaking one at a time, and sometimes all together, they told the Porter the story of the Russian Prisoner.

"Well, I must say," said Perks; but he did not say it--whatever it was.

"Yes, it is pretty awful, isn't it?" said Peter, "and I don't wonder you were curious about who the Russian was."

"I wasn't curious, not so much as interested," said the Porter.

"Well, I do think Mr. Gills might have told you about it. It was horrid of him."

"I don't keep no down on 'im for that, Missie," said the Porter; "cos why? I see 'is reasons. 'E wouldn't want to give away 'is own side with a tale like that 'ere. It ain't human nature. A man's got to stand up for his own side whatever they does. That's what it means by Party Politics. I should 'a' done the same myself if that long-'aired chap 'ad 'a' been a Jap."

"But the Japs didn't do cruel, wicked things like that," said Bobbie.

"P'r'aps not," said Perks, cautiously; "still you can't be sure with foreigners. My own belief is they're all tarred with the same brush."

"Then why were you on the side of the Japs?" Peter asked.

"Well, you see, you must take one side or the other. Same as with Liberals and Conservatives. The great thing is to take your side and then stick to it, whatever happens."

A signal sounded.

"There's the 3.14 up," said Perks. "You lie low till she's through, and then we'll go up along to my place, and see if there's any of them strawberries ripe what I told you about."

"If there are any ripe, and you *do* give them to me," said Phyllis, "you won't mind if I give them to the poor Russian, will you?"

Perks narrowed his eyes and then raised his eyebrows.

"So it was them strawberries you come down for this afternoon, eh?" said he.

This was an awkward moment for Phyllis. To say "yes" would seem rude and greedy, and unkind to Perks. But she knew if she said "no," she would not be pleased with herself afterwards. So--

"Yes," she said, "it was."

"Well done!" said the Porter; "speak the truth and shame the--"

"But we'd have come down the very next day if we'd known you hadn't heard the story," Phyllis added hastily.

"I believe you, Missie," said Perks, and sprang across the line six feet in front of the advancing train.

The girls hated to see him do this, but Peter liked it. It was so exciting.

The Russian gentleman was so delighted with the strawberries that the three racked their brains to find some other surprise for him. But all the racking did not bring out any idea more novel than wild cherries. And this idea occurred to them next morning. They had seen the blossom on the trees in the spring, and they knew where to look for wild cherries now that cherry time was here. The trees grew all up and along the rocky face of the cliff out of which the mouth of the tunnel opened. There were all sorts of trees there, birches and beeches and baby oaks and hazels, and among them the cherry blossom had shone like snow and silver.

The mouth of the tunnel was some way from Three Chimneys, so Mother let them take their lunch with them in a basket. And the basket would do to bring the cherries back in if they found any. She also lent them her silver watch so that they should not be late for tea. Peter's Waterbury had taken it into its head not to go since the day when Peter dropped it into the water-butt. And they started. When they got to the top of the cutting, they leaned over the fence and looked down to where the railway lines lay at the bottom of what, as Phyllis said, was exactly like a mountain gorge.

"If it wasn't for the railway at the bottom, it would be as though the foot of man had never been there, wouldn't it?"

The sides of the cutting were of grey stone, very roughly hewn. Indeed, the top part of the cutting had been a little natural glen that had been cut deeper to bring it down to the level of the tunnel's mouth. Among the rocks, grass and flowers grew, and seeds dropped by birds in the crannies of the stone had taken root and grown into bushes and trees that overhung the cutting. Near the tunnel was a flight of steps leading down to the line--just wooden bars roughly fixed into the earth--a very steep and narrow way, more like a ladder than a stair.

"We'd better get down," said Peter; "I'm sure the cherries would be quite easy to get at from the side of the steps. You remember it was there we picked the cherry blossoms that we put on the rabbit's grave."

So they went along the fence towards the little swing gate that is at the top of these steps. And they were almost at the gate when Bobbie said:--

"Hush. Stop! What's that?"

"That" was a very odd noise indeed--a soft noise, but quite plainly to be heard through the sound of the wind in tree branches, and the hum and whir of the telegraph wires. It was a sort of rustling, whispering sound. As they listened it stopped, and then it began again.

And this time it did not stop, but it grew louder and more rustling and rumbling.

"Look"--cried Peter, suddenly--"the tree over there!"

The tree he pointed at was one of those that have rough grey leaves and white flowers. The berries, when they come, are bright scarlet, but if you pick them, they disappoint you by turning black before you get them home. And, as Peter pointed, the tree was moving--not just the way trees ought to move when the wind blows through them, but all in one piece, as though it were a live creature and were walking down the side of the cutting.

"It's moving!" cried Bobbie. "Oh, look! and so are the others. It's like the woods in Macbeth."

Lesson 83

1. Read the second part of chapter six of *The Railway Children.*
2. Why did they think Bobby was heartless? (Answers)
3. Tell someone about the chapter.

It really did seem a little like magic. For all the trees for about twenty yards of the opposite bank seemed to be slowly walking down towards the railway line, the tree with the grey leaves bringing up the rear like some old shepherd driving a flock of green sheep.

"What is it? Oh, what is it?" said Phyllis; "it's much too magic for me. I don't like it. Let's go home."

But Bobbie and Peter clung fast to the rail and watched breathlessly. And Phyllis made no movement towards going home by herself.

The trees moved on and on. Some stones and loose earth fell down and rattled on the railway metals far below.

"It's *all* coming down," Peter tried to say, but he found there was hardly any voice to say it with. And, indeed, just as he spoke, the great rock, on the top of which the walking trees were, leaned slowly forward. The trees, ceasing to walk, stood still and shivered. Leaning with the rock, they seemed to hesitate a moment, and then rock and trees and grass and bushes, with a rushing sound, slipped right away from the face of the cutting and fell on the line with a blundering crash that could have been heard half a mile off. A cloud of dust rose up.

"Oh," said Peter, in awestruck tones, "isn't it exactly like when coals come in?--if there wasn't any roof to the cellar and you could see down."

"Look what a great mound it's made!" said Bobbie.

"Yes," said Peter, slowly. He was still leaning on the fence. "Yes," he said again, still more slowly.

Then he stood upright.

"The 11.29 down hasn't gone by yet. We must let them know at the station, or there'll be a most frightful accident."

"Let's run," said Bobbie, and began.

But Peter cried, "Come back!" and looked at Mother's watch. He was very prompt and businesslike, and his face looked whiter than they had ever seen it.

"No time," he said; "it's two miles away, and it's past eleven."

"Couldn't we," suggested Phyllis, breathlessly, "couldn't we climb up a telegraph post and do something to the wires?"

"We don't know how," said Peter.

"They do it in war," said Phyllis; "I know I've heard of it."

"They only *cut* them, silly," said Peter, "and that doesn't do any good. And we couldn't cut them even if we got up, and we couldn't get up. If we had anything red, we could get down on the line and wave it."

"But the train wouldn't see us till it got round the corner, and then it could see the mound just as well as us," said Phyllis; "better, because it's much bigger than us."

"If we only had something red," Peter repeated, "we could go round the corner and wave to the train."

"We might wave, anyway."

"They'd only think it was just *us*, as usual. We've waved so often before. Anyway, let's get down."

They got down the steep stairs. Bobbie was pale and shivering. Peter's face looked thinner than usual. Phyllis was red-faced and damp with anxiety.

"Oh, how hot I am!" she said; "and I thought it was going to be cold; I wish we hadn't put on our--" she stopped short, and then ended in quite a different tone--"our flannel petticoats."

Bobbie turned at the bottom of the stairs.

"Oh, yes," she cried; "*they're* red! Let's take them off."

They did, and with the petticoats rolled up under their arms, ran along the railway, skirting the newly fallen mound of stones and rock and earth, and bent, crushed, twisted trees. They ran at their best pace. Peter led, but the girls were not far behind. They reached the corner that hid the mound from the straight line of railway that ran half a mile without curve or corner.

"Now," said Peter, taking hold of the largest flannel petticoat.

"You're not"--Phyllis faltered--"you're not going to *tear* them?"

"Shut up," said Peter, with brief sternness.

"Oh, yes," said Bobbie, "tear them into little bits if you like. Don't you see, Phil, if we can't stop the train, there'll be a real live accident, with people *killed*. Oh, horrible! Here, Peter, you'll never tear it through the band!"

She took the red flannel petticoat from him and tore it off an inch from the band. Then she tore the other in the same way.

"There!" said Peter, tearing in his turn. He divided each petticoat into three pieces. "Now, we've got six flags." He looked at the watch again. "And we've got seven minutes. We must have flagstaffs."

The knives given to boys are, for some odd reason, seldom of the kind of steel that keeps sharp. The young saplings had to be broken off. Two came up by the roots. The leaves were stripped from them.

"We must cut holes in the flags, and run the sticks through the holes," said Peter. And the holes were cut. The knife was sharp enough to cut flannel with. Two of the flags were set up in heaps of loose stones between the sleepers of the down line. Then Phyllis and Roberta took each a flag, and stood ready to wave it as soon as the train came in sight.

"I shall have the other two myself," said Peter, "because it was my idea to wave something red."

"They're our petticoats, though," Phyllis was beginning, but Bobbie interrupted--

"Oh, what does it matter who waves what, if we can only save the train?"

Perhaps Peter had not rightly calculated the number of minutes it would take the 11.29 to get from the station to the place where they were, or perhaps the train was late. Anyway, it seemed a very long time that they waited.

Phyllis grew impatient. "I expect the watch is wrong, and the train's gone by," said she.

Peter relaxed the heroic attitude he had chosen to show off his two flags. And Bobbie began to feel sick with suspense.

It seemed to her that they had been standing there for hours and hours, holding those silly little red flannel flags that no one would ever notice. The train wouldn't care. It would go rushing by them and tear round the corner and go crashing into that awful mound. And everyone would be killed. Her hands grew very cold and trembled so that she could hardly hold the flag. And then came the distant rumble and hum of the metals, and a puff of white steam showed far away along the stretch of line.

"Stand firm," said Peter, "and wave like mad! When it gets to that big furze bush step back, but go on waving! Don't stand *on* the line, Bobbie!"

The train came rattling along very, very fast.

"They don't see us! They won't see us! It's all no good!" cried Bobbie.

The two little flags on the line swayed as the nearing train shook and loosened the heaps of loose stones that held them up. One of them slowly leaned over and fell on the line. Bobbie jumped forward and caught it up, and waved it; her hands did not tremble now.

It seemed that the train came on as fast as ever. It was very near now.

"Keep off the line, you silly cuckoo!" said Peter, fiercely.

"It's no good," Bobbie said again.

"Stand back!" cried Peter, suddenly, and he dragged Phyllis back by the arm.

But Bobbie cried, "Not yet, not yet!" and waved her two flags right over the line. The front of the engine looked black and enormous. It's voice was loud and harsh.

"Oh, stop, stop, stop!" cried Bobbie. No one heard her. At least Peter and Phyllis didn't, for the oncoming rush of the train covered the sound of her voice with a mountain of sound. But afterwards she used to wonder whether the engine itself had not heard her. It seemed almost as though it had--for it slackened swiftly, slackened and stopped, not twenty yards from the place where Bobbie's two flags waved over the line. She saw the great black engine stop dead, but somehow she could not stop waving the flags. And when the driver and the fireman had got off the engine and Peter and Phyllis had gone to meet them and pour out their excited tale of the awful mound just round the corner, Bobbie still waved the flags but more and more feebly and jerkily.

When the others turned towards her she was lying across the line with her hands flung forward and still gripping the sticks of the little red flannel flags.

The engine-driver picked her up, carried her to the train, and laid her on the cushions of a first-class carriage.

"Gone right off in a faint," he said, "poor little woman. And no wonder. I'll just 'ave a look at this 'ere mound of yours, and then we'll run you back to the station and get her seen to."

It was horrible to see Bobbie lying so white and quiet, with her lips blue, and parted.

"I believe that's what people look like when they're dead," whispered Phyllis.

"*Don't*!" said Peter, sharply.

They sat by Bobbie on the blue cushions, and the train ran back. Before it reached their station Bobbie had sighed and opened her eyes, and rolled herself over and begun to cry. This cheered the others wonderfully. They had seen her cry before, but they had never seen her faint, nor anyone else, for the matter of that. They had not known what to do when she was fainting, but now she was only crying they could thump her on the back and tell her not to, just as they always did. And presently, when she stopped crying, they were able to laugh at her for being such a coward as to faint.

When the station was reached, the three were the heroes of an agitated meeting on the platform.

The praises they got for their "prompt action," their "common sense," their "ingenuity," were enough to have turned anybody's head. Phyllis enjoyed herself thoroughly. She had never been a real heroine before, and the feeling was delicious. Peter's ears got very red. Yet he, too, enjoyed himself. Only Bobbie wished they all wouldn't. She wanted to get away.

"You'll hear from the Company about this, I expect," said the Station Master.

Bobbie wished she might never hear of it again. She pulled at Peter's jacket.

"Oh, come away, come away! I want to go home," she said.

So they went. And as they went Station Master and Porter and guards and driver and fireman and passengers sent up a cheer.

"Oh, listen," cried Phyllis; "that's for *us*!"

"Yes," said Peter. "I say, I am glad I thought about something red, and waving it."

"How lucky we *did* put on our red flannel petticoats!" said Phyllis.

Bobbie said nothing. She was thinking of the horrible mound, and the trustful train rushing towards it.

"And it was *us* that saved them," said Peter.

"How dreadful if they had all been killed!" said Phyllis; "wouldn't it, Bobbie?"

"We never got any cherries, after all," said Bobbie.

The others thought her rather heartless.

Lesson 84

1. Read the first part of chapter seven of *The Railway Children*.
2. Describe Roberta.
3. Tell someone about the chapter.

I hope you don't mind my telling you a good deal about Roberta. The fact is I am growing very fond of her. The more I observe her the more I love her. And I notice all sorts of things about her that I like.

For instance, she was quite oddly anxious to make other people happy. And she could keep a secret, a tolerably rare accomplishment. Also she had the power of silent sympathy. That sounds rather dull, I know, but it's not so dull as it sounds. It just means that a person is able to know that you are unhappy, and to love you extra on that account, without bothering you by telling you all the time how sorry she is for you. That was what Bobbie was like. She knew that Mother was unhappy--and that Mother had not told her the reason. So she just loved Mother more and never said a single word that could let Mother know how earnestly her little girl wondered what Mother was unhappy about. This needs practice. It is not so easy as you might think.

Whatever happened--and all sorts of nice, pleasant ordinary things happened--such as picnics, games, and buns for tea, Bobbie always had these thoughts at the back of her mind. "Mother's unhappy. Why? I don't know. She doesn't want me to know. I won't try to find out. But she *is* unhappy. Why? I don't know. She doesn't--" and so on, repeating and repeating like a tune that you don't know the stopping part of.

The Russian gentleman still took up a good deal of everybody's thoughts. All the editors and secretaries of Societies and Members of Parliament had answered Mother's letters as politely as they knew how; but none of them could tell where the wife and children of Mr. Szezcpansky would be likely to be. (Did I tell you that the Russian's very Russian name was that?)

Bobbie had another quality which you will hear differently described by different people. Some of them call it interfering in other people's business--and some call it "helping lame dogs over stiles," and some call it "loving-kindness." It just means trying to help people.

She racked her brains to think of some way of helping the Russian gentleman to find his wife and children. He had learned a few words of English now. He could say "Good morning," and "Good night," and "Please," and "Thank you," and "Pretty," when the children brought him flowers, and "Ver' good," when they asked him how he had slept.

The way he smiled when he "said his English," was, Bobbie felt, "just too sweet for anything." She used to think of his face because she fancied it would help her to some way of helping him. But it did not. Yet his being there cheered her because she saw that it made Mother happier.

"She likes to have someone to be good to, even beside us," said Bobbie. "And I know she hated to let him have Father's clothes. But I suppose it 'hurt nice,' or she wouldn't have."

For many and many a night after the day when she and Peter and Phyllis had saved the train from wreck by waving their little red flannel flags, Bobbie used to wake screaming and shivering, seeing again that horrible mound, and the poor, dear trustful engine rushing on towards it--just thinking that it was doing its swift duty, and that everything was clear and safe. And then a warm thrill of pleasure used to run through her at the remembrance of how she and Peter and Phyllis and the red flannel petticoats had really saved everybody.

One morning a letter came. It was addressed to Peter and Bobbie and Phyllis. They opened it with enthusiastic curiosity, for they did not often get letters.

The letter said:--

"Dear Sir, and Ladies,--It is proposed to make a small presentation to you, in commemoration of your prompt and courageous action in warning the train on the --- inst., and thus averting what must, humanly speaking, have been a terrible accident. The presentation will take place at the --- Station at three o'clock on the 30th inst., if this time and place will be convenient to you.

"Yours faithfully,

"Jabez Inglewood.
"Secretary, Great Northern and Southern Railway Co."

There never had been a prouder moment in the lives of the three children. They rushed to Mother with the letter, and she also felt proud and said so, and this made the children happier than ever.

"But if the presentation is money, you must say, 'Thank you, but we'd rather not take it,'" said Mother. "I'll wash your Indian muslins at once," she added. "You must look tidy on an occasion like this."

"Phil and I can wash them," said Bobbie, "if you'll iron them, Mother."

Washing is rather fun. I wonder whether you've ever done it? This particular washing took place in the back kitchen, which had a stone floor and a very big stone sink under its window.

"Let's put the bath on the sink," said Phyllis; "then we can pretend we're out-of-doors washerwomen like Mother saw in France."

"But they were washing in the cold river," said Peter, his hands in his pockets, "not in hot water."

"This is a *hot* river, then," said Phyllis; "lend a hand with the bath, there's a dear."

"I should like to see a deer lending a hand," said Peter, but he lent his.

"Now to rub and scrub and scrub and rub," said Phyllis, hopping joyously about as Bobbie carefully carried the heavy kettle from the kitchen fire.

"Oh, no!" said Bobbie, greatly shocked; "you don't rub muslin. You put the boiled soap in the hot water and make it all frothy-lathery- -and then you shake the muslin and squeeze it, ever so gently, and all the dirt comes out. It's only clumsy things like tablecloths and sheets that have to be rubbed."

The lilac and the Gloire de Dijon roses outside the window swayed in the soft breeze.

"It's a nice drying day--that's one thing," said Bobbie, feeling very grown up. "Oh, I do wonder what wonderful feelings we shall have when we *wear* the Indian muslin dresses!"

"Yes, so do I," said Phyllis, shaking and squeezing the muslin in quite a professional manner.

"*Now* we squeeze out the soapy water. *No*--we mustn't twist them--and then rinse them. I'll hold them while you and Peter empty the bath and get clean water."

"A presentation! That means presents," said Peter, as his sisters, having duly washed the pegs and wiped the line, hung up the dresses to dry. "Whatever will it be?"

"It might be anything," said Phyllis; "what I've always wanted is a Baby elephant--but I suppose they wouldn't know that."

"Suppose it was gold models of steam-engines?" said Bobbie.

"Or a big model of the scene of the prevented accident," suggested Peter, "with a little model train, and dolls dressed like us and the engine-driver and fireman and passengers."

"Do you *like*," said Bobbie, doubtfully, drying her hands on the rough towel that hung on a roller at the back of the scullery door, "do you *like* us being rewarded for saving a train?"

"Yes, I do," said Peter, downrightly; "and don't you try to come it over us that you don't like it, too. Because I know you do."

"Yes," said Bobbie, doubtfully, "I know I do. But oughtn't we to be satisfied with just having done it, and not ask for anything more?"

"Who did ask for anything more, silly?" said her brother; "Victoria Cross soldiers don't *ask* for it; but they're glad enough to get it all the same. Perhaps it'll be medals. Then, when I'm very old indeed, I shall show them to my grandchildren and say, 'We only did our duty,' and they'll be awfully proud of me."

"You have to be married," warned Phyllis, "or you don't have any grandchildren."

"I suppose I shall *have* to be married some day," said Peter, "but it will be an awful bother having her round all the time. I'd like to marry a lady who had trances, and only woke up once or twice a year."

"Just to say you were the light of her life and then go to sleep again. Yes. That wouldn't be bad," said Bobbie.

"When *I* get married," said Phyllis, "I shall want him to want me to be awake all the time, so that I can hear him say how nice I am."

"I think it would be nice," said Bobbie, "to marry someone very poor, and then you'd do all the work and he'd love you most frightfully, and see the blue wood smoke curling up among the trees from the domestic hearth as he came home from work every night. I say-- we've got to answer that letter and say that the time and place *will* be convenient to us. There's the soap, Peter. *We're* both as clean as clean. That pink box of writing paper you had on your birthday, Phil."

It took some time to arrange what should be said. Mother had gone back to her writing, and several sheets of pink paper with scalloped gilt edges and green four-leaved shamrocks in the corner were spoiled before the three had decided what to say. Then each made a copy and signed it with its own name.

The threefold letter ran:--

"Dear Mr. Jabez Inglewood,--Thank you very much. We did not want to be rewarded but only to save the train, but we are glad you think so and thank you very much. The time and place you say will be quite convenient to us. Thank you very much.

"Your affecate little friend,"

Then came the name, and after it:--

"P.S. Thank you very much."

"Washing is much easier than ironing," said Bobbie, taking the clean dry dresses off the line. "I do love to see things come clean. Oh--I don't know how we shall wait till it's time to know what presentation they're going to present!"

When at last--it seemed a very long time after--it was *the* day, the three children went down to the station at the proper time. And everything that happened was so odd that it seemed like a dream. The Station Master came out to meet them--in his best clothes, as Peter noticed at once--and led them into the waiting room where once they had played the advertisement game. It looked quite different now. A carpet had been put down--and there were pots of roses on the mantelpiece and on the window ledges--green branches stuck up, like holly and laurel are at Christmas, over the framed advertisement of Cook's Tours and the Beauties of Devon and the Paris Lyons Railway. There were quite a number of people there besides the Porter--two or three ladies in smart dresses, and quite a crowd of gentlemen in high hats and frock coats--besides everybody who belonged to the station. They recognized several people who had been in the train on the red-flannel-petticoat day. Best of all their own old gentleman was there, and his coat and hat and collar seemed more than ever different from anyone else's. He shook hands with them and then everybody sat down on chairs, and a gentleman in spectacles--they found out afterwards that he was the District Superintendent--began quite a long speech--very clever indeed. I am not going to write the speech down. First, because you would think it dull; and secondly, because it made all the children blush so, and get so hot about the ears that I am quite anxious to get away from this part of the subject; and thirdly, because the gentleman took so many words to say what he had to say that I really haven't time to write them down. He said all sorts of nice things about the children's bravery and presence of mind, and when he had done he sat down, and everyone who was there clapped and said, "Hear, hear."

And then the old gentleman got up and said things, too. It was very like a prize-giving. And then he called the children one by one, by their names, and gave each of them a beautiful gold watch and chain. And inside the watches were engraved after the name of the watch's new owner:--

"From the Directors of the Northern and Southern Railway in grateful recognition of the courageous and prompt action which averted an accident on --- 1905."

The watches were the most beautiful you can possibly imagine, and each one had a blue leather case to live in when it was at home.

"You must make a speech now and thank everyone for their kindness," whispered the Station Master in Peter's ear and pushed him forward. "Begin 'Ladies and Gentlemen,'" he added.

Each of the children had already said "Thank you," quite properly.

"Oh, dear," said Peter, but he did not resist the push.

"Ladies and Gentlemen," he said in a rather husky voice. Then there was a pause, and he heard his heart beating in his throat. "Ladies and Gentlemen," he went on with a rush, "it's most awfully good of you, and we shall treasure the watches all our lives--but really we don't deserve it because what we did wasn't anything, really. At least, I mean it was awfully exciting, and what I mean to say--thank you all very, very much."

The people clapped Peter more than they had done the District Superintendent, and then everybody shook hands with them, and as soon as politeness would let them, they got away, and tore up the hill to Three Chimneys with their watches in their hands.

Lesson 85

1. Read the second part of chapter seven of *The Railway Children*.
2. Write a one-sentence summary of the chapter.

It was a wonderful day--the kind of day that very seldom happens to anybody and to most of us not at all.

"I did want to talk to the old gentleman about something else," said Bobbie, "but it was so public--like being in church."

"What did you want to say?" asked Phyllis.

"I'll tell you when I've thought about it more," said Bobbie.

So when she had thought a little more she wrote a letter.

"My dearest old gentleman," it said; "I want most awfully to ask you something. If you could get out of the train and go by the next, it would do. I do not want you to give me anything. Mother says we ought not to. And besides, we do not want any *things*. Only to talk to you about a Prisoner and Captive. Your loving little friend,

"Bobbie."

She got the Station Master to give the letter to the old gentleman, and next day she asked Peter and Phyllis to come down to the station with her at the time when the train that brought the old gentleman from town would be passing through.

She explained her idea to them--and they approved thoroughly.

They had all washed their hands and faces, and brushed their hair, and were looking as tidy as they knew how. But Phyllis, always unlucky, had upset a jug of lemonade down the front of her dress. There was no time to change--and the wind happening to blow from the coal yard, her frock was soon powdered with grey, which stuck to the sticky lemonade stains and made her look, as Peter said, "like any little gutter child."

It was decided that she should keep behind the others as much as possible.

"Perhaps the old gentleman won't notice," said Bobbie. "The aged are often weak in the eyes."

There was no sign of weakness, however, in the eyes, or in any other part of the old gentleman, as he stepped from the train and looked up and down the platform.

The three children, now that it came to the point, suddenly felt that rush of deep shyness which makes your ears red and hot, your hands warm and wet, and the tip of your nose pink and shiny.

"Oh," said Phyllis, "my heart's thumping like a steam-engine--right under my sash, too."

"Nonsense," said Peter, "people's hearts aren't under their sashes."

"I don't care--mine is," said Phyllis.

"If you're going to talk like a poetry-book," said Peter, "my heart's in my mouth."

"My heart's in my boots--if you come to that," said Roberta; "but do come on--he'll think we're idiots."

"He won't be far wrong," said Peter, gloomily. And they went forward to meet the old gentleman.

"Hullo," he said, shaking hands with them all in turn. "This is a very great pleasure."

"It *was* good of you to get out," Bobbie said, perspiring and polite.

He took her arm and drew her into the waiting room where she and the others had played the advertisement game the day they found the Russian. Phyllis and Peter followed. "Well?" said the old gentleman, giving Bobbie's arm a kind little shake before he let it go. "Well? What is it?"

"Oh, please!" said Bobbie.

"Yes?" said the old gentleman.

"What I mean to say--" said Bobbie.

"Well?" said the old gentleman.

"It's all very nice and kind," said she.

"But?" he said.

"I wish I might say something," she said.

"Say it," said he.

"Well, then," said Bobbie--and out came the story of the Russian who had written the beautiful book about poor people, and had been sent to prison and to Siberia for just that.

"And what we want more than anything in the world is to find his wife and children for him," said Bobbie, "but we don't know how. But you must be most horribly clever, or you wouldn't be a Direction of the Railway. And if *you* knew how--and would? We'd rather have that than anything else in the world. We'd go without the watches, even, if you could sell them and find his wife with the money."

And the others said so, too, though not with so much enthusiasm.

"Hum," said the old gentleman, pulling down the white waistcoat that had the big gilt buttons on it, "what did you say the name was-- Fryingpansky?"

"No, no," said Bobbie earnestly. "I'll write it down for you. It doesn't really look at all like that except when you say it. Have you a bit of pencil and the back of an envelope?" she asked.

The old gentleman got out a gold pencil-case and a beautiful, sweet-smelling, green Russian leather note-book and opened it at a new page.

"Here," he said, "write here."

She wrote down "Szezcpansky," and said:--

"That's how you write it. You *call* it Shepansky."

The old gentleman took out a pair of gold-rimmed spectacles and fitted them on his nose. When he had read the name, he looked quite different.

"*That* man? Bless my soul!" he said. "Why, I've read his book! It's translated into every European language. A fine book--a noble book. And so your mother took him in--like the good Samaritan. Well, well. I'll tell you what, youngsters--your mother must be a very good woman."

"Of course she is," said Phyllis, in astonishment.

"And you're a very good man," said Bobbie, very shy, but firmly resolved to be polite.

"You flatter me," said the old gentleman, taking off his hat with a flourish. "And now am I to tell you what I think of you?"

"Oh, please don't," said Bobbie, hastily.

"Why?" asked the old gentleman.

"I don't exactly know," said Bobbie. "Only--if it's horrid, I don't want you to; and if it's nice, I'd rather you didn't."

The old gentleman laughed.

"Well, then," he said, "I'll only just say that I'm very glad you came to me about this--very glad, indeed. And I shouldn't be surprised if I found out something very soon. I know a great many Russians in London, and every Russian knows *his* name. Now tell me all about yourselves."

He turned to the others, but there was only one other, and that was Peter. Phyllis had disappeared.

"Tell me all about yourself," said the old gentleman again. And, quite naturally, Peter was stricken dumb.

"All right, we'll have an examination," said the old gentleman; "you two sit on the table, and I'll sit on the bench and ask questions."

He did, and out came their names and ages--their Father's name and business--how long they had lived at Three Chimneys and a great deal more.

The questions were beginning to turn on a herring and a half for three halfpence, and a pound of lead and a pound of feathers, when the door of the waiting room was kicked open by a boot; as the boot entered everyone could see that its lace was coming undone--and in came Phyllis, very slowly and carefully.

In one hand she carried a large tin can, and in the other a thick slice of bread and butter.

"Afternoon tea," she announced proudly, and held the can and the bread and butter out to the old gentleman, who took them and said:--

"Bless my soul!"

"Yes," said Phyllis.

"It's very thoughtful of you," said the old gentleman, "very."

"But you might have got a cup," said Bobbie, "and a plate."

"Perks always drinks out of the can," said Phyllis, flushing red. "I think it was very nice of him to give it me at all--let alone cups and plates," she added.

"So do I," said the old gentleman, and he drank some of the tea and tasted the bread and butter.

And then it was time for the next train, and he got into it with many good-byes and kind last words.

"Well," said Peter, when they were left on the platform, and the tail-lights of the train disappeared round the corner, "it's my belief that we've lighted a candle to-day--like Latimer, you know, when he was being burned--and there'll be fireworks for our Russian before long."

And so there were.

It wasn't ten days after the interview in the waiting room that the three children were sitting on the top of the biggest rock in the field below their house watching the 5.15 steam away from the station along the bottom of the valley. They saw, too, the few people who had got out at the station straggling up the road towards the village--and they saw one person leave the road and open the gate that led across the fields to Three Chimneys and to nowhere else.

"Who on earth!" said Peter, scrambling down.

"Let's go and see," said Phyllis.

So they did. And when they got near enough to see who the person was, they saw it was their old gentleman himself, his brass buttons winking in the afternoon sunshine, and his white waistcoat looking whiter than ever against the green of the field.

"Hullo!" shouted the children, waving their hands.

"Hullo!" shouted the old gentleman, waving his hat.

Then the three started to run--and when they got to him they hardly had breath left to say:

"How do you do?"

"Good news," said he. "I've found your Russian friend's wife and child--and I couldn't resist the temptation of giving myself the pleasure of telling him."

But as he looked at Bobbie's face he felt that he *could* resist that temptation.

"Here," he said to her, "you run on and tell him. The other two will show me the way."

Bobbie ran. But when she had breathlessly panted out the news to the Russian and Mother sitting in the quiet garden--when Mother's face had lighted up so beautifully, and she had said half a dozen quick French words to the Exile--Bobbie wished that she had *not* carried the news. For the Russian sprang up with a cry that made Bobbie's heart leap and then tremble--a cry of love and longing such as she had never heard. Then he took Mother's hand and kissed it gently and reverently--and then he sank down in his chair and covered his face with his hands and sobbed. Bobbie crept away. She did not want to see the others just then.

But she was as gay as anybody when the endless French talking was over, when Peter had torn down to the village for buns and cakes, and the girls had got tea ready and taken it out into the garden.

The old gentleman was most merry and delightful. He seemed to be able to talk in French and English almost at the same moment, and Mother did nearly as well. It was a delightful time. Mother seemed as if she could not make enough fuss about the old gentleman, and she said yes at once when he asked if he might present some "goodies" to his little friends.

The word was new to the children--but they guessed that it meant sweets, for the three large pink and green boxes, tied with green ribbon, which he took out of his bag, held unheard-of layers of beautiful chocolates.

The Russian's few belongings were packed, and they all saw him off at the station.

Then Mother turned to the old gentleman and said:--

"I don't know how to thank you for *everything*. It has been a real pleasure to me to see you. But we live very quietly. I am so sorry that I can't ask you to come and see us again."

The children thought this very hard. When they *had* made a friend--and such a friend--they would dearly have liked him to come and see them again.

What the old gentleman thought they couldn't tell. He only said:--

"I consider myself very fortunate, Madam, to have been received once at your house."

"Ah," said Mother, "I know I must seem surly and ungrateful--but--"

"You could never seem anything but a most charming and gracious lady," said the old gentleman, with another of his bows.

And as they turned to go up the hill, Bobbie saw her Mother's face.

"How tired you look, Mammy," she said; "lean on me."

"It's my place to give Mother my arm," said Peter. "I'm the head man of the family when Father's away."

Mother took an arm of each.

"How awfully nice," said Phyllis, skipping joyfully, "to think of the dear Russian embracing his long-lost wife. The baby must have grown a lot since he saw it."

"Yes," said Mother.

"I wonder whether Father will think *I've* grown," Phyllis went on, skipping still more gaily. "I have grown already, haven't I, Mother?"

"Yes," said Mother, "oh, yes," and Bobbie and Peter felt her hands tighten on their arms.

"Poor old Mammy, you *are* tired," said Peter.

Bobbie said, "Come on, Phil; I'll race you to the gate."

And she started the race, though she hated doing it. *You* know why Bobbie did that. Mother only thought that Bobbie was tired of walking slowly. Even Mothers, who love you better than anyone else ever will, don't always understand.

Lesson 86

1. Read the first part of chapter eight of *The Railway Children*.
2. Write a one-sentence summary of the chapter.

Vocabulary

1. Use prefixes to create antonyms for the following words: forgettable, personal, imaginable, complete, destructible, desirable, perfect. (Answers)
2. What prefixes create antonyms?

"That's a likely little brooch you've got on, Miss," said Perks the Porter; "I don't know as ever I see a thing more like a buttercup without it *was* a buttercup."

"Yes," said Bobbie, glad and flushed by this approval. "I always thought it was more like a buttercup almost than even a real one--and I *never* thought it would come to be mine, my very own--and then Mother gave it to me for my birthday."

"Oh, have you had a birthday?" said Perks; and he seemed quite surprised, as though a birthday were a thing only granted to a favoured few.

"Yes," said Bobbie; "when's your birthday, Mr. Perks?" The children were taking tea with Mr. Perks in the Porters' room among the lamps and the railway almanacs. They had brought their own cups and some jam turnovers. Mr. Perks made tea in a beer can, as usual, and everyone felt very happy and confidential.

"My birthday?" said Perks, tipping some more dark brown tea out of the can into Peter's cup. "I give up keeping of my birthday afore you was born."

"But you must have been born *sometime*, you know," said Phyllis, thoughtfully, "even if it was twenty years ago--or thirty or sixty or seventy."

"Not so long as that, Missie," Perks grinned as he answered. "If you really want to know, it was thirty-two years ago, come the fifteenth of this month."

"Then why don't you keep it?" asked Phyllis.

"I've got something else to keep besides birthdays," said Perks, briefly.

"Oh! What?" asked Phyllis, eagerly. "Not secrets?"

"No," said Perks, "the kids and the Missus."

It was this talk that set the children thinking, and, presently, talking. Perks was, on the whole, the dearest friend they had made. Not so grand as the Station Master, but more approachable--less powerful than the old gentleman, but more confidential.

"It seems horrid that nobody keeps his birthday," said Bobbie. "Couldn't *we* do something?"

"Let's go up to the Canal bridge and talk it over," said Peter. "I got a new gut line from the postman this morning. He gave it me for a bunch of roses that I gave him for his sweetheart. She's ill."

"Then I do think you might have given her the roses for nothing," said Bobbie, indignantly.

"Nyang, nyang!" said Peter, disagreeably, and put his hands in his pockets.

"He did, of course," said Phyllis, in haste; "directly we heard she was ill we got the roses ready and waited by the gate. It was when you were making the brekker-toast. And when he'd said 'Thank you' for the roses so many times--much more than he need have--he pulled out the line and gave it to Peter. It wasn't exchange. It was the grateful heart."

"Oh, I *beg* your pardon, Peter," said Bobbie, "I *am* so sorry."

"Don't mention it," said Peter, grandly, "I knew you would be."

So then they all went up to the Canal bridge. The idea was to fish from the bridge, but the line was not quite long enough.

"Never mind," said Bobbie. "Let's just stay here and look at things. Everything's so beautiful."

It was. The sun was setting in red splendour over the grey and purple hills, and the canal lay smooth and shiny in the shadow--no ripple broke its surface. It was like a grey satin ribbon between the dusky green silk of the meadows that were on each side of its banks.

"It's all right," said Peter, "but somehow I can always see how pretty things are much better when I've something to do. Let's get down on to the towpath and fish from there."

Phyllis and Bobbie remembered how the boys on the canal-boats had thrown coal at them, and they said so.

"Oh, nonsense," said Peter. "There aren't any boys here now. If there were, I'd fight them."

Peter's sisters were kind enough not to remind him how he had *not* fought the boys when coal had last been thrown. Instead they said, "All right, then," and cautiously climbed down the steep bank to the towing-path. The line was carefully baited, and for half an hour they fished patiently and in vain. Not a single nibble came to nourish hope in their hearts.

All eyes were intent on the sluggish waters that earnestly pretended they had never harboured a single minnow when a loud rough shout made them start.

"Hi!" said the shout, in most disagreeable tones, "get out of that, can't you?"

An old white horse coming along the towing-path was within half a dozen yards of them. They sprang to their feet and hastily climbed up the bank.

"We'll slip down again when they've gone by," said Bobbie.

But, alas, the barge, after the manner of barges, stopped under the bridge.

"She's going to anchor," said Peter; "just our luck!"

The barge did not anchor, because an anchor is not part of a canal-boat's furniture, but she was moored with ropes fore and aft--and the ropes were made fast to the palings and to crowbars driven into the ground.

"What you staring at?" growled the Bargee, crossly.

"We weren't staring," said Bobbie; "we wouldn't be so rude."

"Rude be blessed," said the man; "get along with you!"

"Get along yourself," said Peter. He remembered what he had said about fighting boys, and, besides, he felt safe halfway up the bank. "We've as much right here as anyone else."

"Oh, 'ave you, indeed!" said the man. "We'll soon see about that." And he came across his deck and began to climb down the side of his barge.

"Oh, come away, Peter, come away!" said Bobbie and Phyllis, in agonised unison.

"Not me," said Peter, "but *you'd* better."

The girls climbed to the top of the bank and stood ready to bolt for home as soon as they saw their brother out of danger. The way home lay all down hill. They knew that they all ran well. The Bargee did not look as if *he* did. He was red-faced, heavy, and beefy.

But as soon as his foot was on the towing-path the children saw that they had misjudged him.

He made one spring up the bank and caught Peter by the leg, dragged him down--set him on his feet with a shake--took him by the ear--and said sternly:--

"Now, then, what do you mean by it? Don't you know these 'ere waters is preserved? You ain't no right catching fish 'ere--not to say nothing of your precious cheek."

Peter was always proud afterwards when he remembered that, with the Bargee's furious fingers tightening on his ear, the Bargee's crimson countenance close to his own, the Bargee's hot breath on his neck, he had the courage to speak the truth.

"I *wasn't* catching fish," said Peter.

"That's not *your* fault, I'll be bound," said the man, giving Peter's ear a twist--not a hard one--but still a twist.

Peter could not say that it was. Bobbie and Phyllis had been holding on to the railings above and skipping with anxiety. Now suddenly Bobbie slipped through the railings and rushed down the bank towards Peter, so impetuously that Phyllis, following more temperately, felt certain that her sister's descent would end in the waters of the canal. And so it would have done if the Bargee hadn't let go of Peter's ear--and caught her in his jerseyed arm.

"Who are you a-shoving of?" he said, setting her on her feet.

"Oh," said Bobbie, breathless, "I'm not shoving anybody. At least, not on purpose. Please don't be cross with Peter. Of course, if it's your canal, we're sorry and we won't any more. But we didn't know it was yours."

"Go along with you," said the Bargee.

"Yes, we will; indeed we will," said Bobbie, earnestly; "but we do beg your pardon--and really we haven't caught a single fish. I'd tell you directly if we had, honour bright I would."

She held out her hands and Phyllis turned out her little empty pocket to show that really they hadn't any fish concealed about them.

"Well," said the Bargee, more gently, "cut along, then, and don't you do it again, that's all."

The children hurried up the bank.

"Chuck us a coat, M'ria," shouted the man. And a red-haired woman in a green plaid shawl came out from the cabin door with a baby in her arms and threw a coat to him. He put it on, climbed the bank, and slouched along across the bridge towards the village.

"You'll find me up at the 'Rose and Crown' when you've got the kid to sleep," he called to her from the bridge.

When he was out of sight the children slowly returned. Peter insisted on this.

"The canal may belong to him," he said, "though I don't believe it does. But the bridge is everybody's. Doctor Forrest told me it's public property. I'm not going to be bounced off the bridge by him or anyone else, so I tell you."

Peter's ear was still sore and so were his feelings.

The girls followed him as gallant soldiers might follow the leader of a forlorn hope.

"I do wish you wouldn't," was all they said.

"Go home if you're afraid," said Peter; "leave me alone. *I'm* not afraid."

The sound of the man's footsteps died away along the quiet road. The peace of the evening was not broken by the notes of the sedge- warblers or by the voice of the woman in the barge, singing her baby to sleep. It was a sad song she sang. Something about Bill Bailey and how she wanted him to come home.

The children stood leaning their arms on the parapet of the bridge; they were glad to be quiet for a few minutes because all three hearts were beating much more quickly.

"I'm not going to be driven away by any old bargeman, I'm not," said Peter, thickly.

"Of course not," Phyllis said soothingly; "you didn't give in to him! So now we might go home, don't you think?"

"*No*," said Peter.

Nothing more was said till the woman got off the barge, climbed the bank, and came across the bridge.

She hesitated, looking at the three backs of the children, then she said, "Ahem."

Peter stayed as he was, but the girls looked round.

"You mustn't take no notice of my Bill," said the woman; "'is bark's worse'n 'is bite. Some of the kids down Farley way is fair terrors. It was them put 'is back up calling out about who ate the puppy-pie under Marlow bridge."

"Who *did*?" asked Phyllis.

"*I* dunno," said the woman. "Nobody don't know! But somehow, and I don't know the why nor the wherefore of it, them words is p'ison to a barge-master. Don't you take no notice. 'E won't be back for two hours good. You might catch a power o' fish afore that. The light's good an' all," she added.

"Thank you," said Bobbie. "You're very kind. Where's your baby?"

"Asleep in the cabin," said the woman. "'E's all right. Never wakes afore twelve. Reg'lar as a church clock, 'e is."

"I'm sorry," said Bobbie; "I would have liked to see him, close to."

"And a finer you never did see, Miss, though I says it." The woman's face brightened as she spoke.

"Aren't you afraid to leave it?" said Peter.

"Lor' love you, no," said the woman; "who'd hurt a little thing like 'im? Besides, Spot's there. So long!"

The woman went away.

"Shall we go home?" said Phyllis.

"You can. I'm going to fish," said Peter briefly.

"I thought we came up here to talk about Perks's birthday," said Phyllis.

"Perks's birthday'll keep."

Lesson 87

1. Read the second part of chapter eight of *The Railway Children*.
2. Tell someone about the chapter.

So they got down on the towing-path again and Peter fished. He did not catch anything.

It was almost quite dark, the girls were getting tired, and as Bobbie said, it was past bedtime, when suddenly Phyllis cried, "What's that?"

And she pointed to the canal boat. Smoke was coming from the chimney of the cabin, had indeed been curling softly into the soft evening air all the time--but now other wreaths of smoke were rising, and these were from the cabin door.

"It's on fire--that's all," said Peter, calmly. "Serve him right."

"Oh--how *can* you?" cried Phyllis. "Think of the poor dear dog."

"The *baby*!" screamed Bobbie.

In an instant all three made for the barge.

Her mooring ropes were slack, and the little breeze, hardly strong enough to be felt, had yet been strong enough to drift her stern against the bank. Bobbie was first--then came Peter, and it was Peter who slipped and fell. He went into the canal up to his neck, and his feet could not feel the bottom, but his arm was on the edge of the barge. Phyllis caught at his hair. It hurt, but it helped him to get out. Next minute he had leaped on to the barge, Phyllis following.

"Not you!" he shouted to Bobbie; "*Me*, because I'm wet."

He caught up with Bobbie at the cabin door, and flung her aside very roughly indeed; if they had been playing, such roughness would have made Bobbie weep with tears of rage and pain. Now, though he flung her on to the edge of the hold, so that her knee and her elbow were grazed and bruised, she only cried:--

"No--not you--*me*," and struggled up again. But not quickly enough.

Peter had already gone down two of the cabin steps into the cloud of thick smoke. He stopped, remembered all he had ever heard of fires, pulled his soaked handkerchief out of his breast pocket and tied it over his mouth. As he pulled it out he said:--

"It's all right, hardly any fire at all."

And this, though he thought it was a lie, was rather good of Peter. It was meant to keep Bobbie from rushing after him into danger. Of course it didn't.

The cabin glowed red. A paraffin lamp was burning calmly in an orange mist.

"Hi," said Peter, lifting the handkerchief from his mouth for a moment. "Hi, Baby--where are you?" He choked.

"Oh, let *me* go," cried Bobbie, close behind him. Peter pushed her back more roughly than before, and went on.

Now what would have happened if the baby hadn't cried I don't know-- but just at that moment it *did* cry. Peter felt his way through the dark smoke, found something small and soft and warm and alive, picked it up and backed out, nearly tumbling over Bobbie who was close behind. A dog snapped at his leg--tried to bark, choked.

"I've got the kid," said Peter, tearing off the handkerchief and staggering on to the deck.

Bobbie caught at the place where the bark came from, and her hands met on the fat back of a smooth-haired dog. It turned and fastened its teeth on her hand, but very gently, as much as to say:--

"I'm bound to bark and bite if strangers come into my master's cabin, but I know you mean well, so I won't *really* bite."

Bobbie dropped the dog.

"All right, old man. Good dog," said she. "Here--give me the baby, Peter; you're so wet you'll give it cold."

Peter was only too glad to hand over the strange little bundle that squirmed and whimpered in his arms.

"Now," said Bobbie, quickly, "you run straight to the 'Rose and Crown' and tell them. Phil and I will stay here with the precious. Hush, then, a dear, a duck, a darling! Go *now*, Peter! Run!"

"I can't run in these things," said Peter, firmly; "they're as heavy as lead. I'll walk."

"Then *I'll* run," said Bobbie. "Get on the bank, Phil, and I'll hand you the dear."

The baby was carefully handed. Phyllis sat down on the bank and tried to hush the baby. Peter wrung the water from his sleeves and knickerbocker legs as well as he could, and it was Bobbie who ran like the wind across the bridge and up the long white quiet twilight road towards the 'Rose and Crown.'

There is a nice old-fashioned room at the 'Rose and Crown'; where Bargees and their wives sit of an evening drinking their supper beer, and toasting their supper cheese at a glowing basketful of coals that sticks out into the room under a great hooded chimney and is warmer and prettier and more comforting than any other fireplace *I* ever saw.

There was a pleasant party of barge people round the fire. You might not have thought it pleasant, but they did; for they were all friends or acquaintances, and they liked the same sort of things, and talked the same sort of talk. This is the real secret of pleasant society. The Bargee Bill, whom the children had found so disagreeable, was considered excellent company by his mates. He was telling a tale of his own wrongs--always a thrilling subject. It was his barge he was speaking about.

"And 'e sent down word 'paint her inside hout,' not namin' no colour, d'ye see? So I gets a lotter green paint and I paints her stem to stern, and I tell yer she looked A1. Then 'E comes along and 'e says, 'Wot yer paint 'er all one colour for?' 'e says. And I says, says I, 'Cause I thought she'd look fust-rate,' says I, 'and I think so still.' An' he says, '*Dew* yer? Then ye can just pay for the bloomin' paint yerself,' says he. An' I 'ad to, too." A murmur of sympathy ran round the room. Breaking noisily in on it came Bobbie. She burst open the swing door--crying breathlessly:--

"Bill! I want Bill the Bargeman."

There was a stupefied silence. Pots of beer were held in mid-air, paralysed on their way to thirsty mouths.

"Oh," said Bobbie, seeing the bargewoman and making for her. "Your barge cabin's on fire. Go quickly."

The woman started to her feet, and put a big red hand to her waist, on the left side, where your heart seems to be when you are frightened or miserable.

"Reginald Horace!" she cried in a terrible voice; "my Reginald Horace!"

"All right," said Bobbie, "if you mean the baby; got him out safe. Dog, too." She had no breath for more, except, "Go on--it's all alight."

Then she sank on the ale-house bench and tried to get that breath of relief after running which people call the 'second wind.' But she felt as though she would never breathe again.

Bill the Bargee rose slowly and heavily. But his wife was a hundred yards up the road before he had quite understood what was the matter.

Phyllis, shivering by the canal side, had hardly heard the quick approaching feet before the woman had flung herself on the railing, rolled down the bank, and snatched the baby from her.

"Don't," said Phyllis, reproachfully; "I'd just got him to sleep."

*   *   *   *   *   *

Bill came up later talking in a language with which the children were wholly unfamiliar. He leaped on to the barge and dipped up pails of water. Peter helped him and they put out the fire. Phyllis, the bargewoman, and the baby--and presently Bobbie, too--cuddled together in a heap on the bank.

"Lord help me, if it was me left anything as could catch alight," said the woman again and again.

But it wasn't she. It was Bill the Bargeman, who had knocked his pipe out and the red ash had fallen on the hearth-rug and smouldered there and at last broken into flame. Though a stern man he was just. He did not blame his wife for what was his own fault, as many bargemen, and other men, too, would have done.

*   *   *   *   *   *

Mother was half wild with anxiety when at last the three children turned up at Three Chimneys, all very wet by now, for Peter seemed to have come off on the others. But when she had disentangled the truth of what had happened from their mixed and incoherent narrative, she owned that they had done quite right, and could not possibly have done otherwise. Nor did she put any obstacles in the way of their accepting the cordial invitation with which the bargeman had parted from them.

"Ye be here at seven to-morrow," he had said, "and I'll take you the entire trip to Farley and back, so I will, and not a penny to pay. Nineteen locks!"

They did not know what locks were; but they were at the bridge at seven, with bread and cheese and half a soda cake, and quite a quarter of a leg of mutton in a basket.

It was a glorious day. The old white horse strained at the ropes, the barge glided smoothly and steadily through the still water. The sky was blue overhead. Mr. Bill was as nice as anyone could possibly be. No one would have thought that he could be the same man who had held Peter by the ear. As for Mrs. Bill, she had always been nice, as Bobbie said, and so had the baby, and even Spot, who might have bitten them quite badly if he had liked.

"It was simply ripping, Mother," said Peter, when they reached home very happy, very tired, and very dirty, "right over that glorious aqueduct. And locks--you don't know what they're like. You sink into the ground and then, when you feel you're never going to stop going down, two great black gates open slowly, slowly--you go out, and there you are on the canal just like you were before."

"I know," said Mother, "there are locks on the Thames. Father and I used to go on the river at Marlow before we were married."

"And the dear, darling, ducky baby," said Bobbie; "it let me nurse it for ages and ages--and it *was* so good. Mother, I wish we had a baby to play with."

"And everybody was so nice to us," said Phyllis, "everybody we met. And they say we may fish whenever we like. And Bill is going to show us the way next time he's in these parts. He says we don't know really."

"He said *you* didn't know," said Peter; "but, Mother, he said he'd tell all the bargees up and down the canal that we were the real, right sort, and they were to treat us like good pals, as we were."

"So then I said," Phyllis interrupted, "we'd always each wear a red ribbon when we went fishing by the canal, so they'd know it was *us*, and we were the real, right sort, and be nice to us!"

"So you've made another lot of friends," said Mother; "first the railway and then the canal!"

"Oh, yes," said Bobbie; "I think everyone in the world is friends if you can only get them to see you don't want to be *un*-friends."

"Perhaps you're right," said Mother; and she sighed. "Come, Chicks. It's bedtime."

"Yes," said Phyllis. "Oh dear--and we went up there to talk about what we'd do for Perks's birthday. And we haven't talked a single thing about it!"

"No more we have," said Bobbie; "but Peter's saved Reginald Horace's life. I think that's about good enough for one evening."

"Bobbie would have saved him if I hadn't knocked her down; twice I did," said Peter, loyally.

"So would I," said Phyllis, "if I'd known what to do."

"Yes," said Mother, "you've saved a little child's life. I do think that's enough for one evening. Oh, my darlings, thank God *you're* all safe!"

Lesson 88

1. Read the first part of chapter nine of *The Railway Children.*
2. Tell someone about the chapter.

It was breakfast-time. Mother's face was very bright as she poured the milk and ladled out the porridge.

"I've sold another story, Chickies," she said; "the one about the King of the Mussels, so there'll be buns for tea. You can go and get them as soon as they're baked. About eleven, isn't it?"

Peter, Phyllis, and Bobbie exchanged glances with each other, six glances in all. Then Bobbie said:--

"Mother, would you mind if we didn't have the buns for tea to-night, but on the fifteenth? That's next Thursday."

"*I* don't mind when you have them, dear," said Mother, "but why?"

"Because it's Perks's birthday," said Bobbie; "he's thirty-two, and he says he doesn't keep his birthday any more, because he's got other things to keep--not rabbits or secrets--but the kids and the missus."

"You mean his wife and children," said Mother.

"Yes," said Phyllis; "it's the same thing, isn't it?"

"And we thought we'd make a nice birthday for him. He's been so awfully jolly decent to us, you know, Mother," said Peter, "and we agreed that next bun-day we'd ask you if we could."

"But suppose there hadn't been a bun-day before the fifteenth?" said Mother.

"Oh, then, we meant to ask you to let us anti--antipate it, and go without when the bun-day came."

"Anticipate," said Mother. "I see. Certainly. It would be nice to put his name on the buns with pink sugar, wouldn't it?"

"Perks," said Peter, "it's not a pretty name."

"His other name's Albert," said Phyllis; "I asked him once."

"We might put A. P.," said Mother; "I'll show you how when the day comes."

This was all very well as far as it went. But even fourteen halfpenny buns with A. P. on them in pink sugar do not of themselves make a very grand celebration.

"There are always flowers, of course," said Bobbie, later, when a really earnest council was being held on the subject in the hay-loft where the broken chaff-cutting machine was, and the row of holes to drop hay through into the hay-racks over the mangers of the stables below.

"He's got lots of flowers of his own," said Peter.

"But it's always nice to have them given you," said Bobbie, "however many you've got of your own. We can use flowers for trimmings to the birthday. But there must be something to trim besides buns."

"Let's all be quiet and think," said Phyllis; "no one's to speak until it's thought of something."

So they were all quiet and so very still that a brown rat thought that there was no one in the loft and came out very boldly. When Bobbie sneezed, the rat was quite shocked and hurried away, for he saw that a hay-loft where such things could happen was no place for a respectable middle-aged rat that liked a quiet life.

"Hooray!" cried Peter, suddenly, "I've got it." He jumped up and kicked at the loose hay.

"What?" said the others, eagerly.

"Why, Perks is so nice to everybody. There must be lots of people in the village who'd like to help to make him a birthday. Let's go round and ask everybody."

"Mother said we weren't to ask people for things," said Bobbie, doubtfully.

"For ourselves, she meant, silly, not for other people. I'll ask the old gentleman too. You see if I don't," said Peter.

"Let's ask Mother first," said Bobbie.

"Oh, what's the use of bothering Mother about every little thing?" said Peter, "especially when she's busy. Come on. Let's go down to the village now and begin."

So they went. The old lady at the Post-office said she didn't see why Perks should have a birthday any more than anyone else.

"No," said Bobbie, "I should like everyone to have one. Only we know when his is."

"Mine's to-morrow," said the old lady, "and much notice anyone will take of it. Go along with you."

So they went.

And some people were kind, and some were crusty. And some would give and some would not. It is rather difficult work asking for things, even for other people, as you have no doubt found if you have ever tried it.

When the children got home and counted up what had been given and what had been promised, they felt that for the first day it was not so bad. Peter wrote down the lists of the things in the little pocket-book where he kept the numbers of his engines. These were the lists:--

GIVEN.

A tobacco pipe from the sweet shop.

Half a pound of tea from the grocer's.

A woollen scarf slightly faded from the draper's, which was the

other side of the grocer's.

A stuffed squirrel from the Doctor.

PROMISED.

A piece of meat from the butcher.

Six fresh eggs from the woman who lived in the old turnpike

cottage.

A piece of honeycomb and six bootlaces from the cobbler, and an

Iron shovel from the blacksmith's.

Very early next morning Bobbie got up and woke Phyllis. This had been agreed on between them. They had not told Peter because they thought he would think it silly. But they told him afterwards, when it had turned out all right.

They cut a big bunch of roses, and put it in a basket with the needle-book that Phyllis had made for Bobbie on her birthday, and a very pretty blue necktie of Phyllis's. Then they wrote on a paper: 'For Mrs. Ransome, with our best love, because it is her birthday,' and they put the paper in the basket, and they took it to the Post-office, and went in and put it on the counter and ran away before the old woman at the Post-office had time to get into her shop.

When they got home Peter had grown confidential over helping Mother to get the breakfast and had told her their plans.

"There's no harm in it," said Mother, "but it depends *how* you do it. I only hope he won't be offended and think it's *charity*. Poor people are very proud, you know."

"It isn't because he's poor," said Phyllis; "it's because we're fond of him."

"I'll find some things that Phyllis has outgrown," said Mother, "if you're quite sure you can give them to him without his being offended. I should like to do some little thing for him because he's been so kind to you. I can't do much because we're poor ourselves. What are you writing, Bobbie?"

"Nothing particular," said Bobbie, who had suddenly begun to scribble. "I'm sure he'd like the things, Mother."

The morning of the fifteenth was spent very happily in getting the buns and watching Mother make A. P. on them with pink sugar. You know how it's done, of course? You beat up whites of eggs and mix powdered sugar with them, and put in a few drops of cochineal. And then you make a cone of clean, white paper with a little hole at the pointed end, and put the pink egg-sugar in at the big end. It runs slowly out at the pointed end, and you write the letters with it just as though it were a great fat pen full of pink sugar-ink.

The buns looked beautiful with A. P. on every one, and, when they were put in a cool oven to set the sugar, the children went up to the village to collect the honey and the shovel and the other promised things.

The old lady at the Post-office was standing on her doorstep. The children said "Good morning," politely, as they passed.

"Here, stop a bit," she said.

So they stopped.

"Those roses," said she.

"Did you like them?" said Phyllis; "they were as fresh as fresh. *I* made the needle-book, but it was Bobbie's present." She skipped joyously as she spoke.

"Here's your basket," said the Post-office woman. She went in and brought out the basket. It was full of fat, red gooseberries.

"I dare say Perks's children would like them," said she.

"You *are* an old dear," said Phyllis, throwing her arms around the old lady's fat waist. "Perks *will* be pleased."

"He won't be half so pleased as I was with your needle-book and the tie and the pretty flowers and all," said the old lady, patting Phyllis's shoulder. "You're good little souls, that you are. Look here. I've got a pram round the back in the wood-lodge. It was got for my Emmie's first, that didn't live but six months, and she never had but that one. I'd like Mrs. Perks to have it. It 'ud be a help to her with that great boy of hers. Will you take it along?"

"*Oh*!" said all the children together.

When Mrs. Ransome had got out the perambulator and taken off the careful papers that covered it, and dusted it all over, she said:--

"Well, there it is. I don't know but what I'd have given it to her before if I'd thought of it. Only I didn't quite know if she'd accept of it from me. You tell her it was my Emmie's little one's pram--"

"Oh, *isn't* it nice to think there is going to be a real live baby in it again!"

"Yes," said Mrs. Ransome, sighing, and then laughing; "here, I'll give you some peppermint cushions for the little ones, and then you run along before I give you the roof off my head and the clothes off my back."

All the things that had been collected for Perks were packed into the perambulator, and at half-past three Peter and Bobbie and Phyllis wheeled it down to the little yellow house where Perks lived.

The house was very tidy. On the window ledge was a jug of wild- flowers, big daisies, and red sorrel, and feathery, flowery grasses.

There was a sound of splashing from the wash-house, and a partly washed boy put his head round the door.

"Mother's a-changing of herself," he said.

"Down in a minute," a voice sounded down the narrow, freshly scrubbed stairs.

The children waited. Next moment the stairs creaked and Mrs. Perks came down, buttoning her bodice. Her hair was brushed very smooth and tight, and her face shone with soap and water.

"I'm a bit late changing, Miss," she said to Bobbie, "owing to me having had a extry clean-up to-day, along o' Perks happening to name its being his birthday. I don't know what put it into his head to think of such a thing. We keeps the children's birthdays, of course; but him and me--we're too old for such like, as a general rule."

"We knew it was his birthday," said Peter, "and we've got some presents for him outside in the perambulator.

As the presents were being unpacked, Mrs. Perks gasped. When they were all unpacked, she surprised and horrified the children by sitting suddenly down on a wooden chair and bursting into tears.

"Oh, don't!" said everybody; "oh, please don't!" And Peter added, perhaps a little impatiently: "What on earth is the matter? You don't mean to say you don't like it?"

Mrs. Perks only sobbed. The Perks children, now as shiny-faced as anyone could wish, stood at the wash-house door, and scowled at the intruders. There was a silence, an awkward silence.

"*Don't* you like it?" said Peter, again, while his sisters patted Mrs. Perks on the back.

She stopped crying as suddenly as she had begun.

Lesson 89

1. Read the second part of chapter nine of *The Railway Children.*
2. Tell someone about the chapter.

"There, there, don't you mind me. *I'm* all right!" she said. "Like it? Why, it's a birthday such as Perks never 'ad, not even when 'e was a boy and stayed with his uncle, who was a corn chandler in his own account. He failed afterwards. Like it? Oh--" and then she went on and said all sorts of things that I won't write down, because I am sure that Peter and Bobbie and Phyllis would not like me to. Their ears got hotter and hotter, and their faces redder and redder, at the kind things Mrs. Perks said. They felt they had done nothing to deserve all this praise.

At last Peter said: "Look here, we're glad you're pleased. But if you go on saying things like that, we must go home. And we did want to stay and see if Mr. Perks is pleased, too. But we can't stand this."

"I won't say another single word," said Mrs. Perks, with a beaming face, "but that needn't stop me thinking, need it? For if ever--"

"Can we have a plate for the buns?" Bobbie asked abruptly. And then Mrs. Perks hastily laid the table for tea, and the buns and the honey and the gooseberries were displayed on plates, and the roses were put in two glass jam jars, and the tea-table looked, as Mrs. Perks said, "fit for a Prince."

"To think!" she said, "me getting the place tidy early, and the little 'uns getting the wild-flowers and all--when never did I think there'd be anything more for him except the ounce of his pet particular that I got o' Saturday and been saving up for 'im ever since. Bless us! 'e *is* early!"

Perks had indeed unlatched the latch of the little front gate.

"Oh," whispered Bobbie, "let's hide in the back kitchen, and *you* tell him about it. But give him the tobacco first, because you got it for him. And when you've told him, we'll all come in and shout, 'Many happy returns!'"

It was a very nice plan, but it did not quite come off. To begin with, there was only just time for Peter and Bobbie and Phyllis to rush into the wash-house, pushing the young and open-mouthed Perks children in front of them. There was not time to shut the door, so that, without at all meaning it, they had to listen to what went on in the kitchen. The wash-house was a tight fit for the Perks children and the Three Chimneys children, as well as all the wash-house's proper furniture, including the mangle and the copper.

"Hullo, old woman!" they heard Mr. Perks's voice say; "here's a pretty set-out!"

"It's your birthday tea, Bert," said Mrs. Perks, "and here's a ounce of your extry particular. I got it o' Saturday along o' your happening to remember it was your birthday to-day."

"Good old girl!" said Mr. Perks, and there was a sound of a kiss.

"But what's that pram doing here? And what's all these bundles? And where did you get the sweetstuff, and--"

The children did not hear what Mrs. Perks replied, because just then Bobbie gave a start, put her hand in her pocket, and all her body grew stiff with horror.

"Oh!" she whispered to the others, "whatever shall we do? I forgot to put the labels on any of the things! He won't know what's from who. He'll think it's all *us*, and that we're trying to be grand or charitable or something horrid."

"Hush!" said Peter.

And then they heard the voice of Mr. Perks, loud and rather angry.

"I don't care," he said; "I won't stand it, and so I tell you straight."

"But," said Mrs. Perks, "it's them children you make such a fuss about--the children from the Three Chimneys."

"I don't care," said Perks, firmly, "not if it was a angel from Heaven. We've got on all right all these years and no favours asked. I'm not going to begin these sort of charity goings-on at my time of life, so don't you think it, Nell."

"Oh, hush!" said poor Mrs Perks; "Bert, shut your silly tongue, for goodness' sake. The all three of 'ems in the wash-house a-listening to every word you speaks."

"Then I'll give them something to listen to," said the angry Perks; "I've spoke my mind to them afore now, and I'll do it again," he added, and he took two strides to the wash-house door, and flung it wide open--as wide, that is, as it would go, with the tightly packed children behind it.

"Come out," said Perks, "come out and tell me what you mean by it. 'Ave I ever complained to you of being short, as you comes this charity lay over me?"

"*Oh*!" said Phyllis, "I thought you'd be so pleased; I'll never try to be kind to anyone else as long as I live. No, I won't, not never."

She burst into tears.

"We didn't mean any harm," said Peter.

"It ain't what you means so much as what you does," said Perks.

"Oh, *don't*!" cried Bobbie, trying hard to be braver than Phyllis, and to find more words than Peter had done for explaining in. "We thought you'd love it. We always have things on our birthdays."

"Oh, yes," said Perks, "your own relations; that's different."

"Oh, no," Bobbie answered. "*not* our own relations. All the servants always gave us things at home, and us to them when it was their birthdays. And when it was mine, and Mother gave me the brooch like a buttercup, Mrs. Viney gave me two lovely glass pots, and nobody thought she was coming the charity lay over us."

"If it had been glass pots here," said Perks, "I wouldn't ha' said so much. It's there being all this heaps and heaps of things I can't stand. No--nor won't, neither."

"But they're not all from us--" said Peter, "only we forgot to put the labels on. They're from all sorts of people in the village."

"Who put 'em up to it, I'd like to know?" asked Perks.

"Why, we did," sniffed Phyllis.

Perks sat down heavily in the elbow-chair and looked at them with what Bobbie afterwards described as withering glances of gloomy despair.

"So you've been round telling the neighbours we can't make both ends meet? Well, now you've disgraced us as deep as you can in the neighbourhood, you can just take the whole bag of tricks back w'ere it come from. Very much obliged, I'm sure. I don't doubt but what you meant it kind, but I'd rather not be acquainted with you any longer if it's all the same to you." He deliberately turned the chair round so that his back was turned to the children. The legs of the chair grated on the brick floor, and that was the only sound that broke the silence.

Then suddenly Bobbie spoke.

"Look here," she said, "this is most awful."

"That's what I says," said Perks, not turning round.

"Look here," said Bobbie, desperately, "we'll go if you like--and you needn't be friends with us any more if you don't want, but--"

"*We* shall always be friends with *you*, however nasty you are to us," sniffed Phyllis, wildly.

"Be quiet," said Peter, in a fierce aside.

"But before we go," Bobbie went on desperately, "do let us show you the labels we wrote to put on the things."

"I don't want to see no labels," said Perks, "except proper luggage ones in my own walk of life. Do you think I've kept respectable and outer debt on what I gets, and her having to take in washing, to be give away for a laughing-stock to all the neighbours?"

"Laughing?" said Peter; "you don't know."

"You're a very hasty gentleman," whined Phyllis; "you know you were wrong once before, about us not telling you the secret about the Russian. Do let Bobbie tell you about the labels!"

"Well. Go ahead!" said Perks, grudgingly.

"Well, then," said Bobbie, fumbling miserably, yet not without hope, in her tightly stuffed pocket, "we wrote down all the things everybody said when they gave us the things, with the people's names, because Mother said we ought to be careful--because--but I wrote down what she said--and you'll see."

But Bobbie could not read the labels just at once. She had to swallow once or twice before she could begin.

Mrs. Perks had been crying steadily ever since her husband had opened the wash-house door. Now she caught her breath, choked, and said:--

"Don't you upset yourself, Missy. *I* know you meant it kind if he doesn't."

"May I read the labels?" said Bobbie, crying on to the slips as she tried to sort them. "Mother's first. It says:--

"'Little Clothes for Mrs. Perks's children.' Mother said, 'I'll find some of Phyllis's things that she's grown out of if you're quite sure Mr. Perks wouldn't be offended and think it's meant for charity. I'd like to do some little thing for him, because he's so kind to you. I can't do much because we're poor ourselves.'"

Bobbie paused.

"That's all right," said Perks, "your Ma's a born lady. We'll keep the little frocks, and what not, Nell."

"Then there's the perambulator and the gooseberries, and the sweets," said Bobbie, "they're from Mrs. Ransome. She said: 'I dare say Mr. Perks's children would like the sweets. And the perambulator was got for my Emmie's first--it didn't live but six months, and she's never had but that one. I'd like Mrs. Perks to have it. It would be a help with her fine boy. I'd have given it before if I'd been sure she'd accept of it from me.' She told me to tell you," Bobbie added, "that it was her Emmie's little one's pram."

"I can't send that pram back, Bert," said Mrs Perks, firmly, "and I won't. So don't you ask me--"

"I'm not a-asking anything," said Perks, gruffly.

"Then the shovel," said Bobbie. "Mr. James made it for you himself. And he said--where is it? Oh, yes, here! He said, 'You tell Mr. Perks it's a pleasure to make a little trifle for a man as is so much respected,' and then he said he wished he could shoe your children and his own children, like they do the horses, because, well, he knew what shoe leather was."

"James is a good enough chap," said Perks.

"Then the honey," said Bobbie, in haste, "and the boot-laces. *He* said he respected a man that paid his way--and the butcher said the same. And the old turnpike woman said many was the time you'd lent her a hand with her garden when you were a lad--and things like that came home to roost--I don't know what she meant. And everybody who gave anything said they liked you, and it was a very good idea of ours; and nobody said anything about charity or anything horrid like that. And the old gentleman gave Peter a gold pound for you, and said you were a man who knew your work. And I thought you'd *love* to know how fond people are of you, and I never was so unhappy in my life. Good-bye. I hope you'll forgive us some day--"

She could say no more, and she turned to go.

"Stop," said Perks, still with his back to them; "I take back every word I've said contrary to what you'd wish. Nell, set on the kettle."

"We'll take the things away if you're unhappy about them," said Peter; "but I think everybody'll be most awfully disappointed, as well as us."

"I'm not unhappy about them," said Perks; "I don't know," he added, suddenly wheeling the chair round and showing a very odd-looking screwed-up face, "I don't know as ever I was better pleased. Not so much with the presents--though they're an A1 collection--but the kind respect of our neighbours. That's worth having, eh, Nell?"

"I think it's all worth having," said Mrs. Perks, "and you've made a most ridiculous fuss about nothing, Bert, if you ask me."

"No, I ain't," said Perks, firmly; "if a man didn't respect hisself, no one wouldn't do it for him."

"But everyone respects you," said Bobbie; "they all said so."

"I knew you'd like it when you really understood," said Phyllis, brightly.

"Humph! You'll stay to tea?" said Mr. Perks.

Later on Peter proposed Mr. Perks's health. And Mr. Perks proposed a toast, also honoured in tea, and the toast was, "May the garland of friendship be ever green," which was much more poetical than anyone had expected from him.

*   *   *   *   *   *

"Jolly good little kids, those," said Mr. Perks to his wife as they went to bed.

"Oh, they're all right, bless their hearts," said his wife; "it's you that's the aggravatingest old thing that ever was. I was ashamed of you--I tell you--"

"You didn't need to be, old gal. I climbed down handsome soon as I understood it wasn't charity. But charity's what I never did abide, and won't neither."

*   *   *   *   *   *

All sorts of people were made happy by that birthday party. Mr. Perks and Mrs. Perks and the little Perkses by all the nice things and by the kind thoughts of their neighbours; the Three Chimneys children by the success, undoubted though unexpectedly delayed, of their plan; and Mrs. Ransome every time she saw the fat Perks baby in the perambulator. Mrs.

Perks made quite a round of visits to thank people for their kind birthday presents, and after each visit felt that she had a better friend than she had thought.

"Yes," said Perks, reflectively, "it's not so much what you does as what you means; that's what I say. Now if it had been charity--"

"Oh, drat charity," said Mrs. Perks; "nobody won't offer you charity, Bert, however much you was to want it, I lay. That was just friendliness, that was."

When the clergyman called on Mrs. Perks, she told him all about it. "It *was* friendliness, wasn't it, Sir?" said she.

"I think," said the clergyman, "it was what is sometimes called loving-kindness."

So you see it was all right in the end. But if one does that sort of thing, one has to be careful to do it in the right way. For, as Mr. Perks said, when he had time to think it over, it's not so much what you do, as what you mean.

Lesson 90

1. Read the first part of chapter ten of *The Railway Children*.
2. Tell someone about the chapter.

When they first went to live at Three Chimneys, the children had talked a great deal about their Father, and had asked a great many questions about him, and what he was doing and where he was and when he would come home. Mother always answered their questions as well as she could. But as the time went on they grew to speak less of him. Bobbie had felt almost from the first that for some strange miserable reason these questions hurt Mother and made her sad. And little by little the others came to have this feeling, too, though they could not have put it into words.

One day, when Mother was working so hard that she could not leave off even for ten minutes, Bobbie carried up her tea to the big bare room that they called Mother's workshop. It had hardly any furniture. Just a table and a chair and a rug. But always big pots of flowers on the window-sills and on the mantelpiece. The children saw to that. And from the three long uncurtained windows the beautiful stretch of meadow and moorland, the far violet of the hills, and the unchanging changefulness of cloud and sky.

"Here's your tea, Mother-love," said Bobbie; "do drink it while it's hot."

Mother laid down her pen among the pages that were scattered all over the table, pages covered with her writing, which was almost as plain as print, and much prettier. She ran her hands into her hair, as if she were going to pull it out by handfuls.

"Poor dear head," said Bobbie, "does it ache?"

"No--yes--not much," said Mother. "Bobbie, do you think Peter and Phil are *forgetting* Father?"

"*No*," said Bobbie, indignantly. "Why?"

"You none of you ever speak of him now."

Bobbie stood first on one leg and then on the other.

"We often talk about him when we're by ourselves," she said.

"But not to me," said Mother. "Why?"

Bobbie did not find it easy to say why.

"I--you--" she said and stopped. She went over to the window and looked out.

"Bobbie, come here," said her Mother, and Bobbie came.

"Now," said Mother, putting her arm round Bobbie and laying her ruffled head against Bobbie's shoulder, "try to tell me, dear."

Bobbie fidgeted.

"Tell Mother."

"Well, then," said Bobbie, "I thought you were so unhappy about Daddy not being here, it made you worse when I talked about him. So I stopped doing it."

"And the others?"

"I don't know about the others," said Bobbie. "I never said anything about *that* to them. But I expect they felt the same about it as me."

"Bobbie dear," said Mother, still leaning her head against her, "I'll tell you. Besides parting from Father, he and I have had a great sorrow--oh, terrible--worse than anything you can think of, and at first it did hurt to hear you all talking of him as if everything were just the same. But it would be much more terrible if you were to forget him. That would be worse than anything."

"The trouble," said Bobbie, in a very little voice--"I promised I would never ask you any questions, and I never have, have I? But-- the trouble--it won't last always?"

"No," said Mother, "the worst will be over when Father comes home to us."

"I wish I could comfort you," said Bobbie.

"Oh, my dear, do you suppose you don't? Do you think I haven't noticed how good you've all been, not quarrelling nearly as much as you used to--and all the little kind things you do for me--the flowers, and cleaning my shoes, and tearing up to make my bed before I get time to do it myself?"

Bobbie *had* sometimes wondered whether Mother noticed these things.

"That's nothing," she said, "to what--"

"I *must* get on with my work," said Mother, giving Bobbie one last squeeze. "Don't say anything to the others."

That evening in the hour before bed-time instead of reading to the children Mother told them stories of the games she and Father used to have when they were children and lived near each other in the country--tales of the adventures of Father with Mother's brothers when they were all boys together. Very funny stories they were, and the children laughed as they listened.

"Uncle Edward died before he was grown up, didn't he?" said Phyllis, as Mother lighted the bedroom candles.

"Yes, dear," said Mother, "you would have loved him. He was such a brave boy, and so adventurous. Always in mischief, and yet friends with everybody in spite of it. And your Uncle Reggie's in Ceylon--yes, and Father's away, too. But I think they'd all like to think we'd enjoyed talking about the things they used to do. Don't you think so?"

"Not Uncle Edward," said Phyllis, in a shocked tone; "he's in Heaven."

"You don't suppose he's forgotten us and all the old times, because God has taken him, any more than I forget him. Oh, no, he remembers. He's only away for a little time. We shall see him some day."

"And Uncle Reggie--and Father, too?" said Peter.

"Yes," said Mother. "Uncle Reggie and Father, too. Good night, my darlings."

"Good night," said everyone. Bobbie hugged her mother more closely even than usual, and whispered in her ear, "Oh, I do love you so, Mummy--I do--I do--"

When Bobbie came to think it all over, she tried not to wonder what the great trouble was. But she could not always help it. Father was not dead--like poor Uncle Edward--Mother had said so. And he was not ill, or Mother would have been with him. Being poor wasn't the trouble. Bobbie knew it was something nearer the heart than money could be.

"I mustn't try to think what it is," she told herself; "no, I mustn't. I *am* glad Mother noticed about us not quarrelling so much. We'll keep that up."

And alas, that very afternoon she and Peter had what Peter called a first-class shindy.

They had not been a week at Three Chimneys before they had asked Mother to let them have a piece of garden each for their very own, and she had agreed, and the south border under the peach trees had been divided into three pieces and they were allowed to plant whatever they liked there.

Phyllis had planted mignonette and nasturtium and Virginia Stock in hers. The seeds came up, and though they looked just like weeds, Phyllis believed that they would bear flowers some day. The Virginia Stock justified her faith quite soon, and her garden was gay with a band of bright little flowers, pink and white and red and mauve.

"I can't weed for fear I pull up the wrong things," she used to say comfortably; "it saves such a lot of work."

Peter sowed vegetable seeds in his--carrots and onions and turnips. The seed was given to him by the farmer who lived in the nice black-and-white, wood-and-plaster house just beyond the bridge. He kept turkeys and guinea fowls, and was a most amiable man. But Peter's vegetables never had much of a chance, because he liked to use the earth of his garden for digging canals, and making forts and earthworks for his toy soldiers. And the seeds of vegetables rarely come to much in a soil that is constantly disturbed for the purposes of war and irrigation.

Bobbie planted rose-bushes in her garden, but all the little new leaves of the rose-bushes shriveled and withered, perhaps because she moved them from the other part of the garden in May, which is not at all the right time of year for moving roses. But she would not own that they were dead, and hoped on against hope, until the day when Perks came up to see the garden, and told her quite plainly that all her roses were as dead as doornails.

"Only good for bonfires, Miss," he said. "You just dig 'em up and burn 'em, and I'll give you some nice fresh roots outer my garden; pansies, and stocks, and sweet willies, and forget-me-nots. I'll bring 'em along to-morrow if you get the ground ready."

So next day she set to work, and that happened to be the day when Mother had praised her and the others about not quarrelling. She moved the rose-bushes and carried them to the other end of the garden, where the rubbish heap was that they meant to make a bonfire of when Guy Fawkes' Day came.

Meanwhile Peter had decided to flatten out all his forts and earthworks, with a view to making a model of the railway-tunnel, cutting, embankment, canal, aqueduct, bridges, and all.

So when Bobbie came back from her last thorny journey with the dead rose-bushes, he had got the rake and was using it busily.

"*I* was using the rake," said Bobbie.

"Well, I'm using it now," said Peter.

"But I had it first," said Bobbie.

"Then it's my turn now," said Peter. And that was how the quarrel began.

"You're always being disagreeable about nothing," said Peter, after some heated argument.

"I had the rake first," said Bobbie, flushed and defiant, holding on to its handle.

"Don't--I tell you I said this morning I meant to have it. Didn't I, Phil?"

Phyllis said she didn't want to be mixed up in their rows. And instantly, of course, she was.

"If you remember, you ought to say."

"Of course she doesn't remember--but she might say so."

"I wish I'd had a brother instead of two whiny little kiddy sisters," said Peter. This was always recognized as indicating the high-water mark of Peter's rage.

Bobbie made the reply she always made to it.

"I can't think why little boys were ever invented," and just as she said it she looked up, and saw the three long windows of Mother's workshop flashing in the red rays of the sun. The sight brought back those words of praise:--

"You don't quarrel like you used to do."

"*Oh*!" cried Bobbie, just as if she had been hit, or had caught her finger in a door, or had felt the hideous sharp beginnings of toothache.

"What's the matter?" said Phyllis.

Bobbie wanted to say: "Don't let's quarrel. Mother hates it so," but though she tried hard, she couldn't. Peter was looking too disagreeable and insulting.

"Take the horrid rake, then," was the best she could manage. And she suddenly let go her hold on the handle. Peter had been holding on to it too firmly and pullingly, and now that the pull the other way was suddenly stopped, he staggered and fell over backward, the teeth of the rake between his feet.

"Serve you right," said Bobbie, before she could stop herself.

Peter lay still for half a moment--long enough to frighten Bobbie a little. Then he frightened her a little more, for he sat up--screamed once--turned rather pale, and then lay back and began to shriek, faintly but steadily. It sounded exactly like a pig being killed a quarter of a mile off.

THIS COURSE IS CONTINUED WITH EP FOURTH READER LESSONS 91-180.

ANSWERS

Lesson 1

quench: satisfy

retort: to say something in answer, typically in a sharp or witty fashion

dismay: distress

Lesson 2

toil: work hard

strife: conflict

Lesson 3

malicious: intending to harm

adrift: lost and confused

Lesson 4

envy: jealousy

Lesson 5

ignorant: lacking knowledge

haste: hurry

inquire: ask

Lesson 6

5. five

6. The first, second and last lines rhyme. The third and fourth lines rhyme.

Vocabulary 1.C 2.C 3.A 4.A 5.C 6.D 7.A 8.C 9.B 10.D

Lesson 7

assure: encourage someone that something will come about

earnest: sincere

grove: a small group of trees

Lesson 8

2. Don't waste time; use your time wisely.

3. AABB

Lesson 9

3. $5
4. $50
5. He says that she's honest by not just taking the $50.
6. Don't let greed cause you to be dishonest.
8. distress: extreme worry or sorrow
   hesitation: pause

Lesson 10

4. Don't be late. It's better to be early.
5. ABCB The first and third lines don't rhyme, but the second and fourth do.
7. adorn: to make more beautiful
   dispute: argument

Lesson 11

coarse: rough
peevish: easily irritated
perplexed: baffled, puzzled

Vocabulary 1. earnest, 2. dispute 3. adorn 4. grove 5. forge 6. envy 7. assure

Lesson 12

reproach: to address someone with disapproval and disappointment
stroke: move your hand across a surface, like petting a cat

Lesson 13

clad: covered
array: an orderly arrangement of something
scarlet: bright red
revere: deeply respect
torment: to cause suffering

Vocabulary: 1.M, 2.F, 3.L, 4.I, 5.R, 6.D, 7.J, 8.C, 9.N, 10.H 11.G, 12.P, 13.E, 14.O 15.Q 16.S, 17.K, 18.B, 19.A

Lesson 14

crevice: narrow opening
prowl: to move around stealthily

Lesson 16

Vocabulary 1B, 2E, 3A, 4C, 5D, 6I, 7H, 8F, 9G, 10J

Lesson 19

3. a rude lack of respect

Lesson 23

3. They pray and thank God.

Lesson 24

3. They throw stones up at the monkeys and the monkeys imitate them and throw nuts down at them.

Lesson 27

3. bridge

Lesson 28

3. in a tree

Lesson 35

2. make shoes/boots

Lesson 38

4. a wild donkey

Lesson 39

2. crystals, He calls them diamonds at first, but they are salt crystals.

Lesson 50

2. He loves their island home.

Lesson 51

3. Fritz

Lesson 54

3. Mother and Francis

Lesson 57

3. Jack was tied up and taken away by islanders ("natives").

Lesson 60

3. Francis

Lesson 62

3. Madame Hirtel (That's like saying Mrs. Hirtel. She and her two daughters were shipwrecked as well.)

Lesson 75
2. coal
3. to steal

Lesson 76
2. He confessed.

Lesson 80
Vocabulary: content-discontent (dismayed, frustrated…there is no one right answer), lazy-tireless, discourage-assure, helpful-hindering, prepared-unprepared (took the easy way out on that one), thoughtful-thoughtless, humble-proud, knowledge-ignorance,   colorful-bland or monotone, dread-anticipation

Lesson 83
2. upset they didn't get cherries when they are being grateful for just being alive

Lesson 86
unforgettable, impersonal, unimaginable, incomplete, indestructible, undesirable,   imperfect (un, in, im are the prefixes I used)

ABOUT

EASY PEASY ALL-IN-ONE HOMESCHOOL

Easy Peasy All-in-One Homeschool is a free, complete online homeschool curriculum. There are 180 days of ready-to-go assignments for every level and every subject. It's created for your children to work as independently as you want them to. Preschool through high school is available and courses ranging from English, math, science and history to art, music, computer, thinking, physical education and health. A daily Bible lesson is offered as well. The mission of Easy Peasy is to enable those to homeschool who otherwise thought they couldn't.

Made in the USA
Monee, IL
14 August 2022

11580150R00208